The Management of Clubs, Recreation, and Sport: Concepts and Applications

Thomas Sawyer
Owen Smith

Sagamore Publishing
Champaign, Illinois

www.sagamorepub.com

Editor: Susan M. McKinney
Book design: Jennifer L. Polson & Anne E. Kolodziej
Cover design: Deborah Bellaire

ISBN: 1-57167-027-0
Library of Congress Number: 98-85173

Printed in the United States.

Dedication

This book is dedicated to our families:

Shawn, Peter, Meghan, Kathi, and Daughn

and

Michael, Timothy, Peggy, and Carolyn

BOOK ADVISORY MEMBERS

◆ ———————————————————— ◆

CONTENTS

ACKNOWLEDGMENTS

◆ ———————————— ◆

Obviously, a book of this nature could not be possible without the involvement and participation of many individuals. Many students and practitioners have contributed ideas and suggested practices to this book. A special thanks to Dr. Jeff James, University of Illinois. His comments and efforts were very useful in refining the manuscript.

We would like to extend our appreciation to the authors and publishers of journals and magazines who have permitted us to use their work to strengthen our ideas.

A special expression of gratitude is extended to Andrea Proyen for her efforts as developmental editor. Her review and suggestions were very valuable in the final development of the manuscript. A special thanks to Susan McKinney for editing the manuscript, and to Jennifer Polson for an excellent job in following the manuscript through the production process. Thanks to Deborah Bellaire for her creative cover design.

Thomas Harrison Sawyer
Owen Russell Smith

FOREWORD

◆ ────────────────── ◆

In an era of the health and fitness entrepreneur, sport has become even more significant and pervasive in American society. Sport has become a multibillion-dollar industry that places unique demands on its personnel and increasingly requires specialized training. Jobs in the sport industry involve a variety of skills applicable to the sport setting and specific to the increasingly complex and multi-faceted areas it represents. Sport management is now recognized by the sport industry as a legitimate profession and field of study in colleges and universities throughout the United States, Canada, and other sport-oriented countries; as a result a new profession has arrived on the scene.

In 1995, resources that addressed managing fitness, recreation, and sport programs in the club environment were, and remain today, limited. Even though the academic field of sport management has flourished since the mid 1980s, including the publication of numerous books related to the various aspects of the field as well as a number of professional and trade journals, it is still difficult to find a book focused on applying sport management theory to the rapidly growing club market. Clubs need appropriately prepared young men and women to manage the various programs in order to be successful in this very competitive industry.

In order to appropriately prepare these young men and women to operate and manage the clubs of today and of the 21st century successfully, there need to be resources available to instruct and prepare them. Our present and future club managers needs to know how to identify and foster the four issues that are vital for the survival of any club facility. These issues are: human resources, sound financial principles, the club market, and facility maintenance and the management of the club facility.

The first and most important issue is human resources. The text's first three chapters provide a broad and rich perspective on three central human resource issues: the selection and training of personnel, the coordination and planning of operations, and the all-important development of programs, which are the life-blood of every facility.

The second issue that needs to be effectively managed in every athletic and fitness facility is sound financial management principles. These principles are: the budgeting process, the enterprise of revenue generation, the challenge of effective promotion, the issue of fundraising, the supreme task of generating repeat business (membership retention), and purchasing issues. In six well-chiseled chapters, Sawyer and Smith focus on these financial factors and forces that determine the success or failure of every sport facility business.

The third issue, so often overlooked in other texts, is the club market. No matter how talented the personnel or how well the enterprise is capitalized, if the market is not prime, the business will never completely fulfill its potential. Sawyer and Smith do a brilliant job explaining to the readers how to analyze and communicate with the market to ensure success regardless of the market situation.

The fourth and final issue to be considered is the facility itself. The authors excel in raising and exploring the central issues relating to facility development, facility management, the legal issues relating to the operation of the facility, and the management of the risks inherent in operating an athletic or fitness facility.

Sawyer and Smith do an excellent job presenting the information in this books in an open, accessible, clear, and compelling manner that raises all the right questions and invites deeper exploration.

This book is tailored around the informational needs of future sport and recreational sport professionals who will be involved in managing professional sport, recreation, and sport facilities; campus recreation programs; community-based sport programs; sport clubs; health and fitness clubs; aquatic facilities; and non-profit youth agency sport programs. This text is ideally suited to classroom discussion and exploration because it raises the issues surrounding the management of club, recreation, and sport facilities in an open and accessible way. This book not only introduces the students to various management, marketing, financial, and legal concepts related to sport; it also shows students HOW to apply the concepts in real-life situations. Sawyer and Smith have provided both educators and students with a wonderfully flexible and adaptable teaching tool that brings to life the entire enterprise of recreation and sport facilities.

John McCarthy
Executive Director
International Health, Racquet, and Sports Club Association
Boston, Massachusetts

PREFACE

◆ ———————————————————— ◆

In an era of great expansion, sport has become even more significant and pervasive in American society. Sport is defined as those activities that have the following characteristics: (1) it is competitive, (2) they have scoring, (3) they have rules, (4) they are played by amateurs and/or professionals, (5) they are played indoors and outdoors, (6) they have components of both fitness and recreation, (7) they provide the participants enjoyment and fun, and (8) they provide entertainment for the spectator. Sport is used in this book in a very broad sense as an "umbrella term" encompassing the ever-growing areas of amateur and professional sport as well as all activities of the fitness and recreation industry. Sport is a multi-billion-dollar industry ranging from fitness, recreation, and sport activities to retail sales to entertainment.

This growing industry places unique demands on its personnel and increasingly requires specialized education. The job requirements in the sport industry involve many skills applicable to the sport setting and specific to the increasingly complex and multifaceted areas it represents. This text provides the reader with enough information on a variety of subjects to know where to proceed without assistance and when it would be wise to seek additional professional assistance.

Since the early 1970s, a new breed of specialists has emerged—the sport manager. Sport management is now recognized as a legitimate field of study in colleges and universities worldwide. In its broadest sense, sport, sport programs, or sport management are terms used to encompass such other terms as activity-based programs, fitness programs, recreation programs or club management, fitness management, recreation management. Therefore, throughout this text the "umbrella" term will be sport management.

Settings for the management of fitness, recreation, and sport activities fall into five primary clusters, each of which contains two or more categories that have similar objectives and provide similar services, but occur in different settings, and/or serve different clientele.

1. Sport for leisure and recreational settings include organizations that provide facilities and programs for organized sport or fitness participation of members, including college and university intramural sport clubs, corporations and companies with sport or *fitness programs*, *private clubs*, and public sport clubs.
2. Sport and athletic settings include organizations that provide management of sorting event, athletes, and/or spectator use, including college and university athletics, professional sport, sport organizations, amateur sport, and sport management services.

3. Sporting goods industry settings include businesses that develop, distribute, and/or promote the sale of sport, recreation, and fitness equipment or clothing, including sport marketing, sport merchandising and retail sales.
4. Settings include businesses that provide lodging and include recreation or leisure programs and/or facilities for their clientele, including hotel, resorts, and travel or cruise businesses, and
5. Agency or club settings include organizations (agency) that use nonprofit funding sources and clubs (for profit organizations) to develop, implement, and manage fitness, recreation, or sport programs, activities, or facilities to meet the needs of the agency or club members or population of governmental districts (e.g., city, county, state, federal), including local government agencies, federal government agencies, voluntary agencies (e.g., YMCA, YWCA, Boys' or Girls' Club or Boys' and Girls' Scouts, health and fitness clubs, and racquet clubs (Kelley, Beitel, Blanton, & DeSensi, 1990).

A major concern for higher education and practitioners is the lack of a variety of textbooks and related resources in this expanding field of study. Some texts are generalized and others are specific. *The Management of Clubs, Recreation, and Sport: Concepts and Applications* is a comprehensive compilation of concepts and practical subject matter published for the recreation and sport management student and practitioner.

Audience

An increasing number of students with a wide variety of backgrounds are selecting sport management as a course of study both at the undergraduate and graduate levels. The intention of this book is to cater to this changing and rapidly growing audience. Further, this book has been written for an upper-division course, such as a capstone course. Students using this text will have a fundamental understanding of basic finance, basic management, basic marketing, and computer utilization. This book will also be a valuable resource for **practitioners.** Instructors at other levels are encouraged to review the content for potential use as well.

Features

Content

This book has been designed as a textbook as well as a practitioner's how-to book. The content focuses on those activities that are the most important for either a club manager, recreational sports manager, or competitive sport manager. Each chapter provides explanations of various management concepts important for the student to understand and how-to information that applies the concepts to realistic situations.

The manuscript is divided into four major parts: (1) managing human resources and the planning process, (2) financial management, (3) marketing, and (4) facility and risk management.

Each major part is divided into chapters. Part I, Chapters 1-3, focuses on managing human resources and the planning process. The second part, consisting of Chapters 4-9, covers the budget process, revenue generation, promotion and advertising, fund-raising, membership retention, and equipment control and purchasing. Part III, Chapters 10-11, focuses on marketing and public relations. The final section, containing Chapters 12-15, covers designing a new facility, facility and event management, legal issues in sport management, and risk management.

Pedagogy

This text uses many pedagogical features to aid the learner's comprehension of many diverse topics. Each chapter contains the following components:

- a listing of **learning objectives,**
- a **short summary** emphasizing the learning objectives for each chapter,
- a series of **self-testing exercises/cases** relating to the chapter, a complete listing of **references,** and
- a listing of **suggested additional reading** that students should read carefully for supplemental information.

Authors' Philosophy as it Relates to Sport Management

Our philosophy is very simple. We believe management is a process of achieving desired results through efficient utilization of human and material resources by employing such managerial functions as planning, organizing, staffing, leading, and controlling. Further, we believe that the process of management is basically the same for all activities, whether it be business, government, education, fitness, recreation or sport. Therefore, when one teaches the basic tenets of management, it applies to all fields of endeavor—management is management. The only thing that changes are the specific circumstances, but the five basic management functions must still be applied–planning, organizing, staffing, leading, and controlling— if the efficient utilization of human and material resources is to be the end result.

Introduction

SPORT AND THE
MANAGEMENT PROCESS

◆ —————————————— ◆

Sport

Sport, in its broadest sense, refers to all recreational and competitive sports, physical and fitness activities, and dance. Sport has become a dominant influence in many societies. No single aspect of any culture receives the media attention given to sport. Sport is big business and continues to grow at a phenomenal rate; it provides the visibility for its star participants to enter the political arena, and become broadcasters or movie stars, or entrepreneurs.

Further, recreational participation in sport continues to grow in popularity each year, driven by increased time for leisure activities and discretionary income to spend on exercise and fitness pursuits. This increase in growth has required development of new undergraduate programs to prepare a new type of sport manager. This new sport manager needs to understand the management process in order for the sport business to be successful.

The Management Process

At one time in America, Europe, and Japan, the world of work was largely composed of individuals working alone, rather than groups of people working together. Farmers produced food for themselves and their families, and, if they were lucky, had a surplus to sell. Potters, silversmiths, and other craft workers produced their goods independently. Families who needed homes built them alone, or with help from their neighbors. Even government was individualized, consisting of a lord or knight who reigned over a relatively small territory.

This individualized work pattern no longer exists in developed countries. Goods such as Boeing 767 airplanes, television sets, and heating and air-conditioning systems could not be replaced efficiently by a single individual. Seldom does one person possess the necessary capital, knowledge, abilities, or resources to "go it alone."

People are needed who can efficiently coordinate the human and material resources required to accomplish desired goals. These people are managers. Accordingly, *management is defined as the process of achieving desired results through efficient utilization of human and material resources*, and has a number of important functions. And *leadership is defined as the art of influencing individual or group activities toward achievement of an organization's goals and objectives*. Over the years a number of interesting leadership theories of management have developed.

Leadership Theories

Over the past 50 years, a number of leadership theories have been developed, however, only a few have gained any popularity. The leadership theories that follow have remained popular in one form or another. Before discussing the leadership theories, it is important to understand that a manager's assumptions about people will influence how he or she behaves as a leader. Therefore, it is appropriate to review Douglas McGregor's Theories X and Y: assumptions about people.

McGregor's Theory X and Theory Y

McGregor (1957) hypothesized that managers generally hold one of two contrasting sets of assumptions about people. He asserted that a manager's behavior as a leader would be influenced by the particular set of assumptions he or she held. Managers with *Theory X* assumptions (see Table 1) are autocratic leaders and rely on coercion, discipline, and penalties to accomplish organization objectives. However, managers with *Theory Y* assumptions (see Table 1) are democratic leaders, emphasize self-management and openly encourage subordinates to seek responsibility and share in the decision making necessary to accomplish organizational objectives.

The first leadership theory to be discussed will be the *trait phase*. The earliest attempts to understand leadership centered on determining what specific traits make a person an effective leader. A trait is generally defined as a distinctive physical or psychological characteristic that accounts for a person's behavior. This was later called the "great man" theory. After a number of years of study, researchers found little evidence for distinguishing leaders from followers. As a consequence, in the 1940s researchers began to question the existence of unique leader traits.

Researchers then shifted their attention to the study of leader behavior. This shift marked the beginning of the *behavioral phase* of leadership research. This phase of research held that leaders may be best characterized by how they behave, rather than by their personal traits. Underlying this phase was the assumption that effective leaders utilize a particular behavioral style that causes others to follow them.

Table 1
Assumptions about People

Theory X

1. The average person has an inherent dislike of work and will avoid it if possible.
2. Most people must be coerced, controlled, directed, and threatened with punishment to get them to put forth adequate effort toward achievement of organization objectives because of their characteristic dislike of work.
3. The average person prefers to be directed, wishes to avoid responsibility, has relatively little ambition, and wants security above all.

Theory Y

1. The expenditure of physical and mental effort in work is as natural as play or rest.
2. External control and threat of punishment are not the only means for bringing about effort toward organization objectives.
3. People will exercise self-direction and self-control in the service of objectives to which they are committed.
4. Human beings learn, under proper conditions, not only to accept but also to seek responsibility.
5. The capacity to exercise a relatively high degree of imagination, ingenuity, and creativity in the solution of organization problems widely, not narrowly, distributed among the population.
6. The intellectual potentialities of the average person are only partially utilized under the conditions of modern industrial life.

Source: Adapted from *The Human Side of Enterprise* by Douglas McGregor, pp. 33-34, 47-48.

A third phase in leadership research is known as the ***situational phase***. Contemporary leadership theories are almost entirely situational in nature. In contrast to earlier theories, which focused on leader behavior, the newer theories attempt to explain effective leadership within the context of the larger situation in which it occurs. The most prominent of these situational theories are Fielder's contingency theory (1967, 1981, 1983), House's path-goal theory (1971, 1974), and Vroom and Yetton's normative theory (1973, 1984). The Contingency Theory defines leader effectiveness in terms of work group performance. It holds that work group performance is contingent upon the match between: (1) a person's leadership style, and (2) the favorableness of the leadership situation. Leadership style refers to a leader's manner of acting in a work situation. Situational favorableness refers to the degree a situation enables a person to exert influence over a work group.

The second situational leadership theory is called Path-Goal Theory of Leadership. This theory describes how leader behavior affects motivation, which depends on a person's belief that effort will lead to performance. The leader's task, in this model, contains two elements: (1) goal element, which is linked to the increased number and kinds of rewards subordinates receive for work-goal attainment, and (2) path-element, which makes the paths to these rewards easier to travel by removing obstacles that inhibit goal accomplishment. House (1974) described four types of leader behavior:

- *Directive leadership* is characterized by a leader who informs subordinates what is expected of them and provides specific guidance on how to do it;
- *Supportive leadership* is epitomized by a leader who is friendly and approachable and shows concern for the status, well-being, and personal needs of subordinates;
- *Achievement-oriented leadership* is illustrated by a leader who sets challenging goals, expects subordinates to perform at their best, and shows confidence that subordinates will perform well; and
- *Participative leadership* is portrayed by a leader who consults with subordinates and asks for their suggestions before making a decision.

The third leadership theory is the Normative Theory of Leadership. It offers normative guidelines for how decisions should be made in a specific situation. In doing so, it focuses on the extent a leader should allow subordinates to share in decision making. Vroom and Yetton (1984) identified the following distinct decision-making methods:

- Autocratic I is characterized by managers solving the problem alone, using whatever is available at the time;
- Autocratic II is portrayed by managers who obtain necessary information from subordinates before making the decision alone;
- Consultative I is illustrated by managers sharing problems with subordinates individually, getting their ideas and suggestions before making the decision;
- Consultative II is epitomized by managers sharing problems with subordinates as a group, getting their ideas and suggestions before making the decision; and
- Group Participation is characterized by managers sharing problems with subordinates as a group and together they make the decision.

Management Functions

The six common managerial functions that should be performed by *sport managers* include (1) planning the use of an organization's resources; (2) organizing the organization's resources; (3) staffing the provision of the organization's human resources; (4) leading the organization in such a way to accomplish its goals; (5) controlling the organization's resources; and (6) decision making for the organization.

Planning is the process of determining the organization's objectives and selecting a future course of action to accomplish them. It includes (1) establishing the organization's objectives, (2) developing premises about the environment in which they are to be accomplished, (3) selecting a course of action for accomplishing the objectives, (4) initiating activities necessary to translate plans into action, and (5) evaluating the outcome of the planning.

Organizing is a procedure by which employees and their jobs are related to each other for accomplishing the organization's objectives. It consists of dividing work among groups and individuals, and coordinating individual and group activities. Organizing also involves establishing managerial authority.

Staffing is a method of assuring that competent employees are selected, developed, and rewarded for accomplishing the organization's objectives. Effective staffing and human resource management also includes establishing a work climate in which employees are satisfied.

Leading is the process of inducing individuals (peers, superiors, subordinates, and non-subordinates) or groups to assist willingly and harmoniously in accomplishing the organization's objectives.

Controlling is a mechanism of assuring the efficient accomplishment of the organization's objectives. It involves (1) establishing standards, (2) comparing measured performance against established standards, and (3) reinforcing success and correcting shortcomings.

Decision making is the key activity at all levels of management and for all aspects of management. Sport managers must make decisions concerning organizing, staffing, leading, controlling, and planning.

The Leadership Grid Theory

Blake and Mouton (1985) developed the managerial grid, which was later refined by Blake and McCanse (1991) as the Leadership Grid. The x-axis of the grid is labeled "concern for production" and the y-axis "concern for people." Each axis is divided into nine sections, numbered one through nine. Values are expressed as a pair of interdependent numbers; the first representing the x-axis (production) and the second representing the y-axis (people). There are five possible combinations, including 1,9 country club management (i.e., thoughtful attention to the needs of people for satisfying relationships leads to a comfortable, friendly organization atmosphere and work tempo); 9,9 team management (i.e., work accomplishment is from committed people, interdependence through a "common stake" in organization purpose leads to relationships of trust and respect); 5,5 middle-of-the-road management (i.e., adequate organizational performance is possible through balancing the necessity to get out the work while maintaining morale of people at a satisfactory level); 1,1 impoverished management (i.e., exertion of minimum effort to get required work done is appropriate to sustain organization membership); and 9,1 authority-compliance (i.e., efficiency in operations results from arranging conditions of work on such a way that human elements interfere to a minimum degree).

Decision Making

Decision making is a key activity at all levels of management. It may be defined as the act of choosing between two or more alternatives. It involves identifying alternatives and selecting the one judged best. This identification and selection can occur under conditions that vary dramatically. In a free-enterprise system, managers make decisions under conditions of certainty, risk, and uncertainty.

A decision is made under conditions of: (1) certainty when a manager knows the available alternatives and the benefits or costs associated with each; (2) risk when a manager knows the alternatives, the likelihood of their occurrence, and the potential benefits (or costs) associated with each but their outcomes are in doubt; and (3) uncertainty when a manager does not know the available alternatives, the likelihood of their occurrence, or their potential outcomes. The latter of these three is the most difficult.

Leadership Grid

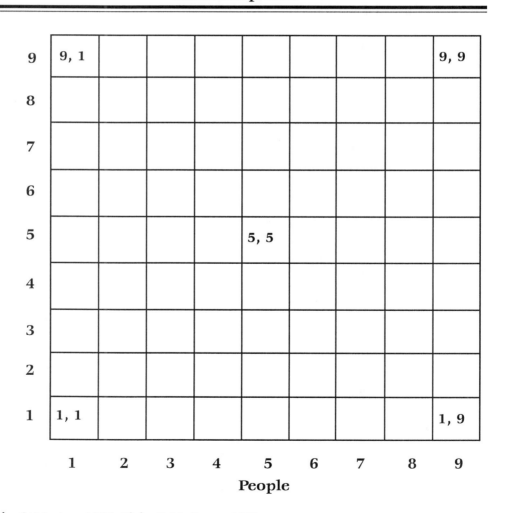

Blake & Morton, 1985; Blake & McCause, 1991.

There are three steps in decision making: (1) available alternatives must be identified, (2) each alternative must be evaluated in light of premises about the future, and (3) based on the preceding evaluation, the alternative with the highest estimated probability of success should be selected. It is in this final step that a plan of action is adopted and the climax of the decision-making process occurs.

What is the Most Appropriate Leadership Theory for Sport Managers to Concentrate On?

The most appropriate leadership theory for sport managers to become acquainted with is situational leadership. The theory that best lends itself to sport managers is the Path-Goal Theory of Leadership. However, sport managers need to pay close attention to their leadership styles as well as their decision-making methods. Sport managers who are as concerned about people as they are about results will be the most successful in the long run.

Management Approaches

The most successful management process is characterized by two major elements—strong leadership and a participative management approach. Leadership has been discussed, now it is time to shift gears and discuss a variety of management approaches that will be best suited for sport managers who are concerned equally about people and results.

Management By Objectives (MBO) is a management approach designed to integrate individual and organization objectives. MBO encourages the meshing of individual and organization objectives. It is a form of participatory management that engages the individual in the assisting management in attaining organizational goals. It is based on the belief that joint subordinate-superior participation in translating overall objectives into individual objectives will have a positive influence on employee performance and organizational goal attainment. The central idea behind MBO is that the mutual establishment and acceptance of objectives will elicit a stronger employee commitment than if a superior unilaterally establishes objectives and imposes them on subordinates. The enhanced commitment by employees who have helped to set personal objectives should, in turn, lead to improved performance. The MBO process is composed of five steps: (1) discuss job requirements with employee; (2) develop performance objectives for the employee that are (a) clear and concise, (b) achievable, (c) challenging, (d) measurable, (e) consistent with overall organization objectives, and (f) accompanied by an anticipated completion date; (3) discuss objectives with employee ; (4) determine mutually agreed upon checkpoints; and (5) evaluate results together (Odiorne, 1965).

Total Quality Management

Total Quality Management (TQM) is a collection of roles and practices that are oriented and strive to always meet or exceed the needs and expectations of the consumer in an ongoing, planned system. What TQM attempts to achieve is a workplace where employees perceive that they have a personal stake in the output. Workers seek to measure against expectations that are achievable and that they have had a hand in setting. Performance is reviewed by their peers and by managers who are active participants in the daily operation of the workplace.

Case Study

Hannibal University

Hannibal University evaluates the productivity of its coaches according to three factors: win-loss record, graduation rates, and gate receipts. Each year these productivity evaluations are used as the basis for individual coaching salary increases and contract extensions.

Further, because Hannibal University is a state-supported university, the state legislature is becoming more interested in coaching productivity. It often complains that coaches only work during the season. "What do they do with the rest of their time?" one legislator complained. "I propose we require the university to provide us with productivity measures similar to those I get in my company," said another legislator, who was a manufacturing executive. Yet another legislator proposed that coaches' productivity be measured by how successful their graduates are at gaining professional sport contracts — "After all, isn't that what college sports is all about?"

Questions

1. What difficulties might there be in measuring individual coach productivity levels by the three factors that Hannibal University uses? What factors would you suggest?
2. What do you think of the legislature's desire to measure coaching productivity? Do you agree or disagree with the proposals and comments from the three quoted legislators?
3. How is productivity measurement likely to differ between coaching, teaching, and manufacturing?
4. As athletic director, how would you deal with this situation?

References

Bedeian, Arthur G. (1986). *Management.* New York: The Dryden Press.

Blake, Robert R., & McCanse, A.A. (1991). *Leadership dilemmas—Grid solutions.* Houston, TX: Gulf Publishing Co.

Blake, Robert R., & Moulton, Jane S. (1981). Grid approaches for managerial leadership in nursing. St. Louis, MO: CV Mosby.

Deming, W.E. (1982). *Quality, productivity, and competitive position.* Cambridge, MA: MIT Center for Advanced Engineering Study.

Drucker, Peter F. (1974). *Management: Tasks, responsibilities, practices.* New York: Harper & Row.

Fielder, Fred E. (1967). *A theory of leadership effectiveness.* New York: McGraw-Hill.

Fielder, Fred E. (1981). Leadership effectiveness. *American Behavorial Scientist, 24,* 619-632.

Fielder, Fred E., & Potter III, Earl H. (1983). In Glumberg, Herbert H. Hare, Paul A., Kent, Valerie, & Davies, Martin F., (Eds.). Dynamics of leadership effectiveness. *Small Groups and Social Interaction. (1)* 407-412. Chichester, U.K.: Wiley.

Hersey, P., & Blanchard, H. (1972). *Management of organizational behavior: Utilization of human resources.* (2nd ed.). Englewood Cliffs, NJ: Prentice Hall.

House, Robert J. (1971). A path-goal theory of leader effectiveness. *Administrative Science Quarterly, 16,* 138-139.

House, Robert J., & Mitchell, Terence R. (1974). Path-goal theory of leadership. *Journal of Contemporary Business, (3)* 81-97.

McGregor, Douglas M. (1957). *The human side of enterprise.* New York: McGraw-Hill.

Odiorne, G.S. (1965). *Management by objectives: A system of managerial leadership.* New York: Pitman Publishing Company.

Vroom, Victor, & Yetton, Philip W. (1973). *Leadership and decision-making.* Pittsburgh, PA: University of Pittsburgh Press.

Vroom, Victor H. (1984). Reflections on leadership and decision-making. *Journal of General Management, (9)* 18-36.

Suggested Readings

Belasco, James A. (1991) *Teaching the elephant to dance.* New York: Penguin Group.

Blanchard, Kenneth, & Johnson, Spencer. (1982) *The one-minute manager.* New York: Wm. Morrow and Company, Inc.

Branvold, Scott. (1995). In Bonnie L. Parkhouse (Ed.), *The management of sport.* (2nd ed.). St. Louis, MO: Mosby.

Canfield, Jack, & Hansen, Mark Victor. (1993). *Chicken soup for the soul.* Deerfield Beach, FL: Health Communications, Inc.

Canfield, Jack, & Hansen, Mark Victor. (1995). *A second helping of chicken soup for the soul.* Deerfield Beach, FL: Health Communications, Inc.

Peters, Thomas J., & Waterman, Robert H. Jr. (1982). *In search of excellence.* New York: Warner Books.

Roberts, Wess. (1987). *Leadership secrets of Attila the Hun.* New York: Warner Books, Inc.

Tucker, Robert B. (1991). *Managing the future.* New York: Berkley Publishing Group.

Wilson, Bradley, R.A., & Glaros, Timothy E. (1994). *Managing health promotion programs.* Champaign, IL: Human Kinetics. See chapters 2, 3, & 4.

PART I

MANAGING HUMAN RESOURCES AND THE PLANNING PROCESS

1

MANAGING HUMAN RESOURCES

◆ ——————————————— ◆

Instructional Objectives:

After reading this chapter the student should be able to:

- understand important legal issues regarding employer-employee relationships,

- delineate the contents of a human resources handbook,

- describe the hiring process and all its components,

- design a performance appraisal process,

- develop a regularly scheduled in-service program,

- understand how to motivate employees,

- describe a termination process,

- discuss important issues regarding employee compensation

- design a grievance procedure for an organization, and

- discuss the value of good communication and listening skills.

Introduction

The most important asset in any organization is its human resources. People are the key to a business' success or failure. The goal is to obtain competent employees and provide the means for them to function optimally. Sport organizations are people-oriented operations. Therefore, the management of human resources, whether it be a manager of the human resource department in a large organization or the owner or manager of a small organization, plays a primary role in the organization. Further, the human problems of management are often the most complex because of the variability of human nature and behavior. This makes the management of human resources of the organization a key to its success. Management of human resources involves all the policies and procedures developed to help employees interact with the organization in both a formal and informal way. The common components of human resource management are the following:

- hiring competent and qualified employees,
- assigning and classifying employees effectively,
- motivating employees to perform optimally,
- stimulating employees' professional growth and development,
- evaluating and compensating employees fairly,
- rewarding employees for their efforts, and
- providing in-service education opportunities.

There are basically two types of employees—professional (salaried) and hourly. These employees can be paid, volunteers, or independent contractors. The professional employees are paid a salary, have a college degree, hold higher-level positions, do not have fixed work schedules, do not punch time clocks, and perform specific duties that do not fit into fixed day/hour schedules (e.g., club manager, program director, marketing director, and instructors). The hourly employees usually have specific day/hour schedules, punch time clocks, may have specified lunch and rest breaks, receive specified vacation time and sick leave and are not expected to work after hours without additional compensation (e.g., custodians, secretaries, maintenance personnel, equipment managers, security officers, and other office personnel).

Some special types of employees are part-time and seasonal employees, volunteers, and independent contractors. Every organization at one time or another has the need for *part-time* personnel. In determining personnel needs, the manager should decide which work tasks can be clustered into jobs that can be accomplished by part-time employees. Part-time positions may include: aerobic dance instructors, fitness instructors, professional trainers, instructors, day care personnel, janitors, secretaries, accountants, lifeguards, ticket sellers, ticket takers, security guards, ushers, emergency technicians, parking lot attendants, and concession personnel, to name a few. These positions need to have job descriptions developed the same as full-time positions.

Some organizations employ *seasonal employees* to meet the demands of their clientele. The summer increases the need for personnel in organizations that cater to school-aged children. Many fitness centers need to employ more personnel for day care centers during the summer months, because younger children are out of school, and during the first quarter of the new year to meet the demands of the increased number of clients after holiday eating binges.

Many tasks and services can be accomplished by *volunteers*. Managers have to determine the specific work tasks (e.g., answering the phone, working the registration desk, working in the day care center, assisting in raising funds). All volunteer positions should have job descriptions. A volunteer service program should be considered and initiated.

When selecting volunteers, the organization should expect that the volunteer will be able to do the following:

- like people,
- accept the clients of the organization and treat them with respect as individuals, rather than to maximize their shortcomings,
- be dependable, sincere, thoughtful, and cooperative,
- have a strong sense of responsibility,
- be able to take action,
- be creative,
- be able to take initiative within the limits of the assigned responsibility,
- be appropriately dressed for the work to be performed,
- enjoy the work assignment in the organization,
- be able to stimulate participation, and
- be physically, mentally, and socially fit to perform the assigned responsibilities.

Finally, many organizations use *independent contractors* to provide services. An independent contractor is someone or another organization that contracts with the organization to provide a specific service, for a specific amount of time, for an agreed upon amount of money. Traditionally, these contracts are for services including: aerobic dance, clerical, custodial, trash collection, laundry, lawn, professional trainers, snow plowing, sports officials, concessionaires, athletic trainers, security personnel, and coaches. The organization pays for the service and the individual or other organization is responsible for paying employer taxes, fringe benefits, and liability insurance. It is imperative that the independent contractor carry liability insurance to cover errors of commission and omission. Another caution is to make sure that the aerobic dance instructor has gained copyright permissions on all the music used in the performance of the contracted service. The organization should not be responsible for the independent contractor's infringement upon the artist's copyright on the music.

All organizations should have a chart that provides a graphic view of the organization's basic structure and illustrates the lines of authority and responsibility of its various members. Employees should be familiar with this chart and understand how their positions and duties contribute to the overall structure.

The limitations of an organizational chart include: (l) it is easily outdated; (2) it fails to show precise functions and amounts of authority and responsibility; and (3) it does not portray the informal relationships that exist.

In a line and staff organization, authority flows from the highest supervisor down through the chain of command to the lowest position. Line personnel provide leadership for a specific unit within the organization. Staff personnel are incorporated into the line organization. Staff are specialists in areas such as program development, contractual services, and assistants to or advisors for line personnel. Table 1-1 depicts the common difference between line and staff functions.

Table 1-1
Line and Staff Functions

Line	Staff
Directs or orders	Advises
Has responsibility to implement activities	Studies, reports, recommends, but does not implement
Follows chain of command	Assists line but is not part of chain
Decides when and how to use staff	Always available for line use
Is the "doing" part of the organization	Is the "assisting" part of the organization

Hiring

Every organization needs to have a manual outlining policies and procedures for recruitment and appointment of personnel. The manager of human resources must have appropriate hiring procedures in place. The components of a hiring process should include the following:

- gaining approval for the position,
- establishing a search and screen committee,
- informing the search and screen committee of the appropriate Affirmative Action and Equal Opportunity Employment statutes,
- developing a job description,
- preparing a position announcement,
- establishing a plan for advertising the position,
- screening the pool of candidates,
- verifying the candidates' credentials,
- interviewing the candidate,
- selecting the final candidate, and
- negotiating the appointment with the selected candidate.

Gaining approval for the position is the first step in any hiring process. Human resource managers and owners are faced with replacing vacant positions or determining whether a new position is appropriate. In either situation a case must be built to justify a replacement or new position. It is best to develop a five-year plan for human resources. The plan is developed based on future business projections and consideration of turnover in personnel (e.g., retirements, emergency leaves, sick leaves, and resignations). This will assist in justifying the need for a replacement or new position or even a redefined position.

Once approval for a replacement, redefined position, or new position has been gained, the next step is to *appoint a search and screen committee.* This may not be necessary in small organizations. You can never be too careful when it comes to recruiting and selecting personnel. The committee should be composed of three to seven people. The members of the committee should be as diverse as the employees and clientele or customers of the organization.

Before the committee starts its work, there should be a meeting to review the Affirmative Action and Equal Employment Opportunity guidelines (Executive Order 11246 which mandates nondiscrimination and affirmative action in public and non-public institutions which receive federal monies over a specified amount). The committee is to develop the job description, the position announcement, search strategy, and to screen the candidate pool down to three to five final candidates. The committee may be asked by a human resources manager to either recommend three to five final candidates with no priority, with a priority order, or select the number one candidate.

Human Resource Development Tip

Nondiscrimination and affirmative action. The Civil Rights Act of 1964 was designed as a national statement against discrimination in occupations, voting, use of public facilities, and public education on the basis of race, color, religion, sex, or national origin. Title VII of the Civil Rights Act of 1964 regarding nondiscrimination in employment was amended by the Equal Employment Opportunity Act of 1972, which extended the coverage of the act, created the Equal Employment Opportunity Commission, and stated additional rules, regulations, and enforcement procedures. The main concept embodied in these acts is that of nondiscrimination.

Nondiscrimination requires the elimination of all existing discriminatory conditions, whether purposeful or inadvertent. Employers, employment organizations, training programs, and labor organizations must carefully and systematically examine all of their employment policies to be sure that they do not, if implemented as stated, operate to the detriment of any persons on grounds of race, color, religion, sex, or national origin. These organizations must also ensure that the practices of those responsible in matters of employment, including all supervisors, are nondiscriminatory. These requirements apply to all persons, whether or not the individual is a member of a conventionally defined minority group. In other words, no individual may be denied employment or related benefits on the grounds of his or her race, color, religion, sex, or national origin.

The Age Discrimination In Employment Act of 1967, as amended in 1978, prohibits discrimination against workers between 40 and 70 years of age. This act applies to local, state, and federal governments and to employers with 20 or more employees. In addition, it eliminates mandatory retirement of federal employees.

The Vocational Rehabilitation Act of 1973, and as subsequently amended in 1974, extended these protections to handicapped individuals, and the Vietnam-era Veterans Readjustment Assistance Act of 1974 did the same with regard to such veterans.

Affirmative action requires organizations to make additional efforts to recruit, employ, and promote qualified members of groups formerly excluded, even if that exclusion cannot be traced to particular discriminatory actions on the part of the employer.

It is imperative that every organization establish human resource policies and practices that adhere to the concepts of nondiscrimination and affirmative action whether it is public or nonpublic, whether it has a small or large number of employees, or whether or not it has a government contract.

Job Description

The search and screen committee's task is to ***develop a job description***. The job description should include, but not be limited to: (1) a position title (i.e., the position title should describe generally the responsibilities of the position), (2) the qualifications for the position (i.e., experience, education, certifications), and (3) the responsibilities and duties for the position.

When developing the qualifications for the position be careful not to be too prescriptive. An example of a too-prescriptive set of qualifications would be: "the candidate must have earned a M.A./M.S. degree in exercise physiology, have five years' experience in a club setting, current certification in CPR, and currently hold a director's certification from the ACSM." This set of qualifications may narrow the pool of qualified candidates. A set of qualifications like the following is less restrictive and allows for a larger candidate pool: the candidate will have a B.S. in physical education, adult fitness, sport sciences, recreation and sport management, prefer a M.A./M.S. in physical education, adult fitness or cardiac rehabilitation; have 3-5 years' experience in a clinic, club, college/university, corporate, or hospital setting; have completed a class in CPR from either the American Red Cross or the American Heart Association, prefer current certification; and a fitness instructor or exercise technician certification from the ACSM, prefer director certification. If you are truly searching for a strong candidate, the larger the candidate pool the better.

The duties of any position include four basic components: duty period, tasks to be accomplished, ethical practices, and expectations. Policies concerning responsibilities and expectations common to specific employee groups should be found in a human resources handbook. All organizations should have a human resources handbook (see Table 1-2 for the suggested contents for a human resources handbook).

The job description will not be used only for the search process. Every position, whether it is full-time, part-time, or volunteer should have a job description, which will become the basis of the performance appraisal document. Therefore, it is imperative that the job responsibilities and duties be very detailed and can be evaluated objectively after the candidate is employed. Further, include a statement toward the end or at the end of the responsibilities section that allows the employer some flexibility, such as— "and any other responsibilities or duties assigned in writing by the immediate supervisor." Table 1-3 provides a sample job description for a fitness instructor.

After the job description is completed, the committee will ***design an appropriate position announcement***. A position announcement includes: (1) the position title, (2) a short description of the organization, (3) a summary of the job description, (4) qualifications, (5) application procedure, (6) deadline, and (7) an AA/EEO Employer designation. It is important to be flexible in establishing the deadline. A statement such as "the review of applications will begin September 1, and continue until the position is filled" allows the committee to review later applicants who qualify.

Table 1-2
Components of a Human Resources Handbook

Every organization should have a human resources handbook outlining the responsibilities of the employer and employee. The human resources handbook should include descriptions of, but is not limited to:

- the organizational structure,
- all positions (include a definition of hourly and professional employees,
- part-time/seasonal employee, independent contractor),
- hiring procedures,
- grievance procedures,
- termination procedures,
- the employee performance appraisal process (include a sample
- performance appraisal form),
- the awards system,
- fringe benefit package(s) (e.g., retirement; health, life, and disability
- insurance; liability coverage; vacation time; sick leave; personal leave;
- educational opportunities),
- health/wellness and recreation opportunities,
- inservice education opportunities,
- affirmative action and equal employment opportunity commitment,
- policies related to compliance with the Americans with Disabilities Act,
- procedures to be followed in the case of sexual harassment,
- how and when the employee can review his/her personnel file, and
- how to report any injury (personal and client)

The application procedure should request the following from the applicant: letter of interest, completed application (see Appendices—personnel forms), resume, copies of all current and appropriate certifications, and names, addresses, and phone numbers of three to five professional references. Once the names and addresses are received, a letter should be prepared asking specific questions about the candidate for the reference to respond to in detail. A phone call can be made to clarify answers or ask other questions. Each candidate should be asked for current copies of all certifications. A transcript can be requested prior to offering the position. Table 1-4 provides a sample position announcement for a fitness instructor.

Position Announcement

Once the position announcement has been completed the committee must decide *how, where, and when the position will be announced.* The following are a few common ways of communicating a position announcement: (1) referral and employment agencies, public and private; (2) college and university placement services and bulletin boards in departments of exercise science, kinesiology, physical education, recreation and sport management; (3) professional journals and news-

Table 1-3
Mark Twain Fitness Center
Hannibal, Missouri
Position Description for Fitness Director

Education:
Minimum: BS
Preferred: MA/MS in any of the following areas of expertise: adult fitness, cardiac rehabilitation, exercise science, health promotion, physical education, recreation and sport management or the equivalent.

Certifications:
Minimum: Current CPR (ARC or AMA), Standard First Aid, and ACS:Fitness Instructor Level; Preferred: Director Level ACSM

Experience: Minimum: three years of fitness center management experience; Preferred: five years' experience.

Duties:
- supervise all fitness center personnel, including hiring and evaluating performance,
- recommend and implement policy and procedures for operation of the fitness center,
- maintain client reports, develop applied strategic and operational plans for the fitness center,
- plan and implement appropriate regular inservice education opportunities for all employees,
- develop, recommend, and monitor the budget,
- design and implement a marketing and promotional plan for the center,
- prepare and implement a public relations plan for the center,
- plan and implement appropriate programming that will make the center profitable,
- supervise the purchasing of equipment and supplies,
- oversee the safety of the equipment and facility, and
- any other duties the president of the corporation assigns.

letters; (4) job marts at professional conventions (i.e., American College of Sports Medicine [ACSM], American Alliance for Health, Physical Education, Recreation, and Dance [AAHPERD], International Dance Exercise Association [IDEA], National Strength and Conditioning Association [NSCA], National Recreation and Park Association [NRPA], and the annual Athletic Business Convention to name a few); (5) local newspapers , (6) national/regional newspapers; (7) employee referrals; (8) cooperative fieldwork, internship, or work study programs with colleges and uni-

Table 1-4
Announcing a Position Opening for a Fitness Director at
Mark Twain Fitness Center
Hannibal, Missouri

Mark Twain Fitness Center is located in Hannibal, Missouri about one hour north of St. Louis on the Mississippi River. Hannibal has a population of approximately 50,000 and it is the home of Samuel B. Clemens (Mark Twain was his pen name). The center is located in a newly constructed 75,000-square-foot building with state-of-the-art equipment, swimming pool, locker rooms, strength training area (12,000 square feet), dance exercise area (1,600 square feet), main lobby/lounge, offices, day care center, tanning beds, and much more. The center is privately owned and operated.

The fitness director will be responsible for managing the center, including but not limited to: development of human resources, budgeting, marketing, promotions, public relations, programming, and the safety of the personnel and clients. (A complete job description is available upon request.)

The successful candidate will minimally have (1) a B.S. in any of the following areas of expertise: adult fitness, cardiac rehabilitation, exercise science, health promotions, physical education, or recreation and sport management, (2) current certifications in CPR, Standard First Aid, and ACSM fitness instructor level, and (3) three years of fitness management experience.

For those interested in applying for this position send the following to: Tom Sawyer, President, Mark Twain Fitness Center, Inc., 1946 Huckleberry Lane, Hannibal, Missouri, 44321; (1) letter of interest, (2) current resume, (3) copies of all current certifications, (4) names, addresses, and phone numbers of five references, and complete an application that will be sent to you upon receipt of your letter of interest. The review of applications will begin on September 1, 1995, and continue until the position is filled.

MTFC is an AA/EEO Employer

versities; and (9) job listings on the Internet or World Wide Web. It is customary to allow at least 10-20 working days for people to respond to the position announcement.

When developing the recruitment strategy, the committee must be conscious of preparing a realistic budget. The search budget will include not only the recruitment aspects but also related to long distance calls, postage, transportation, lodging, and meals. Therefore, it is important to establish early financial benchmarks for the entire hiring process.

As the deadline nears for the initial screening to begin, the committee should establish a procedure for *screening the pool of candidates*. The first step in screening candidates is organizing each candidate's file to determine which files are complete. Only those files that are complete are to be reviewed by the committee. A complete file would include, for example, letter of application; current resume; names, addresses and phone numbers of references; copies of certifications; and possibly a valid high school or college transcript.

Next, each member of the committee will review all completed candidate files and select their top 10-15 candidates. After this process is complete, the committee will meet to narrow the pool to 10-15 potential semifinalists. Each of the semifinalists will be called to see if he/she is still interested in the position, then letters will be sent to each continuing candidate's references to gather more information and to validate the candidate's credentials, and each candidate will be interviewed over the telephone by the committee. The interview questions must be appropriate (see Table 1-5 for examples of appropriate and inappropriate questions). At the conclusion of this process, the committee will narrow the field to three to five finalists to be interviewed on-site.

The above process is appropriate for all professional employees but may not be for other employees, such as clerical, receptionists, and housekeeping. The process for nonprofessional personnel would not be as elaborate. For example, when hiring a person for housekeeping, the applicant would complete a standard application and complete any appropriate pre-employment tests. The human resources manager would check all references from the application, review the results of the test(s), and interview the candidate with the housekeeping supervisor.

Interviewing

All candidates must be interviewed prior to hiring. The interview is for both the candidate and the organization. The candidate is deciding whether or not the position and organization are a match for his/her skills and personality. The organization is concerned about whether the candidate is a good match for the organization. Table 1-5 outlines the interview process.

The on-site interview can range from a few hours to a few days. The length of time depends on the position, whether it be professional or support staff. The more influential the position, the longer the interview. An on-site interview should include time with the committee and others who will interact with the position. After the interview has been completed, the committee will meet to discuss and rank each candidate. At the conclusion of this meeting, a recommendation should be forthcoming to the human resources manager.

Once the finalist has been chosen it is time to make an offer of appointment. This can be done by the human resources manager or specific supervisor. The initial offer should be the best possible, but be prepared to make a counter offer if appropriate. The hiring process is a two-way street. The employer is looking for the best possible candidate who will best fit into the organization, and the candidate is looking for the best possible employment situation working within a supportive and friendly environment. In the end the organization selects the person, and the person selects the organization. The formalization of these commitments by both parties takes the form of a contract or a letter of appointment signed by both parties.

Table 1-5
Interviewing Candidates

Questions related to sex, age, race, religion, national origin, or disability are inappropriate when interviewing candidates for positions.

Common sense, courtesy, and professional approach are the cardinal rules for successful interviewing. Treat women, men, minority applicants or persons with disabilities in the same professional manner. You should remember to:

- Ask the same general questions and require the same standards for all applicants.
- Treat all applicants with fairness, equality, and consistency.
- And follow a structured interview plan that will help achieve fairness interviewing.

Discriminatory behavior is improper even when it is not intended. The appearance can be as important as the reality. The fact that you ask certain questions not related to the job wouldn't necessarily show that you mean to discriminate, but such questions can be used, and have been used, in a discriminatory way. The following suggestions should be helpful in ensuring that no federal or state equal employment opportunity laws are violated in the interview:

1. Only ask questions relevant to the job itself. Because improper significance might be given to questions regarding marriage plans or family matters, do not inquire into:

   - marital status or non-marital arrangements; what the husband/wife does, questions regarding spouse earnings,
   - how the husband/wife feels about the candidate's work life, travel requirements, possible relocation,
   - medical history concerning pregnancy or any questions relating to pregnancy (the EEOC has ruled that to refuse to hire a female solely because she is pregnant amounts to sex discrimination), and
   - whether there are children, how many, and their ages.

2. Be professional and consistent in addressing men and women. Either use first names or last for all candidates and persons involved in the recruitment.

3. Applicants with disabilities should only be asked questions relevant to the job. Do not inquire into:

   - past or present serious illnesses or physical/mental conditions,
   - the nature or severity of an apparent disability,
   - problems an individual may have had because of a disability, and
   - how a person became disabled.

You may inquire the following:

- whether the individual needs any reasonable accommodations or assistance during the hiring or interviewing process,

(CONT.)

Table 1-5 Cont.

- about the individual's ability to perform essential job functions with or without a reasonable accommodation, and
- about attendance at prior jobs if the question is asked of all candidates and is limited to days off or days late for any reason (not specifically days missed due to disability/illness).

4. In making a selection or recommendation, avoid making assumptions such as the following:

- Supervisors might prefer men or women or employees of certain ethnic/racial origins or colleagues who do not have physical disabilities.
- Clients or coworkers might not want to deal with men or women or minorities or persons who have physical disabilities.
- The jobs might involve travel or travel with the opposite sex or members of certain ethnic/racial backgrounds which might be thought to disqualify the applicant.
- The job might involve unusual working conditions which might be thought to disqualify the applicant.

5. Since the American system of law presumes that a person is innocent until proven guilty, records of arrest without conviction are meaningless; thus, it is inappropriate to inquire about an arrest record. It is appropriate to inquire about an applicant's conviction record for security-sensitive jobs.

6. If you're going to discuss the town or city, mention everything and do not try to overemphasize the town's aspects as a family place in which to live and bring up children. Also, do not assume that your town or city is not the place for a single person or for minorities. Mention the town's lakes, urban areas, or whatever might be relevant. It is important to understand a single person may be interested in buying a house rather than just renting an apartment.

7. In general, avoid references to a candidate's personal happiness (i.e., social and/or sexual).

8. Do not indicate that you're interested in hiring a woman or minority person or person with a disability as a statistic to improve your organization's AA/EEO profile. You are offering an opportunity to be considered for the position based on qualifications.

    There are so many things not to do or say—what can you talk about? You can discuss:

- the individual's qualifications, abilities, experience, education, and interests,
- the duties and responsibilities of the job,
- where the job is located, travel, equipment, and facilities available,
- career possibilities and opportunities for growth, development, and advancement, and
- the organization's missions, programs, and achievements.

The use of a written contract or letter of agreement is recommended so that obligations of the employer-employee relationship are explicitly stated. The contract or letter of appointment should be developed in consultation with legal counsel (see appendix for a sample letter of appointment).

The appointment policy should include a statement such as: "Appointment is based on consideration of educational qualifications, appropriate certifications, and demonstrated achievement in the area of _____ in relation to the goals of the _____ organization and the position to be filled. In making a letter of appointment signed by both parties, recommendations for appointment to the board, commission or owners, the executive takes into account the judgements of professional peers. This statement guarantees certain procedures, which include assessment of an individual's educational background and past achievements, recommendations to the executive by a selection committee, and the executive's recommendation to the board, commission or owner.

Recruitment

Recruiting strong and effective employees is the key to the success of any organization. The efforts in the area of recruitment are critical to the future of the organization. One mistake can spell doom for an organization.

An important question to be answered when filling positions is whether it is desirable to fill the positions from within the existing staff through promotion or transfer or to seek outside applicants. It is the philosophy of many organizations always to look first within to promote loyal and competent employees before bringing in new outside personnel. This practice has the advantage of building staff moral and a conscious effort by employees to achieve and thus earn their way to more desirable positions. It rewards loyalty and provides a strong base for tradition and standardization of operation. However, outsiders may have qualifications superior to any current members of the organization. They will be more likely to provide new ideas and approaches to their assigned duties. In most cases, it is best to solicit applicants from both within and outside the organization. Careful judgement will then produce the best selection from the potential candidates. If the internal candidate is selected, in the end he/she will be stronger because of the process.

In-service Training

Training personnel is not a luxury, it is a necessity. Personnel can never be too well trained to perform their responsibilities. The training program should be for all personnel. No employee should be exempted from training.

Providing regular, planned, and systematically implemented in-service education programs for the staff can only benefit the organization and staff member. The education program(s) should be based on the needs of the individual(s) in relation to the demands of the job. The employee and employer should see the process as career development designed to make the employee a more effective member of the organization.

The human resources manager should develop an ongoing staff development program. This program should be composed of the following elements: (1) new staff orientation (see Table 1-6), (2) safety training (e.g., C.P.R. and first aid), (3) career development, and (4) technology upgrades. A few examples of staff development seminars or workshops are time management, communication skills, risk assessment and management, or increasing computer skills. These are only a few examples of the need for staff development which will continue to increase in a rapidly changing society.

The new staff orientation should include a discussion of:

- organization history, structure, and services,
- area and clients served by the organization,
- organization policies and regulations,
- relation of managers and human resources department,
- rules and regulations regarding—wages and wage payment, hours of work,
- overtime, safety (accident prevention and contingency procedures), holidays and vacations, methods of reporting tardiness and absences, discipline and grievances, uniforms and clothing, parking, fringe benefits, identification badges, office space, key(s), and recreation services, and
- opportunities—promotion and growth, job stabilization, and suggestions and decision making.

Common Errors of In-service Education Programs

It is important for the human resources manager to avoid the following errors when designing an in-service education program:

- feeding too much information at one time,
- telling without demonstrating,
- lack of patience,
- lack of preparation, failure to build in feedback, and
- failure to reduce tension within the audience.

Human Resource Development Tip

Knute Rockne often said that anybody could be a good teacher if he or she were able to master four simple principles of teaching:

- tell 'em what you want them to do in a way they understand you,
- show 'em what you want done,
- let 'em do it without interference from you, and
- correct 'em in a positive manner rather than negatively.

Evaluating Employee Performance

All employees should be evaluated. The evaluation period varies from six weeks for new employees to annual performance reviews for established employees. The evaluation should take the form of a performance appraisal. The performance appraisal is drafted by using the job description for the position as well as the mutually agreed upon annual performance objectives.

A performance appraisal (i.e., work plan, progress review, annual performance review) (see appendix for sample forms) is a systematic review of an individual employee's job performance to evaluate the effectiveness or adequacy of his or her work. Performance appraisals are the essence of human resources management. They are the means for evaluating employee effectiveness and a basis for producing change in the work behavior of each employee. Performance appraisals should be used as learning tools.

The task of assessing performance is a difficult and extremely complex undertaking. For this reason, significant planning and supervisory time should be devoted to the appraisal process. All organizations should require annual performance appraisals of all employees. In every case, they provide the opportunity for employee and supervisor to discuss the employee's job performance and to identify any desired redirection efforts. The human and financial resources devoted to conducting performance appraisals pay off in the long haul. It is valuable for both large and small organizations.

Other purposes for performance evaluations are to:

* provide employees with an idea of how they are doing,
* identify promotable employees or those who should be demoted
* administer the salary program,
* provide a basis for supervisor-employee communication,
* assist supervisors in knowing their workers better,
* identify training needs,
* help in proper employee placement within the organization,
* identify employees for layoff or recall,
* validate the selection process and evaluate other personnel activities (e.g., training programs, psychological tests, physical examinations),
* improve department employee effectiveness,
* determine special talents
* ascertain progress at the end of probationary periods (i.e., new employees or older employees with performance difficulties),
* furnish inputs to other personnel programs, and
* supply information for use in grievance interviews.

Human Resource Development Tip
The performance appraisal must be based on the job description and job relevant criteria, and not on unrelated personal characteristics or vague items not related to job performance.

Personnel Records

A personnel file should be established as a depository for all pertinent information concerning the employment status and productivity of each employee. These files serve the purpose of recording all aspects of employment status including, but not limited to: position title, job description, contract provisions, an accounting of benefits, accumulated sick leave, vacation time, awards received, performance appraisals, disciplinary actions, letters of commendation, salary history, home address and phone number, person(s) to contact in case of emergency, name of spouse and children, social security number, income tax data, life and/or disability insurance, and family physician.

Personnel files are confidential. When an item is placed into a personnel file, the employee must be notified. The employee may have access to his/her personnel file at any time under the guidelines established by the Freedom of Information Act. The employer cannot maintain a secondary personnel file that contains information that the employee is not aware exists. It should be general practice that only an employee's supervisor(s) have access to personnel files. Care must be exercised to protect the confidentiality of the employee. There should be policies and procedures established for the handling and accessibility of personnel files.

Rewards System

A rewards system, whether intrinsic or extrinsic, is essential to maintaining employee morale. People need to feel that their efforts are appreciated, or they will seek appreciation elsewhere. An intrinsic reward is personal—"I know I am doing a good job." The person feels good about him or herself. Extrinsic rewards are tangible and are provided by the organization. Common extrinsic rewards are salary increases above the average provided, promotional opportunities, bonuses not attached to salary, payment for attendance at conferences, special recognition dinners, and newspaper recognition.

The rewards system should be developed by the human resources manager. The system should concentrate on celebrating personnel for jobs well done. There should be a specific line item in the annual budget to cover all costs for the system.

Fringe Benefits

It is essential that a fringe benefit packet be established for all personnel in the organization. Fringe benefits typically include group health insurance (i.e., including prevention coverage, doctor visits, surgical interventions, drug purchases, eye and dental coverage), group term life insurance, disability insurance (Rehabilitation Act 1973, Veterans Readjustment Assistance Act 1974, Vocational Rehabilitation Act 1973), retirement programs, contributions to social security, leaves of absence for various reasons (e.g., personal emergency, death in the family, and jury duty), vacations, sick leave, holidays, and tuition assistance for advanced education.

The health benefits program should be administered by the human resources manager. The fringe benefits packet needs to be budgeted. The organization should not pay for the entire program, but share the costs with the employees (i.e., the organization will pay 80% of the medical plan and the employees will pay 20%).

Healthcare Plans

There are four different types of healthcare plans on the market today: **HMOs,** or health maintenance organizations, purport to lower the cost of care by regulating who patients can see for healthcare and what treatments they receive. For example, an HMO usually requires the patient to see a primary care physician first, who will determine whether to refer him or her to a specialist for a specific problem. **PPOs**, or preferred provider organizations, are similar to HMOs and will allow the patient to see only "approved" doctors who belong to the PPO network. **Indemnity plans**, such as the traditional Blue Cross/Blue Shield, allow patients to visit the doctor and specialist of their choice, but tend to be more costly than managed care plans. MSAs, medical savings accounts, offer an option for small companies (no more than 50 employees). **MSAs** are private accounts funded by an employee's pre-tax contributions that are used to pay for routine medical expenses. The plans are paired with catastrophic health insurance policies to cover the costs of serious illnesses. However, MSAs are available on a limited basis under a pilot program approved by Congress.

Selecting an Employee Healthcare Plan

With so many options in employee healthcare coverage today, club operators often accept the policy carrying the lowest price tag. But with healthcare, the old adage certainly rings true: You get what you pay for. It is not wise anymore to shop for a policy based only on price. There are too many other variables that can affect the quality of your insurance program. The following is a checklist of questions to answer when selecting your own facility's employee healthcare plan.

What are the Costs?

The club manager should not select a plan simply because it offers the lowest premium. Other ancillary costs (e.g., catastrophic illness or injury coverage) could drive up the price employees will pay for health insurance.

In addition to the monthly premium, check the cost of the co-payment (i.e., the amount you pay for office visits or hospital services) and the amount of any deductible (i.e., the amount you have to pay out-of-pocket before any insurance coverage applies). The club manager should investigate if there are any extra costs (e.g., for emergency care or visits to out-of-plan doctors).

Can You Choose a Doctor?

Some plans, such as point-of-service, allow employees to choose any doctor. Others, like managed-care plans, require employees to choose a doctor from an approved list of physicians affiliated with their healthcare network. If management selects a plan that limits choice of doctors, the plan should (1) offer a choice of physicians within a reasonable distance of the employees' homes or club, and (2) be affiliated with hospital(s) located near the club.

Does It Offer Access to Specialists?

The plan should have a procedure for visiting a specialist for treatment or consultation. A managed-care plan requires that employees be referred to a specialist by their primary care physicians.

Are There Coverage Limits?

The sport manager needs to understand what the proposed plan covers (i.e., prescription drugs and medical supplies). He or she should ask if the plan places a limit on how much it will pay for a specific injury or illness, or if it limits some forms of treatment.

How Much of the Premium Dollar Is Spent on Health Care?

Representatives of the various plans should be able to explain how much they spend on health care, and how much goes toward profit and administrative costs. Some plans spend as little as 60 cents of every dollar on healthcare. However, the better plans spend closer to 80 cents of every dollar on healthcare.

Does the Plan Have a Good Reputation?

Ask for the names of other employers who are offering their workers the healthcare plan being reviewed. It is important to gauge whether the plan has a good reputation with patients in the community. Further, ask local doctors if they are satisfied with the level of care the plan allows.

Can It Provide Excellent Informational Materials?

The club employees need to be made fully aware of the benefits any plan offers. Therefore, it is important that the plan under consideration offers good informational materials so the employees know all the details. It also helps if a representative of the company can come and answer questions.

Does It Deliver What It Promises?

What actually happens when an employee calls the plan's member telephone number? Can he or she get questions answered immediately by the designated representative? A good test of a plan's effectiveness is to simply perform a test-run ahead of time. Call the 800 number the company has provided. How long is it before someone picks up the phone?

Staff Compensation—Beyond the Paycheck

Most fitness facilities cannot afford to pay the employees as much as they deserve. But when it comes to employee compensation, there are alternatives to cash incentives. Monetary rewards are obviously a great way to compensate employees, but not the only way. In lean times, club operators have to get creative to demonstrate an appreciation of employees.

Following are several ways in which you can further compensate and motivate staffers:

- *Offer fringe benefits.* Providing benefits such as medical, dental, life and disability insurance may sound obvious, but many club operators neglect to offer their employees participation in these plans because of the cost. However, merely offering access to a plan does not necessarily mean the club covers the entire cost. It is common that company employees pay a portion of the monthly premiums. Fringe benefits can help a club attract and retain quality employees. For example, healthcare benefits are particularly appealing to more mature employees who might be supporting a family and need high-quality insurance plans.
- *Participate in a retirement plan.* Retirement savings accounts such as company-sponsored 401(k)s can attract and retain more mature employees. The club should match employee contributions to the plan, it helps remind participants that they have a stake in the success of the company, too.
- *Send them to school.* Allow employees to attend educational industry conferences. This can happen in several ways: by awarding paid time off and paying for an employee to attend a conference or seminar series as part of an in-service program; by awarding "points" for billing over a certain number of hours; or by awarding "points" for retaining a certain number of clients.
- *Throw a party.* Hosting occasional staff parties can help boost morale and foster a sense of spirit while thanking employees for all of their work. The employees should be encourage to invite their spouses or special friends.

- *Offer professional growth.* Support employees' professional growth and networking efforts by occasionally running educational programs in the club facility—perhaps by arranging for a speaker to talk about time management or customer service. The club should consider paying for at least one professional membership per employee annually. This will encourage employees to continue their growth and development. Further, the club management should establish a tuition reimbursement program that pays up to $3,000 in educational expenses annually. These educational benefits strengthen the structure of the organization as much as they improve the individual.
- *Provide access.* A membership in the club is a boon for many staffers, but take it a step further by offering access to ancillary services, such as, allowing staffers to attend any of the facility's wellness seminars.
- *Say "thanks."* A simple acknowledgment of a job well done or a certification recently attained can go a long way toward making an employee feel appreciated. Traditional employee-of-the-month programs should be spontaneous and meaningful. The following are ideas that might be useful: (1) At your next staff meeting, offer a round of applause for deserving employees. (2) Leave a message of praise on an individual's voice mail. (3) Write a handwritten note of thanks and send it to an employee's home.
- *Give time off.* For some employees, paid time off can be more rewarding than paid overtime. In fact, recent national employment studies show that, if given the choice, most of today's busy workers would rather have paid time off than more money in their paychecks.
- *Target rewards.* The sport manager might offer to the diligent and trustworthy employee who opens the club early every morning a certificate for a week's worth of free coffee. Or, give the most improved salesperson a subscription to an industry magazine. Be creative and surprise the employees with the unexpected.
- *Compensate for performance.* The management could develop a bonus pool that rewards employees based on the success of their department as well as the success of the club as a whole. For example, employees share in a pool that rewards them for profits beyond a predetermined base. This encourages everyone to run their departments more efficiently.
- *Reward employment anniversaries with certain privileges, benefits or rewards.* This procedure sends the subtle message to the rest of the staff that management values longevity.
- *Offer discounts.* Another strategy is to offer employees amenities, such as massages, tanning, pro shop purchases, restaurant meals, clinics and lessons, and discounts on, on-site childcare. These types of things are quality-of-life benefits that people really like.

Guidelines for Motivating Employees

Good leaders understand their human resources and the organization well enough to develop a clear vision of the future and can excite the human resources to follow the path into the future. Effective and successful leaders are those who establish and accomplish the goals and objectives of the organization. But they can not be successful without assistance from the human resources. These leaders need to be able to motivate the employees to release their potential work capabilities. The leaders must create a motivating environment. This can be done by implementing the following guidelines:

- making a commitment to motivation as an essential organizational goal,
- becoming aware of individual employee needs through observation and communication, learning their strengths and weaknesses, and allowing for differences,
- providing structured informal opportunities for individuals to communicate personal and career goals to their supervisors,
- assisting employees in achieving personal goals by accomplishing organizational goals,
- acknowledging a job well done as soon as possible and making such a practice consistent,
- establishing work objectives with individual employees as well as appropriate timelines for completion,
- scheduling formal, ongoing performance appraisal sessions in which employees and supervisors review work accomplishments, employee growth, employee performance assessments for future positions, and creating new objectives for interesting and challenging work,
- consulting with employees, their supervisor and colleagues when performance problems appear,
- providing opportunities to obtain vocational, leisure, or personal counseling to assist in making decisions and solving problems,
- removing roadblocks in the physical or administrative areas that may be demotivating,
- providing amenities that will bring pleasure (e.g., artwork, plants, coffeemaker, vending machines, or brighten the environment),
- enhancing supervisory approaches and strategies if they are not adequate;
- providing human and technical resources to assist employees,
- assessing strategies and approaches for creating a motivating environment on a continuous basis,
- providing opportunities for employees to obtain knowledge and skills through appropriate training, and enhance interpersonal relationships among colleagues, subordinates, and supervisors, and
- furnishing payoffs or rewards that have meaning to the individual for successful performance.

Termination

Termination, like appointment, is a two-way street: the person may choose to leave the organization, or the organization may decide that the person must leave. Whichever is the case, policies and procedures need to be established and placed in the human resources policy and procedure manual. There are two policies that need to be developed. The first relates to when an individual is considering termination (i.e., quitting). This policy might say, "All personnel are expected to give due notice in writing of intention to leave the organization, whether by resignation or retirement. Due notice is construed as not less than _____ for supervisory personnel, and _____ for all other personnel."

Procedures for terminations by the employee should include, but not be limited to the following:

*   an indication of the persons to whom written notice should be sent,
*   a statement regarding turning over such things as reports, records, and equipment, and
*   completion of an exit interview.

The second policy, which is the most sensitive of all human resource policies, for organization termination of the employee. The policy might read: "Termination of a staff member is based upon consideration of quality of performance in relation to achievement of the goals of the organization. The judgements of peers and supervisors are taken into account by the executive when recommending terminations to the board."

The following are questions that should be answered prior to considering termination by the organization:

*   How is quality performance considered?
*   What are the roles of the peers and supervisor(s)?
*   When is notice given?
*   How is notice given?
*   What, if any, severance pay?
*   What about the employees' due process?
*   How are the specific reasons for termination communicated?

Either the human resources manager or immediate supervisor will complete the dismissal.

Grievance Policy

All organizations need to establish a grievance policy and appropriate procedures to guarantee the employees' due process rights. The individual who is either terminated or disciplined has the right to due process. This aspect is generally covered by a policy on grievance and provides detailed procedures of implementation. The policy and procedures developed should have the intent to resolve differences at the lowest level of the professional relations and as informally as possible (see Table 1-6 for a sample grievance procedure).

Table 1-6
Sample Grievance Procedure

Due process is the right of the individual to appeal a decision made about him/her with which he/she disagrees. The grievance policy for an organization outlines the process by which an employee can appeal a decision. A grievance policy should include:

Step 1: If an employee feels unjustly or unfairly treated or disciplined, the employee must first take up the complaint with the immediate supervisor. The supervisor must reply to the employee's complaint within five (5) days.

Step 2: If no mutually satisfactory settlement of the complaint results from Step 1, a meeting of the next level supervisor, the immediate supervisor, and aggrieved employee shall take place no later than three (3) working days; following the referral of the complaint to Step 2. The next level supervisor must reply to the employee's complaint within five (5) working days.

Step 3: If the grievance has not been satisfactorily resolved at Step 2, the aggrieved employee and a representative, if desired, will be granted the opportunity to meet with the appropriate administrative official and the director of human relations or designee(s). (In grievances involving questions relating to allegations of discrimination because of sex, sexual orientation, age, disability, creed, race, or national origin, the affirmative action officer will participate in a fact-finding and advisory capacity with the director of human relations or a designee(s).) This meeting should take place no later than five (5) working days following the referral of the grievance to Step 3. The director of human relations will reply to the employee's grievance within five (5) working days.

Step 4: Should the grievance fail to be resolved at Step 3, the employee may request its referral to the head of the organization for review and final disposition.

It is important for all supervisors to know how to deal with complaints and grievances non-emotionally and fairly.

Sexual Harassment Policy Development

Sexual harassment is the imposition of unwanted sexual requirements on a person or persons within the context of an unequal power relationship. There are many forms of sexual harassment in the workplace including, but not limited to: unwelcome physical touching, hugs and kisses; physically cornering someone; sexual jokes, derogatory sexual names, pornographic pictures; promises of reward or threats of punishment coupled with sexual advances. Men as well as women may be the victims of harassment, and women as well as men may be harassers. The victim does not have to be of the opposite sex from the harasser.

Since 1976, the courts and the U.S. Equal Employment Opportunity Commission (EEOC) have defined sexual harassment as one form of sex discrimination. As such, it violates Title VII of the 1964 Civil Rights Act (42 U.S.C. §2000e-5-9) which guarantees that a person shall not be discriminated against in an employment setting because of race, color religion, sex, or national origin.

In the workplace, sexual harassment occurs when a person who is in a position of authority, influence, or can affect another person's job or career uses the position's authority to coerce the other person (male-female; female-male; female-female; male-male) into sexual acts or relations or punishes the person if he or she refuses to comply.

It is important that the organization's human resources handbook have a policy and procedures to assist employees faced with this type of action. Such a policy might read as follows:

> Unwelcome sexual advances, requests for sexual favors, and other verbal or physical conduct of a sexual nature constitute sexual harassment when (1) submission to such conduct is made either explicitly or implicitly a term or condition of an individual's employment, (2) submission or rejection of such conduct by an individual is used as the basis for employment decisions affecting such individuals, or (3) such conduct has the purpose or effect of unreasonably interfering with an individual's performance or creating an intimidating, hostile, or offensive environment.

Note: All policy statements developed should be reviewed by legal counsel before implementation of the policy.

The policy rests on three conditions established by the EEOC:

- submission to the conduct is made either an explicit or implicit condition of employment;
- submission to or rejection of the conduct is used as the basis for an employment decision affecting the harassed employee; and
- the harassment substantially interferes with an employee's work performance or creates an intimidating, hostile, or offensive work environment.

A sexually hostile work environment can be created by:

- discussing sexual activities,
- unnecessary touching,
- commenting on physical attributes,

- displaying sexually suggestive pictures,
- using demeaning or inappropriate terms, such as "babe,"
- ostracizing workers of one gender by those of the other, and
- using crude and offensive language.

All staff in positions of authority need to be sensitive to the hazards in personal relationships with subordinate employees. When significant disparities in age or authority are present between two individuals, questions about *professional responsibility* and the *mutuality of consent* to a personal relationship may well arise.

Human Resource Development Tip

In determining if your own conduct might be unwelcome, ask yourself, "Would my behavior change if someone from my family was in the room or would I want someone from my family to be treated this way?"

Further, if it happens to you or another employee, what should you do? Hoping the problem will go away or accepting it as "the way things are" only perpetuates and encourages such inappropriate behaviors. It is important that the organization outlines a similar procedure as follows: (1) report the incident immediately, (2) know your rights and the organization's policies and procedures, (3) keep a written, dated record of all incidents, and any witnesses, (4) consider confronting the harasser in person or writing the harasser a letter (i.e., outlining the facts of what has occurred, how you feel about the events, and what you want to happen next), and (5) evaluate your options and follow through.

False accusations of sexual harassment can be prevented if the following suggestions are taken seriously:

- schedule one-on-one meetings in businesslike settings, preferably during the daytime,
- leave doors open,
- focus on the purpose of meeting,
- respect the personal space of others, and
- limit touching to the conventional handshake.

The charge of sexual harassment is not to be taken lightly by a charging party, a respondent, or any member of the organization. Both the charging party and the respondent may anticipate a confidential, impartial review of the facts by the human resources manager.

Americans with Disabilities Act

The Americans with Disabilities Act (ADA) Public Law 101-336 (July 26, 1990) provides certain protections for those with statutorily defined disabilities in the areas of: employment, government services, places of public accommodation, public transportation, and telecommunications. Health clubs, fitness and exercise facilities, health care provider offices, day care or social service establishments, as well as gymnasiums, health spas and other places of exercise, recreation, or sport are all covered under the ADA.

Disability means, with respect to an individual, a physical or mental impairment that substantially limits one or more of the major life activities of such individual; a record of such an impairment; or being regarded as having such an impairment. The phrase physical or mental impairment includes, but is not limited to, such contagious and noncontagious diseases and conditions as orthopedic, visual, speech, and hearing impairments, cerebral palsy, epilepsy, muscular dystrophy, multiple sclerosis, cancer, heart disease, diabetes, mental retardation, emotional illness, specific learning disabilities, HIV disease, tuberculosis, drug addiction, and alcoholism.

The phrase *major life activities* means functions such as caring for one's self, performing manual tasks, walking, seeing, hearing, speaking, breathing, learning, and working.

The phrase *has a record of such an impairment* means one has a history of or has been misclassified as having a mental or physical impairment that substantially limits one or more major life activities.

The ADA is a federal anti-discrimination statute designed to remove barriers that prevent qualified individuals with disabilities from enjoying the same employment opportunities that are available to persons without disabilities. Like the Civil Rights Act of 1964 that prohibits discrimination on the basis of race, color, religion, national origin, and sex, the ADA seeks to ensure access to equal employment opportunities based on merit. It does not guarantee equal results, establish quotas, or require preferences favoring individuals with disabilities over those without disabilities. Rather it focuses on when an individual's disability creates a barrier to employment opportunities, the ADA requires employers to consider whether reasonable accommodation could remove the barrier. The ADA establishes a process in which the employer must assess a disabled individual's ability to perform the essential functions of the specific job held or desired. However, where that individual's functional limitation impedes such job performance, an employer must take steps to reasonably accommodate, and thus overcome the particular impediment, unless to do so would impose an undue hardship. Such accommodations usually take the form of adjustments to the way a job customarily is performed, or to the work environment itself. An accommodation must be tailored to match the needs of the disabled individual with the needs of the job's essential functions.

Guidelines for Managing AIDS in the Workplace

HIV/AIDS is a serious health problem. Many people do not understand the disease and make certain inappropriate judgements. It is important for organizations to develop a response to AIDS in the workplace. The following principles are a starting point for the development of a policy relating to AIDS in the workplace (developed by the Citizens Commission on AIDS for New York City and Northern New Jersey):

- People with HIV/AIDS infection are entitled to the same rights and opportunities as people with other serious or life-threatening illnesses.
- Employment policies must, at a minimum, comply with federal, state, local laws and regulations.
- Employment policies should be based on the scientific and epidemiological evidence that people with HIV/AIDS infection do not pose a risk of transmission of the virus to coworkers through ordinary workplace contact.
- The highest levels of management and union leadership should unequivocally endorse nondiscriminatory employment policies and educational programs about HIV/AIDS.
- Employers and unions should communicate their support of these policies to workers in simple, clear, and unambiguous terms.
- Employers have a duty to protect the confidentiality of employees' medical information.
- Employers and unions should undertake education for all employees in order to prevent work disruption and rejection by coworkers of an employee with HIV/AIDS.
- Employers should not require HIV/AIDS screening as part of general pre-employment or workplace physical examinations.
- In those special occupational settings where there may be a potential risk of exposure to HIV/AIDS (e.g., health care, exposure to blood or blood products), employers should provide specific, ongoing education and training, as well as the necessary equipment to reinforce appropriate infection control procedures and ensure that they are implemented.

Guidelines for Communicating with People

"If there is one single problem that all organizations have in common it's lack of communication" (Ailes, 1988, 124). Every organization and person within the organization needs to improve upon communication skills. The 10 most common problems relating to communication are:

- lack of initial rapport with listeners,
- stiffness or woodenness in use of body,
- presentation of material is intellectually oriented, forgetting to involve the audience emotionally,

- speaker seems uncomfortable because of fear of failure,
- poor use of eye contact and facial expression,
- lack of humor,
- speech direction and intent unclear due to improper preparation,
- inability to use silence for impact,
- lack of energy, causing inappropriate pitch pattern, speech rate and volume, and
- use of boring language and a lack of interesting material.

There are seven essential components for successful communication to exist, including:

- content ... is it accurate?
- clarity ... is it clear?
- credibility ... is it the truth?
- context ... does it fit the situation or circumstances? Is it appropriate to the audience?
- continuity ... do ideas flow from one to another?
- consistency ... are thoughts and words consistent?
- channels ... are adequate means established for the carrying of the message, and the receipt of communication?

Good communication starts with good *conversation.* If you converse well, then you should be able to transfer that ability to a lectern or TV or any other format. To gauge your conversational skills, you need constructive, critical feedback from someone else; spouse, friend, or co-worker to candidly appraise your conversational skills, based on these criteria:

- Are you self-centered or "other"-oriented?
- Do you try to dominate conversations?
- Do you talk too much, overexplain, or lecture others? Are you a complainer?
- Do you draw other people out on topics they're clearly interested in discussing?
- Are you a sympathetic listener?
- Do you smile, laugh easily, and respond to others genuinely?
- Do you have interesting things to say?
- Can you discuss subjects besides your job or home life?
- Do you occasionally use colorful language?
- Do you avoid trite expressions?
- Are you lively or dull?
- Do you speak in a monotone and without enthusiasm?
- Do you get on to the point quickly and engagingly or do you belabor points?
- Are you passive and nonresponsive or active in the give-and-take on conversation?
- Do you encourage monologues or dialogues?
- Do you ask others open-ended questions that draw them out?

- Are your questions "closed," prompting just one-word responses? Open-ended questions often begin with how or what; they elicit detail. You may need to use closed questions occasionally, as in this series of questions. You can recognize closed questions because they often begin with *do you …*
- Do you pontificate or do you ask others how they feel about a subject?
- Are you open, candid, direct, and friendly or tight-lipped, secretive, elliptical, and aloof?

Effective communication must be a two-way process. Communication must flow two-ways … from the sender to the intended recipient. Communication can take place through a person's actions and inactions, as well as by one's speech and writings. Communication can be deliberate, incidental, or accidental; however, the fundamental concept of communication is clear. In order to have effective communication, both the sender and the recipient of the message(s) must interpret what is sent/received in an identical fashion.

There are numerous barriers to good communication that lessen the effectiveness of the message(s) being sent. The message may not even be received because of deficiencies in (1) the manner in which the message is communicated, (2) the message itself, (3) various obstructions, and (4) because of some defect with the intended recipient.

Some of the factors that can affect the effectiveness of communication attempts include the following:

- use of specific language … meaning of words,
- misinterpretations of words or terms,
- political differences,
- religious beliefs,
- prejudices,
- superstitions,
- age,
- poor choice of communication medium,
- interference,
- lack of clarity,
- words taken out of context,
- use of words with more than one meaning,
- timing of the communication,
- circumstances surrounding the communication, and
- pride.

Listening Tips

Here are some tips that can assist managers and employees to become better listeners:

- Relax and clear your mind if someone is speaking, so that you're receptive to what they're saying.
- Never assume that you've heard correctly, because the first few words have taken you in a certain direction. Most listening mistakes are made by people who only hear the first few words of a sentence, finish the sentence in their own minds, and miss the second half.
- Learn to speed up your point of contact as a listener. The second you hear a sound coming from another person, concentrate quickly on the first few words. That will get you started correctly.
- Don't tune out a speaker just because you don't like his or her looks, voice, or general demeanor. Stay open to new information.
- Don't overreact emotionally to the speaker's words or ideas—especially those that may run contrary to your usual thinking. Hear the other person out.
- Before forming a conclusion, let the speaker complete his or her thought.
- Then, evaluate by distinguishing in your mind specific evidence presented (good) versus generalities (bad).
- Part of listening is writing down things that are important. You should always have paper, a pencil, a notebook, or a card in your pocket. Throughout the day, many important things are discussed, but by the close of business, you don't remember the details. How many of you have found a phone number on a scrap of paper in your handwriting with no name attached? So take notes to listen, to remember later, and to document, if necessary.
- People will often say one thing and mean something else. As you grow in your listening sophistication it is important to listen for *intent* as well as *content*. Watch as you listen. Be sure that the speaker's eyes, body, and face are sending signals that are consistent with the speaker's voice and words. If something sounds out of sync, get it cleared up. Many people are afraid of looking foolish if they ask for clarification because it will seem as if they weren't paying attention. Better to have the speaker repeat a message on the spot than to set off a chain reaction of misunderstanding.
- Human communication goes through three phases: reception (listening), information processing (analyzing), and transmission (speaking). When you overlap any of those, you may short-circuit the reception (listening) process. Try to listen without overanalyzing. Try to listen without interrupting the speaker.
- The other major failing of people in listening is simple distraction. To listen correctly you must be able to reprioritize immediately. The second you hear sound coming toward you, focus and say to yourself: "This is important." Keep your eye on the speaker. Don't fiddle with pens, pencils, paper, or other distractions.

Summary

Human resource management is the key to a successful organization. A strong impartial set of human resource policies and procedures is critical to the health of an organization. This chapter has identified the steps to be taken when recruiting, hiring, training, motivating, and evaluating personnel, the appropriate policies to be developed regarding sexual harassment, ADA, and AIDS in the workplace, and the steps to improve employee and employer communication.

Learning Objective 1: Understand important legal issues regarding employer-employee relationship.

The policies and procedures regarding hiring, interviewing, evaluating, discrimination, sexual harassment, ADA, and AIDS in the workplace are examples of legal issues regarding employer-employee relationships. It is important for any human resources manager to be cognizant of these and other legislative enactments.

Learning Objective 2: Delineate the contents of a human resources handbook.

The human resources handbook should include such categories as employee recruitment, hiring process, evaluation, organizational chart, employee classification, inservice education, fringe benefits, personnel records, discrimination, sexual harassment, ADA, AIDS, and employer-employee communication.

Learning Objective 3: Describe the hiring process and all its components.

The hiring process includes evaluating employment needs, developing job description announcements, interviewing process, and selection. This process is the most important process in any organization. It can determine the organization's future.

Learning Objective 4: Design a performance evaluation process.

A performance evaluation should be based on two important documents—the employee's job description and the mutually agreed upon annual performance document. The job description describes the duties of the employee. Further, each employee should have an annual performance document outlining what tasks should be completed within mutually established time lines. The combination of these two documents should be the foundation for the performance appraisal.

Learning Objectives 5: Develop a regularly scheduled in-service program.

The human resources manager should develop an in-service program for all employees. The in-service program should be both general and specific in nature. All employees need in-service programs to keep them focused and prepared to complete their tasks more effectively.

Learning Objectives 6: Understand how to motivate employees.

It is important for all levels of management to understand how to motivate employees. A poorly motivated employee can cause the organization problems. A properly motivated employee becomes a great asset to the organization.

Learning Objectives 7: Describe a termination process.

The human resources manager must establish a clear and simple termination policy for both employees who wish to relocate and the employer who needs to eliminate ineffective employees. The process must include due process for all employees.

Learning Objective 8: Design a grievance procedure for an organization.

The grievance procedure must be clear, simple, and employee-friendly. The procedure should be designed to protect employee due process rights.

Learning Objective 9: Discuss the values of good communication and listening skills.

A good communication network is a key to a successful organization. The employee and managers at all levels need to understand how to communicate with each other and listen to each other's concerns and ideas. Many differences can be resolved if employee-employer feel comfortable talking with each other. Effective communication increases the trust level with the organization.

Case Study

You have been hired as the manager of a new privately-owned fitness, recreation, and sport facility in Fairfax, VA just south of Washington, D.C. You have been charged with the initial responsibility of hiring all the staff. The facility contains an indoor and outdoor pool, indoor and outdoor tennis courts, indoor soccer field, outdoor fields for softball and soccer, racquetball courts, strength center, cardiovascular center, dance exercise studio, day care area, eating facilities, locker room space, and health spa area with sauna, steam room, and hot tub. You will need to hire assistant managers, clerical support, receptionists, a tennis pro, racquetball pro, personal trainers, custodians, officials, dance exercise instructors, swimming instructors, lifeguards, kitchen staff, and more.

1.   What would you do first?
2.   What steps would take in recruiting this staff?
3.   What should be the steps in the hiring process?
4.   How would you evaluate the personnel?
5.   How would you organize the in-service training programs?

References

Ailes, Roger. (1988). *You are the message: Secrets of the master communicator.* Homewood, IL: Dow Jones-Irwin.

Americans with Disabilities Act (ADA). Public Law 101-336 [S.993], July 26, 1990; 42 U.S §12101- 12213 (1991).

Civil Rights Act 1964; 42 U.S.C. §2000e-5 - 2000e-9. Executive Order 11246.

Rehabilitation Act of 1973; 29 U.S.C. §791.

Veterans Readjustment Assistance Act of 1974.

Vocational Rehabilitation Act of 1973; amended 1974.

Suggested Readings

Grossman, Arnold H. (1989). *Personnel management in recreation and leisure services,* (2nd ed.). Reston, VA: American Alliance for Health, Physical Education, Recreation, and Dance.

Herbert, David L. (1992). *The Americans with Disabilities Act: A guide for health clubs and exercise facilities.* Canton, OH: Professional Reports Corporation.

Horine, L. (1991). *Administration of physical education and sport programs.* Dubuque, IA: Wm. C. Brown & Benchmark.

Jensen, C.R. (1988). *Administrative management of physical education and athletic programs.* (2nd ed.). Philadelphia: Lee & Febiger.

2

THE PLANNING PROCESS

◆ ——————————————— ◆

Instructional Objectives

After reading this chapter the student should be able to:

• describe the planning process,

• appreciate the planning process,

• identify the different types of plans that might exist in a typical enterprise,

• recount the importance of strategic planning,

• assess an enterprise's strengths and weaknesses,

• recognize the 10 biggest pitfalls to successful planning, and

• list some benefits of objectives.

Introduction

Planning is the process of determining the organization's goals and objectives and selecting a course of action to accomplish them within the environment and within and outside the organization. Its primary purpose is to offset future uncertainties by reducing the risk surrounding the organization's operations. It requires the organization to review its internal accomplishments (strengths) and challenges (weaknesses), and external opportunities and threats. During this process, the organization will develop a SWOT chart (i.e., the depiction of internal strengths and weakness, and external opportunities and threats of the organization and identify connections within the organization as well as externally that will allow the organization to become strategically competitive in the future [see Figure 2-1]). This process is best facilitated by the use of brainstorming.

Figure 2-1
A Connections SWOT Chart

Internal Strengths List (accomplishments)	Internal Weaknesses List (challenges)
External Opportunities List	External Threats List

The best way to identify items under each category is through the use of brainstorming with the organization's employees and others outside the organization. The category "external opportunities" relates to those unique favorable circumstances that the organization might be able to take advantage of in the future. The external threat category refers to those circumstances that might be harmful to the organization if not carefully understood.

Brainstorming

Brainstorming, developed by Alexander F. Osborn (1888-1966), involves forming a group of six to eight members who are presented with a problem and asked to identify as many potential solutions as possible. The session usually lasts from 30 minutes to an hour. At least two days before a session, group members are given a one-page summary of the problem they are to consider (Hussey, 1991). There are four rules of brainstorming: (1) **criticism is prohibited**—Judgement of ideas must be withheld until all ideas have been generated. (2) **"freewheeling" is welcome**— The wilder and further out the idea the better. It is easier to "tame down" than to "think up" ideas. (3) **quantity is wanted**—The greater the number of ideas, the greater the likelihood of an outstanding solution. (4) **Combination and improvement are sought**— In addition to contributing ideas of their own, members are encouraged to suggest how the ideas of others can be improved, or how two or more ideas can be combined into still another idea.

The Steps in the Planning Process

There are five steps in the planning process, including establishing objectives, developing premises, decision making, implementing a course of action, and evaluating the results (Wright, 1994).

Step 1: Identifying internal and external connections and relationships

The initial step in the planning process is identifying internal strengths (accomplishments) and weaknesses (challenges), and external opportunities and threats (concerns). This information is placed into a SWOT analysis chart which will assist in the identification of connections and relationships relating to the internal organizational environment and external environment.

The following is an example of a SWOT for an intercollegiate sport program:

Internal Strengths	*Internal Weaknesses*
In compliance with Title IX	Need to work on equal pay issues
Graduation rate is 65%	Need to increase graduation rate
In compliance with NCAA rules	Insufficient funding
Above win/loss record overall	Ticket sales down dramatically
A well-organized booster club	Fund-raising below expectations
Stable coaching staff	Need more women coaches
Stable administrative staff	Need more women administrators

External Opportunities	*External Threats*
Sport's entertainment value	Saturated entertainment market
Low unemployment	Low paying service jobs
Increasing population	Over-55 age group increasing the fastest

Step 2: Establishing objectives

The next step in the planning process is the establishment of organization objectives. Objectives are an essential starting point because they provide direction for all other managerial activities. Objectives are generally based on perceived opportunities that exist in an organization's surrounding environment.

Based on the above SWOT chart that lists external opportunities one object might be: XYZ University will capture 45% of the local entertainment dollar.

Step 3: Developing premises

Once organization objectives have been established, developing premises about the future environment in which they are to be accomplished is essential. This basically involves forecasting events or conditions likely to influence objective attainment.

According to the noted futurists Alvin Toffler and John Naisbett, the aging Baby Boomers and Generation Xers have one thing in common—their love for American sport. They predict that the entertainment industry will increase by 50% by the year 2000, and that sport will capture nearly 70% of the growth. Over the past decade, the number of successful professional sports has nearly doubled and

the traditional sports continue to expand. Therefore, it is fair to assume that intercollegiate sports will benefit from this overall growth in the entertainment industry.

Step 4: Decision making

After establishing objectives and developing premises, the next step is selecting the best course of action for accomplishing stated objectives from the possible alternatives. There are three phases of decision making: (1) available alternatives must be identified, (2) each alternative must be evaluated in light of the premises about the future and the external environment, and (3) the alternative with
the highest estimated probability of success should be selected.

Institution XYZ brings together a task force to develop a series of action
plans for achievement of objectives established. This task force will be composed
of a variety of stockholders, such as, university administration, athletic administrators, coaches, faculty, students, student athletes, local community leaders, alumni,
and fans. The task force will review the objectives and corresponding premises
and then establish a number of viable action plans. The action plan for capturing
45% more of the local entertainment dollar might go something like this: (1) the
university will select a marketing company to develop a five-year marketing plan
aimed at capturing additional entertainment market share, (2) the university will
implement the new marketing strategies by increasing public relations and promotional activities, and (3) the university will retain an advertising company to
develop an advertising campaign.

Step 5: Implementing a course of action

Once a plan of action has been adopted, it must be implemented. Plans alone
are no guarantee of success. Managers must initiate activities that will translate the
plans into action.

Each objective and its action plan should become the responsibility of a
specific group or administrator to implement. The action plan should be implemented step by step along a specific time table. The assistant athletic director,
responsible for marketing, will solicit marketing proposals and select the marketing proposal that best suits the university's needs. Further, he or she will organize
the staff to implement the marketing plan. Finally, he or she will solicit advertising
proposals for the advertising campaign and select the one best suited to the university.

Step 6: Evaluating the plan

Plans and their implementation must be constantly monitored and evaluated. All managers are responsible for the evaluation of planning outcomes. Comparison of actual results with those projected is necessary, as well as to refine
plans.

The athletic director will request the planning team to establish results and
an appropriate time table for completion for each objective and action plan. Upon
completion of each objective and action plan, a comparison will be made to see
whether or not each objective was completed appropriately.

Classification of Plans

Plans can be viewed from a number of different perspectives. From the viewpoint of application, plans can be classified in terms of *functional areas* (e.g., marketing plans, production plans, human resource management plans, financial plans). Plans may also be classified according to the *period of time* over which they are projected (e.g., short- or long-range) or with respect to their *frequency of use* (standing versus single-use). The nature of functional plans is evident. However, further explanation is needed for period of time and frequency of use plans.

Short- and long-range plans are the most popular classification of plans. In practice, however, the terms short-range and long-range have no precise meaning, but rather express relative periods of time. These plans are interrelated in at least two respects. First, they compete for the allocation of resources. Consequently, there can be a dangerous tendency to sacrifice long-term results for short-term gains. Second, short-range plans should be compatible with long-range plans. It is usually difficult, if not impossible, for long-range plans to succeed unless short-range plans are accomplished. Thus, both are important in achieving an organization's objectives.

The term short-range is often titled "Operational" in many organizations, and long-term has been changed to "Applied Strategic." These terms will be used interchangeably throughout the remainder of the chapter.

There are three criteria most often used in determining the length of a plan: (1) how far into the future an organization's commitments extend; (2) how much uncertainty is associated with the future; and (3) how much lead time is required to ready a good or service for sale (Paley, 1991).

Planning by most effective organizations is often done on a "rolling" basis. This simply means those organizations that develop applied strategic plans for a five-year period and two-year operational plans are updating both plans on an annual basis. As the current year of a five-year plan closes, it is extended or rolled forward to include a new fifth year. This procedure allows an organization to revise its plans on the basis of new information and to maintain a degree of flexibility in its commitments. A general guideline is to refrain from formalizing plans until a final commitment is absolutely necessary (Fogg, 1994).

Standing plans are used again and again, focusing on managerial situations that recur repeatedly. Standing plans include policies, procedures, and rules.

Policies are general statements that serve to guide decision making. They are plans in that they prescribe parameters within which certain decisions are to be made. Policies set limits but they are subject to interpretation because they are broad guidelines. Table 2-1 provides examples of policies. Notice that each example is purposefully broad and only provides a general guideline subject to managerial discretion. However, each statement does prescribe parameters for decision making and, thus, sets limits to the actions of organization members.

A *procedure* is a series of related steps that are to be followed in an established order to achieve a given purpose. Procedures prescribe exactly what ac-

Table 2-1
Examples of Policies

Customer Service:	It is the policy of this organization to provide customers with the finest service possible within limits of sound financial principles. [Interpretation = What are the limits of sound finance?]
Employee Benefits:	It is the policy of this organization to provide its employees with acceptable working conditions and an adequate living wage. [Interpretation = What is acceptable and adequate?]
Promotion from Within:	It is the policy of this organization to promote qualified employees from within organization ranks whenever possible. [Interpretation = What is meant by qualified or feasible?]
Gifts from Suppliers or Vendors:	It is the policy of this organization that no employee shall accept any gift from any supplier or vendor unless it is of nominal value. [Interpretation = What is nominal?]

tions are to be taken in a specific situation. Procedures are similar to policies in that both are intended to influence certain decisions. They are different in that policies address themselves to single decisions, while procedures address themselves to a sequence of related decisions. Table 2-2 shows how an organization might write procedures for processing a bill of sale.

Table 2-2
Procedure for Processing a Bill of Sale

Step 1:   Prior to recording, all noncash sales will be forwarded to the credit department for approval.

Step 2:   Following the necessary credit approval, all bills of sale will be presented to production scheduling for an estimated production completion date.

Step 3:   Subsequent to production scheduling, all bills of sale will be delivered to the accounting department where they will be recorded.

Step 4:   Pursuant to their processing in the accounting department, all bills of sale will be filed with the shipping department within 24 hours.

Rules are different from policies and procedures in that they specify what personal conduct is required of an individual. Stated differently, rules are standing plans that either prescribe or prohibit action by specifying what an individual may or may not do in a given situation. Therefore, the statements "eye goggles must be worn," "no swimming alone," "no smoking," "no drinking on premises" are all examples of rules. Rules are usually accompanied by specifically stated penalties that vary according to the seriousness of the offense and the number of previous violations. Unlike policies that guide, but do not eliminate discretion, rules leave little room for interpretation. The only element of choice associated with a rule is whether it applies in a given situation. Of the three forms of standing plans discussed, rules are the simplest and most straightforward. They are without question the narrowest in scope and application.

Single-use plans are specifically developed to implement courses of action that are relatively unique and are unlikely to be repeated. Three principal forms of single-use plans are **budgets, programs,** and **projects.**

A *budget* is a plan that deals with the future allocation and utilization of various resources to different activities over a given time period. Budgets are perhaps most frequently thought of in financial terms. However, they also are used to plan allocation and utilization of labor, raw materials, floor space, machine hours, and so on. A budget simply is a tool that managers use to translate future plans into numerical terms. Further, they are a method for controlling organization operations (see Chapter 4 for a thorough consideration of budgets).

Programs are typically intended to accomplish a specific objective within a fixed time. Table 2-3 offers six guidelines for effective program development.

Table 2-3
Guidelines for Effective Program Development

1. Divide the overall program into parts, each with clearly defined purpose.
2. Study the necessary sequence and relationships between the resulting parts.
3. Assign appropriate responsibility for each part to carefully selected individuals or groups.
4. Determine and allocate the resources necessary for the completion of each part.
5. Estimate the completion time required for each part.
6. Establish target dates for the completion of each part.

Projects are usually a subset or component part of a specific program. Accordingly, projects often share some of the same characteristics as the overall programs of which they are a part. Projects are less complex than their supporting programs and, are, by definition narrower in scope. Table 2-4 summarizes the various standing and single-use plans.

Table 2-4
Summary of Standing and Single-use Plans

Type	Definition	Example
Standing Plans		
Policy	A general statement that guides decision making.	"Preference will be given to hiring the handicapped."
Procedure	A series of related steps that are followed in an established order to achieve a given purpose.	Filing for travel expenses reimbursement.
Rule	A statement that either prescribes or prohibits action by specifying what an individual may or may not do in a specific situation.	"No eating at work stations."
Single-use Plans		
Budget	A plan that deals with the future allocations and utilization of various resources to different enterprise activities over a given time.	Allocation and utilization of machine hours.
Program	A plan typically intended to accomplish a specific objective within fixed time.	Membership Recruitment Program.
Project	A subset or component part of a specific program.	Telemarketing project.

Strategic Planning

Strategic planning, unlike operational planning which focuses on more direct aspects of operating an organization, focuses on an organization's long-term relationship to its environment (Wright, Pringle, Kroll, & Parnell, 1994). The strategic plan should be developed through participatory involvement by all members of the organization and its clients. By focusing on an organization as a total system, strategic planning recognizes that all organizations face many uncontrollable elements within the environment. Competitors' actions, economic conditions, regulatory groups, labor unions, and changing customer preferences represent factors over which an organization achieves its objectives. Therefore, strategic planning concerns itself with shaping an organization so it can accomplish its goals. A strategic plan attempts to answer such questions as (Antoniou, 1994):

- What is the organization's business and what should it be?
- What business should the organization be in five years from now? 10 years?
- Who are the organization's customers and who should they be?
- Should the organization try to grow in this business or grow primarily in other businesses?

Objectives

Objectives are those ends that an organization seeks to achieve by its existence and operation. There are two essential characteristics of an objective: (1) objectives are predetermined, and (2) objectives describe *future* desired results toward which *present* efforts are directed. There are eight *key result areas* in which all organizations should establish objectives according to Peter F. Drucker—market share, innovation, productivity, physical and financial resources, profitability, manager performance and development, worker performance and attitude, and social responsibilities (1964).

There are two ways to establish objectives. The first is the *entrepreneurial method.* According to this method, objectives are established by an entrepreneur (top management or stockholders). An organization's objectives are defined as the entrepreneur's objectives. The entrepreneur ensures that employees' actions are consistent with these objectives by paying them—salaries, bonuses, or pensions—to support the goals.

The second method is the *consensual method.* In this method, the objectives of an organization are established by the general consent of those concerned. Organization members share in setting the objectives and conflict is eliminated by identifying common or consensual goals.

The Planning Premise

Once enterprise objectives have been established, developing planning premises about the future environment in which they are to be accomplished is essential (Hoffman, 1993; Hamel & Prahalad, 1994). Unfolding environmental conditions almost invariably influence enterprise objectives, forcing modifications in both current and anticipated activities. Premises, which attempt to describe what the future will be like, provide a framework for identifying, evaluating, and selecting a course of action for accomplishing enterprise objectives.

The Components of Applied Strategic and Operational Plans

The *applied strategic plan* is composed of a situational analysis, highlights, introduction, vision statement(s), value(s), mission statement, internal environment, external environment, connections, major action plans, action priorities, monitoring and evaluating, and review, approval, and commitment (Goodstein, 1993). The *situational analysis* has five sections including a description of the geographical location and pertinent demographics (e.g., population, economic indicators, industry, average income, etc.), a description of the organization, a SWOT summary, an overview of major strategies and plans, and organization progress since last review.

The *highlight* section describes major challenges, customer/client needs, and major accomplishments. The *introduction* provides the reader with a brief description of the planning process and the people involved in the process. The *vision statement* describes the dream of the future for the organization. The *values* section describes that which is desirable or worthy of esteem by the organization (e.g., fostering a "we care" image with our clients). The *mission statement* is a statement outlining the purpose and mission of the organization. The *internal environment* is composed of a description of the organization's strengths (accomplishments) and weaknesses (challenges), and the *external environment* consists of a description of the organization's external opportunities and threats (concerns). After the internal and external environments have been analyzed, a series of *connections* are established based on the relationships found in the analysis. From the connections, a series of *major action plans* are established. The actions plans are then translated into *major action priorities*. These major action priorities are the foundation for the one- or two-year operational plan. The applied strategic plan must have established *monitoring and evaluating* procedures in place to assure the proper implementation of the plan. Finally, there must be *review, approval, and commitment* steps established for the final acceptance of the plan.

The *operational plan* includes the following components: major action priorities, problem, project summary, priority issue(s), background, vision of success, goals and objectives of the plan, and action plans (strategies, objectives, baseline data, and action steps).

Each major action priority will have a specific *problem(s)* that will be resolved at the completion of the project. The *project summary* describes briefly the project that will be undertaken by the organization. Each project will have one or more *priority issues* to be tackled during the project. Each major action priority will have a section that outlines the historical significance of the issue(s) relating to the action priority. This section is called *background*. The authors of the operational plan will describe a *vision of success* for each major action priority. Each major action priority will have one or more *goals* and a series of *objectives* for each goal.

Each major action priority has an *action plan*. The action plan can have one or more *strategies* that can have one or more *objectives*. Each action plan has *baseline data* to be used to compare what was with what is. This comparison over the years will establish progress. For each action plan there will be a series of *action steps*. Each action step will outline the *resources* to be used to complete the step, who is *responsible* for the completion of each step, and when the project will *start* and *complete*.

Tips for Writing Plans

The following are a few tips that may assist the organization planner in preparing the applied strategic or operation plans:

- Include a table of contents describing the overall content and organization of the plan, including page numbers.
- Format the plan consistently, using the same style for sections, subsections, headings, and subheadings, etc., with a consistent use of numbers or letters for headings.
- Number all pages consecutively.
- Spell out and define all acronyms so that readers unfamiliar with the organization's programs and operations will understand the plan.
- Write clearly and concisely, with short declarative sentences and active verbs.
- Order the plan elements, provide cross-references when necessary, and develop a topic or subject index so that a reader can follow major ideas, themes, throughout the document.
- Make all references to other documents, plans or reports clear and specific enough to allow a reader to easily find the item or section referenced.
- Include in an appendix any information that is not critical to understanding the plan, but which provides useful background or context.
- Structure the plan in a way that will permit sections to be excerpted and distributed to specific audiences, and which will permit changes, edits, or updates without revising the whole plan.
- Test the understandability of the document by having it reviewed by individuals who were not directly involved in its development.
- On each section, type its computer file name (to speed retrieval in the future). In addition, during the draft process, include date/time code (to keep track of the most up-to-date revision). During the draft process, it helps to also hand write the draft (revision) number in the corner as each revision is printed or establishing a watermark (Draft Document 1).

What are the Pitfalls of Planning?

Strategic planning is a process requiring great skill. It can be frustrating and require a great deal of time. An inability to predict the future can create anxiety and feelings of inadequacy. The 10 biggest pitfalls to successful planning are (Nolan, 1993; Poirier, 1996):

1. Top management assumes that it can delegate its planning function and, thus, not become directly involved.
2. Top management becomes so involved in current problems that it spends insufficient time on planning. As a consequence, planning becomes discredited at lower levels.

3. Failure to clearly define and develop enterprise goals as a basis for formulating long-range goals.
4. Failure to adequately involve major line managers in the planning process.
5. Failure to actually use plans as a standard for assessing managerial performance.
6. Failure to create a congenial and supportive climate for planning.
7. Assuming that comprehensive planning is something separate from other aspects of the management process.
8. Creating a planning program that lacks flexibility and simplicity and fails to encourage creativity.
9. Top management fails to review and evaluate long-range plans that have been developed by department and division heads.
10. Top management makes intuitive decisions that conflict with formal plans.

Summary

The need for planning stems from the fact that virtually all enterprises operate in a changing environment. The uncertainty resulting from environmental change makes planning a necessity in all but the simplest circumstances. This chapter has identified the phases of the planning process, commented on the importance of planning, examined the scope and application of different types of enterprise plans, introduced the concept of strategic planning and discussed pitfalls in planning.

Learning Objective 1: Describe the planning process.

The planning process is composed of five repetitive and interactive phases that must be considered simultaneously. During each phase, an enterprise should look ahead and back to determine how other phases affect implementation at a particular time. The five phases of the planning process are: (1) establishing goals and objectives, (2) developing premises, (3) decision making, (4) implementing a course of action, and (5) evaluating results.

Learning Objective 2: Appreciate the importance of planning.

Planning is important for at least four basic reasons: (1) it helps enterprises succeed, (2) it provides direction and a sense of purpose, (3) it helps managers cope with change, and (4) it contributes to the performance of other managerial functions.

Learning Objective 3: Identify the different types of plans that might exist in a typical enterprise.

Plans can be classified in terms of (1) functional areas (i.e., marketing plans, production plans, personnel plans, financial plans and so forth), (2) period of time (i.e., short- versus long-range), and (3) frequency of use (i.e., standing versus single-use).

Learning Objective 4: Recount the importance of strategic planning.

Strategic planning is important because it serves to define an enterprise's overall character, mission, and direction.

Learning Objective 5: Assess an enterprise's strengths and weaknesses.

The assessment of an enterprise's strengths and weaknesses involves considering a range of factors related to a specific industry and the positioning of a company within the industry.

Learning Objective 6: Recognize the 10 biggest pitfalls to successful planning.

These 10 pitfalls to successful planning apply to all types of organizations and activities within an organization.

Learning Objective 7: Recount the characteristics of an objective.

Objectives are predetermined and stated in advance, and describe future desired results toward which present efforts are directed.

Learning Objective 8: List some benefits of objectives.

Objectives serve as: (1) guidelines for action, (2) constraints, (3) a source of legitimacy, (4) standards of performance, and (5) a source of motivation.

Review and Discussion Questions

1. As the successful CEO of a major league baseball team, comment on the role of planning in the management process.
2. Assume you are the athletic director of an Ivy League university. Despite its importance, you seem to resist planning. What are some of the reasons you might offer to explain your behavior?
3. Imagine you are the human resource manager of a medium-size sporting goods company with facilities in seven states. As part of an orientation program for a new group of employees, you have been asked to comment on the company's policies, procedures, and rules. What explanations and examples would you give?
4. As an expert in planning, you have been asked by the vice president for student affairs of your university to prepare a strategic plan for managing the university's athletic program over the next ten years. How would you define the specific market segments to be served? What key capabilities would be required to most effectively serve the defined target markets? Outline a realistic program for developing and maintaining these key capabilities.

5. Fantasize that you have been appointed President of the Dallas Cowboys. Explain how you would avoid the biggest pitfalls to successful planning.
6. As the successful head coach of a nationally recognized university basketball program, explain what your objectives will be for the upcoming season. Of what benefit are these objectives to you and your team?

Case Study

You are Tate Alexander. You have just inherited $75,000 (after taxes) from your grandfather. You graduated from a good sport management program in the Midwest and have thought of entering the sport bar business because you like it. You would like to move to a warm climate, so you are considering several smaller cities in Arkansas, Texas, or Alabama.

Your present first choice has a population of about 100,000. The city is not contiguous to others. You have heard the population is about one-fourth upper class (income above $75,000), one-third lower class (income below $15,000).

At present there are 12 bars of the quality you would like to run in this city. Four of the bars have changed management in the last year. Three others previously went bankrupt. You have heard that several of the bars are barely managing to continue operation.

You would like to run a very nice, rather expensive sport bar with an accompanying steak restaurant. You are wondering if you should go ahead.

Questions to be answered:

*   What kind of planning should you do before you decide to go ahead on this project in this city?
*   What additional environmental search should you carry out?
*   What objectives should you set up?
*   Can you ever make a decision like this on the basis of planning premises and studies alone?

References

Antoniou, Peter H. (1994). *Competitiveness through strategic success.* Oxford, OH: Planning Forum.

Drucker, Peter F. (1992). *Managing for the future: The 1990s and beyond.* New York: Dutton.

Fogg, Davis C. (1994). *Team-based strategic planning: A complete guide to structuring, facilitating, and implementing the process.* New York: American Management Association.

Goodstein, Leonard David, Nolan, Timothy M., & Pfeiffer, William J. (1993). *Applied strategic planning: A comprehensive guide.* New York: McGraw-Hill.

Hamel, Gary, & Prahalad, C.K. (1994). *Competing for the future.* Boston: Harvard Business School Press.

Hoffman, Alan N., & O'Neill, Hugh M. (1993). *The strategic management casebook and skill builder.* Minneapolis/St. Paul: West Publishing.

Hussey, David E. (1991). *Introducing corporate planning: Guide to strategic management.* New York: Pergamon Press.

Naisbett, John, & Aburdene, P. (1990). *Megatrends 2000.* New York: Morrow and Company.

Nolan, Timothy M. (1993). *Plan or die: 10 keys to organizational success.* San Diego, CA: Pfeiffer & Co.

Paley, Norton. (1991). *The strategic marketing planner.* New York: AMACOM.

Poirier, Charles C. (1996). *Avoiding the pitfalls of total quality.* Milwaukee, WI: ASQC Quality Press.

Toffler, Alvin. (1970). *Future shock.* New York: Random House.

Wright, Peter L., Pringle, Charles D., Kroll, Mark J., & Parnell, John A. (1994). *Strategic management: Text and cases.* Boston: Allyn and Bacon.

Suggested Readings

Burton, E. James, & McBride, W. Blan. (1991). *Total business planning: a step-by-step guide with forms.* New York: Wiley.

Certo, Samuel C., & Peter, J. Paul. (1993). *Case in strategic management.* Homewood, IL: Austen Press.

Covello, Joseph A., & Hazelgren, Brian J. (1995). *Your first business plan.* (2nd ed). Naperville, IL: Sourcebooks Trade.

Harrison, Mike. (1993). *Operations management strategy.* London: Pitman.

Hudson, William. (1993). *Executive economics: forecasting and planning for the real world of business.* New York: Wiley.

Kahrs, Kristin (Ed.), & Koek, Karin E. (Contributing Eds.). (1995). *Business plans handbook: A compilation of actual business plans developed by small business throughout North America.* New York: Gale Research.

Michelson, Bart, McGee, Mike, & Hawley, Len. (1994). *Consensus team decision making for strategic leaders.* Washington, D.C.: National Defense University.

Nutt, Paul C., & Backoff, Robert W. (1992). *Strategic management of public and third sector organizations.* San Francisco: Jossey-Bass Publishers.

3

PROGRAMMING FOR SUCCESS

◆ ———————————— ◆

Instructional Objectives

After reading this chapter the student should be able to:

• understand the dynamics of developing a program,

• be able to describe the most common tournaments available for scheduling,

• understand the dynamics of developing a schedule,

• comprehend the process required for expanding or reducing a program, and

• be able to perform a program assessment.

Introduction

The term "program development" as used in this chapter refers to the total learning experiences provided to consumers to achieve the objectives of health, fitness, physical activity, recreation and sport. It is concerned with the component parts of all the programs in each of the five areas as well as with the resources (e.g., facilities, financial, human, and technological) involved in implementing those learning experiences. The overwhelming trend in American society today is to provide carefully planned programs based on the following considerations: (1) the abilities, needs, and wants of the customer/client, (2) the needs of society in general, (3) the social-psychological aspects of society that influence learning, and (4) the marketability of the products/services developed to meet the needs and wants of the customer/client.

Program Development

Program development involves a large number of personnel who plan and implement the programs. There are many factors that influence program development that need to be considered and reviewed before final approval is provided. A number of approaches have been and are being used to develop programs. These approaches have different components and steps to follow as programs are developed.

Personnel Responsible for Program Development

The responsibility of program planning falls on the shoulders of a number of people and organizations. The planners include: management personnel (program directors), staff, professional organizations, customers/clients, parents, community leaders, and other professionals such as medical personnel, lawyers, architects, and corporate leaders.

The *management personnel* (program directors) play a key and vital role in the planning process. They serve as the (1) creators of the catalytic force that sets the planning in motion, (2) facilitators for the planning process, and (3) sustainers of the development process. Further, they provide the leadership that encourages and stimulates interest in providing optimal experiences; clears the barriers (e.g., time, place, space, and resources) that might impede the accomplishment of the task, and implements the appropriate recommendations for a program plan. Finally, program directors are responsible for pulling together teams that can work cooperatively and effectively together, provide them with a charge or challenge, and supply them with the necessary motivation as well as adequate financial, human, and technical resources to accomplish the task of designing a quality program.

The *staff* members (e.g., dance exercise instructors, personal trainers, swimming instructors) are at the grassroots levels of program development. They will be key members of the team that develops programs. The staff members contribute experience and knowledge and provide data to support the directions of program development. Staff input and perceived ownership are necessary before a program is designed and implemented.

The professional organizations (National Recreation and Parks Association [NRPA], American Association for Leisure and Recreation [AALR], National Association for Sport and Physical Education [NASPE], American Alliance for Health, Physical Education, Recreation and Dance [AAHPERD], Society for the Study of the Legal Aspects of Sport and Physical Activity [SSLASPA], and North American Society for Sport Management [NASSM]) (see Table 3-1) are some of the many groups and agencies who can help in program planning. These groups may provide program guides, consulting services, and advice that will prove to be invaluable in the planning of any program. Before embarking on a program development adventure you should first consider what professional groups or agencies can be of assistance and contact them early on in the process. There is no need to

Table 3-1
National Professional Associations

- National Recreation and Parks Association [NRPA] 22377 Belmont Ridge Road, Ashburn, VA 20148 703/858-0784 http://www.nrpa.org

- American Alliance for Health, Physical Education, Recreation, and Dance [AAHPERD] 1900 Association Drive, Reston, VA 20191-1599 703/476-3400

- National Association for Sport and Physical Education [NASPE] 1900 Association Drive, Reston, VA 20191-1599 703/476-3410 naspe@aahperd.org

- Sport Management Council 1900 Association Drive, Reston, VA 20191-1599 703/476-3410 naspe@aahperd.org

- American Association for Active Lifestyles and Fitness [AAALF] 1900 Association Drive, Reston, VA 20191-1599 703/476-3430 aaalf@aahperd.org

- Council on Facilities and Equipment [CFE] 1900 Association Drive, Reston, VA 20191-1599 703/476-3430 aaalf@aahperd.org

- American Association for Leisure and Recreation [AALR] 1900 Association Drive, Reston, VA 20191-1599 703/476-3472 aalr@aahperd.org

- National Association for Girls and Women in Sport [NAGWS] 1900 Association Drive, Reston, VA 20191-1599 703/476-3450 nagws@aahperd.org

- The Society for the Study of the Legal Aspects of Sport and Physical Activity [SSLASPA] 5840 South Ernest Street, Terre Haute, IN 47802 812/2372186 pmsawyr@scifac.indstate.edu

- North American Society for Sport Management [NASSM] Suite 334, 106 Main Street, Houlton, ME, USA 04730-9901 [for US membership] Faculty of Physical Education & Recreation, University of New Brunswick, Fredericton, NB, Canada E3B 5A3, 506/453- 4575; FAX 506/453-3511; nassm@unb.ca; http://unb.ca/web/sportmanagement/index.html

reinvent the wheel. The old wheel may only need a small amount of adjustment to meet your needs.

The *customers* should play a part in program development. Their collective thoughts in regard to what constitutes desirable activities for program delivery are important. Customers today are more actively involved in expressing their program needs or desires. They want to be heard, identified, and participate in planning the various activities and experiences that a quality program should provide to its customers. Therefore, it is important that customers be part of the planning team. The customers can be surveyed (written or oral), placed on a program development committee, or involved in a focus group.

The *parents* and *community leaders* many times can assist in communicating with the public what an organization is trying to achieve. These two groups can make significant contributions by supplying information regarding desired outcomes when dealing with youth or public school programs. It is important to include representation from these two groups in order to develop any program in an effective and efficient manner. However, parents rarely impact collegiate programs or private health and racquetball clubs. Yet, community leaders can impact both of these groups.

Factors that Influence Program Development

There are 11 factors that either directly or indirectly influence program development. The 11 factors include the following:

(1) climate and geographical considerations, such as average temperatures for each season, amount of rain and snow, prevailing winds, northeast, northwest, southeast, southwest, north central, and south central,

(2) economic and social forces, including above average, average, or below average economic climate, and more upper and upper middle class, more lower and lower middle class, or more middle class,

(3) population demographics, such as the number of upper, upper-middle, middle, lower-middle and lower class people, number of single males and females, number of married couples, size of population in the following classifications preschool, elementary school, middle school, high school, college, over 24, over 30, over 40, over 50, over 60, over 70, over 80, over 90, number employed; unemployment rate; one household families,

(4) the community, such as blue collar, white collar, farming/rural, urban, suburban,

(5) federal, state, and local legislation and regulations, including laws or regulations affecting recreational use of property, sale of alcohol, employment laws related to children,

(6) professional organizations, such as programming suggestions from any of the national professional associations listed earlier in this chapter,

(7) attitudes of managers and consumers, including positive, negative, caring, cooperative,

(8) staff, such as not enough staff, poorly prepared staff, well trained staff, adequate staff,

(9) research, including gathering as much information about the proposed program as possible,

(10) facilities and equipment, such as knowing the facility can accommodate the proposed program and equipment will be available for the participants; and and

(11) competition, including describe the level of competition (i.e., youth, middle/high school, college, adults, senior citizens, Special Olympics.

Program Development Components

The components for effective program development are: (1) establishing that a need exists for program development, (2) appointing a diverse planning team to specify the specific areas of need, (3) organizing personnel for planning, (4) identifying program objectives, (5) generating program solutions, (6) selecting the program design, (7) implementing the program design, and (8) evaluating the program. The program director needs to be sure that all the planning components are in place before proceeding.

Program Development Steps

The major steps involved in program development include (1) determining the objectives, (2) analyzing the objectives in terms of the program, (3) analyzing the objectives in terms of activities, (4) providing program guides, and (5) assessing the program based on predetermined outcomes (Patton, Corry, Gettman, & Graf, 1986).

In *determining the objectives,* the planning team should consider studying such factors as the developmental program trends, needs and wants of the consumers, competitor's programs, and technological advances so that objectives may be clearly formulated to meet market demands.

After the objectives have been determined based on the understanding of the consumers' characteristics, needs, and wants, they should be analyzed in terms of the program and activities. The analysis should consider the various constraints associated with the objectives and assign relative emphases to the various phases of the program. Further, the analysis must focus attention on the activities needed to achieve the set objectives. Do these activities allow for the objectives to be met?

Each program developed needs to have a program guide for its participants and its marketing endeavors. The program guide contains descriptions and schedules of all planned activities. Further, they provide opportunities for marketing products/services to the organizations various markets.

All programs need to be assessed. Assessment represents the culmination of the program development process. It defines the end result of the program and compares it with what the program expected to achieve during the developmental stages. Assessment, like program development, is a dynamic process that helps to determine the progress being made in meeting program objectives. It should identify strengths, weaknesses, and omissions, and show where needed resources or emphases might be shifted in order to improve the program. Further, it assists the consumers in determining their own progress within the program and is useful to the management for interpreting and reporting program outcomes to its consumers and board.

Five Common Approaches to Programming

There are five common approaches to programming. They include programming by (1) objectives, (2) desires of the participants, (3) perceived needs of the participant, (4) cafeteria style, and (5) external requirements (Bucher & Krotee, 1993).

Programming by objectives is the most contemporary of all approaches to planning programs. Inherent in selecting this approach are these assumptions:

- The programming team is able to conceptualize the activity process.
- The programming team is skilled in writing performance objectives.
- The objectives so stated are consistent with the objectives of the participants in the activity.
- The program's success or failure will be fairly evaluated by whether the program has or has not realized its objectives.

This approach to planning should be based on four solid planning principles including the following:

- The needs of the consumer—activities should be designed to meet the anticipated needs and wants of the consumers.
- Life enhancement—programs should enhance the quality of life.
- Assessment—programs should be formally and regularly evaluated in terms of their planned purposes.
- Participant readiness—programs should be related to participant readiness and abilities.

Programming by desires of the participants approach is a very popular method. It allows for consumer involvement in the process. This involvement can be accomplished through written surveys or focus groups. The following assumptions are inherent in this approach:

- Desires of the participant groups can be ascertained.
- Health, fitness and recreation programs are an important need.
- Programming teams are able to understand which activities meet which desires in most individuals.
- Programming teams are able to know when desires have been met or satisfied.

The planning principles involved in this approach include the following:

- All programs should be designed to meet the needs and interests of the consumer.
- All programs should encompass a diversity and balance in substance and consumer.
- All programs should encompass a diversity and balance in substance and organizational patterns. This diversity should embrace a variety of skill levels relating to both genders, noncompetitive to highly competitive activities, and a variety of financial arrangements (e.g., free to special costs, schedule for activities, and format for participating in terms of size of activity groups).
- All programs should be set in a safe environment.

Programming by perceived needs of the participant makes the following assumptions:

- The programming team is a professional in the fields of health, fitness, physical activity, recreation, and sport, and knows and understands what others will want and need.
- The programming team is in a better position than anyone else to know what others want.
- Consumers are unable to identify program-activity desires.
- Consumers are anxious to be told what they are interested in.
- Generally people are much the same, and time and money are saved by avoiding an expensive input system while the programming team/programmer designs what will be satisfactory.

This approach uses the following programming principles:

- All programs should be designed to utilize creatively all facilities and areas available.
- All programs should be efficiently organized and planned so that maximum participation is available.
- All programs should be nondiscriminatory and allow for true diversity (in clusion).
- All programs should be staffed by top-quality leaders who understand and accept their role in providing these services.
- All programs should have an interrelationship and progress sequences from one level to another.

Programming by cafeteria style is based on the ensuing assumptions:

- Consumer interests are constantly changing, and the least expensive way to satisfy these interests is to offer a wide variety of programs and let consumers indicate their preferences by their own selection. The programming team cannot know every possible interest area. Therefore, this smorgasbord is a fair device to uncover interests in a participant group. However, the programming team might want to consider a survey instrument to reduce operating costs.
- Guiding principles of programming can be met by offering diverse programs through which any potential participant can find at least one attractive activity.
- Many people do not know what they want and if the programming team/programmer is unsure, this approach provides a useful compromise.

The guiding principles to employ with this approach are:

- All programs should tap all possible resources within the area of their jurisdiction.

- All programs should provide an opportunity for adventure and new, creative experiences.
- All programs should be compatible with the economic, social, and physical abilities of the potential consumers.

Programming by external requirements (standards) is based on the following inherent assumptions:

- If the external standard is met, the program is good, that is, satisfying to the users.
- Those persons involved in setting the standards are able to make quality judgements about the local situation.
- Standards generally represent minimums; therefore, to exceed the standard would indicate higher quality in the program experience.

Programming by external requirements is a style for which the ensuing guiding principles should be considered (Lewis & Appenzeller, 1985):

- All programs should have diversity and internal balance.
- All program planning should adhere to carefully developed standards for both design and administration.
- All programs should be delivered through a system of highly qualified leadership.
- All programs should utilize the full resources available to the planning agency.

Developing Program Schedules

A program is as good as the schedule developed to implement it. Sport managers need to take great care in developing schedules. The development process requires great attention to detail.

Scheduling—How-to

It is important for the programming team to understand scheduling patterns of the customer whom the organization serves. Scheduling has at least four distinct and different patterns: (1) seasons such as fall, winter, spring, and summer; (2) block periods such as two-, three-, four-, or eight-to-ten-week periods; (3) monthly or weekly; and (4) daily timeframes such as sessions held during the early morning [6-9am], morning [9am-12noon], early afternoon [12-3pm], late afternoon [3-6pm], early evening [6-9pm], and late evening [9-11pm].

Effective scheduling distinguishes every successful program level, whether at the youth level or interscholastic or intercollegiate or professional. Unless a high level of agreement between the mission of the organization and the schedule(s) generated is obtained, the sport program will suffer the consequences of less than adequate performance. The success level of each activity or unit within an overall program rests, in a great part, on the construction of a well-planned schedule.

As an example of schedule development, the following questions might be used as a guide for the development of a successful and competitive sports schedule for either an interscholastic or intercollegiate sport program (Lewis & Appenzeller, 1985):

- What is the standard of competition sought for each sport program? What is the expected level of success for each team?
- What is the participation level? How should participants be grouped by age, gender, experience, size, or skill?
- What are the financial parameters governing the construction of the schedule?
- What geographical/travel limitations exist? Are there conference affiliations to be considered?
- What is the policy governing the mode of transportation utilized for trips?
- Is it necessary or desirable to arrange schedules to enable two different teams from the same institution to travel together to a common opponent?
- Relative to some sports, is there a limit on how many contests per week are academically permissible? How many contests can be played during one day? Is there a difference or a preference for weekday versus weekend day contests? Can contests be played on Sunday?
- Are contests permitted to be scheduled during vacation periods that fall within the sport season?
- Are teams who qualify permitted to participate in postseason tournament competition? What are the ramifications if postseason participation falls during examination periods or after the academic year is concluded?
- What considerations are given to vacation periods—Christmas, New Year's, Easter, summer?

These questions can be modified to be used for youth programs as well as public baseball, basketball, soccer, softball, or volleyball leagues. The programming team should develop a series of questions that can guide them through the scheduling process, no matter what they are scheduling.

If an institution is a member of a conference, there will most certainly be guidelines and agreements relative to scheduling that should be understood by those making the schedules. Likewise it is quite important for the sport director to be aware of scheduling parameters set forth by the national or state governing bodies to which the institution belongs.

Once a scheduling policy has been established and adopted by the organization, other questions need to be considered before the scheduling team can draft the schedule, such as (Lewis & Appenzeller, 1985):

- What facility considerations exist? Is the facility shared with others? If the facility is shared, what priorities for usage have been established so that equity exists and conflicts can be avoided?

- What are the goals of the program? How many contests, if any, should be scheduled in different divisions? If scheduling against a lower-division opponent, how strong is the opponent? What effect would a defeat to a lower or higher-division opponent have on the morale or team ranking?
- What days of the week are preferred for scheduling of contests? Is spectator attendance an important factor, and how is it affected by day or time of contest?
- Should contest days and times be consistent from week to week? Do the participants on the team tend to have one day per week when it is better not to schedule contests because of academic reasons?
- Does the organization have a policy about scheduling a contest on the Sabbath? Are there participants who cannot play on certain religious holidays or days?
- Is Monday a good day to schedule a contest if it follows a weekend of no competition or practice?
- When should away trips be scheduled (i.e., short trips during the week and longer trips over the weekend)?
- What are the vacation periods and holidays that fall during the season? How should the schedule address these?
- When is the first permissible contest date of the season?
- What national or state sport organizations rules may impact noneducational institution scheduling?
- Which opponents should be scheduled early in the season?
- How should the strong opponents be spread throughout the season?
- What kind of home and away balance is desired?
- How does a long trip affect the next competition?
- What are the considerations of a long trip and how should long trips be balanced from year to year?
- How many contests should be played during a long trip?
- What considerations exist for contest starting times?

A good schedule is the end result of meeting the stated philosophy and policies of the organization. The following is an example of a good educational institution schedule (Lewis & Appenzeller, 1985):

- includes all members of the conference (if the institution belongs to a conference),
- includes a few non-conference games that encompass the following:
  - at least one probable win,
  - at least one ranked team, and
  - at least one respectable opponent with name recognition and are a toss-up competitive situation,
- includes at least a 50/50 split between home and away contests,
- generates maximum financial rewards,
- includes no more than two games at home or two on the road consecutively,
- creates fan interest,

- gives a fair chance to:
    - have a winning season, and
    - gain postseason opportunities,
- is reasonable in terms of travel,
- includes opponents that have reasonably similar academic standards, and
- maximizes geographical, institution, and individual player(s) exposure.

The Mechanics of a Sound Schedule

Organization is the key to success in almost any administrative function, and scheduling is no exception to the rule. Scheduling at best is a complex task requiring a great deal of patience. The greatest assets in scheduling teams must possess are patience, the ability to negotiate, and attention to detail.

The following records must be kept regarding the schedule: records of ideas, thoughts, phone calls, correspondence, past schedules, future schedules, agreements to play, contest contracts (e.g., actual contracts, when sent, received, and returned), officials' contracts, officials' roster, and details of successes and concerns (Railey & Tschauner, 1993).

All contests within a schedule should have contracts or agreements even in youth league operations. The following is a checklist for what should be included in an agreement (Railey & Tschauner, 1993):

- dates the agreement is entered into,
- site of the contest,
- date of the contest,
- time of the contest,
- eligibility regulations of participants,
- financial agreements, if any,
- auditing requirement, if required,
- complimentary ticket arrangements for both teams,
- number of sideline passes for both teams, if appropriate,
- number and location of visiting teams,
- number of seats for team parties,
- admission of band and cheerleaders, if appropriate,
- control of ticket prices,
- admission of game workers,
- media agreements,
- programming concession rights,
- game officials,
- special event rights (e.g., Band Day),
- additional games to be played as part of the original contract agreement,
- conditions of failure to comply with the contract,
- terminations of the contract clause, and
- additional miscellaneous agreements.

Program Assessment

The programming team must complete a thorough assessment of the program(s) on a regular basis. The following questions need to be answered prior to embarking on the evaluation journey (Parkhouse, 1996):

- What is the philosophy behind the program developed?
- What personnel and customer/client behaviors represent the minimum acceptable competence for the program?
- Can you verify that all of the personnel make safety a priority?
- Do the personnel maintain appropriate, proper, and accurate records?
- Are the facilities safe, adequate, and cost effective for the program offerings?
- Is equipment maintained, distributed, collected, and stored properly and safely?
- Does the program offer equal access to all persons regardless of gender, race and ethnicity, and socioeconomic status?
- Are the program offerings the best use of financial resources?

The approach taken in evaluating the program(s) should be dictated by the needs of the organization and its customers. Effective and efficient program evaluation requires careful planning. There are six steps that will lead you to a successful evaluation. They are the following:

- reflect on organizational philosophy(ies),
- identify key roles,
- assess evaluation needs,
- develop an evaluation plan,
- implement the evaluation plan, and
- review and revise the evaluation plan.

Types of Tournaments Available and the Selection Process

The following is a brief description on how to organize a successful tournament (Byl, 1990; Gunsten, 1978). The selection of a tournament is based on the goals of the program. The programming team/programmer should answer the following questions before selecting a particular type of tournament:

- Do you want all players/teams to play an equal number of contests?
- Does it matter whether the number of contests is the same per player/team?
- Do you want all the contests to be close games?
- Does it matter if there are a few lopsided contests?
- How important is it to know who comes in first, second, third, fourth, or fifth?

The common types of tournaments used in programs are: single elimination, double elimination, round robin and extended. There are variations to these, such as multilevel, round-robin, double-split, triple-split, and quadruple-split.

A single-elimination tournament is best used for postseason competition after the completion of a round-robin tournament. The advantages of a single-elimination tournament are the format is easy to use and understand, it accommodates a large number of entries, requires few games, and requires few playing areas. The disadvantages are that each participant is guaranteed only one game, accurate seeding is crucial, and does not maximize the use of multiple playing areas.

A double-elimination tournament is best used when time and playing areas are limited and final standings are important. The advantages of a double-elimination tournament are that each participant is guaranteed two games, a participant who loses once can still win the championship, it requires few playing areas, and it is a better measure of ability than a single-elimination tournament. The disadvantages are that some players play many games and others play few, it takes many rounds to complete, and it does not maximize use of multiple playing areas.

A *round-robin* tournament is best used for league play and whenever standings are essential. The advantages of a round-robin tournament are that all players play each other, so true standings result, seeding is unimportant, it uses multiple playing areas effectively, and no one is eliminated. The disadvantages are that it requires many games, and many games may be lopsided.

Extended tournaments are best for individual sports in recreational settings. The advantages of extended tournaments are that they can be conducted over any length of time, the number of games per entry can be limited, they require little supervision, and no one is eliminated. The disadvantage is that the number of contests depends upon participants' initiative in challenging.

Process for Expanding or Reducing and/or Eliminating a Program

After completing the assessment, the programming team has a number of options regarding the future existence of the program. These options include maintaining, expanding, reducing, or eliminating the program. Before any of these options can be selected the following must be considered:

- the human resources available or affected,
- the financial resources available or affected,
- the facility resources available or affected,
- the equipment resources available or affected,
- the effects on other related or tangential program offerings,
- the effect on overall programming, and
- the effect on the customer base.

Anytime a program is modified in any way, it has a domino effect on all other activities within the organization. It may appear to be a simple modification on the surface, but it could cause major problems with other related and non-related activities within the organization. Any recommendation for modification must be reviewed carefully in the context of the whole organization, and not merely the area of suggested change.

Expanding a Program

The Hannibal High School administration has approved the expansion of the sport offering for girls with the addition of softball. The following will need to be accomplished over the next two years: (1) raise $100,000 to cover the start-up costs, (2) construct lighted softball field, spectator areas, concessions, restrooms, and storage building, (3) purchase two sets of uniforms for 24 girls, (4) purchase expendable supplies and equipment such as bats, balls, talc, bases, bat weights, batting helmets, ball bags, batting cages, safety screens, benches, scoreboard, replacement light bulbs, mowing equipment, and more, establishing a budget for operations to include the coaches' salaries, transportation, officials, balls, replacement uniforms, athletic training equipment and supplies, and more, and (5) hire two coaches.

Reducing a Program

John Q. Smith University decided after many years of losing seasons and deficit budgets to eliminate football scholarships. This decision required these tasks to be completed, including the following: (1) notify each players of his options—to remain at the university and complete his studies but not play football or transfer to another scholarship program without loss of eligibility, (2) reconstruct the competition schedule to play other non-scholarship teams, (3) reduce the coaching staff, (4) reduce the size of the traveling team to 45, (5) reduce the number of players to 50, and (6) reduce the recruiting program drastically.

Eliminating a Program

The Riley Town Board directed the parks superintendent to eliminate the play at Mudd Park to make way for a new indoor arts and crafts building. Prior to the decision, the parks superintendent determined the effect of losing the playground to related and tangential programming as well as overall programming and the customer base. It was found that the loss of the playground would not be detrimental to the customer base or over programming as long as an alternate space could be found. The park superintendent arranged for parts of the playground to four other playgrounds in the park system of playgrounds.

Summary

Learning Objective 1: Describe the dynamics of developing a program.

The programming development committee or program director must establish the needs of the organization and involve a diverse group of people to assist in the development of programs to meet the needs. This diverse body should include customers, management, staff, and local community leaders.

Learning Objective 2: Describe the most common tournaments available for scheduling.

The most common tournaments used in scheduling include round robin (provides maximum participation), double-elimination, and single-elimination (provides the least amount of participation). The round-robin tournament requires the greatest amount of time, while the single-elimination can be completed in the shortest amount of time.

Learning Objective 3: Describe the dynamics of developing a schedule.

Those involved in scheduling need to take into consideration many factors as they develop the schedule of events. Schedules must be reviewed carefully by the developers. As the schedule unfolds, developers need to make note of any complications and successes, so that modifications can be included in the next schedule.

Learning Objective 4: Describe the process required for expanding or reducing a program.

Expanding a program is a pleasant experience, whereas reducing a plan is most often frustrating and painful for all involved. In both situations, program directors need to involve a diverse group to review the situation and recommend a number of options to the program director to rectify the situation. Expansion as well as reduction can be difficult but manageable if planned for properly.

Learning Objective 5: Describe program assessment.

All programs should be assessed regularly to ascertain whether the activities have been successful in meeting the needs that they were developed to meet. The program director should review the effectiveness of the programs and the personnel, facilities, and equipment involved in implementing the program. The program director should also involve the participants in the assessment of the program.

Case Study

A.   You have been selected as the new athletic director for a large high school in Indiana near the Illinois border. The name of the high school is Harry Truman. The high school has 2,100 students. There are two other high schools in the city-county school district. The other high schools have 2,000 and 450 students, respectively. Harry Truman High School has 10 boys sports including (Fall) cross country, football, soccer, and tennis; (Winter) basketball, swimming, wrestling; (Spring) baseball, golf, and track and field; and 10 girls sports including (Fall) cross country, golf, soccer, volleyball; (Winter) basketball, gymnastics, and swimming; (Spring) softball, tennis, and track and field. The high school is not in a conference.

1. How would you establish scheduling policies and procedures?
2. Who would be involved in developing the schedule?
3. What must be considered when developing the overall schedule?
4. What type of tournament scheduling will be used for holiday tournaments?
5. How should the schedule be assessed?

B.   You have been hired as the sport program director for a large city park and recreation department. The department offers programs for youth, high school students, college students, and adults of all ages. The sports offered include: flag football, soccer (indoor and outdoor), roller blade hockey, ice hockey, basketball, softball, baseball, tennis, golf, swimming and diving, and racquetball. All teams and individuals pay a fee to enter the various leagues. The department develops the schedule after all sign-ups are completed.

1. How will you prepare for the development of the schedule?
2. Who will be involved in the scheduling?
3. What must you consider when developing the schedule?
4. What kind of tournaments will be used in the scheduling process?
5. How will the schedule be assessed?

References

Bucher, Charles A., & Krotee, March L. (1993). *Management of physical education and sport.* (10th ed.). Boston: Mosby Year Book.

Byl, John. (1990). *Organizing successful tournaments.* Champaign, IL: Leisure Press.

Gunsten, Paul H. (1978). *Tournament scheduling: The easy way.* Winston-Salem, NC: Hunter Textbooks, Inc.

Lewis, Guy, & Appenzeller, Herb. (1985). *Successful sport management.* Charlottesville, VA: Michie Company.

Patton, Robert W., Corry, James M., Gettman, Larry R., & Graf, Joleen Schovee. (1986). *Implementing health/fitness programs.* Champaign, IL: Human Kinetics Publishers.

Parkhouse, Bonnie L. (1996). *The management of sport: Its foundation and application.* (2nd ed.). St. Louis, MO: C.V. Mosby Year Book.

Railey, Jim H., & Tschuaner, Peggy R. (1993). *Managing physical education, fitness and sports programs.* (2nd ed.). Mountain View, CA: Mayfield Publishing Company.

Suggested Readings

Kestner, James L. (1996). *Program evaluation for sport directors.* Champaign. IL: Human Kinetics Publishers.

Parks, Janet B., & Zanger, Beverly R.K. (Eds.). (1990) *Sport and fitness management: Career strategies and professional content.* Champaign, IL: Human Kinetics Publishers.

Wilson, Bradley R.A., & Glaros, Timothy E. (1994) *Managing health promotions programs.* Champaign, IL: Human Kinetics Publishers.

PART II

◆

FINANCIAL MANAGEMENT

4

THE BUDGET PROCESS

◆ ———————————————— ◆

Instructional Objectives

After reading this chapter the student should be able to:

- discuss the role of budgeting in operational planning,

- understand the relationship between budget documents,

- identify the sequence for preparing various budget documents,

- analyze trends using historical and management data,

- identify internal and external factors impacting budget preparation,

- prepare an operating budget, and

- understand the function of a capital budget.

Introduction

Managers of sport-related organizations have many tools and resources available to assist them in making decisions. Sound financial decisions require information from a wide variety of sources such as staff, accountants, consultants, sales representatives, boards of directors, and customers. There are several tools managers can use in this process, beginning with documents used to enter financial data on a daily basis, and progressing through summary documents that usually include balance sheets and profit and loss statements. From all of these resources, management must develop a financial plan that will provide the basis for a successful operation for the next fiscal period. That financial plan is the operating budget.

Another budget that must be prepared is the capital development budget. This is a budget plan that states in priority form what the organization intends to acquire or build that is nonrecurring in nature and generally has a life span of at least 10 years. Examples of projects included in a capital budget would be enlarging a fitness activity area by adding on to an existing building, renovating the watering system on a golf course, purchasing additional land for expansion purposes, or purchasing new vehicles.

Operating Budgets

An operating budget is used for projecting and quantifying program objectives within a recreation, club, or sport organization. In other kinds of organizations, the terms production, sales, or service objectives might be used in lieu of program objectives. A budget can also be considered a plan that uses dollars in both revenue (income) and expenditures (see Table 4-1), to project what the organization can do in the coming year, or in the case of capital budgets, over a period of perhaps five years.

Once a budget is established, it becomes a tool to monitor and control expenditures. It is also a method of keeping management honest through control. This is especially true with a public agency, whose primary source of revenue is tax dollars, and profit and loss statements are not part of the accounting process (Mikesell, 1986).

Table 4-1
City of Terre Haute, Indiana
Department of Parks and Recreation
Rea Park Golf Course Budget 19XX

Projected Revenue

Season Ticket Sales and Greens Fees	290,000
Golf Carts	130,000
Golf Driving Range	20,000
Other Income	1,485

Projected Expenses

Operational Expenses	
Salaries & wages	92,046
Payroll tax	9,200
Employee benefits	0
Clubhouse supplies	3,563
Cart Maintenance, Winter service	7,000
Cart repairs	581
Golf range expenses	3,187
Office supplies	846
Building maintenance	1,973
Utilities	13,000

(Cont.)

Table 4-1 Continued

Education	0
Course supplies	1,250
Equipment repairs	1,112
Insurance	6,000
Miscellaneous	<u>5,000</u>
Total	**147,672**

Golf Course Maintenance

Salaries and wages	92,406
Payroll taxes	9,200
Chemicals	67,800
Seed and sand	6,790
Fuel and lubricants	4,358
Course supplies	1,500
Small tools	700
Trees and tree maintenance	0
Irrigation	2,500
Equipment repairs	15,000
Building utilities	4,000
Landscaping	3,500
Education	0
Security	0
Fees	290
Miscellaneous	<u>5,000</u>
Total	**147,672**

Equipment Purchases

Maintenance equipment	25,000
Golf cart fleet rotation	36,000
Range equipment	0
Miscellaneous	<u>327</u>
Total	**61,327**

Capital Improvements

New roof for club house	16,255
Electrical upgrade—club house	<u>3,187</u>
Total	**19,442**

Total Expense Projection	**441,485**

To develop a budget, the organization must establish goals and objectives for each program or unit. Without knowing what each unit plans to do, it is impossible to project either revenues or expenses that will be meaningful. After goals and objectives have been identified, along which units are responsible for specific goals and objectives, the costs for labor, supplies, services, and equipment are calculated. Expected revenues are based upon projected demand and receipts from appropriated funds, if the agency receives tax dollars. Public agencies may also generate revenues from fees and charges for goods or services, which would be considered non-appropriated revenues. In the case of private or commercial entities, revenues will be based on projected demand for goods or services.

When preparing a budget, the prudent manager needs to avoid making the budget too complex and overly detailed. Too much detail can actually inhibit effective management by denying flexibility in budget decision making. Another pitfall is preparing budgets based solely on historical data without predicting what increases might be forthcoming. For example, a facility manager might be told by upper-level management to expect a 4% general increase in the budget for next year. The easiest way to prepare the budget for the next fiscal period then would be to simply change each item in the budget to reflect a 4% increase. Certainly this saves a great deal of time but would rarely reflect the reality of what will actually happen.

Finally, the manager should recognize that budgets must be flexible. Budgets are actually an educated estimate (guess) of what is necessary for the agency to operate during the coming fiscal period. Things will change as a result of a myriad of circumstances, therefore the budget should provide the flexibility to meet those changes. For example, cold, snowy weather can result in dramatically lower attendance in any activity, which would consequently result in a loss of revenue. Management must have the flexibility to transfer funds from one account to another to allow expenses to be covered in cases like this.

Budget Objectives

Establishing realistic objectives is vital to any organization. Objectives must be identified in program planning, capital construction, personnel, and all other elements within an organization to provide for effective budgeting. Objectives must be measurable and time sensitive. Any effort to manage an organization's finances must include such basic objectives as being able to pay bills (liquidity) and to generate enough revenue from all sources to continue to operate over the long haul.

Advantages to Budgeting

Without a sound budget, management lacks a plan for forecasting future costs as well as revenues. The budget, therefore, is the cornerstone of good financial planning, (Bullaro & Edginton, 1996). The four major advantages to budgeting identified by Edginton and Griffith, (1983, pp. 195-196) are the following:

1. The budget translates programs and other services into financial terms.
2. The budget provides a mechanism for appraising staff, officials, and other interested parties in the financial operations of the organization.
3. Budgeting provides a means for systematically identifying and evaluating procedures, programs, and other services.
4. The budget provides a record of the financial transactions that take place within the organization itself and with other persons and organizations.

Finally, the budget, over time, shows others that the organization has planned either very well or very poorly. It assists the management in completing the plan on time and within budget. Budgets are planning as well as control tools.

Liquidity

By comparing total revenues to total expenses, a manager will know how much cash is available to pay bills. This process sounds simple enough but varies in complexity depending on the type and size of operation. A public school athletic department, for example, does not generate revenue for every sport, and usually generates revenue during peak months such as during the football and basketball seasons. Weak revenues during football season due to bad weather or poor win-loss records could have devastating effects on liquidity during the spring sports season, when few, if any, revenues are generated, even though expenses such as travel or field maintenance may be high. On the other hand, a fitness center or a pro-shop will usually generate higher revenues in close conjunction with higher expense periods, (Bullaro & Edginton, 1986).

When a new operation starts up, it is essential that adequate cash reserves are available to pay expenses until revenue generation can catch up and exceed expenses. The ability to pay bills in this case will be in the form of cash reserves generated from loans, investors, savings, or some other source (Epperson, 1977).

Profitability

Since the mid-1980s, declining tax revenues have forced managers of public organizations to build budgets based on programs paying their own way as has always been the case in the commercial sector. This is not to say that all public programs are going to become totally entrepreneurial in nature, but certainly as tax revenues decline, managers of government-supported sport programs have to look for other sources of income (see Chapter 5). In many cases, program costs can be transferred directly to participants (Howard & Crompton, 1983).

Not-for-profit agencies are not directly concerned with profit per se, but these agencies must also strive to improve revenues from all sources. If new programs are to be developed, facilities renovated, or new construction realized, more funding has to be generated.

Components of the Financial Process

Identifying and discussing all of the procedures and documents necessary to understand everything that goes into a complete financial plan for sport management is beyond the scope of this chapter, even this text. Crompton and Howard's text, *Financing Sport* (1995), is an excellent resource to gain a broad perspective of the intricacies of finance in sport.

The type of financial records an agency should keep depends on the type of agency (public, private, not-for-profit, commercial). The accounting process, however, can be illustrated by a five-step diagram, (Figure 4-2), (Crossley & Jamieson, 1988, adapted from Harmon, 1979).

Figure 4-2
The Accounting Process

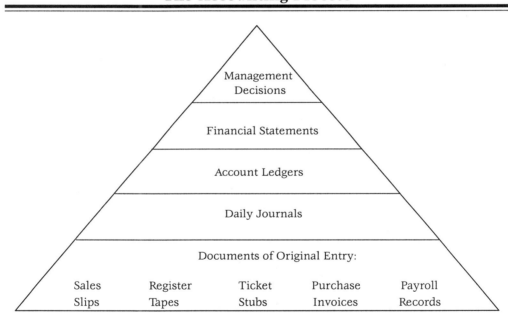

Documents of Original Entry

Documents of original entry refer to those documents that are recorded on a daily basis and reflect the income and expenses of the day's business. In the case of payroll records (Figure 4-2), time cards are often recorded on a daily basis, but are part of the overall records for the payroll period. The amounts of each of the daily documents are recorded in a daily journal. In turn, the data in the daily journal is transferred into a specific account ledger. Each asset, liability, and financial activity has its own account ledger. On a timely basis, usually monthly, or quarterly, a financial statement, balance sheet, and a profit and loss (P&L) statement is prepared. When the various financial statements are prepared, management then has data to use in making decisions.

The amount of time and effort required to build an operating budget varies greatly. There are some basic considerations, however, that are required at all levels of management. Budgets are compiled for a variety of organizational units. For example, each department or operational unit will have a budget. Within departments each program will have a budget. Within programs, each activity could prepare a budget. In addition, a specific facility such as a swimming pool or fitness center would have a separate budget. All of these budgets would be incorporated into the budget of the next higher level, and so on, until all of the data is assembled into a master operating budget (Howard & Crompton, 1988).

Steps Used In The Budget Process

There are five steps that are commonly used in the budget process: collecting data, application of various analysis techniques, identification of other factors that have or may impact operations, calculation of the actual dollars required, and review and interpretation of the budget (Horine, 1991).

Collecting Budget Data

There are several sources sport managers can use to collect data necessary for budget preparation.

Employee Input. In collecting data for the budget, management must examine data from a variety of sources, most of which are historical. This process should use data collected from employees, statistical analysis, and managers. Employees below mid-level management have information that can be invaluable from many perspectives. Employees are the grassroots users of equipment and supplies. They know best what does and does not work. They should have the opportunity to make that information available to supervisors and others in management so that their knowledge and experience can contribute to budgeting decisions.

Statistical Input. Statistics the manager needs are: how income and expenses compare for a given period of time (variance analysis), usage and participation data, program evaluation reports, inventory levels, and other sources as appropriate.

Forecasting. To build a budget, management must be able to forecast, or predict with some degree of confidence, what expected revenues and expenses will be for the next fiscal period. Forecasting must be made for both existing programs as well as anticipated new programs.

1. *Existing Program Forecasting.* To forecast needs in existing programs, program evaluation needs to have occurred. From these data, decisions on existing programs can be made.

Use/Participation. Is use/participation expected to remain the same, increase or decrease?

Economy. How will projections for the local economy affect use/participation patterns?

How will economic projections affect the cost of goods and services?

Program Trends. Are existing programs consistent with local, regional, and national trends; if not, what adjustments need to be made?

Equipment Replacement. What equipment needs to be replaced this fiscal period? Where is equipment failure or safety most vulnerable?

Facility/Equipment Replacement/Renovation. What facilities/equipment need to be renovated that are not currently identified for renovation? What facilities/equipment need to be replaced that are not currently identified? Facility/equipment replacement/renovation is included during annual budget preparation, but data will be included in the organization's capital improvement budget.

2. *New Program Forecasting.* Many of the same questions, but from a different perspective can be asked when compiling budget data for new programs.

Use/Participation. Who will be the participants in the new program? What will be the extent or frequency of participation?

Equipment Requirements. What new equipment will be required? If none, will existing equipment experience greater use and therefore a shorter service life?

Facility Requirements. What demands will the new program have on existing facilities? What impact will increased demand have on wear and tear, maintenance costs, custodial costs, increased hours of operations, increased utility costs, etc.?

Personnel Requirements. Will the new program require new personnel, or retraining of existing personnel? Will additional personnel hours be required? Will the program require specialized training? If so, can training be conducted on site, or must personnel train elsewhere?

Supply Requirements. Will new supplies have to be identified and ordered? If so, in what quantities? Does storage space exist for new supplies? Will new supplies require specialized requirements not currently available?

Applying Trend Analysis

Past budgets should be examined to attempt to identify financial trends that have developed. This can be done by examining the financial statement for the current month and comparing with past months of the fiscal year, comparing the current month with the current budget, comparing the current month with the same month last year, comparing year-to-date data with the same information of the previous year, and actual performance year-to-date with budget year-to-date (Horine, 1991).

Other factors can impact operations, and therefore budget preparation, which do not come directly from past budget data. These can be termed internal and external factors. Internal factors are those occurrences that come from within an organization that will affect budgeting in addition to those previously mentioned in forecasting. Such factors may include cost of living increases for employees, changes in organization policies, changes in management structure, change in management personnel, and other factors that may be unique to the organization.

External factors are those that occur outside an organization and that the organization has little or no control over. Some examples of these factors would be program trends, changes in law, the economy, changes in the tax base, or even the weather.

Calculating the Dollars Required

After all data have been collected and analyzed, dollar amounts should be calculated and applied to various accounts. Expenses should be based on input from the three methods of forecasting, i.e., employee, statistical, and managerial input. Income can be forecast using those methods as well. Most managers estimate expenses based on anticipated increases in the cost of living and/or suppliers forecasts for price increases. Income, on the other hand, is usually projected to be somewhat less than actually hoped for.

Review and Interpretation

When the budget has been completed, at a given level, but before it is presented for approval at the next higher level, it must be reviewed and interpreted with as much staff involvement as possible and practical. It is important that the staff understand what the financial picture for the organization will be for the coming fiscal year. Management must be satisfied that the budget numbers appear to be reasonable, and justifications for decisions are clearly stated.

Clearing up any questions or concerns that staff may have is vital before the budget is presented to an approving body such as a governing board. If questions from staff are not sufficiently answered, or concerns are not addressed before presentation, some staff could present their own ideas to individuals on a governing board resulting in the presenter being "blind-sided" by a board member. It is far better that staff understand what is in the budget and have the opportunity to express their concerns and be satisfied with or at least understand, the budget proposal before it is presented.

In the end, the operating budget is most often the result of experience and a combination of the "best guess" based on available data, and a "gut" feeling of where the organization should be going financially.

Capital Budgets

Capital budgets provide for expenditures to purchase assets that have service life expectancies of at least five years. In the case of buildings, the expectancy is usually 10 years or more. Examples of capital expenditures include virtually any building, equipment, motor vehicles, and computers. Capital expenditures are usually high and occur at infrequent intervals. This is not to infer that capital costs will not occur each fiscal year, but the specific requirement such as construction of a fitness center will not be an annual item in the capital budget. Therefore, the capital budget is usually prepared and maintained separately from the operating budget (Mikesell, 1986).

Capital budgeting requires physical as well as financial planning. Careful physical planning is essential because of the long-term service associated with capital projects. A mistake involving a capital project will be around for many years. Physical planning involves more than design considerations. In the case of new construction, improper selection of the building site that causes a disruption of traffic flow, or prohibits expansion of another structure might well be a mistake that cannot be corrected after construction has begun. Part IV of this text will address specifics of design and maintenance of facilities and the relationship to capital planning.

Financial planning addresses the issues of how the capital project will be funded and, if the cost of the project must be recovered, what the source of repayment revenues will be and over what period of time payments are to be made. In the case of collegiate sport facilities, many universities are uniting with their home communities to raise funds for large athletic facilities that can also be used for public assembly events such as concerts, ice shows, and circuses, that benefit the entire area. Hulman Civic Center on the campus of Indiana State University is one example, and the Lexington Civic Center (Rupp Arena) in Lexington, Kentucky is another (Lewis & Appenzeller, 1985).

Governmental agencies have a variety of options available that other organizations do not. Municipal governments can levy special taxes to help fund construction of large sports arenas such as the RCA Dome (formerly the Hoosier Dome) in Indianapolis, Indiana. Residents of Indianapolis and Marion County were assessed millions of dollars to provide the financial base for construction of that facility.

Not-for-profit agencies often have capital fund donation drives to raise money for major projects. The target market for these drives often includes corporations as well as members of the agency as well as foundations and individual benefactors. Commercial organizations, on the other hand, must rely on other sources for capital improvements or acquisition. Equipment is most often replaced by regularly placing funds in a depreciation account. When equipment reaches the end of its service life, the money to replace the equipment should be in hand. Other capital projects may have to be financed through loans, sale of stock, or other means.

Budgeting for a Sport Program

Budgeting for a sport program is difficult at best. The common expenses found in the average interscholastic sport program include coaching salaries, sport administrators' salaries, athletic trainer's salary or contract with a sport medicine clinic, clerical salary, part-time personnel salaries, maintenance personnel salary, officials fees, tournament fees, transportation costs, uniforms, expendable supplies, telephone and long distance, cellular phone, beeper, office supplies, postage, and more. The common revenue includes ticket sales, concession sales, programs, advertisement, and donations.

The expenses are somewhat different for intercollegiate sports. The intercollegiate program has all the expenses mentioned for interscholastic sports plus scholarships, more coaches, more administrators, overnight and meal expenses for players, recruiting, public/media relations, conference fees, guarantees paid to visiting teams to assist in reducing their travel costs, and more. The revenue side is expanded as well to include merchandise sales, reserved seating, parking concession, guarantees from away games to assist in covering expenses, conference and tournament revenue-sharing, and more.

The professional programs are even more complicated. Their expenses include player salaries ($50 - over $100 million), revenue-sharing with city, larger administrative staffs, greater promotional efforts and public relations programs, rental for facility, league fees, and more. They also have a greater revenue machine which includes the beer concession, major merchandise and souvenir sales, TV/Radio revenue, luxury boxes, VIP parking, major restaurant sales, and more.

The budget process in sport is no different then in any other industry. The final objective is different for each level. The amateur programs seek to balance the budget and allow for some growth each year. The professional programs expect to make big dollars. Many people and organizations invest in professional sport organizations and expect to gain something for the investment.

Summary

An important part of the budget process is understanding the relationship between the budget documents and the sequence for preparing them.

Learning Objective 1: Discuss the role of budgeting in operational planning.

The process of identifying during operational planning the internal and external factors affecting operations is another essential part of the budget process. Budgets are prepared using all of these data along with historical information from other financial periods and staff input from all levels of the organization. Further budgets prepared without information of past performance, without staff input, or without consideration of internal or external factors that could affect operations have the potential for financial disaster for an organization.

Learning Objective 2: Understand the relationship between budget documents.

Documents of original entry provide the initial data for accounting purposes. Without accurate and timely entry of financial data, budget preparation becomes very difficult indeed. Entries in daily journals are recorded into accounts, which are assets or liabilities for specific activities. The summary financial document, which is the financial statement or a profit and loss statement, or a balance sheet, is prepared for management review and discussion.

Learning Objective 3: Identify the sequence for preparing various budget documents.

Since the budget is a tool to monitor and control expenditures, it is important to first understand the organization's goals and objectives. The goals and objectives outline the extent of programming or action to be taken by the organization. These programs require expenditures. After identifying the programs it is fairly easy to describe the various costs and revenues that can be expected. The goals and objectives outline the programs and the programs provide the information for developing the budget—expenses and income.

Learning Objective 4: Analyze trends using historical and management data.

The better read person always has a leg up on his/her competition. It is important to gather and subscribe to industry journals and newsletters, and to read about what is happening nationally and internationally in one's field of interest. Identifying and applying information about trends always allows an organization to be on the cutting edge and be able to take advantage of opportunities.

Learning Objective 5: Identify internal and external factors impacting budget preparation.

As one learns to monitor the budget, he or she begins to recognize internal and external factors that may impact the budget. Managers must be aware of their internal and external surroundings at all times. The manager's knowledge about these factors establishes his or her level of power. Power is knowledge—do your homework!

Learning Objective 6: Preparing an operational budget.

This can be fun and also very frustrating. An operational budget cannot be prepared without knowing what the expenses might be and the projected revenue. A budget is an educated guess that must be monitored regularly. Each time an operational budget is prepared, it becomes more accurate because previous years' experiences can be factored in and there are fewer unknowns. Maintain historical data, watch the inflation rate, understand the ups and downs of revenue generation and cash flow, and be patient.

Learning Objective 7: Understand the function of a capital budget.

The operational budget is designed for daily operations. The capital budget is designed for the purchase of expensive equipment that has a life or for facility development and construction. It generally is for onetime expenditures.

Self-testing Exercise

1. Assume you are the golf superintendent for the Rea Park Golf Course, and therefore use the budget depicted in Appendix 1. You have received a brochure advertising a workshop for greenskeepers that promises to demonstrate ways to reduce course maintenance costs by 15% for those successfully completing the workshop. The workshop fee, related travel, and per diem expenses will cost $1,000 per person.

    a. If the claims of the workshop are true, where would the 15% savings most likely occur?

    b. Would the cost of the workshop be a good investment? Why?

2. You decide to send your maintenance supervisor to the workshop. Realizing that any savings will not be available until next year, where will you find the $1,000 in this year's budget? Justify your decision.

3. Using the basic budget format in Appendix 1, construct a budget for the city's slow pitch softball all-star team to travel to the regional championship tournament in a city 275 miles distant. The entry fee is $750. There are 15 players/coaches on the team. The tournament is expected to last two days. With the cooperation of a local club, or recreation agency, track a single monthly expense, (i.e., utility bill) through the accounting process from receipt to payment.

4. Discuss the relationship between programs and budgeting. Which comes first?

5. You are having an open house at your new fitness center to attract new customers. You will not charge a fee for this event. Plan a budget that will include refreshments, staff to demonstrate equipment, conduct mini-exercise programs, etc. and materials for publicizing the event. The open house is planned for the first Saturday in October from 5:00 p.m. until 8:00 p.m.

References

Bullaro, J., & Edginton, C., (1986). *Commercial leisure service.* New York: MacMillan Publishing Company.

Crossley, J., & Jamieson, L. (1993). *Introduction to commercial and entrepreneurial recreation.* Champaign, IL: Sagamore Publishing.

Edginton, Christopher R., & Griffith, Charles A. (1983). *The recreation and leisure service delivery system.* Philadelphia: Saunders College Publishing.

Ellis, T., & Norton, R. L. (1988). *Commercial recreation.* St. Louis, MO: Times Mirror/Mosby College Publishing Co.

Epperson, A. (1977). *Private and commercial recreation: A text and reference.* New York: John Wiley and Sons.

Haggerty, T., & Patton, G. (1984). *Financial management of sport related organizations.* Champaign, IL: Stipes Publishing, Co.

Harmon, P. (1979). *Small business management.* New York: D. Van Notrand.

Horine, L. (1991). *Administration of physical education and sport.* Dubuque, IA: Wm. C. Brown Company.

Howard, D. R., & Crompton, J. L. (1983). *Financing, managing and marketing recreation and park resources.* Dubuque, IA: Wm. C. Brown Company.

Howard, D. R., & Crompton, J. L. (1995). *Financing sport.* Morgantown, WV: Fitness Information Technology, Inc.

Lewis, G., & Appenzeller, H. (1985). *Successful sport management.* Charlottesville, VA: The Michie Company,.

Mikesell, J.L. (1986). *Fiscal administration: Analysis and application for the public sector.* Chicago: Dorsey Press.

Suggested Readings

Apostolou, N. G., & Crubley, D. L. (1988). *Handbook of governmental accounting and finance.* New York: John Wiley and Sons.

Axlerod, D. (1995). *Budgeting for modern government.* New York: St. Martin's Press.

Berman, B., & Evans, J. (1979). *Retail management: A strategic approach.* New York: MacMillan Publishing Company.

Merrill Lynch. (1979). *How to read a financial report.* New York: Pierce Fenner, and Smith, Inc.

5

REVENUE GENERATION

◆ ——————————————— ◆

Instructional Objectives

After reading this chapter the student should:

• be able to prepare a plan to develop a concessions program from selecting the most appropriate concessions, drafting an RCP proposal, and constructing a concessions agreement,

• appreciate the value of a pro shop and hair salon concession,

• be able to prepare a plan to develop a corporate sponsorship program
from selecting the most appropriate corporations, setting the price, and
drafting the sponsorship agreement,

• understand the value of licensing,

• understand how-to, and

• be able to understand financing facility construction.

Introduction

There are many sources of revenue generation for clubs, recreation organizations, and sport programs. The primary sources of revenue generation are: (1)
membership fees, (2) tax revenue, (3) ticket sales, (4) admission fees, (5) concession, (6) sponsorship, and (7) licensing. *Membership fees* are fees collected by a
club or agency to control access to facilities, programs, etc. to those who have paid
dues. *Tax revenues* are collected by governmental bodies having the legal authorization to levy taxes. Governmental bodies include federal, state, county, and local

units. Within local units, there are several taxing bodies including school districts, park districts, and city governments that offer the kinds of services appropriate to this text. The primary difference between districts and city government regarding tax revenues is that district tax revenues go directly to the district. In most city governments, tax revenues go into a general fund where they are allocated to various departments through budgets approved by a city council, mayoral system, or perhaps a city manager system. *Ticket sales* can be applied to any single event, or a series of events (season tickets) and can usually be purchased in advance of the event. Ticket events differ from events charging an admission fee in that ticketed events are most often associated with spectator events, whereas events with admission fees are usually those where the customer is a participant or user of a facility such as a swimming pool, theme park, campground, etc. *Admission fees* therefore, are those fees charged at the time a person enters a facility and includes authorization to use most, if not all, services within the facility.

Concessions can include parking, food, merchandise, or hair salons. *Sponsorships* are partnerships with corporate entities to assist financially with a particular project or sport event in order to gain a higher public profile. *Licensing* affords the organization an opportunity to generate revenue through the comercial use of its name, logo, or slogan.

There are a number of other sources employed to generate revenue, including, but not limited to: advertising profits, beauty shop receipts, donations, equipment rental income, food sales, franchising receipts, fund-raising dollars, league/conference revenue, leasing revenue, trademark or endorsement revenue, merchandise sales, parking, team guarantees, and television contract income. Clubs, recreation organizations, and sport programs are always seeking ways to generate more revenue to meet the budgetary demands of programming. Without adequate revenue, an organization cannot meet its financial commitments and eventually will have to close its doors. This chapter will be devoted to a discussion of auxiliary sources of revenue generation besides membership fees, tax revenue, or ticket sales.

Concessions

A concession is a privilege granted by a government, company, or organization such as, (a) the right to use land, as for a specified purpose; (b) a government grant of land forming a subdivision of a township; (c) the right or a lease to engage in a certain activity for profit on the lessor's premises (i.e., a refreshment, parking, merchandising, fireworks, child-care, or beauty care concession); and (d) the land, space, etc. so granted or leased (Howard & Crompton, 1995). The concessionaire is the holder of a concession granted by the government, company, or organization. There are five concessions that impact club, recreation, and sport programs— food service, merchandising (i.e., pro shop, souvenir stand), beauty shop, child-care, and parking.

In-house and Contracted Concessions

The advantage of managing in-house concessions is that it provides total control. The facility manager can decide what prices to charge, the quality of the goods/products sold, and whether or not to open the area without having every decision become a negotiating session with the concessionaire. Many managers feel they are maximizing their revenues by cutting out the middleman, the concessionaire.

On the other hand, other managers say they do not want the headaches and hassles that a food service (for example) brings, such as scheduling of hourly part-time employees, purchasing perishable foodstuffs, determining what stands will open, whether or not the sanitation policies are enforced, and who might be stealing cash. Further, many facility managers do not have the necessary resources (i.e., personnel, budget) to operate a variety of concessions effectively, nor do they have the freedom to establish autonomous purchasing and personnel offices. Concessionaires do provide proven systems of operations and a network of facilities that help each other with new menu ideas, management trends, bulk purchasing, national pricing, personnel training, and personnel advancement. Finally, a concessionaire can provide its own capital for equipment, thereby freeing the facility's money for other projects.

The real key to a successful concession operation, whether contracted or in-house operations, is the on-site concessions manager. The on-site concessions manager is the person who controls the operation of the concession and is the facility manager's communication link to the concession management. The responsibilites of the on-site concessions manager include purchase, preparation, and display of the product, control of inventory, selection and training of staff, and overall supervision of the operation. The decision to contract or self-operate needs to be evaluated both quantitatively and qualitatively. The answer will be dependent on the facility's unique requirements and on the management staff's capabilities and desires.

Components of a Concessions Contract

One reason many facility managers self-operate today is that they have had bad experiences with concessionaires in the past. "They were uncooperative," "they were penny-pinchers," "they were too interested in their bottom line and not the good of the facility" are often-quoted phrases heard by many who contract with concessionaires. These complaints can be eliminated for the most part by understanding the concessionaires' business philosophy and financial objectives. Therefore, before entering into any concessionaire contract, seek interested parties through a Request for Concessionaire Proposal (Table 5-1).

Table 5-1
Suggested Components for Request
for Concessionaire Proposal

- date submitted
- name/address/phone & fax numbers/e-mail address
- principal contact
- historical background of company (i.e., date organized; state incorporated in; list of owners, partners, or officers; bank references; list of current clients)
- full description of business philosophy
- full description of financial objectives (i.e., pricing strategies, quality of goods/products, payroll, operating costs, capitalization, and profit projections)
- commission
- equipment to be provided for concession
- insurance coverage
- a full description of personnel training programs
- advertising and promotion efforts (i.e., television, radio, print, point-of-purchase, out door, transportation, in-house, other) (Wong, 1993)

After receiving the Request for Concession Proposal (RCP), the manager should make sure that all information is correct. The manager should involve a consultant to evaluate the information that the prospective concessionaires have provided on the RCP. Once the concessionaire has been chosen, the next step is to negotiate a concessionaire agreement.

The concessionaire agreement is the key to a successful concessions program. The agreement should establish clearly the parameters by which concessionaires should operate. It should provide the concessionaire with an equitable return for their work. The components of a concessionaire agreement are found in the appendix.

There are two basic financial arrangements: the traditional commission agreement and the management fee agreement. The latter has been growing in acceptance in recent years. The commission agreement provides for the concessionaire to pay the organization a predetermined percentage of the gross receipts. There are three commonly recognized advantages of commission agreements: it eliminates the risk of financial loss to the facility, simplifies the auditing of the concessionaire's operation, and insulates the facility from daily operating decisions (Howard & Crompton, 1995).

The management fee agreement provides for the concessionaire to receive a management fee, typically stated as a percentage of *gross* receipts and a profit incentive, which is a percentage of the *net* profits. There are five commonly recognized advantages of a management fee arrangement: it develops a partnership of mutual interest between concessionaire and organization; provides the potential for increased revenues to the organization; offers the organization greater control and flexibility for concessions operations; eliminates the typical adversarial rela-

Tennis club pro shop at Wright Patterson Air Force Base. (Photo: O. Smith)

tionships found in many concession contracts; and encourages regular input from the organization's management (i.e., product quality, staffing levels, and special pricing for unique events).

Pro Shops

An increasing number of health and fitness centers, racquet clubs, and recreation facilities are buying into the theory that pro shops can generate a significant revenue stream. Pro shops give organizations one more area to generate revenue. If a pro shop is run well and selling the right products at competitive prices, it should be turning a handsome profit.

Attractive displays help sales in a pro shop. (Photo: O. Smith)

The vast majority of health, fitness, golf, and tennis clubs have a pro shop within their walls. The average annual revenue was $25,000. However, those clubs that operate their shops in prominent locations, rather than behind the desk, within the facility report annual sales of $200,000 and beyond.

The successful pro shops have the following characteristics: (1) prominent locations that require members to enter and exit through; (2) personalized service with competitive pricing; (3) catalogs for customers to share with friends; (4) merchandise their goods/products (i.e. displaying goods/products in an appealing way); (5) consider themselves retail outlets; (6) innovative goods/products; (7) concentrate on apparel and accessories; (8) stock regularly needed supplies (i.e., feminine hygiene products; golf, racquet, and tennis balls; wrist, knee, or ankle wraps; nutritional drinks and supplements; weight-lifting gloves; athletic footwear); and (9) licensed merchandise.

Hair Salon

In an effort to capitalize on the "looking-good, feeling-good" focus of their members, many health and fitness clubs are adding beauty salons to help pick up where exercise leaves off. The number of health and fitness club-based beauty salons is on the increase. Nearly 15% of health and fitness clubs operate on-site salons.

The reasons for entering the beauty salon business are because it is (1) another revenue center, (2) a convenience for club members, (3) a strategic way to build and sustain membership, and (4) a logical extension of a full menu of services and programs. However, be aware that women tend to have fierce loyalties to their hairdressers and sometimes stick to a favorite for years. Therefore, it takes a lot of relationship building to establish a stable clientele.

The salon should be located close to the entrance. The following design tips should be considered: (1) proper ventilation for removing the fumes and scents, (2) provide between 100 to 200 square feet per chair, (3) place a single-station chair in a position that can easily flip around from sink to mirror, (4) adequate plumbing to accommodate the sinks required, (5) sufficient electrical supply to each station with ground fault interrupters installed near water sources, and (6) nonslip floor.

The equipment to be purchased will be determined by the services offered. The services offered could be hair cutting, coloring, facials, manicures, and pedicures.

With a comfortable space and a good operator on board, most owners say club-based salons carry little risk. The salon can be an in-house operation or contracted to an independent contractor.

Body Heat Fitness Center, a privately-owned fitness center, offers a wide range of ancillary services, including a hair salon. (Photo: O. Smith)

Food Concession

The food concession can be a gold mine if handled appropriately. Many stadia and arenas are expanding their options from the traditional concession stand to include favorite fast food options (i.e., McDonalds, Hardees, Pizza Hut, Taco Bell, Burger King, etc.). The greatest amount of profit in the concessions business is from soft drink sales followed by popcorn, hot dogs, tacos and cheese, candy, and beer. A concession open from dawn to dusk must be flexible offering breakfast, lunch, and dinner favorites that are fast and convenient. People expect to pay more at a concession stand than elsewhere because of the convenience factor. The food concession will be successful if the customers' needs and wants are known, and a clean fresh atmosphere with friendly convenient and fast service is provided.

Management Tip

Despite the benefits of franchising, there are substantial costs and complications involved. The management needs to be careful before entering into a franchising agreement.

The food concession must be conveniently located to the customer. It should have plenty of counter space, hot and cold running water, adequate electricity to operate a popcorn popper, microwave, refrigerator and freezer, and a warming unit, and storage space. The floor should be tiled with an adequate number of drains for cleaning. On the customer side there should be plenty of space to accommodate a large number of people.

Parking

The parking concession can be profitable but it has liabilities. The manager, before charging for parking, must ensure that the following has been accomplished: (1) purchase an adequate liability insurance policy for the space, (2) provide adequate surfacing for the proposed traffic, (3) ensure safe entrance and exit areas, (4) provide adequate lighting, (5) plan for immediate snow and ice removal, (6) establish an emergency plan for the space, (7) ensure adequate supervision and security is available, and (8) provide for the safety of the pedestrians. After the manager has accomplished the above, it is time to decide how many spaces will be for the handicapped, VIPs, and regular customers. The greatest amount of money will be made from VIP parking.

Child- or Adult-Care

Many of the new stadia and arenas are providing space for child-care. Some of the health and fitness facilities are providing both child-care and adult-care. Adult-care is for those older adults who are now living with their children rather than in a nursing home. The children want to use the health and fitness facility but cannot leave aging mom or dad home alone. This a new problem for the "Baby Boomer" generation and many service providers are recognizing the need for adult-care.

Most states have regulations regarding child-care facilities and personnel. Before deciding to provide temporary child-care, review state statutes, and regulations. It may be a requirement to become licensed to provide such care. However, normally this temporary service is considered to be baby sitting, not child-care, as defined by state statute.

The space provided for child-care should have the following: a bathroom, clean walls with graphic designs, carpeted floor, safe toys, audio system, and a video system. For the adults the suggestions are similar with the following exceptions: no toys are needed, graphics on the walls would be different, and reading material should be provided.

Childcare is an important service to adult participants. Dodge Gym at Wright Patterson Air Force Base. (Photo: O. Smith)

Souvenir and Licensed Products

All professional sports and many of the large intercollegiate programs (i.e., Notre Dame, Michigan, Penn State, UCLA, Kentucky, etc.) generate large sums of money from the sale of souvenir and licensed products. Kids young and old love to wear clothing with their favorite team's name, logo, or slogan. When a dad takes his son to the ball game he purchases the traditional soda and hot dog, baseball cap, souvenir ball, and baseball cards that are momentos of the big occasion. The sale of souvenirs and licensed apparel and other merchandise is an important source of revenue as well as great advertisement that should not be overlooked. Disney and Warner Brothers have taken the concept to its greatest levels.

Corporate Sponsorship

A corporate sponsorship is the purchase of rights from an organization, either in cash, products or services, to pursue corporate communication or targeting objectives through predetermined activities and through the use of any images and symbols associated with the organization's activities to the benefit of the corporation.

Brooks (1990a, 1990b, 1994) and others have indicated the key to the corporate connection is contained in three important concepts in the successful production and sale of a product: (1) corporations are not involved in organization marketing; but rather, they are involved in communication, and health, fitness, physical activity, recreation, and sport organizations provide the communication medium; (2) organizations can provide one way to gain access to ready-made consumer segments; and (3) organizations can help marketers attach an image to their product(s) to differentiate them in the marketplace.

A sponsorship within the corporate marketing framework is not philanthropy, but it is business. It must serve the interests of four constituent groups, including (1) the business interest of the sponsoring company, (2) the best interests of the event and its participants, (3) as a positive impact on the sponsor's direct customers (i.e., dealers and retailers who sell its products), and (4) as a benefit to the customers who buy those products. Further, it must create an identity (i.e., link between the identity of the event and the identity of a brand or product), increase sales, promote business-to-business contacts, constituent benefits (i.e., vacation appeal of the region, enhanced facilities, improved sales for local retailers), and business customers.

According to Wilkinson (1986), corporations buy into a variety of event sponsorships for a number of reasons: (1) demonstrate good citizenship, (2) generate positive visibility, (3) increase sales, (4) generate favorable media interest and publicity, and (5) compete with other companies. However, Ensor (1987), indicates that there are several criteria that may be necessary elements in a sponsorship arrangement, including corporate signage at the event, newspaper and television coverage, merchandising, and product sampling.

Sponsorship Proposal

There is no standard sponsorship proposal/agreement format. The format should be creative and neat. The informational content should include: (1) objectives of the sponsorship program, (2) profile/background of sponsoree, (3) promotional opportunities available, (4) levels of sponsorship (i.e., exclusivity, primary, subsidiary official supplier), (5) sponsor benefits, (6) fee structure, (7) contract length and renewal options, and (8) evaluation methodology.

Before drafting a proposal the planner should be able to answer the following questions: How would you describe the organization? What is the event to be sponsored? What impact do you have on the local economy? What is the purpose of your event? How will the organization involve the community, that is, local business, cultural groups, and local residents? Will the event heighten public awareness about the organization or activity? How does the event allow sponsors to reach out and touch their consumers? Is the event based on another similar successful event? Why is the event unique? What are the advantages for sponsors who tie in to the event?

The law as it pertains to sponsorship agreements is not well defined. This should alert managers to be very careful when constructing a sponsorship agreement. The manager should consult an attorney to make sure all matters are included in the contract in clear language with mutual understanding.

What are the Various Levels of Involvement for a Sponsor?

There are four common levels of involvement for sponsors, including exclusive sponsor, primary sponsor, subsidiary sponsor, and official supplier (Brooks,

A bulletin board provides information on ways to prevent injury. Wright Patterson Air Force Base. (Photo: O. Smith)

1994). An *exclusive sponsor* has the sole financial commitment for an event; the sponsor may even own the event. However, usually the sponsor has a major say in the organization of the event.

A *primary sponsor* has made a major financial commitment, but shares with one or more companies that are providing a smaller financial commitment. The primary sponsor has the best opportunity to maximize exposure opportunities with minimal effort and financial risk; but, still can have a major say in how the event is organized and managed.

A *subsidiary sponsor* is a company that is providing a smaller financial commitment behind a primary sponsor. These sponsors generally have exclusivity of sponsorship within a product category. The product and service is frequently essential to the event (i.e., Nevco scoreboards for baseball, basketball, or softball; timing devices for track or swimming events; ice cleaning machines).

An *official supplier* is on the same level as a subsidiary sponsor but the products are not crucial to the competition. Again, like the subsidiary sponsor, the official supplier generally has exclusivity within a product category (i.e., sunglasses, soft drinks, snack foods, sunscreen, feminine hygiene products, etc.).

Customizing a Sponsorship Package

After establishing the sponsorship category, the next step in designing the sponsorship package is to customize it to fit the needs of the sponsor (see Appendix—Sample Sponsorship Agreement). Brooks (1990b; Howard & Crompton, 1995), suggests the following should be considered when customizing sponsorship packages:

Official status. What is the appropriate sponsorship category? What specific language should be written into the contract?

Sponsorship fee. What is the fee? How does the sponsor pay the fee? When does the sponsor pay the fee? Is the fee refundable for any reason? Is there a pre-payment requirement (down payment)?

Title rights. Will the sponsor's name appear in the title? Will the product name appear in the title? How will the trophy be named? Who will present the trophy or prizes?

Television exposure. Who owns and controls the TV rights? Does the sponsor have rights of first refusal on television advertising spots? Is there a ratings guarantee? How will the ratings be established? Will there be a rebate if ratings fall below this guarantee? How is the rebate to be calculated? Can the sponsor use TV video footage in its regular advertising? Does the sponsor need to obtain permission prior to using video clips for commercial reasons? Who is responsible for negotiating television time?

Public relations and media exposure. Will key personnel (i.e., executive director, coach, student-athlete) mention the sponsor's name when the press interviews them? Will media releases include the sponsor's name? Who is responsible for media releases? Can the sponsor develop its own media marketing campaign?

Logo use. Under what conditions can the sponsor use organization logos or trademarks? Who owns the special logos or trademarks? Can the sponsor use the logo or trademark to promote its own image and products? Does the sponsor have merchandising rights (i.e., can it make and sell souvenir items)? Who owns the license for the merchandised items?

Signage. How many banners, patches, pins, placards, arena boards, flags, or community announcement boards can the sponsor use? What size? For how long?

Where can a sponsor place banners? What can appear on them? When should they be taken down? Who puts them up and takes signage down? Who is responsible for making the signage? Who is responsible for paying for the signage? How should the signage be attached to the walls within the facility?

Advertising rights. In what ways can the sponsor use the organization's event for advertising purposes? Will the sponsor's name be on stationary? Will the sponsor's name be in the program? Can the sponsor use event photographs for product promotion and general media advertising? Who gives permission to use the photographs in advertising? Are there limitations on the use of photographs?

Hospitality rights. Does the sponsor have access to a hospitality tent or room? Where can the sponsor place the tent? Does the sponsor get free memberships or tickets to give to clients, or for other use?

Point-of-sale promotion. Can the sponsor sell products on-site? What kinds of products cannot be sold? Who gets the profits from on-site sales? Can the sponsor run on-site or off-site promotions associated with the sponsorship? Can the sponsor team up with other companies to form cooperative promotions?

Direct-mail lists. Will mailing lists of members, ticket holders, student-athletes, or parents be made available to the sponsor? What form of promotions can the sponsor undertake with these mailing lists? Can the sponsor sell the mailing lists? Can the sponsor trade the mailing lists?

Product sampling. Will there be a product display and sampling locations? What type of products can a sponsor display? Will any type of products be banned?

Legal liabilities. Who is responsible for injuries to spectators, participants, officials or personnel? What if it rains? What if it snows? What if there are TV transmission problems?

Future options. How many years does the sponsorship last? Does the sponsor have renewal options? How many years does the option last? How do you determine the sponsorship fee in the future?

Clientele use. Will clientele (i.e., customers, clients, student-athlete) make personal appearances on behalf of the sponsor? Will key personnel (i.e. managers, coaches, athletic directors) attend pre- or post-competition parties? Will clientele wear the sponsor's name during events?

What are Possible Sponsor Benefits?

Organizations seeking corporate sponsorships might consider providing some items from this partial list of merchandising opportunities and sponsor benefits (Brooks, 1994):

- Season tickets for event(s) or memberships, reserved seating, and/or general admission (i.e., complimentary, discount, full purchase availability, blocks for charity use);
- Yearbook, program, press guide, and/or scoreboard advertisement (i.e., complimentary, discount, full purchase availability);
- Scoreboard/P.A. exposure (i.e., copy only, copy and art, number of times/game/event, complimentary, discount, use of on-air talent lead-ins, drop-ins, live announcer [on camera, off camera], special promotion spots [complimentary, charge, reuse off station]);
- Special event nights (i.e., free tickets, special meeting room, souvenirs, first-ball ceremony, scoreboard/P.A. mention, invitations [quantity, number of times/year]);
- Arena signage (i.e., availability, number [complimentary, charge]); and
- Special items (i.e., use of VIP room, use of luxury box, league/press passes, parking passes, use of stadium, use of highlight film, product music at stadium).

Howard and Crompton (1995) emphasizes it is important to sell the above benefits to potential sponsorships. An organization must be more than merely provide a list of items, but rather, consider waht the potential sponsor would like to as a benefit.

Pricing a Sponsorship

Sponsorship agreements are in a constant state of flux due to increased competition, an ever-changing economy, and a volatile marketplace. Brooks (1990b), indicates there are three general ways to approach sponsorship pricing, including cost-plus strategy, competitive market strategy, and relative-value strategy. In the *cost-plus strategy,* a calculation is made determining what the real costs are to offer a sponsorship package and then a predetermined percentage for profit is added. The only tricky aspect of this strategy is determining the percentage of profit. The main risk in this strategy is that it tends to neglect the needs of the target company.

At the other extreme is the *competitive market strategy.* This strategy is based on what managers think the market will bear given the competitive environment. The manager should review the following before establishing a price: (1) degree of primary consumer match with company's target market; (2) size of the primary consumer base; (3) potential media publicity; (4) sales opportunity; (5) psychological association, and (6) exposure opportunity.

The final strategy is *relative value.* The manager in this strategy shows the targeted company the relative value of a sponsorship package. For this strategy to be successful, the manager must have an excellent knowledge of the market value of what he/she is offering, as well as its value to the company.

Licensing

Consumer demand for logoed apparel (an industry generating $4 billion in annual retail sales) has provided professional and amateur sport programs the ability to financially benefit through licensing, which grants a second party the right to produce merchandise bearing their logos for a royalty fee (Irwin, 1993). These royalty charges, approximately 10 percent of the manufacturers' wholesale price, have generated multimillion dollar revenues for major professional and amateur sport organizations. Licensing has also grown to include corporate sport businesses like Nike and Adidas, sporting events such as the Olympics, Wimbledon, and college bowl games and nearly 200 colleges and universities nationwide.

Colleges and universities and a number of large high schools that have established licensing programs as a means of generating supplemental revenues often locate them in the department of athletics, and a large portion, if not all, of the institutional licensing royalty revenue is deposited in the athletic budget. Several institutions, such as Notre Dame, Michigan, and Penn State, are generating nearly $1 million annually from licensing.

The administrator seeking to identify alternative revenue sources for a college or high school athletic program, minor-league team, or amateur sporting event need look no further than the team, school, or event logo. The following operating procedures may help new entries into the sport licensing industry (Irwin, 1991, 1993, & 1996):

(1)   The initial procedure for the licensing program administrator should be to examine all available descriptive marks to determine which ones may be commercially attractive.

(2)   Actively recruit licensees and screen all manufacturers expressing an interest in obtaining a license to produce logged products through an application process. Typically, a manufacturer is asked to supply information regarding financial stability, marketing and distribution channels, production capabilities, projected sales performance and a list af current licensing references.

(3)   The manager must decide whether the licenses executed should be on an exclusive or non-exclusive basis. The non-exclusive agreement enables numerous manufacturers to produce merchandise in the same product category (i.e., apparel, ceramics or headwear), while the exclusive agreement restricts the number of manufacturers for each product category to one. While each method has certain advantages, the exclusive agreement provides the licensor greater leverage in negotiating licensing fees, expedites communications between the parties and helps combat unauthorized use of logos.

The exclusivity of the agreement may be based on product categories and geographic regions that include local, regional, national and international distribution. A number of sport licensing programs have executed joint-use licenses, where the licensed merchandise bears the logos of two or more organizations and the royalties are split by the parties. The NCAA, for example, executes joint agreements with national championship participants, and Major League Baseball and the MLB Players Association employ joint agreements for the use of player likenesses on trading cards, apparel, and videos (Irwin, 1996).

(4)   License revocation or non-renewal may occur for failure to comply with the terms of the agreement, a decrease in quality or a lack of productivity. Several sport programs establish royalty production standards for licensees, the NCAA requires licensees to generate a minimum of $10,000 annually and the NBA commands annual royalty payments of $185,000 from national retail distributors (Irwin, 1993). It is considered standard procedure to require licensees to pay a negotiable advance royalty payment, typically considered to be earnest money, which may be applied toward future royalties owed.

(5)   As product liability issues have arisen, it has become necessary to request an actual product sample for approval prior to distribution. This is highly emphasized for sporting equipment merchandise that is licensed bearing the organization's logos, as the organization may be held legally accountable for defective equipment or merchandise.

(6)   Regularly scheduled compliance reviews, inspections of licensees' manufacturing and accounting procedures, are conducted by a number of sport licensing programs. Licensing auditors are available for compliance review assistance.

(7)   An effective licensing program requires protection against unauthorized use of logos, symbols or designs through market surveillance and immediate contact with unauthorized vendors. Policies against unauthorized use should be in writing and should be designed by an attorney, who will issue cease and desist letters to offenders and represent the organization in legal proceedings.

(8)   Authorized licensees are often the best resource for detection of unauthorized vendors of logos, since this competition has a direct effect on their profits. Manufacturers are sometimes unaware that authorization for logo use must be secured; however, most vendors are familiar with the market

value of sport logos and the necessity to obtain a license for logo reproduction.

(9)   In an effort to expedite the detection of unlicensed merchandise, major sport licensing programs require licensees to place some type of special identification on goods. Consumers have become familiar with the *" Officially licensed Product of..."* hang tag or sticker required by many professional sport leagues.

(10)   Federal and state trademark laws have traditionally provided the legal foundation for licensing activities. In an effort to secure legal protection, a majority of logos have been registered as trademarks.

(11)   Familiarizing the public with the licensing program operations and your intent to enforce legal protection will limit unauthorized use of logos.

(12)   Finally, promoting the availability of licensed products should have a significant effect on revenue production. Low cost, accessible promotional mediums available to the sport licensing director include complimentary advertising space in event programs, public address announcements, press releases to local media and advertising space negotiated to be included in television or radio packages. Several sport licensing programs require licensees to advertise their licensed products, while other forms of print and broadcast advertising may be obtained through ticket trade-outs to keep the promotional costs to a minimum.

A complete promotional mix includes paid advertising on TV and radio and in newspapers and trade publications, and a direct mail campaign is also possible. The costs of direct mail may be reduced by asking a licensee, with prominently displayed merchandise, to underwrite the production and mailing charges.

Staffing a licensing program at the correct level is critical. One full-time licensing director seems to be the norm, but the size of support staffs tend to vary. Factors in determining the appropriate staff size would be market size, the number of products licensed and the number of licensees (Irwin, 1991).

An alternative to hiring staff is to contract with a professional licensing agency to operate your program. A licensing agency provides a professional staff sensitive to licensing technicalities, legal consultation, the ability to tap into the agency's existing licensee bank, regularly scheduled compliance reviews and marketing assistance. Additionally, the licensing agent can prove to be a valuable asset in negotiating international licenses for those programs with such a market (Irwin, 1991). The primary disadvantage is that the licensing agency's fee can amount to 30 % of the annual licensing revenues, considerably more than an internal program might cost. However, initially an organization might decide to contract with a licensing agency and then later on when revenues will support full-time staff, discontinue the contract.

Financing Facility Construction

There are a number of ways in which facilities can be financed. There have been and will continue to be serious questions regarding the economic value of sport facilities. Whether or not there is a proven value they will be built. The most common ways to finance sport facilities have been by using taxes, private investment, federal grants, luxury seat fees, guaranteed federal bonds, city bonds, county bonds, and/or state bonds. Many facilties today are financed by using multiple financing stragedies as listed above rather then relying on only one source of revenue. Regan (1996) indicates the proper financial team needs to be assembled in order to design, organize, and finance a public, private, or public/private facility. The members of a successful financial team should include issuer/owner, facility management representative, feasibility consultant, examination accountant, business plan consultant, financial advisor, architect, cost estimator, design builder, construction manager, senior underwriter, co-underwriter, bond council, and issuer's council.

Taxes

There are a variety of taxes that have been levied to assist in raising funds for the construction of new stadiums, arenas, race tracks, parks, aquatic centers, and more. Some examples of the user or sales taxes used to generate funds include: hotel/motel tax (bed tax), restaurant tax, auto rental tax, taxi or limosuine tax, "sin taxes" (e.g., liquor, tobacco), sales tax, road tax, utitility tax, property tax, capital improvement tax, and others. The most popular of these taxes are hotel/motel, restaurant, and auto rental taxes. These taxes are used most frequently by tourists or fans. Miller (1997) and Taback (1995) agree that these taxes are very popular in legislatures, considered to be appropriate user taxes, and are rising faster than any other kind of levy.

The manager should be concerned about the continual use of such taxes, because they can generate citizen discernment and political unrest. The tourist and fan is as concerned about being taxed inappropriately as is the local citizen in any metropolitan location. If the voter becomes frustrated, politicians begin to look for ways to reduce unrest and many times they resort to reduced taxes.

Tax Abatements

A tax abatement will exempt the facility's assets from property taxation for a given period of time (e.g., 10 or 20 years). It may be for all or for a portion of the tax. Abatement programs exist in approximately two-thirds of the state (Howard & Crompton, 1995). Tax abatements are a strategy used by governments to stimulate private sector investment and and create employment in their communities. These abatements can be substanial and are rarely denied.

Private Investment

As public monies decline, complexities for gaining such dollars increase, and questionable economic impact on the community continues, many stakeholders prefer the private-sector investment strategy. The politicians and taxpayers see private-sector investment as a way to avoid a long-term tax commitment and guarantee to the citizens other perceived needs for the community. There are a variety of ways to secure private sector investment, including cash, in-kind contributions (e.g., materials, equipment, land, expertise), naming rights for the entire facility or parts, concessionaire exclusivity, sponsorship packages, donations, life insurance packages, lease agreements, luxury seats, reserved parking, licensing rights, merchandise revenue, vendor/contractor equity, preferred seating packages, advertising rights, bequests and trusts, endowments, securities, etc.

Federal and State Grants

The Federal government and many states provide monies through grants for redevelopment projects in areas targeted for economic renewal. A community with an identified redevelopment/economic renewal zone should prepare and submit a grant application. These grants can be worth millions of dollars.

Joint Financing Between Public and Private Entities

Another method for financing facilities which is gaining popularity is shared or joint financing. The public entities contribute state appropriations, funding site improvements, parking lots or garages, low-cost financing, access to or owner of valuable real estate, tax inducements and incentives, and control over the permit and zoning process. The private entities contribute managerial expertise and efficiency (Biam, 1985) as well as money securement through naming rights, lifetime seating arrangements, sponsorship agreements donations, lease agreements, concessionaire exclusivity, and restaurant agreements. The sharing concept allows each entity to assist the other without overburdening either in the process. Finally, the liability of any one entity can be reduced through strategic use of contractual language, insurance, and/or indemnification agreements (Miller, 1997).

Bonds

The issuing of bonds is the most common way for a city to generate the needed money for facilities (Howard & Crompton, 1995; Miller, 1997). A **bond** is simply an interest-paying debt (Howard & Crompton, 1980). In the public sector, generating funds for infrastructure projects through bond referendums is often more successful than locally generated tax dollars.

The interest rate on bonds is directly related to the level of risk investors incurred. The level of risk is identified as a rating (i.e., AAA rating = highest quality and lowest probability of default, whereas a C, CC, or CCC rating = defaults very probable). The ratings are established by two major rating agencies—Moody's Investor Service, Inc. and Standard and Poor's Corporation. Many cities are insuring their bonds as a tactic that gives buyers more confidence and encourages a higher bond rating, leading to lower interest rates.

Government agencies use two types of bonds to construct infrastructure projects—full-faith and credit obligations or non-guaranteed debt.The full-faith and credit *obligations* can claim any portion of the taxes levied and other revenues of the government entity issuing the bonds (Mikesell, 1991). The government has guaranteed the bonds through its authority to levy taxes. Bonds issued with this full-faith and credit provision are called general obligation bonds (Howard & Crompton, 1995). The advantages of these bonds are two-fold—ease of sale and reduced cost because of tax guarantee.The disadvantages include required voter approval, taxpayers' concern over value to them of facilities, and increase local debt ties up monies, making the funding of future projects more difficult (Miller, 1997).

The second funding mechanism open to governmental entities is called non-guaranteed bonds. These bonds are not backed by the full-faith and credit provision. But they are sold on the basis of repayment from other designated revenue sources (Howard & Crompton,1995).If the other designated revenue sources fall short of the debt, the government does not have to pay the difference.There are five major advantages,including: (1) voter approval not required in most states; (2) does not count against the debt capacity and, therefore, leave monies left for other needed capital projects; (3) those who most benefit from the facility pay for it; (4) the pressure to be profitable often secures better management and customer service; and (5) the need to distinguish between resident and non-resident users is eliminated (Howard & Crompton, 1980, 1995; Miller, 1997).The disadvantages include investors taking a greater risk, and higher costs to the government entity in interest payments.There are three common mechanisms used in this arena—revenue bonds, certificates of participation, and tax increment financing.

Revenue Bonds

Revenue bonds are most frequently backed by the revenue accruing from the project. In these cases the facility must generate sufficient funds to cover the operating costs, maintenance expenses, and annual principal and interests payments (Howard & Crompton, 1995). Initially this may be a very challenging task. However, these bonds could be backed by other designated revenue streams, such as hotel/motel taxes, restaurant taxes, or sales taxes.

Certificates of Participation

Certificates of participation are backed by revenue from the lease-purchase agreement with the facility they are used to finance (Howard & Crompton, 1995). This involves the government entity purchasing or constructing the facility and then leasing portions of the facility to the general public. Payments are subject to annual appropriations by the issuing government.

Tax increment financing is becoming more popular to have urban areas identified as areas for redevelopment (Howard & Crompton, 1995). Once identified, then tax increment financing (TIF) is available. As Miller (1997) indicates, real estate developed using TIF is attractive to stakeholders, since tax increase are not necessary. Rather, the bonds and developmental costs are repaid from the generated property taxes associated with the newly developed real estate. The only drawback to TIF-generated funds is that use has been predetermined and precludes use of the property tax monies for other projects not directly related to the original renewal. Most states, however, include a definition of how long the property tax dollars can be captured, the types of development costs that can be financed, and the location and size of the area subject to TIF opportunities (Michael, 1987; Regan, 1996; Miller, 1997).

Special Authority Bonds

Sometimes infrastructure projects are built with funds by special public authorities (e.g., New York Port Authority, New York Power Authority, Tennessee Valley Power Authority), which are entities with public powers that are able to operate outside normal constraints placed on governments (Howard & Crompton, 1995). Primarily, this has been used as a way to circumvent public resistance to a project. Further, this eliminates a need for a public referendum. There have been a number of sport facilities constructed using authority financing, including Three River Stadium, Georgia Dome, and Oriole Park at Camden Yards.

Summary

The main sources of revenue generation for clubs, recreation organizations, and sport programs are (1) membership fees, (2) tax revenue, and (3) ticket sales. There are a number of auxiliary sources employed to generate revenue, including, but not limited to: advertising profits, hair salon receipts, donations, equipment rental income, food sales, franchising receipts, fund-raising dollars, league/conference revenue, leasing revenue, license or trademark or endorsement revenue, merchandise sales, parking, sponsorship income, team guarantees, and television contract income.

Learning Objective 1: Be able to prepare a plan to develop a concession program.

A concession is a privilege granted by a government, company, or organization that may include (a) the right to use land, as for a specified purpose; (b) a government grant of land forming a subdivision of a township; (c) the right or a lease to engage in a certain activity for profit on the lessor's premises (i.e., a refreshment, parking, merchandising, fireworks, child-care, or beauty care concession); and (d) the land, space, etc. so granted or leased. While a concessionaire is the holder of a concession granted by the government, company, or organization.

Learning Objective 2:Appreciate the value of a pro shop and hair salon concession.

An increasing number of health and fitness centers, racquet clubs, and recreation facilities are buying into the theory that pro shops can generate a significant revenue stream. Pro shops give organizations one more area to generate revenue.

If a pro shop is run well and selling the right products at competitive prices, it should be turning a handsome profit.

In an effort to capitalize on the looking-good, feeling-good focus of their members, many health and fitness clubs are adding beauty salons to help pick up where exercise leaves off. The number of health and fitness club-based beauty salons is on the increase. Nearly 15% of health and fitness clubs operate on-site salons.

Learning Objective 3: Be able to prepare a plan to develop a corporate sponsorship prgram.

Brooks and others have indicated the key to the corporate connection is contained in three important concepts in the successful production and sale of a product: (1) corporations are not involved in organization marketing; but rather, they are involved in communication, and health, fitness, physical activity, recreation, and sport organizations provide the communication medium; (2) organizations can provide one way to gain access to ready-made consumer segments; and (3) organizations can help marketers attach an image to their product(s) to differentiate it in the marketplace.

Learning Objective 4: Understand the value of licensing.

Licensing is granting a second party commercialized use of a trademark. Technically, licensing can (1) legally protect the names associated with designs that are created for various organizations; (2) promote the organization in the extended marketplace; and (3) realize financial profits from the commercial demand for the organization's name and designs.

Self-testing Exercise

1. You are the assistant athletic director for business operations for a large high school (2,500 students) in the Midwest. Due to across-the-board budget cuts by the school board, the athletics budget must look to other revenue sources for funding. For the past 20 years, the band boosters club has sold concessions at all home athletic events and used proceeds to fund the marching band and other music programs which get no money at all in the school budget other than music faculty salaries. Concession sales generate slightly more than $10,000 each year in profits. Describe the steps necessary to one of

the following: 1) having the athletic booster club take over the concession sales operation to fund athletic events; 2) assume shared responsibility with the music boosters, therefore sharing profits; or 3) identifying other sources of revenue because the band boosters have an "ironclad" agreement with the school board through the year 2020.

2. As athletic programs director for a large metropolitan park and recreation department, you have a dream of hosting a marathon, mini-marathon, or perhaps a triathlon in your city. You have everything you need in terms of facilities, volunteers, and administrative support, but the director has told you the event must be entirely self-supporting. The only real answer is to obtain a sponsor for the event. Develop a proposal to be presented to a potential sponsor. What sponsors would you approach? What potential sponsors might be inappropriate for this type of event?

3. As owner and operator of an 18-hole golf course (non-PGA) you want to expand your retail sales operation. Currently, you stock only cold drinks, snacks and golfing supplies such as new and used balls, tees, and a limited selection of gloves. Your customers have suggested that you might attract more players if you had golfing merchandise for sale. You have the space to provide about 300 square feet of merchandise display, and another 500 square feet that could be used as merchandise storage area. What considerations must you examine before deciding what resale items you would stock, services you would provide such as club re-gripping, club repair, etc.?

References

Alexander, Ruth H. (1995). *The economic impact of licensing logos, emblems, and mascots*. Paper presented at the Seventh Annual Sport Law Conference, Jekyl Island, GA.

Annual industry report. (1993). *Team Licensing Business, (5)*5, 15.

Baim, D.V. (1994). *The sports stadium as a municipal investment.* Westport, CT: Greenwood Press.

Brooks, Christine, M. (1990a). Sponsorship: Strictly business. *Athletic Business, (14)*10, 59-62.

Brooks, Christine M. (1990b). Sponsorship by design. *Athletic Business, (14)*12, 58-62.

Brooks, Christine M. (1994). *Sports marketing: Competitive business strategies for sports*. Englewood Cliffs, NJ: Prentice-Hall.

Ensor, Richard J. (1987). The corporate view of sports sponsorship. *Athletic Business, (11)*9, 40-43.

Howard, Dennis R., & Crompton, John L. (1980). *Financing, managing, and marketin recreation & park resources*. Dubuque, IA: Wm. C. Brown Publishers

Howard, Dennis R., & Crompton, John L. (1995). *Financing sport.* Morgantown, WV: Fitness Information Technology, Inc.

Irwin, Richard (1991). A license to profit. *CAM Magazine, (3)*1, 18-23.

Irwin, Richard (1993). In search of sponsors. *Athletic Management, (5)*3, 10-16.

Irwin, Richard. (1996). *Sport licensing*, 306-324. In Parkhouse, Bonnie L. (Ed.), *The management of sport: Its foundation and application* (2nd ed.). St. Louis, MO: C.V. Mosby Year Book.

Irwin, Richard, Stotlar, David, K., & Mulrooney, A.L. (1993). A critical analysis of collegiate licensing policies and procedures. *The Journal of College and University Law, (20)*3, 97-109.

Irwin, Richard, & Stotlar, David, K (1993). Operational protocol analysis of sport and collegiate licensing programs. *Sport Marketing Quarterly, (2)*10, 7-16.

Lazarus, Bruce I. (1991). Franchising in a park and recreation setting. *Journal of Physical Education, Recreation, and Dance, (62)*9, 48-50.

Lustigman, Alyssa. (1994). Sweat shops. *Club Industry, (10)*1, 24-26, 30.

Michael, J. (1987, October). Tax increment financing: Local redevelopment finance after tax reform. Government Finance Review, pp. 17-21.

Miller, Lori K. (1997). Sport Business Management. Gaithersburg, MD: Aspen Publications.

Mikesell, J.L. (1991). Fiscal administration: Analysis and applications for the public sector. Pacific Grove, CA: Brooks/Cole.

Monahan, Julie. (1994). Looking good. *Club Industry, (10)*4, 14-17.

Regan, T.H. (1996). Financing Sport. In B.L. Parkhouse, (Ed.), *The management of sport*. St. Louis, MO: Mosby-Year Book.

Stotlar, David, K. (1992). Sport sponsorship and tobacco: implications and impact of Federal Trade Commission v. Pinkerton Tobacco Company. *Sport Marketing Quarterly, (1)*1, 13-17.

Stotlar, David, K. (1996). *Sponsorship*, 290-305. In Bonnie L. Parkhouse, (Ed.), *The management of sport: Its foundation and application* (2nd ed.). St. Louis, MO: C.V. Mosby Year Book.

Taback, L. (1995, November). Heavy lifting: How cash-strapped cities generate revenue on the backs of people passing through. *Ambassador, 78*, 30-31.

Tiersten, Sylvia. (1990). Licensing and franchising. *Fitness Management, (6)*12, 36-39.

Tobin, Dan. (1988). Franchising: Can it work? *Club Industry, (5)*1, 29-30, 32-35, 58-59.

Wilkinson, D.G. (1986). *Sport marketing institute*. Willowdale, Ontario: Sport Marketing Institute.

Wong, Glenn M. (1988). *Essentials of amateur sports law*. Dover, MA: Auburn House Publishing Company.

Suggested Readings

Journals

Sports Marketing Quarterly
Team Licensing Business
The Merchandising Reporter
Trademark World

Books

Association of Collegiate Licensing Administrators (ACLA): *Resource book.* East Lansing, MI: ACLA

Association of Collegiate Licensing Administrators (ACLA): *Licensee handbook.* East Lansing, MI: ACLA

Howard, Dennis R., & Crompton, John L. (1995). *Financing sport.* Morgantown, WV: Fitness Information Technology, Inc.

Parkhouse, Bonnie L. (1996). *The management of sport: Its foundation and application* (2nd ed.). St. Louis, MO: C.V. Mosby Yearbook

Law Cases

Boston Professional Hockey Association, Inc. v. Dallas Cap and Emblem Manufacturing, Inc., 510 F.2d 1004 (1975).

National Football League Properties, Inc. v. Dallas Cap and Emblem Manufacturing Company, 327 N.E.2d 247 (Ill.App.Ct. 1975).

National Football League Properties, Inc. v. Consumer Enterprises, Inc., 327 N.E.2d 242 (Ill.App.Ct. 1975).

Stop the Olympic Prison v. USOC, 501 F.Supp. 1112, 1118-21 (S.D.N.Y. 1980).

National Football League, Inc. v. Wichita Falls Sportswear, Inc., 532 F.Supp. 651 (W.D. Wash. 1982).

University of Pittsburgh v. Champion Products Inc., 686 F.2d 1040 (3rd Cir. 1982), *cert. denied*, 459 U.S. 1087, 103 S.Ct. 571, 74 L.Ed.2d 933, 51 U.S.L.W. 3460 (1982).

University of Georgia Athletic Ass'n v. Latte, 756 F.2d 1535 (11th Cir. 1985).

San Francisco Arts and Athletics, Inc. v. United States Olympic Committee, International Olympic Committee, 483 U.S. 398, 107 S.Ct. 2971, 97 L.Ed.2d 427 (1987).

6

PROMOTIONS AND ADVERTISING

◆ ———————————— ◆

Instructional Objectives

After reading this chapter the student should:

- understand how promotion fits into a marketing plan,

- be able to plan a promotional campaign,

- understand the functions of sales promotion,

- be able to describe personal selling,

- understand how to retain memberships,

- be able to describe how to select an advertising firm and the function of advertising,

- understand how the advertising budget is developed, and

- be able to select which media should be used and how to create an advertisement.

Introduction

Promotions, another of the "Ps" (i.e., place, price, product, promotions, and public relations), is a catch-all category for any one of a variety of marketing efforts designed to stimulate consumer interest in, awareness of, and purchase of the service, product, or program. Promotion is the vehicle that (Johnston, 1986): (1) carries the message about the services, products, and programs; (2) positions them in the market; and (3) develops the appropriate image for the services, products, and programs.

Promotion includes the following forms of marketing activities (Lamphear & Frankel, 1990): (1) advertising, (2) personal selling (i.e., any face-to-face presentation), (3) publicity (see Chapter 10 for greater detail), and (4) sales promotion (i.e., a wide variety of activities including displays, trade shows, free samples, introductory free classes, coupons, giveaways, and exhibitions).

The Importance of Promotion in the Overall Marketing Program

Many people consider "selling" and "marketing" to be synonymous terms. However, selling is only one of the many components of marketing. Selling is the personal process of assisting and/or persuading a prospective customer to buy a commodity or a service or to act favorably upon an idea that has commercial significance to the seller (Mullin, Hardy, & Sutton, 1993).

Promotion is a form of selling, but is the all-inclusive term representing the broad field. Selling suggests only the transfer of title or the use of personal salesmen. Promotion includes advertising, personal selling, sales promotion, and other selling tools. Promotion is the first phase of sales. It describes the product or service and outlines why it is important to own the product or subscribe to the service. A good promotional piece prepares the prospective buyer for the sale. There are a number of promotional marketing strategies that are used in marketing.

The two most widely used methods of promotion are personal selling and advertising. Other promotional methods/strategies are (Brooks, 1994): (1) sales promotion, which is designed to supplement and coordinate personal selling and advertising efforts (i.e., store displays, trade shows and exhibitions, and the use of samples or premiums; (2) mail-order advertising and selling; (3) automatic vending; (4) auctions; (5) telemarketing; (6) product differentiation; (7) market segmentation; (8) trading up; (9) trading down; (10) use of trading stamps or frequent flyer miles; and (11) branding a product or service.

The Promotional Campaign

A promotional campaign is a planned, coordinated, integrated series of promotional efforts built around a single theme or idea and designed to reach a predetermined goal. The first step in developing the campaign is establishing the goals and determining the campaign strategies. The manager should answer the following questions when developing campaign strategies (Johnson, 1996):

- What is the relative emphasis to be placed on primary versus secondary demand stimulation?
- What balance is desired between the immediacy of the action-response and the duration of the response?
- Does the organization influence everyone a little bit or a few people intensively?
- At what point is the management targeting the organization's emphasis on the spectrum between brand awareness and brand insistence?

• What issues, products or services features (i.e., both the organization's and the competitor's) will the organization stress?

Early in the course of planning the campaign, management should decide what selling appeals will be stressed. This decision will be based to a large extent upon the specific objectives of the campaign and the research findings concerning the buying motives and habits of the customers.

Most campaigns revolve around a central theme. This theme should permeate all promotional efforts and tends to unify the campaign. A theme is simply appeals dressed up in a distinctive, attention-getting form. As such, it is related to the campaign's objectives and the customers' behaviors. It expresses the product's benefits. Frequently the theme is expressed as a slogan (e.g., Nike's "Just Do It"; Ford's "Quality is Job One").

The key to success in a campaign depends largely on management's ability to activate and coordinate the efforts of its entire promotional task force and the physical distribution of the product or service. In a successfully implemented campaign, the efforts of all involved should be meshed effectively. The advertising program will consist of a series of related, well-timed, carefully placed ads. The personal selling effort can be tied in by having the salesperson explain and demonstrate the products or services benefits stressed in the ads. Sales-promotional devices such as point-of-purchase display materials need to be coordinated with the other aspects of the campaign. Personnel responsible for the physical distribution activities must ensure that adequate stocks of the product are available prior to the start of the campaign.

The Promotional Mix

Determining the promotional mix (i.e., advertising, personal selling, sales promotions) can be difficult for management if an external promotional professional is not part of the promotional team. However, if management takes into consideration such things as (Johnson, 1996): (1) the factors that influence the promotional mix (e.g., money available for promotion, nature of the market [geographical scope, concentration, and type of customers], nature of the product or service, and stage of the product's or service's life cycle); (2) the questions of basic promotional strategy in order to illustrate the effect of the influencing factors (e.g., when should personal selling [see Table 6-1] and advertising [see Table 6-2] be main ingredients; when should promotional efforts by retailer be stressed; when should manufacturer-retailer cooperative advertising be used; is retailer promotion needed when manufacturer emphasizes advertising; if a retailer emphasizes personal selling, does he/she need to advertise; and should promotional activity be continued when demand is heavy or exceeds capacity?); and (3) the quantitative data from a research study to show the practical applications of the analytical material.

What is Sales Promotion?

Sales promotion is those activities, other than personal selling, advertising, and publicity, that stimulate consumer purchasing and dealer effectiveness, such as displays, shows and expositions, and demonstrations. Sales promotion (Mullin, Hardy & Sutton,1993):(1) informs and persuades groups through tools and methods controlled by the organization itself;(2) deals with nonrecurring and nonroutine matters; (3) exists as a plus ingredient in the marketing mix (i.e., an organization can exist profitable without sales promotion);and (4) serves as a bridge between advertising and personal selling—to supplement and coordinate efforts in these two areas.

Table 6-1
When Should Personal Selling Be the Main Ingredient?

Personal selling will ordinarily carry the bulk of the promotional load when:

- the organization is small or has insufficient funds with which to carry on an adequate advertising program;
- the market is concentrated;
- the personality of the salesperson is needed to establish rapport or create confidence;
- the product has a higher unit value;
- the product/service requires demonstration;
- the product/service must be fitted to the individual customer's needs;
- the product/service is purchased infrequently; or
- the product involves a trade-in.

Table 6-2
Criteria for Deciding Whether or Not to Advertise

Advertising works best when the seller wishes to inform many people quickly (e.g., change in hours, a special sales promotion, or a new credit policy). There are five criteria that should be considered when deciding whether or not to advertise. The five criteria are as follows:

- The primary demand trend for the product or service should be favorable;
- There should be considerable opportunity to differentiate the product or service;
- The product or service should have hidden qualities;
- Powerful emotional buying motives should exist for the product or service; and
- The organization must have sufficient funds to support an advertising program adequately.

There are many services rendered by sales promotion to aid in the selling of products and services of an organization. These services are outlined in Table 6-3.

Table 6-3
Services Rendered by Sales Promotion

Customer Services:
- To educate or inform the consumer about the product or service through the production of booklets and manuals, delivery of demonstrations, and offer free consulting.
- To stimulate consumers through giveaway programs or premium services.

Dealers/distributors:
- Conduct training programs.
- Provide consultation to management.
- Install free displays.

Personal Selling

There are five steps to effective personal selling, including (Brooks, 1994): pre-sale preparation, prospecting (locating) for potential buyers, pre-approach to individual prospects, sales presentation, and post-sale activities. *Pre-sale preparation* is to make certain that the salesperson is prepared. This means that the salesperson must be well acquainted with (Peterson & Colacino, 1990) (1) the service, product or program, (2) the market, and (3) the techniques of selling. The salesperson should know as much as possible about (Lewis & Appenzeller, 1985): (1) the motivation and behavior of the target markets to be pursued, (2) the nature of the competition, and (3) the business conditions prevailing in the market.

Prospecting (location of) for potential consumers is the next step in the process. At this juncture, the salesperson is involved in establishing a profile of the ideal consumer for this service(s), product(s), and program(s). The salesperson should (Mullin, Hardy, & Sutton, 1993; Brooks, 1994; Lewis & Appenzeller, 1985): (1) examine past and present consumers, (2) ask present customers about new leads, (3) research consumers of competitors, (4) regularly read lists of building permits, real estate transactions, births, and engagement announcements, and (5) contact former consumers and/or alumni for new leads. The final product of this research is a list of potential consumers.

The next step is the ***pre-approach to individual prospects.*** Before calling on prospects, the salesperson should learn (i.e., what services, products, or programs the prospect is now using; what the prospect's reaction is to them; personal habits, likes, and dislikes of the prospect) about the person or company that is to be approached as a new consumer of the service(s), product(s), or program(s) offered by the organization.

The actual ***sales presentation*** of the salesman will start with an attempt to attract the prospect's attention. Next, the salesperson will try to hold the customer's interest while building a desire for the service, product, and program. Then the salesman will try to close the sale. All through this presentation, the salesman must be ready and able to meet any hidden or expressed objections that the prospect may have.

There are four approaches to attracting a customer's attention. In the simplest approach, the salesperson merely greets the prospect, introduces him- or herself, and states what is being sold or the reason for the call. Another approach is to start the presentation with — "I was referred to you by . . . " The third approach has the salesperson suggesting the product benefits by making some startling statement, such as, "If I can reduce your cost by 25% on an introductory offer, and at the same time provide you all benefits and a free T-shirt, are you interested?" The final approach is simply to walk in and show the services brochure, product, or program brochure to the prospect.

The ***post-sale activities*** are important to an effective selling job. Normally, sales success depends upon repeat business. Satisfied customers will furnish leads. They are also the best salespersons for the organization. The salesperson should (Irwin & Sutton, 1995): (1) reassure the customer by summarizing the service's, product's, and program's benefits and pointing out how satisfied he/she will be with its performance; (2) ascertain that all points in the sales contract and the guarantee are clearly understood; and (3) provide instruction for the new owner, if necessary.

Selecting an Advertising Firm

If the organization is unable to maintain an in-house advertising operation, it is advisable to interview and select a local agency to serve the organization. If an outside agency is engaged, the performance must be constantly monitored so that more than simple advertisement placement is accomplished. The agency should advise the organization of the most appropriate advertising media plan for the organization. Finally, the agency should have a good sense of promotion and public relations. The average charge by an outside agency is a 15% commission for each advertisement placement.

The Function of Advertising

Advertising consists of all the activities involved in presenting to a group, a nonpersonal, oral or visual, openly sponsored message regarding a service, product, or program. This message, called an *advertisement,* is disseminated through one or more media and is paid for by the identified sponsor (Johnson, 1996).

There is a significant distinction between advertising and an advertisement. The advertisement is simply the message itself (Johnson, 1996). Advertising is a process (Johnson, 1996). It is a program or a series of activities necessary to plan and prepare the message and get it to the intended market. Another point is that the public knows who is behind the advertising because the sponsor is openly identified in the advertisement itself. Further, the payment is made by the sponsor to the media which carry the message. These last two considerations differentiate advertising from propaganda and publicity.

Fundamentally the only purpose of advertising is to sell something—a service, product, or program. The intent may be to generate a sale immediately or at some time in the future. Nevertheless, the basic objective is to sell. Stated another way, the real goal of advertising is effective communication; that is, the ultimate effect of advertising should be to modify the attitudes and/or behavior of the receiver of the message.

The general goal of advertising is to increase profitable sales, but this goal is too broad to be implemented effectively in an advertising program. It is necessary to establish some specific objectives that can be worked into the program. A few examples of these more limited aims are listed below (Brooks, 1994; Johnson, 1996):

- support a personal selling program,
- reach people inaccessible to salesmen,
- improve dealer relations,
- enter a new geographic market or attract a new group of customers,
- introduce a new product or a new price schedule,
- increase sales of products,
- expand membership sales,
- counteract prejudice or substitution, and
- build goodwill for the organization and improve its reputation by rendering a public service through advertising or by selling of the organization behind the service, product, or program.

The Advertising Budget

The advertising program budget is developed by considering the following components:

- *Expenses*
  - (1) the number and size of printed advertisements (internal and external sources),

(2) the number and length of radio spots,

(3) the number and length of television spots,

(4) the number of billboards in use,

(5) personnel, and

(6) office expenses

- *Income*

(1) advertisement space sold, and

(2) trade outs [It is possible to increase the advertising schedule for a program on a noncash basis (trade-outs—tickets or memberships for free advertising) if the attraction and manager are willing to allow a radio station (it is less common for television and the printed media to enter into trade-out agreements) to be the program's official media sponsor. Never allow a media sponsorship to be construed as a sponsorship exclusive. Offer the media sponsor a promotional exclusive and clearly retain the right to advertise anywhere else it is appropriate.

The annual budget should include funds each year to advertise the schedule of services, products, and programs in local newspapers in a format that people can clip out and retain on a month-to-month basis. Many organizations also publish a weekly or monthly in-house newsletter that is used as a direct-mail piece as well as a handout at the facility.

Depending on the organization's philosophy, advertising can generate income by selling space for advertising in a variety of media throughout the organization's facility(ies). The possibilities include (Mullin, Hardy, & Sutton, 1993; Brooks, 1994; Johnson, 1996): (1) scoreboard systems, (2) concourse display cases, (3) lobby displays, (4) point-of-sale displays, (5) Zamboni, (6) in-house publications, (7) message centers, (8) outdoor marquees, (9) upcoming program display cases, (10) membership packages, (11) concession product containers, (12) indoor soccer wall boards, (13) baseball/softball outfield fence, (14) scorer tables, and (15) contest programs. There are a number of potential advertisers for these spaces and, in particular, for concession products. Concession product vendors are willing to advertise their names and products on concession containers. This coupled with discount sale promotions will increase food and beverage sales for the organization as well as its vendors.

Selecting the Media

Advertising strategy varies from program to program and season to season depending on the nature of the anticipated audience or market. Where to place an advertisement is governed generally by funds available.

Management must determine what general types of media to use. Newspapers, magazines, radio, television, and billboards? If newspapers, local or regional? If television is selected, will it be local, national network, or spot telecasting?

Objective of the advertisement. Media choices are influenced both by the purpose of a specific advertisement and by the goal of an entire campaign. If an advertiser wants to make last-minute changes in an advertisement, or if he/she wishes to place an advertisement inducing action within a day or two, he/she may use newspapers, radio, or television. Magazines are not so good for this purpose because the advertisement must be placed weeks before the date of publication.

Media circulation. Media circulation must match the distribution patterns of the service, product, or program. Consequently, the geographic scope of the market will influence the choice of media considerably. Furthermore, media should be selected that will reach the desired type of market with a minimum of waste circulation. Media used to reach a teenage market will be different from those used to reach mothers with young children.

Requirements of the message. Management should consider the media that are most suitable for the presentation of the message to the market. Meat products, floor coverings, and apparel are ordinarily best presented in pictorial form; thus radio is not a good medium for these lines. If a product, such as insurance, calls for a lengthy message, outdoor advertising is poor. If the advertiser can use a very brief message, however, as in the case of salt, beer, or sugar, then billboards may be the best choice. Television can be used to show pictures, but not detailed ones.

Time and location of buying decision. The advertiser should select the medium that will reach the prospective customer at or near the time and place that he/she makes the buying decision. For this reason, outdoor advertising (billboards) is often good for gasoline products and hotels/motels. Grocery store advertisements are placed in newspapers on Thursday nights or Friday mornings in anticipation of heavy weekend buying.

How are Advertisements Created?

Before creating the advertisement, the sport manager should remember that the main purpose of advertising is to sell something and that the advertisement itself is a sales talk. The advertisement may be a high-pressure sales talk, as in a hard-hitting, direct-action advertisement; or it may be a very long-range, low-pressure message, as in an institutional advertisement. In any case, it is trying to sell something. Consequently, it involves the same kind of selling procedure as a sales talk delivered by a personal salesman. That is, the advertisement must first attract attention and then hold interest long enough to stimulate a desire for the service, product, or program. Finally, the advertisement must move the prospect to some kind of action. The desired action may lie anywhere within a virtually unlimited scope of possibilities, ranging from an immediate change in overt behavior to a slowly changing attitude or thought process.

Creating an advertisement involves the tasks of writing the copy, including the headline, selecting illustrations that may be used, preparing the layout, and arranging to have the advertisement reproduced for the selected media.

The copy in an advertisement is defined as all the written or spoken material in it, including the headline, coupons, and advertiser's name and address, as well as the main body of the message. The illustration, whether it is a photograph, drawing, reproduction of a painting, cartoon, or something else, is a powerful feature in an advertisement. Probably the main points to consider with respect to illustrations are: (1) whether they are the best alternative use of the space, and (2) whether they are appropriate in all respects to the advertisement itself. The layout is the physical arrangement of all the elements in an advertisement. Within the given amount of space or time, the layout man must place the headline, copy, and illustrations. Decisions are made regarding the relative amount of white space and the kinds of type to be used. A good layout can be an interest-holding device as well as an attention-getter. It should lead the reader in an orderly fashion throughout the entire advertisement.

Summary

Promotion is the vehicle that carries the message about the services, products, and programs, positions them in the marketplace, and develops the appropriate image for the services, products, and programs. Promotion is a key part of the total marketing program.

Learning Objective 1: Promotion as a part of the marketing plan.

The marketing plan includes market research, target marketing, distribution, evaluation, and the five "Ps"—place, price, products, promotions, and public relations. The director of promotions, armed with the definition of the market, the client, and the client needs and wants, responsibility is to stimulate consumer interest in, awareness of, and purchase of the service, product or program.

Learning Objective 2: Planning a promotional campaign.

Once the director of promotions or sport manager understands the market, the service or product or program, and the consumer needs and wants, he/she can develop the promotional campaign. A promotional campaign is a planned, coordinated, integrated series of promotional efforts built around a single theme or idea and designed to reach a predetermined market. There are four main components of a campaign—the advertising program, personal selling effort, sales promotional devices, and physical distribution activities.

Learning Objective 3: The function of sales promotion.

Sales promotion are those activities that stimulate consumer purchasing and dealer effectiveness, such as displays, shows and expositions, and demonstrations.

Learning Objective 4: A description of personal selling.

Personal selling is a collection of activities that increases the opportunity for a sale. The common steps used in personal selling are pre-sale preparation, locating potential buyers, pre-approach to individual prospects, sales presentation, and post-sales or follow-up activities.

Learning Objective 5: Membership retention.

Maintaining membership begins the moment the new customer enters the establishment. Each customer must feel a connection with the facilities and personnel almost immediately and throughout the first year of membership.

Learning Objective 6: Selection of an advertising firm, and the function of advertising.

Selecting an advertising firm is similar to selecting a physician. Advertising firms have specialty areas. Review each firm, including previous advertising campaigns, client references, a sample advertising plan for your organization, and commission.

Advertising is used to distribute a sponsored message regarding a service, product, or program to the marketplace.

Learning Objective 7: The advertising budget.

The advertising budget consists of expenses to advertise in the media and income generated by advertisement space sold by the organization for use in organizational documents.

Learning Objective 8: Selecting the media, and creating the advertisement.

When selecting the media to be used in an advertising program, the sport manager must consider the resources available, the objective of the advertisement, media circulation, requirements of the message, and time and location of buying decision.

Before creating an advertisement, the purpose of the advertisement must be well defined. The creation process involves writing copy, preparing the layout, and arranging to have the advertisement reproduced for the selected media.

Self-testing Exercises

1.   Develop a promotional plan for an annual interscholastic holiday basketball tournament comprised of eight teams from across the state. This will be a combined boys and girls tournament. It will be held between Christmas and New Year's.
2.   You have been hired as a salesperson in charge of group sales for the Charleston Sluggers, a single-A baseball team in Charleston, South Carolina. What will be your personal selling strategy for the upcoming baseball season?
3.   You have talked the board of directors into investing in an advertising plan. What steps will you take in selecting an advertising firm? What will you provide the advertising firm with to assist them in developing an advertising plan? How will you select the media to be used in this campaign? Prepare an advertising budget for the project.

4.   You have just been hired to replace a manager at a local health and fitness club. The membership base had been eroding slowly over the past five years, but recently the losses were growing extremely fast. What will your plan be to gain new members and retain current as well as new members? The management has set a goal of retaining 90% of all members over the next two years.

References

Barrett, Bob. (1993). Ten tips for better member retention. *Club Industry, (9)*1, 41-52.

Brooks, Christine. (1994). Sports marketing: Competitive business strategies for sports. Englewood Cliffs, NJ: Prentice-Hall.

Clemens-Silence, Michele. (1991). Aerobics retention. *Fitness Management, (7)*9, 40-41.

Irwin, Richard L., & Sutton, William A. (1995). Keeping the customer satisfied. *Athletic Management, (7)*3, 18-24.

Johnson, A. T. (1986). Economic and policy implications of hosting sports franchises. *Urban Affairs*.

Johnson, John R. (1996). *Promotion for sport directors*. Champaign, IL: Human Kinetics.

Lamphear, Molly Pulver, & Frankel, Eleanor. (1990). Filling the seats. *CAM Magazine, 2*:7, 27-31.

Lewis, Guy, & Appenzeller, Herb. (1985). *Successful sport management*. Charlottesville, VA: The Michie Company.

Mullin, Bernard J., Hardy, Stephen, & Sutton, William A. (1993). *Sport Marketing*. Champaign, IL: Human Kinetics.

Peterson, James A., & Colacino, Dennis L. (1990). Marketing for profits. *Fitness Management, (6)*1, 24-27.

Seifer, Jan. (1987). Ten management guidelines to boost member retention. *Athletic Business, (11)*10, 66-68.

Suggested Readings

Howard, Dennis R., & Crompton, John L. (1995). *Financing sport*. Morgantown, WV: Fitness Information Technology, INC.

Latora, Carl. (1994). Athletics in the '90s. *Athletic Management, (5)*6, 21-27

Parkhouse, Bonnie L. (1996). *The management of sport: Its foundation and application* (2nd ed.). St Louis, MO: C.V. Mosby Year Book.

White, Jim. (1991). The direct route. *CAM Magazine, (3)*1, 40-43.

7

FUND RAISING

◆ ─────────────── ◆

Instructional Objectives

After reading this chapter the student should:

- be able to describe the function and purposes of fund-raising,

- understand how to develop and implement a fund-raising campaign,

- appreciate the characteristics of givers and what they give,

- understand how to conduct a direct mail campaign and increase audiences,

- understand what steps to take to successfully pass a bond referendum, and

- appreciate how to finance a sport facility.

Introduction

All organizations have the need for additional funds beyond the normal revenue sources (i.e., membership fees, ticket sales, guarantees, post-season opportunities, radio and television contracts, concessions [food, merchandise, and parking], franchising, licensing agreements, sponsorships etc.). There are, of course, many legitimate and logical reasons why additional funding is needed to support programs, such as program expansion, facility renewal or expansion, inflation, changing priorities, increase in unemployment with markets, and a decrease in the purchasing power of the consumers within the markets. Without successful fund-raising programs, exciting promotions, and an excellent public relations program (see Chapter 11), the organization could be forced to reduce or eliminate marginal programs and sport teams, layoff personnel, reduce hours of operation, or close facilities. Therefore, it is imperative for sport managers to develop strong programs in fund-raising and promotions. An effective, efficient, and successful fund-raising program will allow the organization to grow and prosper in today's very competitive financial environment.

Fund-raising is the art of *soliciting money* for charitable organizations, schools, colleges/universities, political parties, and many other worthy projects and organizations. Many organizations define fund-raising as anything that increases revenue, including: concessions, deferred giving, donations, grants, merchandising, licensing, promotions, and sponsorships. This chapter will focus on fund-raising related to donations.

Guidelines for a Fund-raising Program

One of the biggest errors made by novices as well as experienced fund-raisers is to seek something new, different, and unique when it would be far better to adopt a program that has been successful. Why reinvent the wheel? The challenge should not be to originate activities, but to be creative in the implementation of those things that have produced results elsewhere. There are a multitude of events and projects that are appropriate for fund-raising activities. Stier (1994), discusses over 70 plans for events that have been used successfully by others, in his book, *Fundraising for sport and recreation: Step-by-step plans for 70 successful events*.

It is vital that an overall plan for fund-raising be developed using the following guidelines (Stier, 1994): (1) fund-raising must be program specific; (2) a prospect list must be developed; (3) an accounting system must be established; (4) an acknowledgement and follow-up system must be devised; (5) a timetable must be established; (6) the organization will do better if it is classified as a non-profit (not-for-profit) 501 (c)(3) tax-exempted corporation; (7) a board of directors must be formed and a legal binding contract be drawn requiring the board to review and monitor funds periodically; (8) the overall plan should have short- [one to two years] and long- [three to five years] range goals and objectives; (9) the goals and objectives (projects) should be prioritized; (10) all activities, policies, and procedures should be kept simple; (11) an attorney and certified public accountant should be involved in the early phases of the fund-raising program; (12) in selecting projects, choose those that are cost-effective and appropriate for the organization to sponsor; and (13) a training program should be established for staff and volunteers to prepare them for the tasks and a formal and informal means of appreciation needs to be established for all volunteers and community members.

Addressing Preliminary Issues

A fund-raising program is a major commitment for any organization. Therefore, it is very important for the manager to be able to answer the following questions in detail: Is there a definable financial need? Can fund-raising activity meet the program's needs? Is this the only way, or the best way, of meeting the needs? Is the program itself worthy of support? Is there adequate and competent leadership activity? Are there sufficient volunteers? Is there an organization support infra-structure capable of achieving the successful conclusion of the fund-raising effort? Is there a support organization in existence? Could this organization be recognized as the official representative of the athletic program in terms of fund-raising? Is there a positive reputation and image of the support organization in the eyes of the various constituencies?

Other questions to be considered: How much will it cost to raise the desired amount? What are the downside risks and liabilities? Will the program be cost-effective in terms of money, time, effort, personnel, and other resources? Are the necessary resources available? What are the requirements in terms of time to reach the objective(s)? Can the objectives be reached in that time? What legal matters will be of concern (i.e., incorporation, tax-exempted status, mailing permit, taxes, special permits, insurance, etc.)? Can the end results stand up to close scrutiny of various constituencies? Is the financial and political climate conducive to success?

Resources Necessary to Conduct a Successful Fund-raising Program

Fund-raising, if not planned properly, can be a resource drag. There are a number of resources necessary for conducting any fund-raising project. These usually include: time, personnel (i.e., internal/external and paid/volunteer), equipment (i.e., computers, printers, fax machine, filing cabinet), supplies (i.e., paper, stationary, envelopes, file cards, file folder, postage), facilities, reputation and image of the organization, the organization's past accomplishments and achievements, seed funding to start projects, and other non-personnel (i.e., members, students, parents, community members, friends of the organization).

Key Components of a Fund-raising Program

There are seven components of a fund-raising program. Each of the components must be integrated in order to develop a successful program. The components are the following (Stier, 1994; Howard & Crompton, 1995):

(1) *What:*
   (a) the establishment of a mission, purpose, and function statements;
   (b) development of short- and long-term goals and objectives, and
   (c) prepare appropriate strategies to implement the action plans within a suitable time frame;

(2) *Where:*
Fund-raising should take place in many venues inside as well as outside the organization (see Table 7-1);

(3) *Why:*
No fund-raising program or project should be developed unless there are justifiable needs that can be utilized in the development of the case statement [a case statement is an embellished need statement];

(4) *When:*
  (a) fund-raising, like fruit, is time-sensitive and there are good times and bad times in every community to mount a fund-raising campaign;
  (b) a time should be carefully chosen that allows for maximum penetration into the community;
  (c) the campaign should be designed in time-sequenced events that follow an established priority of importance, and
  (d) the most commonly implemented fund-raising efforts are one-time events, repeatable projects, and annual events that are either one-time or repeatable projects.

(5) *By Whom:*
  A key to any fund-raising program or project's success is the people involved. There must be involvement of paid staff, volunteers (i.e., members, students, parents, community leaders, friends of the organization), and other external sources.

(6) *Categories or vehicles of giving:*
  There are a number of categories utilized in fund-raising projects, including major donor programs, capital programs (i.e., building campaign), annual scholarship appeals, annual giving campaigns for the total program, annual special events or projects, annual giving campaigns for special purposes, annual giving campaigns on an unrestricted basis, deferred/planned giving (i.e., proceeds from life insurance or wills), memorial giving programs (i.e., in memory of someone), gifts-in-kind (i.e., donations of professional time or equipment), and general endowment programs;

(7) *Feasibility:*
  The manager and fund-raising committee need to develop an assessment process for evaluating all projects or events to determine:
  (a) how successful a project or event might be,
  (b) whether or not to proceed with the project or event, and
  (c) what should be done to improve the project or event before it is repeated.

Table 7-1
Common Models Used in Fund-raising

The most commonly used models for fund-raising are (Lewis & Appenzeller, 1985; Stier, 1993; Howard & Crompton, 1995):

  (1) person-to-person solicitation,
  (2) single-person cultivation,
  (3) door-to-door solicitation,
  (4) telephone solicitation (telemarketing),
  (5) contest of chance (i.e., 50/50 drawing, raffle, lottery, casino nights), and
  (6) direct mail solicitation

Committees Used in Fund-raising Projects

Not many fund-raising projects are undertaken without a number of key committees, particularly to support public school and not-for-profit fund-raising efforts. These committees may be composed of both paid staff and volunteers. The most commonly utilized committees are (Stier, 1993, 1994): (1) site selection, (2) publicity and promotion, (3) equipment and supplies, (4) finance, (5) refreshments and hospitality, (6) invitation and program, (7) ticket, (8) decorations, (9) prizes, (10) security, (11) cleanup, and (12) project assessment.

Examples of Fund-raising Events

There are many events that can be used for fund-raising by organizations; the only thing that limits a manager is his/her imagination. Here are a few suggestions of fund-raising events: athletic contests, clinics/workshops; youth sport camps/clinics; fun nights; team/individual athlete photos; flea markets/consignment sales; car washes; swim-, walk-, run-, bike-a-thons; invitational tournaments; novelty athletic events (i.e., Harlem Gobletrotters, King and His Court, donkey baseball/softball); craft and hobby shows/sales; rummage/white elephant/garage sales; shows (i.e., baseball cards, musicals, etc.); exhibitions, bazaars, festivals, fairs, and carnivals; rodeos; celebrity and regular golf tournaments; hole-in-one contests; card and board games; excursions; house/garden tours; fashion shows; professional wrestling events; haunted houses; Christmas and Santa Claus workshop; ghost dinners; celebrity roasts; dances; sponsoring camping, boating, or recreational equipment shows; athletic hall of fame; auctions; road races; meet the coaches lunch/breakfast; Monday night football club; wine and cheese/ice cream socials; reunion of championship teams; alumni games; pancake breakfast/Jonah's fish fry; and meet the team night . . . barbecue . . . annual pig roast.

Fund-raising Support Groups

Fund-raising support groups, such as athletic or band booster clubs, are very useful tools in the fund-raising arsenal. These groups are composed of members, parents, and community supporters who are all volunteers.

There are seven steps in the establishment of support groups, including: (Lewis & Appenzeller, 1985): (1) recognition of the need for such a group; (2) communication with management, board members, and/or appropriate school officials; (3) consultation with representative of various internal and external constituencies; (4) establishment of general principles and guidelines for the support group; (5) recognition of potential pitfalls that should be avoided (i.e., overzealous boosters, selecting proper accounting methods, establishment of priorities, relationship between support group and organization, planning for continuity); (6) dissemination of information about the organization and its purpose; and (7) determination of the organizational structure of the group through the establishment of articles of incorporation, bylaws, and rules of operation.

The rules of operation, unlike the articles of incorporation and bylaws, are simplified operational codes not used for establishing a non-profit tax exempt status. See appendix for an outline for establishing a set of rules of operations for a support group (Lewis & Appenzeller, 1985; Stier, 1993).

Contributors to fund-raising usually receive some kind of benefit for their donations. These benefits might be any of the following or a combination of the following: preferred parking, complimentary or reduced ticket prices or the privilege to purchase tickets in a particular location, special event ticket priority, dinner and banquet seating priority, plaques or other gift items to recognize donors, invitations to special events, VIP lounge privilege membership card, periodic newsletters, press guide(s) and other publications, mention and recognition in game programs, away game ticket priority, travel with specific teams, access to press box or special areas for special teams and/or events, specific apparel to identify donors and contributors, a private booth for home contests or events, auto decals, free golf at college/university course, free or reduced membership in college/university health/wellness center, scholarship named after donor, building named after donor, dinner to honor donor, and perpetual award given in donor's name.

Characteristics of Volunteers

No organization has enough staff to adequately raise funds through solicitation. Therefore, volunteers become critical to any fund-raising effort. The volunteer plays the role of a loyal community supporter of the organization involved in raising funds for vital projects. They can easily influence colleagues, newer members, former classmates, and other community leaders of the importance of a project and the need for the funds. Volunteers are great ambassadors of goodwill.

The manager of any organization involved with volunteers must understand how to best involve them in the organization. Volunteers need supervision and attention just as do the employees and customers (Stier, 1993).

Stier (1993) and Meagher (1995) suggest the following when dealing with volunteers:

- Remember the 25% rule—25% of the volunteers will do nearly all that is asked of them.
- The 20% rule—refers to those individuals who are truly effective, who are the real producers and "result-getters."
- Volunteers have feelings, so make them feel valuable and wanted, treat them with respect, and provide them with special privileges to reward them for their contributions.
- Volunteers have needs, satisfy them.
- Volunteers have suggestions, seek their input.
- Volunteers have specific interests, provide options and alternatives for them to do.
- Volunteers have specific competencies, recognize these skills and do not attempt to place square pegs in round holes.
- Volunteers are individuals working with other individuals, encourage them to work as a team, not as competing individuals.

- Volunteers are not (usually) professionals within the organization or profession. Treat them with a special understanding and empathy.
- Volunteers are not paid staff, do not involve them in staff politics.
- Volunteers desire to be of assistance, let them know how they are doing (feedback), answer their questions, and provide good two-way communications.
- Volunteers have the potential to be excellent recruiters, especially through networking, of other potentially helpful volunteers.
- Volunteers can be trained to assume a variety of roles within the fund-raising process.
- Volunteers are able to grow in professional competency with appropriate and timely training, motivation, and opportunity.

How Should a Direct-Mail Promotion Be Developed?

An effective direct mail promotion starts with designing an appropriate eye-catching mailing piece. It is important to establish a budget before considering any design concepts. The type of design can vary from a four-page direct-mail piece on glossy paper to printing in black ink on colored paper. A high-quality, four-color product leaves an impression of a quality program. Four-color printing provides maximum impact if you can afford it; but a talented graphic designer can often create a professional look by using quality black and white photos and two-color printing, or even by printing one color on colored paper.

The designer should minimize copy and maximize pictures, since pictures are worth a thousand words, and in our busy society, people will not take the time to read a lot of copy. The package should be designed so it is exciting, because it is competing for people's attention in a hectic, media-saturated society.

The next decision to be made is whether to use a self-mailer or envelope. A self-mailer requires no envelope, thereby saving money on printing. It also has the advantage of not requiring the recipient to open the envelope, which is a major hurdle for direct mail. Creating an attractive or original design for the piece is one way to eliminate a recipient's belief that the self-mailer is trivial. On the other hand, an envelope with an inserted brochure and letter is the more traditional approach. When using an envelope, it is important to create an envelope that is intriguing enough to motivate the recipient to open it.

Another option is to use postcards, which are inexpensive to print, can be custom-printed to creatively deliver the message, and are very effective in the right situation. For example, if you want to invite people to an annual event that requires minimal explanation, consider mailing a postcard. Postcards can also be used to remind customers to renew memberships or tickets.

It is difficult to decide whether or not to pay for the return postage on envelopes or cards that you want returned by the prospect. At 1997 rates, using a business-reply permit means an extra cost of approximately 5¢ per piece in printing, plus $85 for a business reply permit, 32¢ for each envelope or 21¢ for each postcard returned, and an 8¢ handling fee from the post office for each piece returned. Many direct mail specialists believe that prepaying the postage increases the return rate enough to justify the added expenses.

The use of personal letters is very cost effective with the technology of high-speed laser printers. Similarly, a window envelope adds a more personalized touch and allows you to avoid using the non-personalized adhesive computer labels. Window envelopes also provide the letter with a more professional look, which is important when you are mailing to an untested market. Window envelopes are more expensive than standard envelopes.

The budget should include items such as the design and printing costs for the mailing piece, envelopes, inserts, letters, the cost of postage, procurement of the mailing list(s), and the cost of a mailing service. The 1997 cost of mailing a standard first-class letter was 32¢ and a letter first-class pre-sorted, 28¢. However, the non-profit bulk rate for the same letter was only 11.5¢, and mailing bulk also provides a higher weight limit. The disadvantage of bulk-rate mail is that it is delivered at the slowest rate—anywhere from two days to three weeks. However, bulk rate is still the most cost-effective way to send direct mail pieces. There must be at least 200 pre-sorted pieces mailed at the same time. Further, the best method and most cost effective to affix postage is by use of a postage meter. It appears to be first-class mail and treated with a higher-priority by the recipient. A preprinted bulk-rate permit sends a clear signal that the piece is bulk mail, and therefore may be perceived as a lower-priority item.

If the postal costs are a concern, make arrangements with a bank or utility company to place the piece in the firm's monthly statement. This enables the organization to save money on postage and perhaps, reach a preferred audience. However, do not expect to generate more than one percent return on this type of mailing.

Finally, you must clearly communicate your message in the direct mail piece. The quality of the promotional piece must be consistent with the quality of the service, product, or program. Further, studies have surprisingly found that people are more likely to read a two-page letter than only a one-page letter.

Summary

All large and small organizations have the need for additional funds beyond the normal revenue sources (i.e., membership fees, ticket sales, guarantees, post-season opportunities, radio and television contracts, concessions [food, merchandise, and parking], franchising, licensing agreements, sponsorships etc.). There are, of course, many legitimate and logical reasons why additional funding is needed to support programs, such as program expansion, facility renewal or expansion, inflation, changing priorities, increase in unemployment with markets, and a decrease in the purchasing power of the consumers within the markets.

Learning Objective 1: Describe the function and purpose of fund-raising.

Fund-raising is the art of soliciting money for charitable organizations, schools, colleges/universities, political parties, and many other worthy projects and organizations. Many organizations define fund-raising as anything that increases revenue.

One of the biggest errors made by novices as well as experienced fund-raisers is to seek something new, different, and unique when it would be far better to adopt some program that has been successful. Why reinvent the wheel? The challenge should not be to originate activities but to be creative in the implementation of those things that have produced results elsewhere.

Learning Objective 2: How to develop and implement a fund-raising campaign.

A fund-raising program is a major commitment for any organization. If not properly planned it can be a resource drag. The successfully organized fund-raising program has seven components. The sport manager should spend considerable amount of time defining the characteristics of the givers most likely to become involved in a fund-raising program or project sponsored by the organization. He/she should understand why people contribute to a fund-raising campaign.

Support groups, like athletic or band booster clubs, are very useful tools in the fund-raising arsenal. These groups are composed of members, parents, and community supporters, who are all volunteers.

Learning Objective 3: Characteristics of givers and why they give.

No successful fund-raiser can function without answering the following key questions: (1) What are the characteristics of the givers most likely to give to our cause? (2) Why do these people give to our organization?

Learning Objective 4: Conducting a direct mail campaign and increase audiences.

An effective direct-mail promotion starts with designing an appropriate eye-catching mailing piece. It is important to establish a budget before considering any design concepts.

Learning Objective 5: Understanding a bond referendum.

Government-sponsored health, fitness, physical activity, recreation, and sport programs raise funds for major projects through bond referendums. Bond referendums are often more successful in generating funds for infrastructure projects than locally generated tax dollars. Bonds are a publicly supported financial package.

Learning Objective 6: How to finance a sport facility.

Sport arenas, stadiums, and multipurpose facilities are financed in one of three ways—public, private, or joint public/private. There are several mechanisms available in structuring public sector involvement in sport facility development, expansion, and renovation, such as general obligation bonds, revenue bonds, certificates of participation (lease appropriations bonds), and tax increment bonds.

Self-testing Exercise

1. You are a fund-raising consultant who has been employed by a local youth soccer association to raise $75,000 to construct a soccer field complex with a combination concession stand, public restrooms, and storage for field equipment. How will you organize the soccer association for the fund-raising task?

2. As the new Twain High School sport director, you are faced with an all too common problem with high school sport programs—inadequate funding. The high school does not have a sport booster club or any fund-raising organization. At your last high school, the booster club was responsible for raising over $50,000 annually for the sport program. You decide to prepare a proposal for a sport booster club to be presented to the board of trustees for approval. Prepare the proposal.

3. You and a number of close business friends are interested in constructing a public spectator soccer stadium in your community. The population of this midwestern city is over one million. The economy is very diverse. They have elected you as chairman of the group. The group has completed plans for the structure and gained estimates of costs. Your next task is to secure financing for the project. What steps will you take to secure the funding?

References

Howard, Dennis R., & Crompton, John L. (1995). *Financing sport.* Morgantown, WV: Fitness Information Technology, Inc.

Lamphear, Molly Pulver, & Frankel, Eleanor. (1990). Filling the seats. *CAM Magazine, (2)*7, 27-31.

Lewis, Guy, & Appenzeller, Herb. (1985). *Successful Sport Management.* Charolettesville, VA: The Michie Company.

Meagher, John W. (1995). Right on the money. *Athletic Business, (19)*8, 67-70.

Stier, William F., Jr. (1994). *Successful sport fund-raising.* Dubuque, IA: WCB Brown & Benchmark Publishers.

Stier, William F., Jr. (1993). Project profit. *Athletic Management, (4)*2, 44-46.

Suggested Readings

Mullin, Bernard J., Hardy, Stephen, & Sutton, William A. (1993). *Sport marketing.* Champaign, IL: Human Kinetics Publishers.

Parkhouse, Bonnie L. (1996). *The management of sport: Its foundation and application* (2nd ed.). St. Louis, MO: C.V. Mosby Year Book.

Prince, Russ Alan, & File, Karen Maru. (1994). *The seven faces of philanthrophy—A new approach to cultivating major donors.* San Francisco: Jossey-Bass Publishers.

Stier, William F., Jr. (1994). *Fundraising for sport and recreation: Step-by-step plans for 70 successful events.* Champaign, IL: Human Kinetics Publishers.

8

MEMBERSHIP RETENTION

◆ ———————————— ◆

Instructional Objectives

After reading this chapter the student should:

• understand why customers or fans decide not to renew their memberships or season tickets,

• be able to describe the costs of recruiting new customers,

• understand how to develop an in-service training program for staff to comprehend why customers or fans renew their memberships or season tickets,

• be able to deal with complaints effectively,

• understand basic membership retention strategies,

• be able to develop strategies to maintain season ticket holders, and

• understand why a student-athlete chooses to participate or withdraw from sports.

Introduction

Customer retention statistics show that 50% of all new customers drop out of their programs within six months (Winters, 1994). The average fitness facility loses 40% of its entire customer base each year. Some would say, "No problem!" There is an unlimited supply of new customers. Nearly 80% of the U.S. population do not belong to a club. However, the club industry estimates it costs six times more money to get a new customer than to keep an existing one. When management factors in training and promotions, the rapid turnover of salespeople, and the hiring and training of new sales staffers, the six times figure appears to be conservative. Club profits come from retention, not replacement of customers. If the retention rate is improved by only 5%, a club can expect net profits to double, due to the lower cost of retaining customers as opposed to recruiting new ones.

The existing customers know the facility and how to use the equipment. If they are satisfied with the club and its services, they will recommend the club to their family and friends, which provides the club with a ready source of inexpensive new customers. A direct benefit of all this is that the cost of generating new customers is reduced. Customer retention is the name of the game in club management. Any number of factors contribute to *customer (member) retention* and key among them is customer relations. It is definitely more important to keep customers. The customer base covers operating expenses and provides a profit, but retaining customers is not a simple process. In 1995 the average length of a club membership was 1.63 years for multipurpose clubs and 1.4 years for fitness-only facilities.

Fan retention, like customer retention, is critical in interscholastic, intercollegiate, and professional sports. These sport enterprises cannot survive unless the fans continue to purchase tickets. The successful sport managers have learned that the fans come first and the fans are never wrong.

Why Do Customers or Fans Decide Not to Renew Their Memberships or Season Tickets?

It is not hard to understand that the campaign to retain customers begins the day a person joins a club or purchases a sport ticket. The critical time period is the first year of membership or the first few games attended by a fan. This period of time is when most people decide whether they will stay with the club or sport team or let their membership lapse (see Table 8-1 and 8-2).

How to Gather Knowledge from Current Customers or Fans to Guide the Renewal Process

How well does the sport manager know the customer or fans: Does he/she know how old they are? Their level of income? Their family structure? The specific needs? Does he/she know why they come to this fitness club or sport team? Why do some of them come more often than others? Why do some stop coming altogether?

Many club or franchise owners or managers actually know very little about their customers. Some, however, have learned to gather, retain, and organize information on their customers, and how to use this information to increase and maintain business. Getting this type of information does not have to be expensive. A sophisticated computer system, and special software is not needed. An expensive consultant is not required. The sport manager does not need to be a mathematician or an expert at consumer research. All that is needed is an understanding of a few simple points about a very simple and effective business tool. A tool that can be used to provide management information about the customer base. That tool is a customer survey.

Table 8-1
Why Customers Drop Out

The following are the common reasons why customers drop out:

- failure to receive enough attention,
- failure to receive appropriate guidance during the first year of membership,
- failure to lose weight as quickly as perceived,
- failure to transform their body composition overnight,
- failure not to get into physical shape as quickly as perceived,
- lack of proper orientation for using the facilities, equipment or personnel,
- failure to see results from the program designed,
- club does not meet expectations,
- poorly maintained facility or equipment,
- do not feel as though he/she belongs,
- loss of motivation to continue program,
- the visit to the club was not enough,
- the club does not cater to his/her needs,
- not a family affair,
- the benefits do not outweigh the costs, and
- employees are not personable or friendly.

Table 8-2
Why Sport Teams Lose Fans

There are a number of reasons why sport teams lose fans, including the following:

- they did not feel as though they were important,
- cost outweighs enjoyment,
- dirty facilities,
- boring food service,
- poor seating,
- inconvenient parking,
- no luxury seating,
- no picnic areas,
- no non-smoking areas,
- no non-drinking areas,
- no place to change the young children,
- no day care facilities,
- no playground for young children,
- souvenirs too expensive,
- no other entertainment but the game itself,
- team is not exciting,
- team fails to win consistently, and
- no opportunities to meet the players.

Customer surveys, like the customer profile system depicted in Table 8-3, are a key tool used by thousands of businesses to provide the kind of information they need to increase business, introduce products or services that will meet with a strong consumer response, determine why some never "got off the ground," and ascertain what kinds of customers currently belong or attend so similar customers can be sought and added to the customer base.

Table 8-3
Customer Profile System

A Customer Profile System (CPS) assists in making sure the participants or ticket holders are satisfied customers—and loyal members or fans. A CPS is an after-marketing strategy to assist managers in retaining customers (Irwin & Sutton, 1995). It is important to create a CPS that enables the organization to develop and maintain personal relationships with the customers. The CPS serves as a type of dialogue between the actions and interests of the consumer and the organization.

The potential of what can be accomplished through the establishment of a CPS and related marketing efforts depends upon two factors (Irwin & Sutton, 1995): (1) what information will be compiled in the CPS, and (2) how consistently and aggressively this data will be used. There are four important features in developing the CPS database (Irwin & Sutton, 1995): (1) addressability—ensures that the CPS provides communication with every identifiable customer and enables the organization to communicate with all current customers; (2) consumer purchasing histories—enables the marketer to monitor attendance patterns and purchasing behaviors of the various customer groups; (3) flexibility— the CPS must be flexible enough to be able to segment customers for specifically designed/targeted communications; and (4) accountability—a quantifiable way to assess the number of people who are members or customers.

A CPS software program can easily be stored on a single personal computer. The CPS program can be developed by the organization by using Lotus 1-2-3 or any other data base software program. Storage and utilization are dependent upon the size of the organization and the number of individuals who will be accessing the information simultaneously or during the course of an average work day. The data obtained for the CPS should be updated annually by using a Customer Profile Sheet completed by all customers at time of purchase.

After building the database, the organization can begin after-marketing. Its applications are only limited by the manager's imagination. A few uses for the data base could be customer satisfaction surveys, analyzing customer groups, promoting other and special events, tracking members' purchasing and attendance habits, and to set a benchmark or reference point for future analysis.

The business survey can be used to: (1) increase business, (2) introduce new programs to customer base, (3) determine why existing programs are not getting the attention they were designed for, (4) ascertain more about the existing customer base to encourage renewals and go out and prospect for similar customers, and (5) determine why customers have decided not to renew membership or season tickets.

However, surveys will not: (1) fully identify best prospects' characteristics, wants, and needs; (2) determine why elements of a program are working or not working; (3) monitor how perceptions of the facility, equipment, and services are changing over time; or (4) explain why some programs are successful and others are failures.

Yet, surveys can assist in: (1) effectively defining the market and help marketing dollars go further; (2) becoming more familiar with the existing and potential customers; (3) determining how customers perceive the facilities, equipment, programs, and services; (4) positioning or repositioning facility among other competitors in the same marketplace; and (5) identifying the kinds of program benefits that can be converted into advertising that sells.

When does the sport manager need to conduct a survey? It depends on what you need to know and whether that information is available from any other source, such as marketing magazines, trade magazines, or research journals. Before deciding to conduct a survey, the sport manager should ask the following questions:

*   What do I need to know?
*   Why do I need to know?
*   How much do I want to know?
*   When do I need the information?
*   How much is the information worth to me?
*   Can I afford to make an uninformed decision?

Once the sport manager has decided to use a survey, he/she needs to determine the best type of survey to utilize. There are three types of surveys, including: (1) a mail survey where the respondent is asked to read, interpret, and answer the questions posed, (2) a telephone survey executed by trained operators who ask the questions and are also available to explain ambiguous queries, and (3) a personal survey conducted face-to-face by trained interviewers who are also available for interpretation of questions. Mail surveys are the easiest and most cost effective to prepare, as well as the most common.

How many customers or prospects should be surveyed: The answer to the question depends to a large degree on the information to be gathered. If it is the existing customers, then the manager will select what he/she is comfortable with. For example, if it is decided a decision can be made with 1,000 responses, and felt that a 20% response rate can be obtained, then it would be necessary to mail 5,000 surveys chosen randomly from the 10,000-member customer base. If the response rate was only 10% then 10,000 surveys would have to be mailed. If the manager wants to know more about the people who are not current customers, the manager will need to rely on a purchased list or a list of prospects that the organization has gathered.

The actual preparation of the survey instrument is the most difficult part of conducting a survey. However, a sport manager can do it effectively, if aware of a few simple points, including the following:

- Wording must be simple and easy to understand. The instrument must be easy to read.
- Frame questions so that they can be answered in a straightforward fashion. Avoid open-ended questions (e.g., "What do you think about the proposed water aerobic program?") because they result in a wide variety of responses that can be difficult to categorize and quantify. Instead, frame the question in the following way—"How would you rank your interest in the water aerobics program?"—and then give a series of responses that provide brief descriptive phrases so that respondents can simply check their choice (also known as a forced-answer item). Do not the forget to include an "others" category.
- Do not ask leading questions—"Would you be interested in registering for the water aerobics program, if it were held every Wednesday at 7 PM?"— but rather ask the question this way—"When would you be interested in registering for a water aerobics program?"—followed by a list of days and times for the respondent to select from.

When would you be interested in registering for a water aerobics program:

__ Monday	__ 5 pm
__ Tuesday	__ 6 pm
__ Wednesday	__ 7pm
__ Thursday	__ 8 pm
__ Friday	__ 6 am
__ Saturday	__ 12 noon
	__ Other _____

- Do not make the survey look too complicated or time-consuming. The survey should not be more then two pages, preferably only one. A simple one-page survey that is easy to read will receive a high rate of return.
- Make the survey look important by attaching a cover letter on the organization's letter head and the survey printed on quality paper.
- The use of premiums have been found to greatly increase response rate. The two most commonly used are money/gift certificates and ball point pens. When choosing a premium, make sure that it is something the respondent will find desirable, something that does not introduce a bias, and it is small and light enough to be easily delivered, and not so expensive as to make the cost of conducting the survey prohibitive.
- Encourage a quick response by providing an additional premium for those who return the survey within five days.
- Offer respondents a checkoff for a copy of the results. This has been shown to significantly increase response.
- Plan on sending a follow-up reminder with a survey two weeks after sending the initial mailing, and a postcard reminder two weeks after the first follow-up.
- Avoid confidential areas and technical jargon.
- Include a brief cover letter from the manager describing the purpose of the survey and its importance.

- Protect the respondents' confidentiality.
- Provide a return, self-addressed, postage-paid envelope.

Finally, checking on bias is an extremely important step in assuring accuracy in the responses to the survey. Determining bias can easily be accomplished by selecting a small sample of non-respondents and use a telephone interview to get their responses to a small number of survey questions, then compare their answers to the original respondents. If you find contamination use other data or switch the method from mail survey to either telephone or personal interviews or discard the contaminated data.

Retaining Memberships

Extending memberships is a constant challenge for club operators. Without a doubt, members are the foundation of the club industry. Experts (Seifer, 1987; Clemens-Silence, 1991; Barrett, 1993) maintain that the campaign to keep members must begin the day the person joins the club and it must be ongoing. The first year is the most critical year. Table 6-4 describes a number of tips for better member retention (Seifer, 1987; Clemens-Silence, 1991; Barrett, 1993).

The successful clubs in membership retention have four fundamental strategies that play a critical role in maintaining high levels of membership satisfaction (Seifer, 1987; Barrett, 1993):

Quality programming. The club management must regularly and consistently implement creative and enjoyable programs that everyone in the club can participate in—from club to individual competitions.

The personal touch (TPT). Seek and select personnel who have good interpersonal skills and can establish a rapport with the members. Make sure the front-desk staff and on-floor trainers and instructors know members, greet them by name and ask about their workout and progress. While it is helpful to select personnel knowledgeable about fitness, employees with people skills may be preferable. People skills are hard to teach, but fitness knowledge can easily be gained. Finally, call members regularly to see how they are doing or ask why they have not been working out lately. Show that management is really concerned about the well-being of the members. Concerned and happy employees translate into happy comfortable members.

Club atmosphere. The management should implement regular special events and socials (e.g., Easter party for kids, St. Patrick's Day social event, Halloween party for kids, New Year's Eve social) to create and maintain a friendly and caring club atmosphere. Further, the management should consider selling clothing and other merchandise with club logo, and publishing a regular club newsletter. All of these opportunities assist the people to identify with a club. It is more likely for those members who identify with the club to maintain their annual memberships.

Staying informed. It is extremely important to solicit membership input regarding all aspects of the club operations. Use focus groups or a suggestion box at the front desk to solicit members' concerns or complaints. Ask all personnel to carefully listen to members, especially the maintenance staff. Or go into the sauna or steam room yourself and listen to what members are saying.

Understanding the positive influences. Retention largely depends on understanding the positive influences before the negative consequences are realized. One way a manager can improve retention is by identifying the areas which he/she can control, such as instructors, safety, fun, appropriate classes, atmosphere, group unity, rewards, and cleanliness of the facility (see Table 8-4).

Table 8-4
Membership Retention Tips

- Adopt a club-wide retention philosophy and appropriate action strategies,
- Give the members what they want and need,
- Assimilate new members right away,
- Target high-risk members (e.g., low-use members, general fitness members),
- Develop and implement program with retention in mind,
- Seek and select with retention in mind (people pleasers),
- Offer incentives to your members,
- Operate according to the fun factor vs. the pain factor,
- Get the staff involved with retention, and
- Divide retention responsibility among personnel.

The most powerful bonds for retaining members are established by instructors. A good dance exercise leader (or any instructor for that matter) will use the following customer strategies (Clemens-Silence, 1991): (1) show a sincere interest in the customer, (2) be enthusiastic during instruction and cheerfully provide guidance, (3) develop a personal association and relationship with each customer and learn their names, (4) consider the various reasons why a person exercises and allow for individual differences, (5) initiate customer follow-up when several unexplained absences occur in succession, (6) participate in the exercise sessions, (7) honor special days (e.g., birthdays, anniversaries, special holidays) or exercise accomplishments with extrinsic rewards such as T-shirts, ribbons or certificates, (8) attend to orthopedic and musculoskeletal problems, (9) counsel customers on proper exercise clothing and foot apparel, and (10) motivate to make long-term exercise commitments.

Table 8-5
How to Motivate Customers to Renew

Motivating current club members to renew their memberships is much more cost-effective than seeking new members. The secret to a high renewal rate is frequently a highly satisfied and motivated staff. The following 10 management guidelines will assist in boosting membership retention:

- Seek, select, train, and retain highly qualified and motivated employees,
- Direct all sales personnel to call new members within the first few days after closing the sales to inquire about the instructional staff, locker accommodations, guest utilization and general satisfaction with the club,
- Send all new members a thank you card (salesperson),
- Prepare and send a personal welcome letter from the club manager to all new members,
- Maintain all club operations, including membership, on a computer,
- Send birthday and anniversary cards to members,
- Develop a number of member incentives (e.g., 50% discount on a first massage or free court time and group instruction for those novices who have never tried racquetball,
- Implement special annual promotions with incentives for renewals in the off-season,
- Develop good programming for the social, instructional, and recreational needs of the members (e.g., club-organized activities, such as vacation trips, weekend getaways, cruises, card games, movies, dances, contests, fund-raisers, lecture series, or introductory classes in scuba diving, windsurfing, dancing, tennis, hiking), and
- Guarantee all members a well-managed, well-maintained facility with good programming and proper incentives.

Finally, there are a number of personal and program factors that influence customer retention rates that the manager must consider. The personal factors that influence customer dropout rates include smoking, inactive leisure time, inactive occupation, blue-collar worker, Type-A personality, increased physical strength, extroverted, poor credit rating, overweight/overfat, poor self-image, depressed, hypochondriacal, anxious, introverted, and low ego strength. The program factors are inconvenient time/location, excessive cost, high-intensity exercise, lack of exercise variety, exercises alone, lack of positive feedback or reinforcement, inflexible exercise goals, low enjoyability ratings for running the programs, and poor exercise leadership. Other factors include such things as lack of spousal support, inclement weather, excessive job travel, injury, medical problems, and job change/loss.

Costs of Recruiting New Customers

The cost of recruiting new customers or fans varies from organization to organization. The components of the cost are similar but the actual cost attributed to each component varies. The cost components include (1) advertising in print, over the radio, and on the television; (2) telephone calls to follow up with potential client; (3) sales commissions; (4) sales and processing time; (5) development of cold prospect lists (i.e., people who are in target market but not stake holders in the club); (6) direct mailings to target market; (7) printing direct mailing pieces; and (8) telemarketing. These costs can range from as little of 15% of the membership fee to well over 45%. The cost of renewing a membership is minimal in comparison.

Staff Training to Maintain Customers or Fans

Management and customer or fan retention are so intertwined, yet many organizations leave membership in the hands of sales personnel who are only interested in new weekly sales numbers. Before relying on this method of sales, however, it is important to carefully examine the costs of acquiring new customers, as well as the market the customers are drawn from. Instead of actively seeking new customers, why not look at attracting renewals?

Renewals are cost-effective because they are proven buyers who are already satisfied customers or ticket buyers. In addition, very few clubs have such a large base of new customers that they can afford to overlook renewals as a real source of income. The key to customer retention is developing highly motivated employees who enjoy people and their jobs. Sport managers who establish good management policies resulting in highly motivated employees are likely to be those who have high membership retention rates or very loyal fans.

The sport manager should develop a regular in-service program for a staff and an orientation program for all new personnel. These programs should include how to: (1) answer the phone (Good Morning, XYZ Fitness Club or Spokane Stars, how may I direct your call?), (2) welcome customers or fans (Hello, how are you today?), (3) respond to customer or fan questions, (4) deal with complaints (see Figure 8-6), (5) assist customers with their programs, (6) maintain equipment and facilities, (7) clean locker rooms, spas, saunas, steam rooms, and equipment, (8) create an enjoyable experience (people do not just join a club, they join a lifestyle, and are looking for reliability, assurance, and responsiveness), (9) be reliable and responsive, (10) small talk with customers or fans (How are you?; How is the workout going?; How is the game?; Happy Birthday!; Happy Anniversary!), and (11) do something special for the customer (shining shoes in the locker room, offering water to customers during the workouts, handing out towels in the weight room, suggesting the best seating available, telling regular fans of any special promotions coming in the future).

Table 8-6
How to Deal with Complaints

Dealing with customer complaints is necessary when providing services to the public. Employees must deal with people almost every waking hour. Therefore, it is not surprising that employees are faced with complaints from the customer. The following are steps that can be used in handling complaints (Lewis & Appenzeller, 1985; Helitzer, 1992; Bucher & Krotee, 1993; Railey & Tschauner, 1993):

- direct the conversation away from a public area (The last thing you want to do is to put on a show for the passersby and you do not want others to hear anything negative about services or programs),
- maintain eye contact (Sincerely look the customer/client in the eye, and say, "I am sorry there is a problem. How can I be of service?),
- let the customer/client vent (This accomplishes two things: it airs the precise nature of the problem, allowing the listener to gain enough information and time to better respond to the complaint, and it allows the customer/client to let off steam),
- take notes [if possible] (Ask if you can take a few notes, this will allow the customer/client to understand that the organization takes his/her complaint seriously),
- repeat the complaint back to the customer (People who are upset often do not communicate well. Reading the complaint back ensures that the specific nature of the complaint is understood),
- solve the problem immediately [if at all possible] (Try to suggest a solution right away. If that is not possible, outline the steps that will be taken to resolve the problem),
- acknowledge complaints that cannot be solved, and
- do not tolerate abuse (Simply say, "I am not in the position to tolerate that kind of language or behavior. Once you settle down, I will try to help you.").

Retention Strategies—Retention is a Complete Package

Customer retention begins the moment a prospect signs his or her name on the customer's contract. After all, customers or season ticket holders will only renew their membership or season tickets if they are a valued part of the organization. The following are strategies that can be successfully used to keep customers or fans:

Staff Preparation and Motivation for Customer Retention

Recognizing that there is a large source of potential revenue in current and past customer lists is the beginning of good management. However, employing staff, who have good personal skills and can establish a rapport with customers is a key to success. After completing the hiring process, the sport manager should develop an in-service training program to prepare staff for the task of customer retention. The ensuing steps will create a reasonable set of goals to motivate employees to increase customer retention:

1.   The management, in consultation with the staff, should develop a plan for customer retention. The management should establish bimonthly meetings that are informative, well-researched, and exciting for all to attend. Allow time for staff customers to present new retention ideas.
2.   The sport manager should maintain (a) a positive attitude in these meetings to further excite and elicit good ideas from the staff, and (b) good leadership and direction.
3.   Communication should be the key word for all management and staff. Courtesy should be demanded of all employees, not just toward customers, but toward each other. Being courteous can have a remarkable effect on attitudes and camaraderie, and can help foster a positive team attitude.
4.   Establish a specific set of goals regarding customer retention for all employees. This should be an overall or long-term goal to be reached through small, evenly paced steps that are reasonably attainable, yet require moderate effort on everyone's part. This allows for vision and accomplishment with a sense of achievement.
5.   Along with the goals there should be a reasonable level of expectation for success. If you expect more, you get more; when you expect less, you get less than expected.
6.   Consistency is sorely needed in any endeavor for it to be successful. Slight manipulation and rethinking should be the norm when expectations are not met. Overhauls should be avoided at all costs.
7.   A well-designed employee incentive plan based on customer retention can be an extremely effective tool in enlarging not only gross sales, but net sales as well.
8.   A staff needs to understand not only anatomy but also how to communicate with customers of all different ages, skill levels, personalties, schedules, and interests. People respond to people. And retention is about keeping people happy and active.
9.   Finally, the wise sport manager will make sure the front-desk staff and on floor trainers and instructors know customers, greet them by name, and ask about their workout. While it is helpful to hire individuals knowledgeable about fitness, employees with people skills may be more preferable. Fitness knowledge can be taught, but people without natural people skills find it extremely difficult to modify their attitudes and personalities to become people oriented.

Customer Retention Strategies

Once the sport manager has developed an effective staff that is motivated and responsive, the following should be accomplished:

1. The sales personnel should call new customers within the first few days after closing the sale to inquire about contact with instructional staff, locker needs, guest utilization, and general satisfaction with the organization. This is the beginning of the creation of a sales/customer relationship that should not only spin off new referrals, but also cement the customer's commitment to the facility for future renewals.

2. Good retention programs include group programming that runs six to eight weeks—with a beginning and end. These programs must have a leader, an achievement recognition system, and a mechanism to track results. The most important ingredient for group programs is an instructor who creates a fun environment.

3. The wise manager gets the staff involved with customers. Staffers should play an active role in a program in which customers accumulate organization points or "dollars" that can be put toward special premiums. Staff can collect, distribute, and answer questions regarding club points, making employees more approachable to customers. Staff involvement gives customers a reason to go up to staffers and talk to them. Communication is essential to retention.

4. Organizations are selling a service, and no one likes to be forgotten right after the sale. In addition to follow-up calls, a personalized note of thanks from the salesperson to a new customer is a nice thought.

5. Within the first week of membership, the new customer should receive a welcome call from the manager.

6. Once a customer joins, the staff has a period of 30 days to fully integrate that person into the club. Providing fitness assessments is an important part of that integration process. And as with any type of health analysis, customers must feel comfortable providing personal information to the club staff. If the customer is comfortable with the staff, it can help to create a bond between the customer and the staffer.

7. Offering customers fitness assessment and body composition analysis builds a strong relationship between clients and club staff and, therefore, serves as a valuable retention tool.

8. The key to maintaining a strong customer and staff relationship is to periodically retest and reevaluate customers to make sure they are on track. In this way, the staffer can offer the feedback customers need to stay motivated in their fitness programs.

9. The new customer's name, address, phone number, e-mail address, birthday, anniversary, wife's birthday, children's birthday, and other dates of interest should be entered into the computer. The Personal Touch: Notices can be sent to the customer on these special occasions, cards can be sent to remind customer of customer renewal dates, congratulation notices can be sent when the customer has received an honor from work or a family customer has received an honor or the customer has met a predetermined goal, etc.. Computer software can be purchased that will allow front-desk personnel to run a customer's card through the computer card reader, and if it is the customer's birthday, the computer plays happy birthday.

10.   Ascertain customers' interests and link them to the interest areas or services available.

11.   Buddy new customers with established customers or a member of the staff, doing so will help make the organization more personalized and make the customer feel wanted.

12.   Organize a "welcome" party periodically for the new customers to introduce them more thoroughly to the facilities, staff, and other customers.

13.   Special incentives can be provided to new customers, including a 50% discount on the first massage, free court time, 10% discount in the pro shop, annual promotions with incentives for renewals during a specified time period (months before they are due).

14.   Organize activities, such as vacation trips, weekend getaways, cruises, card games, movies, dances, Halloween party, Christmas Party, Easter Party, contests, fund-raisers, lecture series, or introductory lessons in nutrition, scuba diving, windsurfing, dancing, tennis, massage or hiking, are just the tip of the iceberg.

15.   Make sure the facilities are attractive, clean, safe, and well-maintained.

16.   Be sure the equipment is not broken, and it is clean, safe, and well-maintained. Add new equipment periodically to increase customer interest.

17.   Implement creative and enjoyable programs that everyone in the club can participate in. Good programming for the social, instructional, recreational, and competitive needs cannot be overlooked. Each program needs a marketing plan, a goal, and a budget to succeed. Programming is about marketing to the customer who already has bought you. It has to include sociability, camaraderie, fun, leadership, direction, and constant service. People are more likely to work out on their own if they are receiving programming that makes them happy on a consistent basis.

18.   Use focus groups or a suggestion box at the front desk to gain input from customers regarding concerns or complaints. Ask maintenance staff what they are hearing in the locker room. Deal with problems before they turn customers off.

19.   Club Atmosphere: Run special events and socials regularly to create and maintain a friendly atmosphere. Consider selling T-shirts, caps, water bottles, jackets, sweat suits, sweat shirts, key chains, glasses, mugs, and other items bearing the club's logo. Publish a regular club membership, making sure customers' names appear. The more people identify with a club, the more likely they are to stick with it over time.

20.   Multiple visits with a trainer who can assess a customer's fitness level and design a program are necessary early on. Reevaluation opportunities are a necessity. Trainers on the floor need to be accessible and know when and when not to approach customers.

21.   Offer customers who encourage an existing customer to renew $4 off of the monthly dues for up to one year. On slow months double the dues offer to $8.

22.   Initially show new and deconditioned customers only four strength-training machines (one for each muscle group) and one cardiovascular machine. When the new customer visits the club 15 times, they are shown how to use more machines. This strategy keeps the customer from being overwhelmed with all the new equipment, but is still getting a good workout. The new customer's goal becomes learning the other machines.

23.   Offer a discount for all renewals, increasing the discount for length of longevity.

The Fan Comes First

Retaining sport fans is a challenging task in this day of high technology and multiple entertainment opportunities that can be enjoyed in one's own living room(see Table 8-7). What makes the sport fan want to return to the ball park, stadium, court, or rink, contest after contest? Sport teams are well-oiled entertainment businesses built by hard-driving sport entrepreneurs. These entrepreneurs have a deep respect for their customers. They offer amenities, including changing

Table 8-7
How Can I Increase the Audience or Memberships?

The following listing is a sample of what can be done to draw customers to the events or the club (Lamphear & Frankel, 1990):

- pre-event entertainment,
- youth games at half-time,
- special group promotions (i.e.,Girl Scouts, Boy Scouts, mother and son outing, father and daughter outing),
- special rates for groups (i.e., senior citizens, ladies night, honor students)
- giveaways (i.e., small basketballs, small footballs, small baseball bats, baseball or painter caps, T-shirts),
- scheduling doubleheaders,
- reduced membership fees,
- shoot-out contest at half time,
- event buses,
- special days (i.e., hometown day, specific town day, specific school day),
- student athletes visiting schools as role models,
- clip-out coupons,
- radio giveaways to listeners (i.e., tickets, free memberships),
- use of a pep band at events,
- team color night (i.e., offer half-price admission to anyone dressed in team's colors), and
- face-painting contest (i.e., encourage students to come early and face-paint each other in an area separate from the event area, and judge the painting jobs providing prizes to the winners at halftime).

tables in restrooms for mothers and fathers with young children, more restroom facilities for women to reduce the waiting, day-care centers for mothers and fathers with young children, nonsmoking and non-drinking seating areas, handicapped areas, barbershops, specialty foods, expensive restaurants, highly recognized fast food establishments (e.g., Pizza Hut, Taco Bell, McDonalds, Hardees, Burger King, Subway), luxury boxes, mini-malls (e.g., souvenir shops, clothing shops, shoe stores, etc.), reasonably priced souvenirs and other licensed products, entertaining scoreboards, reasonable and accessible parking, health and fitness centers, playgrounds and entertainment rides, free parking for season ticket holders, car washing service for fans as they watch the game, assigned parking for fans, and picnic areas.

Further, they provide special entertaining promotional activities, including periodic fireworks, celebrities during opening ceremonies or halftime, contests for the fans prior to games or during halftimes, children wearing any kind of sport uniform gets in free, hat or bat night, team picture night, and family picture with your favorite player. These are all examples of how a sport manager can encourage his or her fans to continue their loyalty to the team.

Summary

Customer and fan retention is the foundation for successful business operations in sport-related organizations. It is definitely important to maintain customers and season ticket holders. The simplest way to complete this task is to treat each customer or fan as if he were the most important person in the world.

Learning Objective 1: Understand why customers decide not to renew their memberships or season tickets.

Most often customers and fans drop out because they are not satisfied with services or results of programs or the attention provided to themselves or their needs.

Learning Objective 2: Be able to describe the costs of recruiting new customers.

There are eight costs to recruiting new customers. These costs vary from location to location. The cost of renewing a membership is minimal in comparison.

Learning Objective 3: Understand how to develop an in-service program training staff to comprehend why customers or fans renew their memberships or season tickets.

A major key to maintaining customers and season ticket holders is knowledgeable, reliable, friendly, and effective staff customers. The sport manager needs to work hard to continually train all staff customers in tactics to maintain custom-

ers and season ticket holders.
Learning Objective 4: Be able to deal with complaints effectively.

The sport manager and each employee needs to understand how to deal with customer or fan complaints. The sport manager should make sure that strategies to deal with complaints are reviewed regularly.

Learning Objective 5: Understand basic customer retention strategies.

There are a number of customer strategies that need to be considered by all sport managers. Not all will fit every situation or organization. The sport manager should make sure that all customers feel they are an integral part of the organization and are important to the organization.

Learning Objective 6: Be able to develop strategies to maintain season ticketholders.

The successful sport teams have loyal season ticket holders because they carter to the fan and his/her needs. The "fan comes first" attitude will make a sport franchise successful.

Learning Objective 7: Understand why a student-athlete chooses to participate or withdraw from sports.

It is crucial for sport managers and coaches to understand why student-athletes participate and withdraw from sports so strategies can be developed to (1) encourage student-athletes to continue their involvement in sport, and (2) recruit new student-athletes.

Self-testing Exercise

1.   You have been chosen as a consultant to determine why the Indian Joe Health and Fitness Club has been having trouble maintaining its membership. How will you determine the problem and what strategies will you suggest for the club to implement to correct the situation?
2.   Develop two simple one-page surveys to be sent to (a) current customer base, and (b) non-renewals.
3.   Visit a local health and fitness club and find out how they: (a) recruit new customers, (b) train staff to work with the customer base, (c) encourage customers to renew, (d) deal with complaints, and (e) survey their customer base.
4.   You are a new club manager. The owner has indicated that the renewal rate is extremely low. You have determined that the staff may be the major cause for low customer retention. You have decided to develop a regular in-service program for staff as the first to increase customer retention. Outline the

in-service program you would use to change the staff's attitude.

5. Contact all the local health and fitness clubs to ascertain what they do to motivate a customer to renew.

6. You have been hired by a local businessman who has purchased a minor league baseball team to be the general manager. The previous owners purchased the franchise for $10,000 but sold it for $500,000. The repeat rate for season ticket holders has declined drastically over the past five years as have the on-site sales. You have been charged by the owner to turn around the attendance dilemma. What are you going to do?

7. Do a survey of the local high school student-athletes and coaches to ascertain why student-athletes participate in sports and why they drop out.

8. How would you deal with a customer's complaint?

References

Barrett, Bob. (1993). Ten tips for better member retention. *Club Industry, (9)*1, 41-52.

Bucher, Charles A., & Krotee, March, L. (1993). *Management of physical education and sport.* (10th ed.). St. Louis, MO: C.V. Mosby Year Book.

Butterfield, Stephen A., Brown, Jr., Bruce R., & Perrone, Jim. (1991). Student athletes' perceptions of high school sports participation. *Physical Educator, 48,* pp. 123-127.

Clemens-Silence, Michele. (1991). Aerobics retention. *Fitness Management, (7)* 9, 40-41.

DeVoe, Dale, & Carroll, Thomas, J. (1994) Student participation patterns: High school coaches' perceptions. *Journal of Physical Education, Recreation, and Dance, 65*(8), pp. 63-70.

Ewing, M.E., & Seefeldt, V. (1990). *American youth and sports participation—A study of 10,000 students and their feelings about sports.* (Special media packet made available from the Athletic Footwear Association, North Palm Beach, Florida).

Grensing, Lin. (1989). Survey power. *Fitness Management, 4*(10), 50-53.

Helitzer, Melvin. (1992). *The dream job: Sports publicity, promotion, and public relations.* Athens, OH: University Sports Press.

Lewis, Guy, & Appenzeller, Herb. (1985). *Successful sport management.* Charlottesville, VA: The Michie Company.

Morgenson, Gretchen. (1992, April 27). Where the fans still come first. *Forbes,* pp. 40-42.

Railey, Jim H., & Tschauner, Peggy Railey. (1993). Managing physical education, fitness, and sports programs. (2nd ed.). Mountainview, CA: Mayfield Publishing Company.

Seiffer, Jan. (1993). Ten management guidelines to boost customer retention. *Athletic Business, 11*(10), pp. 66-68.

Winters, Catherine. (1994). The art of keeping. *Club Industry, 10*(2), pp. 17-23.

Suggested Readings

Trade Magazines

Athletic Business
Club Industry
Fitness Management

9

EQUIPMENT/SUPPLIES MANAGEMENT: PURCHASE AND CONTROL

◆ ——————————————— ◆

Instructional Objectives

After reading this chapter the student should:

- be able to develop guidelines for the selection of equipment and supplies,

- understand what questions to ask when evaluating equipment in general,

- be able to develop guidelines for the purchase of equipment and supplies,

- be able to write specifications for equipment and supplies,

- understand how to implement a labeling system,

- be able to establish guidelines for checking, storing, issuing, and maintaining equipment and supplies,

- appreciate what are the best times to purchase equipment and supplies,

- understand the space requirements needed for an equipment room,

- appreciate what needs to be done to manage an equipment room, and

- understand how to place value on used equipment.

Introduction

A major expense for any sport/fitness-related organization is equipment and supplies. Any responsible organization must make sure equipment and supplies that are purchased will: (1) meet program needs, (2) be of good quality, (3) be acquired through appropriate procedures, (4) be properly secured and accounted for, and (5) be maintained for safe future use. Equipment refers to those items that are nonconsumable, meaning they are used for a period of years. Supplies are those materials that are consumable with use such as paper, pencils, and athletic tape.

Guidelines for Selecting Equipment and Supplies

There are a number of guidelines that management should consider seriously when selecting equipment and supplies for the programs and the facility. The National Operating Committee on Standards for Athletic Equipment (NOCSAE), and the American College of Sports Medicine (ACSM) have developed standards for sport and fitness equipment. NOCSAE was formed to respond to the need for nationally approved and accepted standards for activity and sport. These standards should be part of the first considerations made when considering athletic equipment for purchase. Other guidelines would include the following (Bucher & Krotee, 1993; Sol & Foster, 1992; Walker & Seidler, 1993):

- determine purchasing power (how much money is available),
- begin and maintain a "wish list" of needed and wanted equipment,
- determine organization needs,
- determine quality desired,
- consider whether the product is both budget and maintenance friendly, is manufactured by reputable companies,
- consider whether old equipment can be reconditioned successfully or whether new equipment should be purchased,
- purchase must be based on program goals, objectives, and budget,
- determine the priority need and amount of funds available for purchase,
- consider those persons with disabilities,
- consider only equipment that meets safety standards,
- obtain product information from various and diverse vendors, organizing the information by category and type, and each specific company (e.g., catalogs issued by suppliers, trade journals, industrial advertising material, trade directories [Buyer guides found in *Athletic Business* or *Fitness Management*], trade shows and exhibits, and company sales representatives),
- consider the guarantee, whether or not replacement parts are accessible, the

ease of maintenance, and whether or not it fits properly,
- evaluate the usability of the equipment, making certain that it is adjustable (without sacrificing or compromising performance), is state-of-the-art in terms of both design and safety, and is user friendly for all persons,
- evaluate companies in terms of service record, scientific merit of claims, dependability record, amenities offered, and price (Is it competitive?),
- consider trends in equipment and supplies,
- access current or proposed facilities in terms of size, obstacles that may be present and quantity and type of power, and
- create a floor plan.

Guidelines For Purchasing Equipment and Supplies

It is important for management to develop a number of sound management guidelines regarding the purchase of equipment and supplies. These guidelines should include: standardizing equipment and supplies; supervising the entire process of selection, specification, purchase, storage, and maintenance; maintaining an inventory of materials (equipment and supply inventory computer database); preparing specifications for items to be purchased; securing bids for large purchases and those required by law; deciding on or recommending distribution where materials and supplies are to be purchased; testing products to see that specifications are satisfactorily met; checking supplies and equipment to determine if all that were ordered have been delivered and are in top condition; expediting the delivery of purchases so that materials are available as needed; and seeking new products that meet the needs of the program or facility.

There are some specific guidelines that should be implemented by any organization when considering the purchase of equipment or supplies. These guidelines include such things as the following: (Strauf, 1989a, 1986, 1991; Cardinal, 1990, 1994; Railey & Tschauner, 1993):

- all purchases should be meet the organization's requirements and have management approval,
- purchasing should be done in advance of need,
- specifications should be clearly set forth,
- costs should be kept as low as possible without compromising quality,
- purchases should be made from reputable business firms,
- central purchasing can result in greater economy,
- all requests must have purchase requisitions (a requisition is a request to purchase items),
- local firms should be considered,
- competitive bids should be obtained (for large purchases),
- all purchases must be accompanied by a purchase order (a purchase order is an official request to a vendor to deliver a specific item to a specific location for an agreed-upon price. A voucher is the same thing as a purchase order.),

Sport murals add to an otherwise bland wall. (Photo: O. Smith)

- gifts or favors should not be accepted from dealers,
- a complete inventory and program analysis is essential before purchasing,
- establish friendly relationships with vendors,
- order early, and
- take advantage of legitimate discounts (e.g., quantity discounts, discounts on early orders, closeouts, promotional discounts, inventory reduction discounts, discounts on blemished items, trade discounts, and cash discounts).

Evaluating Equipment Before Purchasing

Equipment should not be purchased without a comprehensive evaluation. The purchaser should ask the following questions before making a final selection (Olson, et al., 1987; Goethel, 1990; Walker & Seidler, 1993):

• *Equipment safety*
Is the equipment safe to use? Are there any obvious design flaws that increase the risk? Might any body parts easily exceed a safe range of motion? Do electronic circuits have redundant safety backups?

• *Equipment usage*
Is the equipment self-instructing, or does it come with mounted instructions? Are electronics user-friendly? Is the equipment easy to use? East to learn? Are the movements familiar or unusual? Are the adjustments sensibly engineered and user-friendly? Does the equipment have inherent motivational characteristics? Is the equipment comfortable? Can users of different sizes adapt to it easily and use it for 20 minutes or more? Is the product accompanied by a comprehensive and well-written instruction manual? Is the product aesthetically appealing? Is the product space efficient?

• *Design and Components*

   Does the product perform the task for which it was designed with fluidity and precision? Is the product quiet during operation, and do moving parts mesh with minimal friction? Does the product appear to be built for the long haul? Are component parts of the highest quality possible? Are upholstery and paint or surface treatments durable?

• *Dealer and Warranty*

   How long and comprehensive is the product warranty? Will the manufacturer provide a written warranty? Will the dealer provide a written warranty? Does the local service agent keep parts in stock? How easily will the service be obtained after the warranty?

• *The Manufacturer*

   How long has the product been on the market? What is the past and future of the manufacturer? Are they likely to be around in three to five years? Will the manufacturer provide documents of numbers on out-of-box failures or warranty repairs? Will the manufacturer or dealer provide instruction? How are the instructors professionally qualified? Will the manufacturer or dealer provide equipment setup/installation? How soon after the delivery can it be done? Does the manufacturer have its own fleet of delivery trucks? Are major component parts manufactured domestically or abroad? Are they built in-house by the manufacturer? Does the manufacturer carry product liability insurance?

• *Miscellaneous*

   Have customers/participants requested the product, or will they find it desirable? Is there brand name value? Is the product faddish? Is it likely to become obsolete quickly? Can it be upgraded by the manufacturer in the future? Have you formed opinions from personal use of the product? Will the dealer or manufacturer provide a list of users? How do current users rate the product? Is your gut feeling that the price is fair and competitive considering the above responses to the questions?

   These questions can be answered in a number of ways. Manufacturers will provide printed materials and verbal descriptions, maintenance procedures, equipment durability, safety features, and warranty information at request. They should also be able to provide information regarding who has purchased their merchandise, and be willing to make that information available to potential buyers. Trade magazines and journals will often contain articles about equipment and supplies. Contacts with operators of similar facilities at conferences and trade shows are invaluable because colleagues will usually offer information regarding equipment they use without regard to bias, and most often it is free advice.

The Procurement Process

The procurement process is that part of a purchasing program that begins with a request for purchase (purchase requisition) and ends with a purchase order (voucher), delivery, and the payment of the invoice. The primary goal of the procurement process is to obtain the desired, high-quality equipment and supplies, on time, and at the lowest possible cost. The following steps are most commonly used in the procurement process (Lewis & Appenzeller, 1985; Kinder, 1993; Bucher & Krotee, 1993): (1) need established, (2) management consultation, (3) initial request made, (4) request reviewed, (5) determine if funds are available, (6) preparation of specifications, (7) receipt of bids, (8) bids compared, (9) recommend appropriate bid for purchase, (10) purchase order to supplier, (11) follow-up, (12) receipt of goods, (13) payment authorized, (14) accountability—inventory control number assigned, and (15) equipment inspected and payment made.

Management Tip

The second largest budgetary item behind personnel is equipment and supplies. Management's responsibility is to make sure the equipment and supplies that are purchased will (1) meet program needs, (2) be of good quality, (3) be acquired through appropriate procedures, (4) be properly secured and accounted for, and (5) be maintained for safe future use.

The Bid Process

It is good business to require a competitive bid process to purchase budgeted items no matter how large or small the organization. The primary advantage of competitive bidding for equipment and supplies is a lower per unit cost. The greatest disadvantage is the length of time it generally takes to get through the bidding process.

The typical bidding process includes (Strauf, 1989a, 1991; Goethel, 1990): (1) writing specifications for approved items to be purchased, (2) advertise for bids from vendors (at least three), (3) receive bids, (4) evaluate bids to ensure all specifications have been met, (5) choose vendor(s), (6) submit the purchase order, (7) receive equipment, and (8) pay invoice after equipment or supplies are verified.

Kettering Ice Arena. City of Kettering Park and Recreation Department. (Photo: O. Smith)

Writing Specifications

Writing a clear, well-defined, and complete set of specifications is most important in assuring that what is ordered is in fact delivered. Preparing written specifications will guarantee a fair comparison of bids when the bidder proposes alternatives. The specifications must be clear, concise, and well defined in order to place upon the seller the responsibility of providing a product that meets the needs of the user. In general, clear descriptions of products being ordered list quantity, quality, size, color materials, brand, model number, catalog number, performance characteristics, assembly/installation requirements, delivery requirements, and acceptable, if any, alternatives may be listed to reduce the possibility of purchasing goods that do not meet the needs of the program.

The preparer at the bottom of the purchase requisition form should make the following statements in upper case and boldface print (Fernandez, 1989; Goethel, 1990, Lunch, 1990):

- "FOB (City) [organization's address] LOCATION"
- "NO SUBSTITUTIONS WILL BE ACCEPTED UNLESS LISTED ABOVE"

The following are specific suggestions that should be concerned when writing accurate specifications:

- *Clothing*
  It is important to include the following when ordering clothing—manufacturer or name brand, style number, fabric content, shrinkage factor, color, colorfastness, sizing, special cuts, and lettering and numbering (be sure to include size, type, style, and color of the letters and numbers desired as well as location [check rule

book], specify whether or not you want tackle-twill or silk-screening, and enclose a diagram of the article of clothing).

• *Shoes*

The purchaser needs to include the following: manufacturer or name brand, style number, shoe material (e.g., upper-leather, mesh, high- or low-cut, soles molded, soles-cleated), and color.

• *Protective equipment*

The following should be considered: manufacturer or brand name, style number, material content (e.g., hard plastic, open-cell foam), certification standards, and accurate sizing.

• *Playing equipment*

The purchaser needs to consider the following: manufacturer or brand name, equipment model number, material content (e.g., leather or synthetic balls), size (e.g., #3 , #4, or #5 soccer ball), and weight (e.g., baseball and softball bats, throwing implements).

When Equipment and Supplies Should Be Purchased

Organizations that are using a bidding system need to understand the process will take between four and six weeks before the purchase order will be released. Depending on whether the product is in stock or has to be ordered by the supplier can add another six to eight weeks to the entire process. Therefore, it is recommended that the purchaser allow between six and 12 weeks for the product to be delivered to the site.

If the organization is involved in purchasing sport equipment and supplies, the following purchasing schedule is recommended (Railey & Tschauner, 1993):

Recommended Sport Equipment Purchasing Schedule		
Sport Season	**Order Date**	**Delivery Date**
Early Spring	October 1	February 1
Late Spring	December 1	March 15
Fall	May 1	August 1
Winter	July 1	October 15

Purchasing Fitness Equipment

The process of outfitting a fitness club with the newest equipment does not have to be a chore. It is important for purchasers to know the right questions to ask dealers/sales personnel whose products catch the purchaser's attention. Ask equipment dealers the following questions before purchasing or leasing any of their machines: How many machines are needed? Do you sell or lease? What is the length of the warranty? What is contained in the warranty? Will you install/set up the equipment? Where can the machine be serviced? What is the worst feature of your product? Do you have references? Who has purchased your equipment? What has been the biggest complaint received about your equipment? What kind of discounts are you offering? Do you offer a test model?

Planners must devote a significant amount of time ensuring that a facility's exercise equipment space is functional, well-stocked, and affordable. The planners should consider the use of a three-phase process (Walker & Seidler, 1993).

Phase I: Identification of Preliminary Factors

There are two main factors that exist prior to equipment selection—total space and budget available for the equipment purchase. When calculating space the planners can use the following average square foot requirements: weight-stack resistance—60, free-weight resistance—70, plate-loaded resistance—60, and cardiovascular equipment—55. The average equipment costs are weight-stack— $2,800, free-weight—$1,000, plate-loaded—$1,600, and cardiovascular equipment —$3,400.

Phase II: Selection Criteria

The following should be considered when selecting equipment— goals and objectives, availability of funding, commercial grade equipment, accommodation rate (user to unit), total body workout, manufacturer history (years in business, customer service record, reputation, and client list), product history (years in production, product warranty, service program, maintenance schedule, and product's special requirements), purchase options (30 days, monthly, or annual), and lease options (at the end of the leasing program, a buyer has the following options: purchase for agreed upon amount, return the equipment, extend the lease, and establish a new leasing program for a new list of equipment).

Phase III: The Action Plan

The list below summarizes the main tasks to consider during the equipment selection:

* identify any existing preliminary factors concerning the amount of space and funds available,
* if limitations exist with the total space or funds available, identify the amount of equipment that can be acquired based on the limitations,

A competitive pool at Wright Patterson Air Force Base. (Photo: O. Smith)

- choose the type of equipment to be included in the exercise equipment area,
- develop a list of criteria to use during product and manufacturer reviews,
- conduct product and manufacturer review,
- make final equipment selections,
- determine the purchasing option that best fits your financial situation, and
- purchase equipment.

Considerations When Purchasing a Complete Fitness Program

Putting together classes and routines can be a lonely and time-consuming process unless the purchaser reaches out and taps into the ever-growing pool of industry resources. Music suppliers and program licensers offer a multitude of different types of music and fitness programming that are current and well researched. Before deciding to purchase fitness programming, ask the following seven questions (Hasler & Bartlett, 1995): What different types of programs are available? Can my staff handle the programming? Are promotional materials, instructional manuals and videos, other program materials and supplier support included in the programming? How much will it cost, initially and on an ongoing basis? Do I have to purchase a franchise to be involved in the program? Do the benefits of purchasing programming outweigh the advantages of putting it together in-house? Are other facilities like mine using the program successfully?

Value of Used Equipment

If you have evaluated your five-year-old or older strength training equipment and found it is no longer attracting the same interest among new or renewing members, you are probably facing some hard questions about what to do next. Turning aging equipment into reconditioned equipment, or into dollars toward new equipment, starts with appraising the equipment (Carr, 1991).

The following questions can be used as a value-appraisal tool for equipment (Carr, 1991).The higher the score on the value-rating tool indicates a greater number of options for the owner.This tool will provide a general idea of the equipment's marketability.

1. **How old is the equipment?**
    0-12 months = 10 points; 13-24 months = 8 points; 25-36 months = 6 points; 37-48 months = 4 points; 49+ months = 2 points

2. **How marketable is the line?**
    Survey the industry to estimate how widespread the use is of lines of equipment similar to yours among other clubs nationwide.
    Among the top three most common lines, and is a late model = 10 points; Among the top three but is an older model = 7 points; a widely used line, not top three, but late model = 7; a well-known line that is less-frequently seen in clubs = 3-5; well-made, but little-known, selected line = 3; plate-load machines and free-weights = 3.

3. **Aesthetic appeal?**
    Chrome, paint, pads: excellent = 5; very good = 4; good = 3; fair = 2; and poor = 1.

    Add one point if paint is silver, white or gray. Subtract one point if paint is red, blue, brown, tan, green, etc.

4. **Total score =**
    21-25 points = an excellent value rating; 16-20 = good; 11-15 = fair; 10 or below= poor.

Equipment Control

There are six general guidelines that should be considered when developing equipment control procedures (Boevers, 1989; Strauf, 1989). They are: (1) all equipment and supplies should be carefully inspected upon receipt, (2) equipment and supplies requiring organization identification should be labeled, (3) procedures should be established for issuing and checking in equipment and supplies, (4) equipment should be maintained and stored in good repair, (5) equipment and supplies should be inventoried and stored properly, and (6) garments should be cleaned and cared for properly.

Walker and Seidler (1993) suggest the following management principles should be considered for a well-managed system of inventory, control, and accountability:
*   a system (computerized if at all possible) of inventory must be established and followed (the system should include an emplacement function, a listing

of items including dates of purchase, an evaluation system, an updating system),
- all equipment and supplies must be counted into the inventory,
- all items that are in use must be officially checked out,
- personnel who sign for equipment and materials are held accountable for same,
- all equipment must be coded and labeled upon arrival,
- old or damaged items that are being eliminated from stock should be removed only by authorized equipment management personnel. Removal of items must be noted in the inventory records, and equipment should be properly disposed,
- written procedures must be followed by all persons,
- systematic inventory checks and continual updating must be conducted,
- instruction must be provided on the proper use and care of the equipment,
- equipment must be returned in the condition it was in when issued,
- the equipment room lock should only be accessed by authorized personnel and should not be on the master,
- all warranties and safety documentation from the manufacturers should be filed appropriately,
- an inspection form should be developed to inspect of equipment that is either freestanding or attached to the facility and a regular inspection schedule should be adopted by the organization, and
- a maintenance record should be maintained for all equipment.

Labeling Systems

The labeling system should be well organized and simple. There are many effective methods of marking equipment and supplies and every imaginative manager develops personalized techniques. The following marking suggestions are offered (Short, 1989): (1) felt tip pen, laundry pen (ideal for fabric items); (2) indelible pencil (for leather products); (3) branding irons (for wood, plastic or leather goods); (4) stencils (fabric); (5) decals (items that have little wear); (6) processed numbers (fabric items by manufacturer); and (7) rubber stamps (leather and rubber items).

Space Requirements for an Equipment Room

When facilities are constructed, five areas have a tendency to be reduced in size—custodial or maintenance space, locker rooms, office and lobby areas, storage spaces and equipment areas (Walker & Seidler, 1993). All these spaces are critical to the efficient operation of any health, fitness, physical activity, recreation, or space facility. Walker and Seidler (1993), suggest that college and university facilities should be approximately 3,000 square feet. Others have suggested equipment storage space should be approximately 20% of the total usable facility space. The American Entrepreneurs Association (AEA) suggests that for every 10,000-100,000 people there should be 1,000-3,000 square feet, 100,000-200,000 people there should be 1,500-4,000 square feet, and 200,000+ people there should be 2,000-10,000 square feet.

The equipment room should be located near locker rooms and multipurpose activity areas. The main entrance into the equipment room should be at least 6 feet wide and 8 feet high. A roll-up door might be more efficient than double-wide doors. The room itself should contain storage shelves, moveable interlocking storage units, a repair area, racks, folding tables, a space to store larger pieces of equipment, laundry equipment (commercial washers and dryers), a small office, distribution counter, and a space to hang equipment from the ceiling (Cox, 1989; Kleinau, 1991). Further, all the cabinets, office, repair space, laundry area, and main entrance need to be secured with appropriate alarms. Finally, the area needs to have installed appropriate environmental controls to maintain the entire area at 70° F with 50% humidity if possible. The area also needs to be well-ventilated.

Management of the Equipment Room

Depending on the size of the organization, it may be necessary to employ personnel to manage the equipment operation. The qualities that an individual(s) should possess are (Boss, 1988; Kinder, 1993; Bucher & Krotee, 1993): (1) good interpersonal skills; (2) knowledge of equipment; (3) good judgement; (4) maturity; (5) integrity; (6) basic accounting skills; (7) basic management skills; (8) computer skills in word processing and spreadsheets; (9) knowledge of equipment care; (10) an understanding of purchasing and bidding procedures; and (11) knowledge of fitting equipment.

The equipment room operation should have the following as priorities: (Boss, 1988; Knickerbocker, 1990): (1) proper fitting of equipment; (2) maintenance of equipment; (3) accountability; (4) practice coordination and cooperation; (5) permanent and daily assignments; (6) cleanliness; and (7) helping each other.

The Athletic Equipment Managers Association (AEMA) announced in 1990 it contracted with Columbia Assessment Services to establish its certification program. AEMA has established the following areas that should be included in an equipment manager's job description: (1) purchasing; (2) fitting equipment and clothing; (3) maintenance; (4) administration and organization; (5) management, professional relations, and education; and (6) accountability for equipment. The association has established an educational program that will give equipment managers a certain level of proficiency in these six areas.

Summary

Equipment and supplies account for a major share of any budget. It is the sport manager's responsibility to make sure the equipment and supplies that are purchased will support the overall program. Further, the manager should make sure that the equipment is purchased from a reputable firm and is the best quality. *Learning Objective 1: Development of guidelines for the selection of equipment and supplies.*

The sport manager is responsible for the selection of all equipment and supplies. Therefore he/she should make sure that appropriate guidelines are followed in the selection of equipment and supplies by the staff. The primary considerations include (1) appropriateness for the program, (2) quality, (3) cost, (4) safety, and (5) life span.

Learning Objective 2: Development of questions to be asked when evaluating equipment.

Before purchasing equipment, it is necessary to learn about the equipment. The purchaser should be aware of many different characteristics of the equipment including the cost, safety record, repair record, durability and dependability, life span, maintenance costs, and flexibility of use. Therefore, it is important for the sport manager to develop a number of questions regarding these and other equipment characteristics to be asked before selecting the most appropriate product.

Learning Objective 3: Development of guidelines for the purchase of equipment and supplies.

The wise sport manager has prepared guidelines to be used by the staff for the purchase of equipment and supplies that include, but are not limited to: proper preparation of a purchase requisition, steps to securing a purchase order, selection of the appropriate vendor, and the bidding process.

Learning Objective 4: Writing specifications for the purchase of equipment and supplies.
It is important to teach staff the appropriate way to prepare equipment purchase requisitions. The more detailed the requisition the better the chances of receiving exactly what you requested. It is the responsibility of the purchasing agent to purchase what you request at the lowest price possible. The purchase requisition should include, at a minimum: name of vendor, name of company that makes the product, a specific product number, color, size, type of fabric, quantity, suggested price, brand name, date wanted, and setup if required.

Learning Objective 5: Designing and implementing a labeling system.

One of the biggest problems with equipment and supplies is theft by participants and staff. It is important to label all permanent equipment. The sport manager must devise a system for labeling all permanent equipment before it is used.

Learning Objective 6: Develop guidelines for checking, storing, issuing, controlling, and maintaining equipment and supplies.

The sport manager needs to develop a tight inventory and maintenance system. The inventory system has two major functions — equipment availability and accountability. A good computerized inventory system will allow the sport manager to press a couple of keys and know exactly what equipment is available and how many items there are in the system. The maintenance system has two major functions as well — increase the life span of equipment and make sure the equipment is safe for use.

Learning Objective 7: Developing a purchasing schedule for equipment and supplies.

Many of the programs administered by sport managers are seasonal. This simple fact requires careful planning in the purchase of equipment and supplies so that they are available at the appropriate time. It is not cost effective to purchase equipment and store it for months before use. Therefore, it is important to develop an annual equipment purchasing plan.

Learning Objective 8: Space requirements for an equipment room.

Equipment rooms are critical to the management of equipment and supplies. However, they receive the least amount of planning and space. The first space to be cut when money becomes tight is storage space. This is an error every sport manager regrets. The storage of equipment and supplies becomes a nightmare all too soon. Therefore, it is important the sport manager and building planners guard storage space as if it were a gold reserve. Careful planning needs to be completed relative to the equipment room. The questions to be asked by planners include what needs to be stored, how much needs to be stored, where should the equipment room be located, how should the area be environmentally controlled, what security measures need to be considered, should the laundry be located near the equipment area, and how many storage areas should there be?

Learning Objective 9: Management of the equipment room.

Does the equipment room need to be managed? This is the first question to be answered. If the answer is yes, then a plan needs to be devised to manage the space or spaces, and the equipment and supplies. The sport manager needs to seriously consider how to best manage the equipment and supplies.

Learning Objective 10: What is the value of used equipment.

All equipment must be evaluated on a regular basis to determine how it fits the needs of the program(s). The sport manager needs to understand when it is best to turn aging equipment into reconditioned equipment or into dollars toward new equipment. Therefore the sport manager needs to be able to appraise the equipment or know someone who can do the appraisal to determine if trading, selling outright, or other options can return cash value to the organization before purchasing new equipment.

Self-testing Exercise

1.   You are the manager of a fitness facility. Some of your customers have made some comments to your staff that other local facilities have more modern equipment that they would like to see in your facility. Your equipment is paid for and your profits are good, but you are concerned that you may lose part of your membership to other clubs if you do not modernize. What guidelines will you use to select new equipment? What will be your source of information to determine what equipment you should consider? How will you evaluate equipment before you decide to purchase?

2.   You are the Director of the local YMCA. You have decided to replace 10 pieces of cardiovascular equipment in your fitness club. You have enough money to purchase the equipment you need. Identify at least three ways in which you can dispose of the used equipment and get a reasonable return on your investment. Assume that all of your equipment has been well maintained and is in good working order. You have had the equipment for five years, with at least three years remaining of reasonable use expected as per manufacturer's specifications. None of the items can be covered under manufacturers warranties when sold.

3.   You are the sports director for a park and recreation department in a mid-sized city of 250,000. Your budget for this year includes enough money to purchase replacement basketball backboards for four community centers. In all, you will be purchasing 24 new backboards. The backboards will be rectangular glass boards with breakaway goals at a cost of $2,000 each. Describe how you would prepare your request for bids, how bids would be advertised, and how bids would be awarded.

4.   You are the equipment manager of a division I-AA football program. The athletic director wants you to develop a procedures manual for checking, storing, issuing and maintaining equipment and supplies for which you are responsible. Develop an outline of what should be included in the manual.

References

Boevers, Gary. (1989). A clean operation. *CAM Magazine, 1*:4, 10-13.

Boss, Jeff. (1988). Equipment handbook is student manager Bible. *Athletic Business, (12)*10, 30-38.

Bucher, Charles A., & Krotee, March L. (1993). *Management of physical education and sport.* (10th ed.). St. Louis, MO: C.V. Mosby Time Mirror.

Cardinal, Bradley, J. (1990). Selecting equipment. *Fitness Management, (6)*2, 37-40.

Cardinal, Bradley, J. (1994). Six steps to selecting exercise equipment. *Athletic Business, (18)*9, 39-46.

Carr, Jeffrey. (1991). Valuing your used equipment. *Fitness Management, (7)*2, 35-38.

Cox, Frank. (1989). Cleaning up. *CAM Magazine, 1*:3, 9-10.

Frost, Reuben B., & Marshall, Stanley, J. (1977). *Administration of physical education and athletics: Concepts and practices.* Dubuque, IA: Wm. C. Brown Company Publishers.

Fernandez, Bud. (1989). Setting it Straight. *CAM Magazine, (1)*3, 11—13.

Goethel, Paul. (1990). Buying equipment without regrets. *Fitness Management, (6)*13, 40-42.

Hasler, Arch E. Jr., & Bartlett, Mark (1995). Equipped for exercise. *Athletic Business, (19)*9, 47-54.

Hauss, Debra S. (1990). Fitness programming. *Club Industry (10)*1, 32-36.

Kinder, Thomas M. (1993). *Organizational management administration for athletic programs.* Dubuque, IA: Eddie Bowers Publishing, Inc.

Kleinau, Jim. (1991). A squeaky clean program. *Athletic Management, (3)*6, 35-38.

Knickerbocker, Bob. (1990). A student hand. *CAM Magazine, (2)*5, 20-21.

Lewis, Guy, & Appenzeller, Herb (1985). *Successful sport management.* Charlottesville, VA: The Michie Company.

Lynch, Daniel J. (1990). How corporations select vendors and products. *Fitness Management, (6)*2, 18-19.

Olson, John, Hirsch, Elroy, Breitenbach, Otto, & Saunders, Kit. (1987). *Administration of high school and collegiate athletic programs.* New York: Saunders College Publishing.

Railey, Jim H., & Tschauner, Peggy Railey. (1993). *Managing physical education, fitness, and sports programs.* (2nd ed.). Mountain View, CA: Mayfield Publishing Company.

Short, Mike. (1989). Label laws. *CAM Magazine, (1)*5, 6-7.

Sol, Neil, & Foster, Carl (Eds.). (1992). *ACSM's health/fitness: Facility standards and guidelines.* Champaign, IL: Human Kinetics Publishing.

Strauf, Dale L. (1989). A bid to save money. *CAM Magazine, (1)*1, 9-10.

Strauf, Dale L. (1989). Anatomy of an efficient equipment purchasing system. *Athletic Business, (13)*1, 48-54.

Strauf, Dale L. (1991). The specifics of specs. *CAM Magazine, (3)*1, 8-9.

Timing is important in buying uniforms. (1981). *Athletic Purchasing and Facilities, (5)*9, 24,26.

Walker, Marcia L., & Seidler, Todd L. (1993). *Sports equipment management.* Boston: Jones and Bartlett Publishers.

Suggested Readings

Sol, Neil, & Foster, Carl (Eds.). (1992). *ACSM's health/fitness: Facility standards and guidelines.* Champaign, IL: Human Kinetics Publishing.

Walker, Marcia L., & Seidler, Todd L. (1993). *Sports equipment management.* Boston: Jones and Bartlett Publishers.

PART III

$\blacklozenge$

MARKETING

10

MANAGING THE MARKETPLACE

♦ ──────────────── ♦

Instructional Objectives

After reading this chapter the student should be able to:

• develop a marketing plan for a club, recreation or sport program,

• understand why marketing research is important,

• recognize various market segments,

• understand about consumer behavior and buying patterns, and

• comprehend what motivates a consumer to purchase a product/service.

Introduction

Most managers consider themselves rather well-informed on the subject of marketing. After all, they read newspapers and magazines, listen to the radio, and watch television commercials, and see how advertisers are trying to persuade people to buy. People purchase products on a self-service basis in warehouse stores and supermarkets. People observe the quality of personal selling as they buy varied products in shopping centers. In short, everybody knows something about marketing—promotion, advertising, selling, and public relations.

Organizations should seriously consider out-sourcing marketing to a professional marketing agency if they cannot afford to employ a part- or full-time marketer. The franchise or large chain organizations pay a monthly flat-fee to the central office for marketing that is done locally as well as regionally and nationally. The small organization needs a marketing program as well to establish and/or gain market share. If the small organization cannot afford a professional marketing agency or one is not available, the information in this chapter will assist the manager in developing a marketing program.

Marketing

Marketing is a total system of interacting business activities designed to plan, price, promote, and distribute want-satisfying products and services to present and potential customers.

The concept of marketing is sometimes confusing. For our purposes, a market will be defined as people with needs to satisfy, the money to spend, and the willingness to spend it.

Sport marketing "consists of all activities designed to meet the needs and wants of sport consumers (i.e., encompasses many types of involvement with sport, including playing, officiating, watching, listening, reading, and collecting) through exchange processes" (Mullin, Hardy, & Sutton, 1993). Sport marketing has developed two major thrusts: the marketing of products and services directly to consumers (e.g., a professional team, college/university team, or a racquetball/health-fitness club), and marketing of other consumer and industrial products or services through the use of sport promotions (e.g., a brewery, soda company, or auto dealer).

The components of marketing consist of: (1) the marketing concept, (2) management process in marketing, (3) marketing research, (4) market, (5) market segmentation, (6) consumer behavior and buying patterns, (7) product, (8) distribution, (9) price system, (10) promotional activities, and (11) place. Once these components are understood, then the cross-impact of the elements of the marketing mix (the five "Ps") can be studied (Brooks, 1991; Railey & Tschauner, 1993).

The Marketing Concept

Managers of sport-related programs increasingly recognize that marketing is vitally important to success. These professionals realize that a business is a marketing organization. This realization is the foundation of the *marketing concept*. These organizations must become market-oriented businesses that emphasize the importance of customer relations.

The marketing concept is based on two fundamental beliefs: (1) all organization planning, policies, and operations should be oriented toward the customer; and (2) profitable sales volume (products or services) should be the goal of the organization. The marketing concept is a philosophy of business that states that the customer's want satisfaction is the economic and social justification of the organization's existence. All organizational activities related to production of products or services, finance, and marketing must be devoted to: (1) determining what the customer's wants are and, (2) satisfying these wants while still making a reasonable profit (Peterson & Colacino, 1990).

The *marketing concept* is defined as an organizational state of mind that insists on the *integration* and coordination of all marketing functions for the basic objective of producing maximum long-range organization profits. The important ingredients of the market concept are: (1) a proper state of mind, (2) the actual coordination of all marketing functions, and (3) the use of professional marketing personnel (Brooks, 1991). The common pitfalls in implementing the market concept are the following: (1) inexperienced personnel, (2) unsound organizational structures, and (3) incomplete integration traceable to personality clashes, lack of executive teamwork, or one-person domination (Lewis & Appenzeller, 1985).

Management Process in Marketing

In the theory of management it is generally recognized that the management or administrative process is comprised of several major managerial functions. These functions are: (1) determining objectives, (2) planning, including the establishment of strategies and action steps, (3) organizing and coordinating, (4) staffing and assembling other resources, (5) operating and directing, and (6) analyzing and evaluation (Brooks, 1994). The remainder of this section will be devoted to the marketing application of the major functions of management.

Determining objectives. An organization must be goal-oriented and -directed to be effective. A marketing plan cannot be developed until the organization establishes its objectives. Ordinarily a firm has different levels of marketing objectives (all related to the organization's overall goals) ranging from its ultimate long-range goals to its specific operational objectives. The broad objective may be to market a volume of goods at a level of profit over the long run that will satisfy the interests of stockholders, owners, and consumers. In marketing, planning and operating decisions must be in line with the goals established by the organization.

Planning. Once the organization has established its goals and objectives, the next step is to determine appropriate strategies and action steps. This process is known generally as planning.

Marketing Tip
Making Your Plan

A complete market plan must answer these eight questions:

1.   *Objectives:* What are we trying to accomplish?
2.   *Target audience:* Who are we trying to reach?
3.   *Research:* What do we know about our target audiences, competition, pricing?
4.   *Themes and messages:* What communications will persuade our target audiences to do, think or act in a manner we would wish them to?
5.   *Action plan:* What are we going to do?
6.   *Evaluation:* How do we judge the success and/or value of what we do?
7.   *Resources:* What allocation of time, people and money will be required to implement the program?
8.   *Priorities and responsibilities:* Who will do what, within what time frame?

Organizing and coordinating. Organizing is the process of arranging activities and the people engaged in these activities in such a way as to achieve the maximum output with the highest degree of efficiency and coordination. This process begins after the goals and objectives have been established and the plan of action determined. The end structure of the process is an organization. In a good organization, the people involved produce more effectively as a group than they could individually.

Coordination is the bringing together of activities within an organization to achieve an organization's goals and objectives. There are four basic forms of coordination—informal, programmed, individual, and group.

Informal coordination includes those spontaneous gestures that lubricate an organization's social processes but are not directly part of task performance. For informal coordination to develop, employees must: (1) know and understand their own goals and objectives and those of their work unit; (2) have a clear understanding of what their jobs require (role clarity); and (3) identify with the organization and be willing to assist in achieving its objectives (Peterson & Peterson, 1990).

Programmed coordination involves establishing routines that channel work unit activities into paths consistent with an organization's overall goals. It should be understood that informal and programmed coordination are not always effective, while individual coordination efforts (i.e., a liaison or facilitator) sometimes are successful in resolving coordination problems. Finally, group coordination facilitated by the use of a coordinating committee appears to be the best means of resolving coordination problems.

The marketing concept implies the coordination of all organizational activities which impinge on the consumer. Yet the organizational proposals and changes made to achieve this coordination can and do result in organizational conflicts between those employees concerned with marketing and those concerned with product development and production. Conflicts occur for two reasons: (1) because each department or section wishes to stress the importance of its own tasks, and (2) because each department or section defines its goals narrowly and in its own interest. It is imperative that the organization requires all units to broadly focus on the organization's goals and avoid a focus that is not an integrated effort.

Staffing and assembling other resources. The key to a coordinated marketing effort is the staff assembled to complete the task. The organization should assemble people who are knowledgeable in marketing overall, advertising, promotion, and sales. These services can be provided by consultants, if the organization does not have the resources to employ full-time personnel in marketing.

Operating and directing. After the goals have been set, the planning accomplished, and the organization established and staffed, then, and only then, the program must be executed. At this point, operating, directing, and motivating become important phases in the marketing plan. In the final analysis, no plan is worth much unless it is carried out effectively. The management functions of operating and directing a marketing plan include operating a sales program, directing an advertising campaign, implementing a promotional plan, and working with a variety of people (e.g., middlemen, customers, suppliers).

Analyzing and evaluating. The final stage of the management process consists of analyzing and evaluating the results of the organization's plans and operations to determine whether or not they met expectations. There are at least four major areas of application of this managerial function with respect to the marketing program (Mullin, Hardy, & Sutton, 1993): (1) the manager or director may analyze net sales volume or marketing costs in total as well as products, services, or customer groups; (2) the performance and productivity of personnel involved in the marketing effort; (3) the evaluation of the effectiveness of the advertising programs; and (4) the evaluation of the performance of middlemen promoting products or services.

Table 10-1
Services Rendered by Sales Promotion

Customer Services

* to educate or inform the consumer about the product or service through the production of booklets and manuals, delivery of demonstrations, and offer free consultation
* to stimulate consumers through give away programs or premium services

Dealers/Distributors

* conduct training programs
* provide consultation to management
* install free displays

Marketing Services

Services are activities, benefits, or satisfactions that are offered for sale or are provided in connection with the sale of goods. There are three types of services most commonly recognized : (1) intangible benefits (e.g., insurance, investments, and some medical services); (2) intangible activities that require the use of tangible goods (e.g., amusements, house rentals, car rentals, transportation, personal training); and (3) intangible activities purchased jointly with products or other tangible activities (e.g., credit, club membership that includes use of spa, free racquetball lessons with club membership) (Lewis & Appenzeller, 1985).

The following are services that may be purchased by recreation and sport consumers (Railey & Tschauner, 1993):

- housing (e.g., rentals of hotels, motels, apartments, houses),
- household operations (e.g., utilities, house repairs, plumbing, landscaping, household cleaning),
- recreation (e.g., rental of recreation equipment, repair of recreation equipment, amusements, entertainment activities),
- health and fitness (e.g., club membership, personal trainers, equipment purchase, equipment repair, home videos, purchase of clothing and shoes, fitness certifications),
- sport (e.g., purchase of tickets, purchase of clothing and shoes, purchase of equipment, team membership, private lessons, concessions, coaching education, sport management education),
- personal care (e.g., laundry, dry cleaning, beauty care, hair cuts),
- Medical and other health care (e.g., dental, surgical, family care, nursing, eye care, hospitalization),
- private education,
- business and professional services (e.g., legal, accounting, management consulting, and marketing consulting),
- insurance and financial (e.g., personal and property insurance, risk management consulting, bank services, credit and loan services, investment counseling, tax services), and
- transportation and communications (e.g., freight and passenger service on common carriers, automobile repairs, automobile rentals, mobile communication and answering service).

Once a service is established it is marketed the same way as you would market a product. A marketing plan is developed and implemented that highlights the service or services provided by the organization.

Market Segmentation

Market segmentation consists of taking the total, heterogeneous market for a product or service and dividing it into several submarkets, each of which tends to be homogeneous in all significant aspects. This division of the market becomes useful when a organization sells the same product or service to different markets through the use of different advertising appeals designed specifically for each homogeneous market. More often, however, market segmentation is accompanied by product or service differentiation—by developing a different product for each market segment to meet the market's need.

Segmenting the market into target markets has emerged as the dominant feature of marketing because organizational resources can be more efficiently channeled to meet the expectations and the needs of a specific group. Each targeted segment is made up of individuals who share more similar behaviors, lifestyles, and goals than does the overall market (e.g., the aged are more concerned with the benefits of regular exercise relating to the maintenance of an independent lifestyle than are younger individuals).

For the sport manager who is interested and involved in marketing, the question is not whether to segment the market, but what degree of segmentation is necessary. The literature suggests four questions that can help in selecting the target market segments (Brooks, 1990, 1991, 1994; Peterson & Peterson, 1991; Loyle, 1994):

- Is the segment measurable?
- Is it large enough?
- Is it reachable?
- Is it responsive?

The manager should rate each target market on the basis of these criteria. The most desirable segments would be those that elicit a positive answer to all four questions.

Further, a target segment must have a sufficient number of potential customers to permit a profitable sales volume. Competition and possible market share must also be considered. Some factors for segmentation are easily identified and measured (e.g., age, gender, income level, educational background, occupation, job market, unemployment levels), and some are not (e.g., lifestyles, attitudes, and self-concepts).

All identifiable target segments are potentially reachable. However, the manager had better ask two basic questions before proceeding: (1) How can you communicate with the specific target segment? (2) How much will it cost? If the target market is not profitable, it should not be pursued.

In order to determine the responsiveness of a targeted market segment, it is necessary to ask two questions: (1) Are the people in this target segment willing to buy the product or service? (2) Can the organization develop marketable products or services, and a strategy for promoting the products or services that will provide the organization an advantage over other products or services? The main challenge is to identify what consumers in the target market need and want and then provide it to them at a price they are willing to pay.

There are four effective ways to segment a market: demographic segmentation (e.g., age, gender, income, occupation, education, and household), geographic segmentation (e.g., urban, suburban, commuting distances, counties, states), psychographic segmentation (e.g., lifestyle, personality, attitudes, self-concept), and behavioral segmentation (i.e., consumers are grouped according to their responses to the features of specific products and services) (Peterson & Colacino, 1990; Peterson & Peterson, 1991).

Marketing Research

Marketing research is the systematic, objective, and exhaustive search for and study of the facts relevant to any problem in the field of marketing (see appendix for the scope of marketing research) (Lewis & Appenzeller, 1985; Brooks, 1994). It includes various subsidiary types of research : (1) market analysis, which is a study of the size, location, nature, and characteristics of markets; (2) sales analysis, which is largely an analysis of sales data; (3) consumer research, of which motivation research is a type that is concerned chiefly with the discovery and analysis of consumer attitudes, reactions, and preferences, and (4) advertising research, which is carried on chiefly as an aid to the management of advertising work (Brooks, 1991; Brooks, 1994).

Using Marketing Research

Marketing research can be used for both quantitative and qualitative marketing analysis of: (1) product or service, (2) pricing policies, (3) promotional policies, and (4) the total marketing program. The following examples demonstrate how marketing research can be useful.

(1) As part of a project to develop a chain of health and fitness centers in Indiana, a health and fitness corporation wanted to know more about the economic aspects of the health and fitness industry in the state. In one phase of the project, marketing research (specifically market analysis) was used to determine the health and fitness characteristics of the typical Hoosier—how often do they exercise, what type of exercise(s) is most popular, do men exercise more than women, what generation is more involved in the health and fitness movement, and how much are they willing to pay for health and fitness services? In addition, the health and fitness corporation wanted to know in some detail what the average exercising Hoosier liked and disliked about health and fitness activities. Once the data was gathered and analyzed, the health and fitness corporation decided to reduce the number of units to be built throughout Indiana. It also was able to determine where best to locate each unit in Indiana.

(2) A major exercise equipment manufacturer was considering whether to add a new piece of equipment to its product line. A marketing research firm was engaged to determine something about consumer reactions and attitudes regarding the product (product or service research). Consumers who were interviewed answered that what they wanted most in the new piece of equipment was light weight, maneuverability, durability, and easy storage. After investing over $100,000 in manufacturing a prototype, the company took the model to a consumer panel for their reactions. The consumers promptly rejected the machine on the grounds that it was too heavy and lacked maneuverability. Management scrapped the prototype and went back to design a machine with less mass, more maneuverability, and hopefully more consumer appeal. Although the company had to write off $100,000, the loss would have been far greater if management had marketed the piece of exercise equipment on a larger-scale commercial basis without the marketing research.

(3) A racquetball racquet manufacturer was trying to decide whether to establish a retail price on its best racquet and insist by contract that the retailer (stores and proshops in racquetball clubs) maintain this price. (This price policy is called resale price maintenance or fair trade.) The manufacturer was aware that two national competitors had employed the policy with a reasonably high degree of success. Here was a job for marketing research (research on pricing policies). All retailers (including proshops) currently handling the product were consulted.

In addition, other dealers (Kmart and Walmart) were asked if they would carry the brand if it had a set price that no one could undercut. On balance, the results showed that a policy of resale price maintenance would be a mistake for this manufacturer. Few new accounts would be picked up, and many established accounts, particularly the large ones, would be displeased. Consequently, the manufacturer discarded the idea.

(4) A health/fitness club chain, with clubs in the Midwest, was concerned about the public's reaction to frequent flyer miles. The chain had been offering frequent flyer miles for a few years and wanted to know whether customers liked this or whether they would prefer a cash discount in lieu of frequent flyer miles. In a few clubs, each customer renewing or joining was offered the alternative of frequent flyer miles or a 2% discount. The researchers (research on promotional policies) found that the customers split about fifty-fifty: half took the discount and half preferred the frequent flyer miles. The percentage of customers selecting the discount, however, was much higher among customers who did not fly or flew infrequently. Consequently, the chain decided to allow customers to choose among the two promotions.

Steps in Marketing Research

Marketing research is best left to marketing research professionals. It is complicated and time consuming. It is recommended that a marketing research consulting firm be engaged to conduct appropriate marketing research for the organization. The components of marketing research are outlined in Table 10-2 (Lewis & Appenzeller, 1985; Mullin, Hardy, & Sutton, 1993; Brooks, 1994).

Table 10-2
Steps in a Marketing Research Project

1. Define the objectives of the project and define the problem,
2. conduct a situation analysis,
3. conduct an informal investigation,
4. plan and conduct a formal investigation,
    * determine the sources of information,
    * determine the methods for gathering data,
    * prepare data-gathering forms,
    * pretest the questionnaire or other forms,
    * plan the sample, and
    * collect the data.
5. tabulate and analyze the data,
6. interpret the data and prepare recommendations,
7. prepare a written report, and
8. follow up the study.

What is a Market?

A sound marketing program starts with a careful quantitative and qualitative analysis of the market demand for the product or service. Further, it is imperative that management from the outset understand and appreciate the fact that the consumer is king. The consumer is the basic determinant of what goods and services will be produced and of where, when, how, and at what price they will be sold. The consumer, up to the limits of disposable income, is free to choose the amount and kind of goods and services purchased.

In the market demand for any given product or service, there are three factors to consider—people with needs, their purchasing power, and their buying behavior. A need is the lack of anything that is required, desired, or useful. The potentially limitless number of needs offers unbounded opportunities for market growth. Satisfying wants may be interpreted as the first step toward satisfying needs. We want something that will answer our needs. The organization must be creative enough to develop a product or service to satisfy peoples' wants and needs.

Consumer Behavior and Buying Patterns

Differences in consumers' habits, their cognitive structures, and their motives cause them to behave differently when buying. Although an individual does not act the same way in all situations, people tend to act consistently. Six groups of consumers by their buying behavior are described in Table 10-3 (Peterson & Peterson, 1991; Railey & Tschauner, 1993; Irwin & Sutton, 1995).

Table 10-3
Consumer Buying Behavior

1. A *habit-determined group* of brand-loyal consumers who tend to be satisfied with the product or brand last purchased.
2. A *cognitive group* of consumers who are sensitive to rational claims.
3. A *price-cognitive group* of consumers who decide principally upon the basis of price or economy comparison.
4. An *impulse group* of consumers who buy on the basis of physical appeal and are relatively insensitive to brand name.
5. A group of *emotional reactors* who respond to product symbols and are swayed by images.
6. A *group of new consumers* who have not yet stabilized the psychological dimensions of their behavior.

Particular characteristics of some products have a psychological influence on buying behavior. There are six classes of products identified by their psychological appeal depicted in Table 10-4 (Lewis & Appenzeller, 1985; Brooks, 1991, 1994; Railey & Tschauner, 1993).

In competitive marketing, product classification may determine many organization policies. Where ego-involvement is present or can be developed, consumer interest in a brand can be built on the basis of the product image. This, in turn, means that the market is highly susceptible to other brands and services. Buyers are not habit-bound. They will switch brands easily. Where ego-involvement exists, sellers must depend heavily on motivational selling.

Table 10-4
Psychological Appeal Products/Services

1. *Prestige products or services* are those that become symbols (e.g., expensive automobile or home, or first-class seating).
2. *Maturity products or services* are those that are typically withheld from younger people because of social customs (e.g., cigarettes or alcohol, or gambling).
3. *Status products or services* are those that impute class membership to their users (e.g., expensive clothes and jewelry, or belonging to the country club with an assigned caddy).
4. *Anxiety products and services* are those that are used to alleviate a personal or social threat (e.g., soaps, perfumes, dentifrices, or going to the beauty salon). These products or services involve ego-defense, whereas the three preceding classes of products are concerned with ego-enhancement.
5. *Hedonic products or services* are those that depend highly upon their appeal to the senses (e.g., snack items, presweetened cereal, fast-food, or design and color). Their appeal is immediate and frequently results in impulse purchases.
6. *Functional products or services* are those that have little cultural or social meaning imputed (e.g., staple food items, fruits and vegetables, or building products).

If ego-involvement is low, product/service image is not important. Brand loyalty is established through product/service identity and familiarity. Once brand loyalties are established, they are very strong. It is much more difficult and costly to break down brand loyalty than to build up ego-involving motives. If you are in the health and fitness field, ego-defense and ego-enhancement are your allies, not enemies. American society is very much ego-centered and ego-enhancement is very important to the baby boomers and Generation X.

Social Class Impact on Marketing

Marketers have come to realize that the concept of social class provides a greater depth of understanding and a better basis for interpreting consumer buying behavior than does income alone. Social classes do exist in America, and a person's buying behavior is more strongly influenced by the class to which he belongs, or to which he aspires, than by income alone. Sociologists suggest that there are five social classes. These five social classes have been developed by using a weighted index consisting of occupation, sources of income, and housing type.

Descriptions of the five classes and the percentage of the population falling into each generally are outlined in Table 10-5 (Irwin & Sutton, 1995).

It is generally accepted that (1) a social-class system is operative in large metropolitan areas and can be delineated, (2) there are far-reaching psychological differences between classes, and (3) consumption patterns are symbols of class membership, and class membership is a more significant determinant of economic behavior than is the amount of income (Brooks, 1991, 1994; Irwin & Sutton, 1995).

Table 10-5
American Social Classes

1. The upper class (.9%) includes the old families and the socially prominent newly rich.
2. The upper-middle class (7.2%) includes successful business people, professionals (e.g., physicians, lawyers, college/university professors), and the best sales people.
3. The lower-middle class (28.6%) is the white-collar class.
4. The upper-lower class (44%) includes factory workers, union labor groups, skilled workers (blue collar workers).
5. The lower-class (19.5%) includes unskilled laborers, racial immigrants, and the unemployed.

Note: The *quality market* is classes 1 & 2 which only represent 8.2% of the total population. It is important that the club, recreation and sport manager understand the social implications upon the market in a particular population area.

Consumers' Motivation to Purchase a Product/Service

Managers need to know and understand what motivates consumers to buy certain products/services from a particular organization. A knowledge of these motives (see Table 10-6 for some of the most important motives) is extremely valuable to everyone who is trying to sell a product/service (Brooks, 1991, 1994; Loyle, 1994; Irwin & Sutton, 1995). Consumers prefer to patronize stores where they perceive they are maximizing money, service, and product benefits while minimizing risks as perceived in terms of product price, acceptability of product/service offerings, and required expenditure of time and effort. Consumers' perceptions of the maximum-benefit, minimum-risk mix will vary according to social class. The higher the level of class the greater the risk the consumer is willing to accept.

Table 10-6
Consumer Patronage Motives

1. Convenience of location
2. Rapidity of service
3. Ease of locating merchandise
4. Uncrowded conditions
5. Ease of parking
6. Price
7. Assortment of merchandise
8. Services offered
9. Attractive facilities
10. Caliber of personnel
11. Purchasing options
12. Security

Buying Patterns

A sport manager should be able to answer questions about *when* people buy products/services—the season, the day of the week, and the time of the day. If seasonal buying patterns exist (e.g., New Year's health and fitness resolutions) the manager should try to extend the buying season. The manager may find that promotional programs will smooth out seasonal fluctuations. *When* people buy influences the product- or service-planning, pricing, and promotional phases of a firm's marketing program.

An organization should consider two factors with respect to *where* people buy—where the buying decision is made and where the actual purchase occurs. For many products and services, the decision to buy is made at home. On the other hand, the decision is often made in whole or in part right at the point of purchase. An organization's entire promotional program must be geared to carry the greatest impact at the place where the buying decision is made. If the decision to buy is made in the club, then attention must be devoted to packaging and other point-of-purchase display materials. Of course, some advertising effort must be directed to the consumer in his home because a totally unknown product, service or brand, no matter how attractively packaged, will usually be rejected in favor of the known brand. If the primary decision to buy is made at home, a substantial promotional effort must be devoted to such advertising media as newspapers, magazines, radio, and television.

The *how* part of consumers' buying habits encompasses several areas of behavior. This behavior affects product/service and pricing policies, promotional programs, and many other management decisions. In turn, price, service, and brand relationships can affect consumer preferences. Some people are highly price-conscious and will select only the lowest-priced item regardless of brand; others will buy the lowest-priced product just as long as it is a known brand; some other people willingly pay a higher price to get the service they desire; and still others believe you get what you pay for.

The current trend in buying preferences is "one-stop" shopping (Seifer, 1987; Barrett, 1993; Brooks, 1994). If the club can offer everything consumers need in one place, it is more likely to retain memberships. Look at the great success of the gas station plus convenience store or the Super Kmart or Walmart stores. Americans want convenience, service, and the lowest prices for the items they wish to purchase. Clubs need to begin thinking about providing more "one-stop" shopping opportunities for their clientele (i.e., in-club restaurants, day care/elder care centers, beauty parlors, convenience store, etc). Some aspects of the club services can become self-service (e.g., cafeteria-style restaurants, self-service convenience stores) but others are not (e.g., day care, elder care, personal trainer, pro shop, beauty shop).

Some people always pay cash; whereas others prefer to buy on credit. Credit does not always mean credit cards (i.e., payroll deduction, three easy monthly payments, quarterly payments). A club may encourage less credit by providing discounts for cash payments.

When determining buying habits with respect to *who* does the family purchasing, there are three areas of consideration: (1) who makes the physical purchase, (2) who makes the buying decision, and (3) who actually uses the product (Peterson & Colacino, 1990). Who buys a product will influence a firm's marketing policies regarding its products/services, channels of distribution, and promotion. Free services (e.g., day care, elder care) may be necessary if women are the main clientele.

Behavioral Characteristics That Influence Marketing Efforts

There are six behavioral characteristics that influence marketing efforts: (1) impulse buying, (2) desire for conformity, (3) limited time, (4) increased leisure time, (5) desire for convenience, and (6) upgraded tastes and desire for elegance (Brooks, 1991, 1994; Peterson & Peterson, 1991; Railey & Tschauner, 1994; Irwin & Sutton, 1995).

Impulse buying is purchasing without advance planning. Impulse buying is often done on a very irrational basis. In the supermarket while waiting at the check out counter, customers are surrounded by many inexpensive items that draw their attention and they often purchase the item(s) without thought. Because of impulse buying, greater emphasis must be placed on promotional programs to get people to the club. If the club has racquetball or tennis courts, a display of either racquets, balls, or gloves could be placed close to the main registration desk to tempt the customers' tendency for impulse buying. Displays must be more appealing because the package must serve as a silent salesperson.

Desire for conformity can be seen in all walks of life. For the past four decades, American society has slowly drifted away from a nation of "rugged individualists" to one of conformists. The health and fitness movement has been a beneficiary of this paradigm shift in America. Executives seem to strive to dress alike, drink alike, join the same clubs, and otherwise follow the prescribed pattern of the "organization man or woman." The fact that most families can afford national mass communication media (e.g., magazines, newspapers, radio, television) is another impetus toward conformity. In short, there is an overpowering drive to be accepted by the group and to be like others. No group remains static in its wants. All are constantly shifting. The key is to determine who or what makes them shift.

Limited time in American society is paramount. The most common statement heard is—"I don't have time" to do this or that. American life, in general, is fast-paced and time is becoming an increasingly precious commodity. Americans want more and more personal services on demand—thus the personal trainer becomes popular to meet wants and needs. The trend is toward personal services, renting a product (e.g., car) or buying a disposable one (paper bath towel), rather than to own an article which requires our time for maintenance and care. The television, cable, and video industries have captitalized on the fitness movement by producing thousands of fitness programs that are available on television early in the morning, during the lunch hour, and in the evening, and in the video stores.

Increased leisure time has become common place for American families. This increased leisure time is great for the club, recreation and sport industries. Managers should recognize that leisure time is interrelated with and influenced by how, when, and where people buy. The sport managers need to be prepared to develop and implement strategies to draw families into their markets and capitalize on the increased amount of free time families have at their discretion.

Desire for convenience, a demand for convenience, ties in with the importance of time. There are 10 kinds of convenience managers need to concern themselves with:

1. *Form*. Products must be available in a wide variety of forms (e.g., soap—liquid, solid or powder);
2. *Quantity.* Goods must be offered in a variety of sizes or quantities desired by the consumers (e.g., shirt —Xsm, Sm, M, Lg, Xlg, XXlg, or balls —one or package of three);
3. *Time.* Products/services must be available at any time the consumer wants them (e.g., 24-hour convenience stores, 24-hour Kmart and Walmart stores, 24-hour health and fitness clubs);
4. *Place*. Sellers must offer opportunities for consumers to shop in the most convenient locations (e.g., locations were it is easy to park, obtain housing, food, and gasoline, and convenient to main highways);
5. *Packaging*. Packages must be easy to find, open, use and store (e.g., racquet-ball or tennis balls packaged in easy to carry resealable containers that can be stored in tight spaces);
6. *Combination*. Combination, or packaging, convenience is found in service industries (e.g., travel industry sells packaged tours, health and fitness industry sells combination memberships— aerobic dance and racquetball or aerobic dance and strength and cardiovascular training);
7. *Automation*. Many consumers dream of a push-button society (e.g., instead of a treadmill one must provide the energy to move the tread, one prefers the ease of pushing a button to engage the motor that operates the tread at different speeds);
8. *Credit*. One of the most significant marketing developments has been the tremendous increase in consumer credit cards and debit cards issued by

hundreds of banks as well as specialty cards issued by many retail companies (e.g., acceptance of Visa, MasterCard, Diners Club, American Express, Discover Card as an accepted method of payment);

9. *Selection*. A seller must offer products or services at convenient prices and in an assortment of colors, materials, or flavors (e.g., male and female personal trainers, club shirts and shorts in a variety of colors and designs); and

10. *Readiness*. Virtually everything the consumer purchases must be ready and easy to use—plug and play (e.g., fitness video, home exercise machines, club exercise equipment) (Seifer, 1987; Barrett, 1993).

Marketing Tip

When consumers make shopping decisions, they do so by balancing commodity costs and convenience. Commodity costs are defined as the amount of money paid to the seller for the goods or services purchased. Convenience costs include expenditures of time, physical and nervous energy, and money (e.g., gasoline, parking, phone calls, and carfare) necessary to obtain the goods and services. Convenience costs are becoming an increasingly significant factor in determining where people decide to shop.

Upgraded tastes and desire for elegance is common in American society. The upgrading of living habits is fostered by both economic forces (increased income) and social forces (i.e., improved education, extensive travel, and the influence of mass communications media). This age of elegance, improved tastes, and gracious living is reflected in changing patterns of consumption and behavior on the part of the consumers. There is an ever-growing appreciation for the need of individuals to improve their health and fitness, be involved in physical activity and recreation, and become involved in sport as a participant, coach or spectator. The upgrading of tastes and income also means that consumers now crave the kind of attention that only the "carriage trade" used to expect and receive. The alert manager is already responding to these behavioral pattern changes.

Product

A *product* is a complex mix of tangible and intangible attributes, including packaging, color, price, manufacturer's prestige, retailer's prestige, and manufacturer's and retailer's services, which the buyer may accept as offering satisfaction of wants or needs. Any change in a physical feature (e.g., color, design, size, packaging) however minor it may be, creates, in effect, a new product. The key to the definition is that the consumer is buying more than a set of chemical and physical attributes. Fundamentally, the consumer is buying want-satisfaction. A wise organization sells product/service benefits rather than just the product/service (e.g., don't sell the steak, sell the sizzle; or don't sell the pain of fitness, sell the change in the body).

Planning for a Product/Service

Product/service planning embraces all activities that enable an organization to determine what should constitute an organization's line of products or services. Ideally, product/service planning will ensure that the full complement of a firm's products/services are logically related, individually justified, designed to strengthen the organization's competitive edge and profit position. The sport manager should appoint a product planning/development committee. The committee should seek answers to the questions outlined in Table 10-7 (Lewis & Appenzeller, 1985; Brooks, 1991, 1994; Railey & Tschauner, 1993).

Table 10-7
Product Planning/Development Questions

1. Which products/services should the organization make or provide and which should it buy?
2. Should the organization expand or simplify its line?
3. What new uses are there for each product/service?
4. Is the quality right for the intended use and market?
5. What brand, package, and label should be used on each product/service?
6. How should the product/service be styled and designed, and in what sizes, colors, and materials should it be produced?
7. In what quantities should each item be produced, and what inventory controls should be established?
8. How should the product line be priced?

Merchandising

Merchandising is the science of determining what the consumer will purchase to meets his or her wants and needs. Further, it is that part of marketing involved with promoting sales of merchandise, by considering the most effective means of selecting, pricing, displaying, and advertising items or services for sale.

Packaging

Packaging is the general group of activities in product planning or service development that involve designing and producing the container or wrapper for a product or a brochure for a new service. There are four reasons for packaging: (1) to protect the product on its route from the manufacturer to the consumer, and in some cases even during its life with the consumer; (2) the packaging implements the organization's promotional program (i.e., a package may be the only significant way in which a firm can differentiate its product or service); (3) increased profit through attractive packaging increases the customer's willingness to spend more for the item; and (4) the final reason is customer convenience (Brooks, 1994).

Price

Pricing is the key activity within the capitalistic system of free enterprise (Lewis & Appenzeller, 1985). The market price of a product influences wages, rent, interest, and profits. The price of a product or a service is a major determinant of the market demand for the item. Price will affect the organization's competitive position and its share of the market. As a result, price has a considerable bearing on the organization's revenue and net profit. Further, the price of the product or service also affects the organization's marketing program. In product planning or service development, for example, if the organization wants to improve the quality of its product or service or add differentiating features, this decision can be implemented only if the market will accept a price increase high enough to cover the costs of the changes.

Main Objectives of Pricing

The are five main objectives in pricing: (1) to achieve target return on investment or on net sales; (2) stabilize prices; (3) to maintain or improve a target share of the market; (4) to meet, follow, or prevent competition; and (5) to maximize profits. For small organizations, like health and fitness or racquet clubs, goals three through five are easiest to achieve (Brooks, 1994; Irwin & Sutton, 1995).

Determining Price

There are a number of very reliable ways of determining a price of a product or service. However, the following six-step price determination procedure has been commonly used for small businesses nationwide for decades: (1) select the target market and estimate the demand for the product or service; (2) choose an image for the product or service; (3) estimate the competitive reaction; (4) designate a price strategy to be used to reach the market target; (5) pick an appropriate pricing policy; and (6) establish the specific price (Mullin, Hardy, & Sutton, 1993; Brooks, 1994).

There are two popular pricing strategies found at either end of the scale that are most appropriate to the pricing of new products or services—"skim-the-cream" and penetration pricing. *Skim-the-cream* pricing involves setting a price that is high in the range of expected prices. There are at least five reasons why skim-the-cream pricing may be particularly suitable for new products: (1) the demand is likely to be less elastic in the early stages of a product's or service's life cycle; (2) it segments the market on an income or buying-power basis; (3) it acts as a strong hedge against a possible mistake in setting the price (i.e., it is easier to lower prices than raise them); (4) high initial prices can often generate more revenues and profits than can low prices in the early stages of market development; and (5) high initial prices can be used to keep demand within the limits of the organization's productive capacity (i.e., low initial price, which brings more business than an organization can handle, may result in the permanent loss of the goodwill of many customers) (Mullin, Hardy, & Sutton, 1993; Brooks, 1994).

Penetration pricing is when a low initial price is set in order to reach the mass market immediately. This strategy can be employed at either the early or late stage of the product's or service's life cycle. Compared with cream skimming, penetration pricing is a more aggressive competitive strategy and is likely to be more satisfactory when the following conditions exist (Mullin, Hardy, & Sutton, 1993; Brooks, 1994): (1) the quantity sold is highly sensitive to price; (2) substantial reductions in unit production and marketing costs can be achieved through large-scale operations; (3) the product faces very strong competition soon after it is introduced to the market; and (4) there is an inadequate high-income market to sustain a skim-the-cream price. Low initial pricing may do two things. First, it may discourage other organizations from entering the field because the investment needed in production and marketing facilities will be too great in light of the anticipated low profit margin. Second, low prices may give the innovator such a strong hold on the market share that future competitors cannot cut into the market.

Price leaders and followers is a method by which the highest quality club in the market increases prices, while others monitor the prestigious club's prices and follow any price changes soon after they change. The price change should mirror that of the prestige club.

Fixed price means that everyone pays the same price for the same membership. Most clubs have a one-price policy. However, *flexible* pricing is used to lure new members into the club. The fixed price in the peak season may be $200 but in the off season the same membership is $99, making the price policy flexible in order to encourage membership growth during the off season.

Setting Price

There are basically three methods commonly used to set price: (1) total cost plus desired profit (cost-plus pricing); (2) cost based on the balance between estimates of market demand and costs of production and marketing (break-even analysis); and (3) costs set by the competitive market (i.e., meet competition, below competitive level, and above competitive level) (Lewis & Appenzeller, 1985; McKenzie, 1986; Mullin, Hardy, & Sutton, 1993; Brooks, 1994). Methods one and three are fairly simple to employ, however, method two is a little more difficult.

Break-even analysis (a pricing tool) involves developing tables and/or charts that will assist an organization in determining at what level of output the revenues will equal the costs, assuming a certain selling price. Sales at levels above the break-even point will result in a profit on each unit, and output below the break-even point will result in a loss.

Increasing Prices

There are commonly three times when prices should be increased: (1) announcement of a major new improvement to the facility or a plan to purchase new equipment; (2) completion of the major improvement or the new equipment has been installed; and (3) during the peak activity season (Mullin, Hardy, & Sutton, 1993; Brooks, 1994).

A rule of thumb to consider is the following: (1) major facility improvements raise the rates by 20-25%; (2) new equipment—10-15%; (3) remodeling —15-20%; (4) annual increases should range between 8-10% (i.e., consider average inflation in the local market and competition before finalizing the increase); and (5) maintain the membership fee price and increase specialized fees (e.g., court fees, dance exercise class fees, swimming fees, professional trainer fees) (Mullin, Hardy, & Sutton, 1993; Brooks, 1994).

Summary

Marketing is a total system of interacting business activities designed to plan, price, promote, and distribute want-satisfying products and services to present and potential customers. While sport marketing consists of all activities designed to meet the needs and wants of sport consumers through exchange processes.

Learning Objective 1: Development of a marketing plan.

The management process in developing a marketing plan consists of six basic functions: (a) determining objectives, (b) planning strategies to reach objectives, (c) organizing and coordinating the various components of the marketing program, (d) staffing and assembling other resources to facilitate the marketing program, (e) implementing and providing direction for the plan, and (f) analyzing and evaluating the results of the marketing program.

Learning Objective 2: Understanding the importance of market research.

Marketing research, which is the systematic search for and study of facts, is a very important aspect of the management process. It provides the information about the market and the customers that is essential in developing the appropriate products and services that will attack the appropriate market share to be successful. Without accurate information, a marketing plan will not be successful.

Learning Objective 3: Recognition of market segments.

Market segmentation consists of taking the total, heterogeneous market for a product or service and dividing it into several submarkets, each of which tends to be homogeneous in all significant aspects. Defining the various segments of the market allows the sport manager to provide services and products that target specific audiences needs and wants.

Learning Objective 4: Understanding consumer behavior and buying patterns.

Consumer behavior and buying patterns are important factors to be considered in determining market segmentation. The successful sport manager understands the consumer in the market, the consumer's behavior, and the consumer's buying patterns. This knowledge of the consumer gives the sport manager an advantage in developing services and products for the consumer as well as marketing the services and products the consumers need and want.

Learning Objective 5: Comprehend what motivates a consumer to purchase a product/service.

It is important to understand the consumer when developing products/services as well as how products are packaged and merchandized. However, the pricing of the product/service is the key to successful sales in the end. It is very helpful to have a well-planned sales promotion campaign to promote the product/service, that has been developed based on what motivates the consumers in a specific market to want to purchase the product/service.

Self-testing Exercise

1. Pick any city in the United States that has a population between 50,000 and 60,000, and describe the overall market. What information would be necessary to gather to be able to accurately describe the market in this area? Where would you go to gather such information? Now that you have gathered the information, how would you describe the market? How would you segment the market if you were the athletic director at a middle-sized institution of higher education interested in increasing men's and women's game attendance? Define the target markets you would use.

2. You have been hired as the golf course manager/superintendent for a nine-hole executive golf course. The course is an old course. The course is short but well-maintained. It is a golf course that is great for beginners. The course does not have a marketing plan. You have a very competent assistant course superintendent. Your first task is to develop a marketing plan for the course that will increase revenue by 50% over the next five years. The fees for the course are as high as they can go and still stay competitive. Therefore, the number of rounds needs to be increased and the expansion of auxiliary golf

sales is necessary. How will you develop the marketing plan? What will your objectives and strategies be in the marketing plan? Who will be involved in implementing and evaluating the plan? How will you evaluate the plan?

3.   You are the general manager of Happy Holidays Fitness and Racquet Club. Happy Holidays is a high-end club (i.e., upper-middle class to upper class), one of four in the area. The club has recently invested in a major remodeling, adding more court space for tennis and racquetball, free weight area, expansion of the dance exercise space, and a proshop. How will you determine the new fee structure for memberships? How will you establish retail prices for items sold in the proshop? In answering each question, describe the steps that you will take and how you will evaluate your pricing structure.

4.   What do you need to do to define consumer behavior and buying patterns? Where will you gather the information? What will you do with the information?

References

Barrett, Bob. (1993). Ten tips for better member retention. *Club Industry, (9)*1, 41-52.

Brooks, Christine. (1990). New aerobic markets. *Fitness Management, (6)*1, 28-31.

Brooks, Christine. (1991). The market-share game. *Athletic Business, (10)*4, 59-63.

Brooks, Christine M. (1994). *Sports marketing: Competitive business strategies for sports.* Englewood Cliffs, NJ: Prentice Hall.

Irwin, Richard L., & Sutton, William A. (1995, April/May). Keeping the customer satisfied. *Athletic Management,* pp. 18-24.

Lewis, Guy, & Appenzeller, Herb. (1984). *Successful sport management.* Charlottesville, VA: The Michie Company.

Loyle, Donna. (1994, November). Take aim at the 40-plus market. *Club Industry,* pp. 17-21.

McKenzie, Bill. (1986). Generating pro shop profits. *Athletic Business, (10)*6, 30-35.

Mullin, Bernard J., Hardy, Stephen, & Sutton, William A. (1993). *Sport marketing.* Champaign, IL: Human Kinetics

Peterson, James A., & Peterson, Susan L. (1991). Target marketing. *Fitness Management, (7)*8, 32-34.

Peterson, James A., & Colacino, Dennis L. (1990). Marketing for profits. *Fitness Management, (6)*1, 24-27.

Railey, Jim H., & Tschauner, Peggy A. (1993). *Managing physical education, fitness, and sports programs.* (2nd ed.). Mountain View, CA: Mayfield Publishing Company.

Seifer, Jan. (1987). Ten management guidelines to boost member retention. *Athletic Business, (11)*10, 66-68.

Suggested Readings

Carter, David M. (1996). *Keeping score: An inside look at sports marketing.* Grants Pass, OR: Oasis Press.

Pitts, Brenda G., & Stotlar, David K. (1996). *Fundamentals of sport marketing.* Morgantown, WV: Fitness Information Technology, Inc.

Stephenson, Harriet, & Otterson, Dorothy. (1995). *Marketing mastery: your seven step guide to success.* Grants Pass, OR: Oasis Press.

Stotlar, David. (1993). *Successful sport marketing.* Dubuque, IA: Wm. C. Brown & Benchmark Press.

11

PUBLIC AND MEDIA RELATIONS

◆ ——————————————— ◆

Instructional Objectives

After reading this chapter the student should:

• be able to competently select a public relations agency,

• be able to discuss the legal aspects of public relations,

• understand how to develop a public relations plan,

• be able to define the difference between internal and external public relations, and

• understand the importance of media relations.

Introduction

A *public relations* program is designed to influence the opinions of people within the targeted market through responsible and acceptable performance, based on mutually satisfactory two-way communication. It has been noted that Abraham Lincoln once said, "Public sentiment is everything. With public sentiment, nothing can fail; without it, nothing can succeed." In order to gain public sentiment, programs must familiarize not only customers/clients but the public in general with all aspects of the services, products, and programs offered. An effective public relations program will open communication lines with the various publics and effectively utilize the media in a manner that competently presents the objectives of the organization to the public at large. Further, it will modify the attitudes and actions of the public through persuasion and integrate them with those of the organization.

Seeking a Public Relations Agency

Olguin (1991) suggested that the following 10 questions be asked before an organization contracts with a public relations agency:

- Does the agency have experience in the health, fitness, physical activity, recreation, and sport industries?
- Do the account executives have experience in these industries?
- Does the agency have a good reputation?
- Will the agency give you a list of references?
- Will you get senior-level management attention?
- Do they know the industries' publications and have media contacts at each?
- Are they a full-service agency with public relations, advertising, direct mail, and promotional capabilities?
- Are they creative? Ask to see other public relations campaigns completed for other organizations in the same or related areas.
- Are they result-oriented?
- Are they good listeners?

Public Relations

A sport organization's public relations program should include, but not be limited to the following:

- serving as an information source regarding organization services, products, and activities,
- promoting confidence that the services, products, or activities provided by the organization are useful and assist people in maintaining, gaining, or regaining their health and fitness,
- gathering support for the organization's programs and fund-raising appeals, stressing the value of active lifestyles and the positive impact they have on health and fitness,
- improving communication among customers, staff, parents and the surrounding community,
- evaluating the organization's services, products, and activities, and
- correcting myths, misunderstandings, and misinformation concerning the organization's services, products, and activities.

Steps in Developing a Public Relations Program

It is important to first agree that a public relations program is necessary for the organization. Once it is agreed that a public relations program is necessary, then resources to develop and implement a public relations plan must be provided. The primary resources required are human, financial, facility space, equipment (e.g., computers, printers, and scanners), and materials (e.g., funds for duplication, phones, postage, printing, software, etc).

Initially, a public relations program planning committee should be established with representation from all facets of the organization. This committee should follow the ensuing steps in the development of a public relations program plan:

- Develop a philosophy statement that encourages the foundation for any good public relations program is outstanding performance,
- Establish a mission statement that encourages the establishment and maintenance of two-way lines of communication with as many related publics as possible,
- Develop a sound uniform public relations policy (i.e., all communication with the public will be handled through the public relations office),
- Establish a set of principles to guide the development of the public relations program, such as:

  - Public relations must be considered internally before being developed externally,
  - The public relations program plan will be circulated to all members of the organization for meaningful input and buy in,
  - The persons selected by the sport organization to implement the public relations plan must have a thorough knowledge of the professional services to be rendered, the attitudes of members of the profession and organization represented, and the nature and reaction of the consumers and all the publics directly or indirectly related to the organization's services, products, or programs, and
  - The public relations office must be kept abreast of the factors and influences that affect the program, and develop and maintain a wide sphere of contacts.

- Identify the services, products, and programs that will yield the greatest dividends.
- Define the various related publics.
- Obtain facts regarding consumers'/clients' and other publics' knowledge level about the organization's services, products, and programs.
- Determine the following before drafting the program plan (Parkhouse, 1996):

  - Is there a handbook or manual of guidelines, or a newsletter to keep members of the organization informed (internal communication)?
  - Is there a system for disseminating information to the media?
  - Is there access to the Internet and if so, does the organization have a web homepage?
  - Is there a booklet, flyer, or printed matter that tells the story of the organization?

- •   Do the members (customers/clients) and staff participate in community activities?
- •   Does the organization hold open houses, clinics, seminars, or workshops?
- •   Are there provisions for a speakers' bureau so that civic and service clubs, schools, and other organizations may obtain someone to speak on various topics relating to the organization's services, products, or programs?
- •   Does the organization have an informational video?
- •   Is inter- and intra-organizational electronic mail utilized to its fullest capacity?

- •   Determine appropriate time lines for implementation and who or what group is responsible for the completion of the task; and
- •   Establish a regular evaluation process for the plan (Helitzer, 1992; Bucher & Krotee, 1993).

Difference Between Internal and External Public Relations

Internal public relations is communicating openly and often with personnel and members. The best promotion for an event can be negated if one of the employees or members gives a disgruntled response to the media. The best promoters of an organization are its employees and members.

External public relations is communicating with the outside publics external to the organization and its employees and members. This communication is done directly with the public(s) and through the media. These are prospective new members.

Outlets for Public Relations

There are numerous avenues for getting the message out to the internal and external publics, including: (1) printed media, (2) pictures and graphics, (3) radio, (4) television, (5) video, (6) posters, (7) exhibits, (8) brochures, (9) billboards and posters, (10) public speaking opportunities, (11) electronic mail, (12) Internet (World Wide Web homepage), (13) direct mail, and (14) telemarketing (Lewis & Appenzeller, 1985; Helitzer, 1992).

The news release can be distributed using a variety of electronic equipment and other means: (1) fax machine, (2) computers, (3) newswire services (i.e., AP), (4) handouts, (5) messenger, (6) express mail, (7) U.S. Mail, and (8) telephone (Helitzer, 1992).

Preparing Radio and Television Public Service Announcements (PSAs)

Radio and television media are powerful and well worth the money spent for public relations. The largest obstacle is obtaining free time, known as public service announcements. The idea of public service will influence some station managers to grant free time to an organization. This may be in the nature of an item included in a newscast program, a spot public service announcement (PSA), or a public service program that might range from 15 to 60 minutes.

Sometimes a person must take advantage of the media on short notice. Therefore, it is important for an organization to be prepared with written plans that can be put into operation immediately. The following are a few guidelines for preparation:

- know the organization's message,
- know the program (i.e., style, format, audience participation, time),
- know the audience (i.e., seniors, teens, upscale, non-consumers, gender),
- tailor the message and presentation to the audience interest, and
- practice—speak in lay terms, be brief and concise.

Communications

There are four things audiences will not forgive speakers for not being: prepared, comfortable, committed, and interesting (Lewis & Appenzeller, 1985; Helitzer, 1992). If the speaker concentrates on being prepared, committed, interesting, and making others comfortable, he/she will become an accomplished communicator in formal speeches as well as in interpersonal communications.

Preparation is essential because whenever a speaker talks to other people, the audience must have absolute confidence that the speaker knows what he/she is talking about. The listeners: (1) must have confidence that you know what you are talking about; (2) should feel that you know more about the subject then they do; (3) will feel that you spent time preparing your subject and analyzing your audience; (4) must feel there is a purpose to your message; and (5) must understand you are prepared to face a hostile or skeptical audience (Lewis & Appenzeller, 1985).

In Table 11-1 (Helitzer, 1992; Railey & Tschauner, 1993) is a preparation checklist that will save you time in preparing your next speech.

It is important for the speaker to be *committed* to the message. This is crucial. Very few speakers freeze up when they feel strongly about something. If you know what you are saying, why you are saying it, and care about what you are saying, you will say it well.

A speaker must be *interesting.* It is vital to the health of the audience. It is difficult to be interesting if you are not committed and vice versa. No audience will forgive you if you are boring.

It is essential to make others *feel comfortable.* But first you must be comfortable with yourself and your surroundings. People who are confident are usually comfortable with themselves. Others take their cues from you, so relax, keep things in perspective, and do not overreact. Maintain your sense of humor and take your work seriously but not yourself.

Table 11-1
Speech Preparation Checklist

1.   Speech preparation

- Evaluate the audience
- Consider the occasion
- Determine the length of the talk
- Determine the purpose of your speech—to entertain, inform, inspire, or persuade (good speeches often combine elements of all four)
- Decide on a central theme (If you cannot write your theme on the back of a a business card, it is too complicated.)
- Develop background knowledge
- Gather facts
- Consider the makeup of the audience
- Find a good opening line or story that relates to the speech (If it does not interest you, it will not interest your audience.)
- The speech can be in either the past, present, or future (Write down three to fivequestions the audience might ask you and answer them as the body of your speech.)

2.   Speech outline

- Introduction (Tell them what you are going to tell them.)
- Body (Tell them)
- Close (Tell them what you have told them and close the door.)

3.   Speech delivery

- Be interesting—use some memorable phrases and quotes
- Support statements with facts and examples
- Practice speech out loud in front of a mirror (also use either a tape recorder or video recorder)
- Time speech (add 20 seconds for actual delivery)
- Consider size of audience and room (adjust volume)
- Take your time to get audience's attention
- Concentrate on good eye contact

Management Tip

Publicity is free, but a sound plan for publicity does not happen by accident. It requires planning and careful execution. Public relations is concerned with attempting to create a favorable public opinion for the organization. Consistent media attention is the overall goal of the publicity plan. There are a number of guidelines that should be followed when developing publicity materials for the media and others, including but not limited to:

- Focus the materials on specific objectives;
- Create materials that are interesting to the editors and the reader and creative in nature;
- Make the materials newsworthy;
- Ensure the materials are accurate and neat;
- Fashion materials so they look professionally complete;
- Furnish background material regarding the submission;
- Provide artwork, graphics, or photographs with the submission;
- Focus manuscript (text) on intended audience;
- Develop and respect all relationships with media contacts; and
- Reinforce all relationships with the media contacts by expressing appreciation for their efforts.

Finally, there are few general pointers that should be considered regarding the interrelationship between the media and the organization's publicity practices:

- It is nice to know someone in the media, but it is not necessary to get free publicity. Editors have numerous pages and hours to fill and in many instances your news release may be very helpful to them. Therefore, do not hesitate to send materials to a media source.
- The key to success with the media is to package the news release in such a way it attracts attention allowing for a more in-depth examination by the editor.
- The best way to communicate with the media is by mail or electronic mail. Avoid using the telephone unless it is an emergency or for returning a call.
- It should be understood that publicity efforts do not have to appear in the most influential media to be wothwhile.

(Peterson, 1991a, 1991b; Olguin, 1991; Helitzer, 1993; Bucher & Krotee, 1993)

Legal Aspects Of Public Relations

The sport manager, when dealing with public relations, may become involved in legal matters in two ways: first with regard to what is written by and about the sports organization by outside sources, and second in the dissemination of information about a sport participant by the public relations office, coaches, or administrators of the organization. A situation may arise where an official of the organization may be asked to comment on a particular participant, coach, or employee. It is precisely this situation which requires careful thought and planning on the part of sport managers.

Occasionally, material written by the news media can constitute defamation which generally involves a communication that causes damage to an individual's good name or reputation. Defamation includes both libel and slander. Libel most frequently refers to communications which are written, printed and seen. Included in this area are the electronic media as well as the print media. Slander, on the other hand, involves messages that are spoken and heard. Regardless of the medium on conveyance, defamation occurs when false information is communicated to at least one other person and causes damage to the subject of the statement. The First Amendment of the U.S. Constitution provides for freedom of speech, but does not extend to defamatory remarks.

In 1964 the U.S. Supreme Court (*New York Times v. Sullivan*) set a precedent for contemporary writers. The court ruled that for a written statement concerning a public official to be libelous, it must be shown that actual intent to cause harm (malice) existed. Further, if a reporter was found to have lacked an intent to cause harm, the libeled person could not recover damages.

This case was also concerned with the legal interpretation of the term Public official. In cases subsequent to *Sullivan,* the concept of public official has been expanded to cover public figures. In sports organizations, the term public figures has been shown to include players, coaches, and administrators. The finding was based on the rationale that since sport exhibitions are provided for public enjoyment, legitimate criticism and comment can be made regarding the performance of the coach, team, or players. The opinions of sports writers and commentators are covered by the First Amendment to the U.S. Constitution which protects freedom of the press.

This broad coverage of the First Amendment to public officials extends only to their public activities. Their private lives do not fall within the same broad coverage as do their professional activities as a public figure. The balance between a sports figure's privacy and the public's right to know is not always clear.

The constitutional protection surrounding this right becomes important to the sports organization in two circumstances. First it can apply to what the media write and say about members of the organization, and secondly, it pertains to what the public relations department produces. It should, therefore, be noted that the writers in a sports organizations' public relations departments have to be as careful about violations as the media professionals.

According to the *Sullivan* ruling, any written material produced about public figures by the public relations professional must be shown to have actual malice to be found libelous. If, on the other hand, the individual cannot be shown to be a public figure, considerable restraint must be exercised.

The spoken word in public relations can also encounter legal difficulties. However, because the spoken word is less permanent than the written word, the courts have made it more difficult for the injured party to prove damages.

Sport managers are often involved with the distribution of photographs (still or motion) of the sports figures in their organization. This raises the issue of an image of an individual as personal property. It is generally illegal to use a person's name or likeness ...without consent by another to advertise its products, add luster to its name, or for any of its other business purposes. This issue has generated several implications for schools and universities, amateur sports bodies, and fitness centers. Before any sport organization uses any picture of its participants or clients, the public relations director should be certain to secure photographic releases.

The wording of such a release might be similar to the following:

> I hereby give those acting on behalf of right and permission to copyright and/or use, reuse, and/or publish, and republish photographic pictures of me. I do hereby waive any right to inspect and/or approve the finished photograph. This consent is given for any photographs which have been taken, are about to be taken, or will be taken.

These statements should be required of all athletes, coaches and administrators in the athletic department. It is also a good idea for all sports organizations to require such releases from employees, club members, or administrators. The sport manager should keep these on file should any question arise concerning the legality of the reproduction of a photograph by the organization.

Finally, several lawsuits have been filed regarding access of reporters to locker rooms. Generally speaking, the press has no right to gather information in places not open to the public. Considerable thought should be given to the development of policies relating to access to locker rooms. These policies should be distributed to all reporters in advance of sport competitions and should be strictly enforced.

Media Relations

In today's modern society with its sophisticated communications media, citizens are virtually bombarded by millions of words, pictures, and publications. Among this myriad of messages, public relations practitioners must find a way for material concerning sports organizations to be read, viewed, and heard. Ideally, the merits of the material should be sufficient in determining people's attitudes and actions. Yet, this is not the case. One must fight for survival and advancement. Some consolation exists in that all other public enterprises or institutions, such as the church, government, and political entities, must face the same challenge. Sports organizations, in general, need to realize that the support enjoyed for decades is fragile and the need for improving public relations programs is obvious.

Meeting the Needs of Media

There exists a major conflict between sports organizations and the media. The media want news and the sports organization wants publicity. This basic tenant often sets up an adversarial relationship between the sports organization and the press. It has been suggested that each group has a predisposition about the wants and needs of the other.

The editor, news director of the radio or television station, and other persons concerned with mass communications must seek programming that is new, appealing, and of interest to their audiences. These people are engaged in a very competitive business—their job is to sell subscriptions, advertising, or time. They must meet the interest and needs of their audiences in order to be competitive. For the news to be effective and interesting, it must contain human interest stories, personal items of success and failure, new programs, and reports on rare or unusual events. Therefore, the sports manager must be creative enough to develop stories within these parameters.

Sources of News

The sport manager has the following typical sources to secure news. This list of potential news provides some indication of the broad base of newsworthy sources which a typical sport organization can utilize. Searching for news is a responsibility of the sport manager or delegated to a public relations specialist. Some news events include the following:

- personnel changes, emphasizing the anticipated benefits to the students, clients, and to the organization,
- new teaching or coaching methods,
- additional services available or planned,
- new equipment or facilities and the use to be made of them,
- humorous incidents involving members, students, teachers, or staff,
- services rendered to the community, such as fund drives, charity activities,
- citizens' awards and recognition ceremonies for participation, contributions, or support of sport-related activities,
- member or student awards, prizes, and recognition,
- staff member trips, conference participation, extended education and the values thereof to students, clients and community,
- unusual field or study trips, stressing their educational values,
- special evening, summer, and extended education programs and their value to local citizens,
- testing programs and their purposes,
- participation in campaigns of civic importance, such as ecology, pollution, special programs for the economically, educationally, physically, or mentally disadvantaged, and others,
- books, articles, creative activities, and other related participation by teachers and staff,

- visits to the campus, store, or fitness center by celebrities and experts, speeches made to layperson's groups and professional groups,
- community relations activities, such as recreation programs for children, adults, and senior citizens,
- use of local experts as guest speakers,
- celebrations of venous anniversaries, such as 10th year of operation, league champions, etc.,
- announcements or coverage of something that is planned or was done for the first time,
- any records of significance, such as school or conference athletic records, or client weight lifting marks,
- national or international contests, such as athletic events, aerobics, or sport art,
- results of surveys, such as community or student interests in sport, extracurricular events, facilities, athletic competition, member exercise patterns, or client buying habits,
- athletically related stories, such as personal motivation, overcoming certain handicaps, personal values attached to athletic participation, background of training or preparation, correlation with academic pursuits, and other human or personal interest stories,
- employment internships, emphasizing the importance of this program in preparing students for vocations and the contributions to the employers in the community, and,
- clinics, workshops, and other special teaching and learning activities (Pronzan & Stotlar, 1992)

Press Conference and Media Relations

Press conferences should occur only when circumstances warrant it. Too many times public relations specialists call press conferences to disseminate information which should properly go in a news release. This causes the press to be wary of press conferences. It must be remembered that a press conference takes a great deal of time out of a reporter's day. Therefore, if the press conference is to be a success, the information must warrant it.

Written invitations should be received from five to seven days in advance of the conference; these should be formal invitations or letters on official stationary of the institution, signed by the host. The invitation should contain all the basic information such as the purpose, time, place, speakers, refreshments, and any other items of interest. The day before the conference, each invitee should receive a telephone call as a reminder to underline the importance of the conference.

A press-kit should be prepared in advance for all who attend the conference. This should contain a news release about the main subject of the conference, a full text of any important explanation or statement that is to be delivered at the conference, several photographs of the primary subjects, and some historical reference material.

When a press conference is held, the following guidelines should be implemented (in order):

1.   Establish a check-in desk; send a press kit immediately to all those who were invited but did not appear.
2.   Arrange to have a photographer on-hand; announce to all that the photographer's services are available at given times; arrange to have the photographer's products delivered immediately in person or by messenger.
3.   Newspaper and television photographers should be accorded full courtesy; it possible, assign a representative of your organization to each photographer to help contact subjects and to fully and properly identify them for the photograph.
4.   Know the deadlines of the newspapers that are most important to you; complete the conference no later than four hours before the deadline; adding any travel time to the four-hour leeway.

If the press conference is to be combined with a social function, consider the advantage of having the social function before or after the main purpose of the conference. If before, then the function can be adjourned at one time for all; if the social function follows the main purpose of the conference, some persons will leave immediately in order to prepare materials for the newspaper, radio, or television and the value of the social function is depreciated.

Press Release and Media Relations

The production of a news release (see Appendix for criteria for news releases) does not get it in print. The public relations professional must do several things to improve the chances of getting the release published. First, the public relations staff must compile and keep up-to-date mailing lists of potential news outlets. This list must be complete with the name of the reporter to whom the release should be routed. The multitude of information which flows to a newspaper is tremendous, and material can get lost in the shuffle if not properly addressed.

Publicity—Getting The Information
Seen, Heard, And Read

Publicity is one of the most important tools used in public relations, but it is not all-important. It cannot be substituted for good work or desirable action. However, it can be used to bring attention to these actions and to the sport organization in general.

Objective of Publicity

The primary objective of publicity is to draw attention to a person, the organization, or an event. An effective publicity program is required to obtain an individual's attention. Publicity will not sell tickets, raise funds, win supporters, retain members, or sell merchandise, but publicity can be helpful in conveying ideas to people so that these ends can be more easily attained.

Effect of Publicity

Publicity should be planned with these guidelines in mind: (1) too much publicity can be poor public relations, because often at a given point people tend to react negatively to excessive publicity; (2) the amount of publicity absorbed is important, not the amount released; (3) the amount of publicity disseminated does not necessarily equal the amount received or used; (4) the nature of the publicity eventually tends to reveal the character of the institution or department it seeks to promote, for better or worse; (5) some publicity an institution or department receives originates from outside sources; and (6) all public relations activities do not result in publicity (7) (Bronzan & Stotlar, 1992).

Principles of Good Publicity and Media Relations

The sport management practitioner can develop confidence and respect by adhering to some basic principles or guidelines. These include the following 10 ideas:

1. Be honest.
2. Don't try to block the news by use of evasion, censorship, pressure or trickery.
3. Be cooperative at all times; be accessible by telephone or in person at all times.
4. Be candid; don't seek trouble, but don't try to hide from it.
5. Don't pad a weak story; this practice tends to weaken credibility.
6. Use facts, not rumors, although initially they may be more detrimental than the rumor. Remember, facts limit the story; rumors tend to remove all boundaries.
7. Don't stress or depend upon off-the-record accounts. Remember, the job of the reporter is to get facts and report the story. Asking the reporter to abide with off-the-record requests is unfair and costly.
8. Give as much service to newspapers as possible. When news occurs, get the story out expeditiously. Hot news is desired by newspaper reporters, so one must be willing and able to supply newspapers with the stories, pictures, statistics they wish, as they want them prepared, and on time.
9. If a reporter uncovers a story, do not give the same story to another reporter. Treat it as an exclusive right.
10. Since news is a highly perishable commodity, remember that newspapers want news, not publicity.

Sport managers should become acquainted with the publishers, the highest ranking officer (the executive editor), the editor, the editorial page editor, and, finally, the managing editor, who is the working head of staff engaged in handling news. In addition to these individuals, a close working relationship is necessary with the sports editor, Sunday desk editor, and society editor. Of course, it is advantageous to also know the editors for the amusements, arts, and business sections.

Positive reinforcement is as important in public relations as it is in sports. One should act promptly to commend all persons involved in carrying a special story, promotional activity, or unusual action. Copies of the commendation should be mailed to all relevant members of the newspaper.

Summary

A public relations program is designed to influence the opinions of people within the targeted market through responsible and acceptable performance, based on mutually satisfactory two-way communication. In order to gain public sentiment, programs must familiarize not only customers/clients but the public in general with all aspects of the services and activities offered.

Learning Objective 1: Competently select a public relations agency.

Selecting a public relations agency is extremely important to any organization's public image. The public relations agency must understand the organization, its services, products, and programs as well as its customer base. Before selecting the agency, review carefully the agency's qualifications and previous work.

Learning Objective 2. Discuss the legal aspects of public relations.

The sport manager is responsible for all public relations from a sporting organization. It is important that he or she understand the legal issues surrounding defamation—libel and slander. This understanding must be passed on to the staff as a preventive measure. More than at any time in history, sport has an extremely high profile and is watched and listened to by millions. One small error in judgement at a critical time can spell disaster for the organization.

Learning Objective 3: Developing a public relations plan.

It is important to first agree that a public relations program is necessary for the organization. Once it is agreed that a public relations program is necessary, then resources to develop and implement a public relations plan must be provided. The primary resources required are human, financial, facility space, equipment (e.g., computers, printers, and scanners), and materials (e.g., funds for duplication, phones, postage, printing, software, etc). An organized public relations program should include serving as an information source, promoting confidence, gathering support, improving communications, correcting misunderstandings and misinformation, and evaluating the organization's services, products, and activities.

Learning Objective 4: Define the difference between internal and external public relations.

Internal public relations is communicating openly and often with personnel and members. The best promotion for an event can be negated if one of the employees or members gives a disgruntled response to the media. The best promoters of an organization are its employees and members.

External public relations is communicating with the outside publics external to the organization and its employees and members. This communication is done directly with the public(s) and through the media. These are prospective new members.

There are numerous avenues for getting the message out to the internal and external publics. They include, but are not limited to: (1) printed media, (2) pictures and graphics, radio, (4) television, (5) video, (6) posters, (7) exhibits, (8) brochures, (9) billboards and posters, (10) public speaking opportunities, (11) electronic mail, (12) Internet (web homepage), (13) direct mail, and (14) telemarketing.

Learning Objective 5: Understanding the importance of media relations.

Publications are most effective if they are prepared correctly, distributed efficiently, and are timely. All publications originating from the sport organization should meet the highest standards, particularly in the use of language, spelling, and grammar. Of course, the message or information conveyed should be subject to as little misinterpretation as possible. Some of the key criteria for sport publications are the following:

1. *Form.* The material should be readable, have sensory appeal, utilize a newspaper or other appropriate layout, and have a broad range of reader interest.
2. *Content.* The material should have cognitive appeal, inquiry satisfaction, source credibility, contrasting points of view, factual information, comprehensiveness, and personal interest.
3. *Response.* The object of the publication is to stimulate interest and action in many cases; this action may be either overt or covert, but in either case one seeks to instill certain attitudes and opinions. The use of slogans, phrases, or axioms that are easily remembered, repeated, and have meaning is a forceful method.

Tact, diplomacy, and friendship are the key laments in relationships with the media. The media can become an ally of the sports organization if the perspective is clear that each group has a job to do, they're not always the same, nor are they mutually incompatible.

Self-testing Exercise

1. What steps would you take in selecting a public relations agency to assist you in making your products, programs, and services something consumers not only need but want to purchase or become a associated with in the future?
2. You have been hired by the Greater Yarmouth YMCA as a consultant to develop a public relations program. What would be the steps taken to develop this PR program? Outline the final product to be presented to the Greater Yarmouth YMCA.
3. Communication, oral or written, is the key to success in a career or an organization. There have been thousands of books written about the art of communication. You are the organizer of the committee to bring an NHL Hockey Team to Mobile. Your first task is to gain strong community support to construct an ice hockey arena. The committee has suggested that you go on the banquet circuit and present the concept to all the civic groups, chambers of commerce, and other key decision-making groups. Therefore, you need to prepare a 20-30 minute speech that will be informative and excite these groups enough to become avid supporters of the concept.

    a. Prepare a 20-30 minute speech
    b. Videotape the speech and review
    c. Present the speech to your colleagues as a rehearsal before hitting the circuit.

4. Develop a consumer relations program for the Palm Beach Fitness and Racquet Club, including initial welcome, member services, follow-up, and consumer relations policies for the club.

References

Bronzan, Robert T., & Stotlar, David K. (1992). Public relations and promotions in sport. Daphne, AL: United States Sports Academy.

Bucher, Charles A., & Krotee, March L. (1993) *Management of physical education and sport.* (10th ed.). St. Louis, MO: C.V. Mosby Year Book.

Helitzer, Melvin. (1992). *The dream job: Sports publicity, promotion, and public relations.* Athens, OH: University Sports Press.

Lewis, Guy, & Appenzeller, Herb. (1985). *Successful sport management.* Charolettsville, VA: The Michie Company.

Olguin, Michael A. (1991) Vital marketing. *Fitness Management, (7)*3, 45-47.

Parkhouse, Bonnie L. (1996) The management of sport: Its foundation and application. (2nd ed.). St. Louis, MO: C.V. Mosby Year Book.

Peterson, James A. (1991a) Ten steps to effective publicity. *Fitness Management, (7)*12, 41.

Peterson, James A. (1991b) The power and nature of publicity. *Fitness Management, (7)*12.

Railey, Jim H., & Tschauner, Peggy Railey (1993) Managing physical education, fitness, and sports programs. (2nd ed.). Mountainview, CA: Mayfield Publishing Company.

Suggested Readings

Ailes, Roger. (1988). *You are the message.* Homewood, IL: Dow Jones-Irwin.
Frank, Milo O. (1986). *How to get your point across in 30 seconds—or less.* New York: Simon and Schuster.

PART IV

---◆---

FACILITY AND RISK MANAGEMENT

12

PLANNING NEW FACILITIES

◆ ─────────────────── ◆

After reading this chapter the student should be able to:

- understand pre-design planning, schematic design, construction documents, bidding, construction phase, and change orders,

- develop spaces and floor plans, and

- select an architect, space planning consultant, contractors, and engineers.

Introduction

By the turn of the century as the sport industry continues to change and expand based on the demands of the baby boomers and generation X (baby busters), the chances of a sport manager becoming involved in a construction project are very likely. A construction project, whether it be new construction or remodeling, is an exciting as well as a growth opportunity for the professional in the sport industry. All professionals need to know and understand building design and be prepared to respond when the opportunity to build a facility presents itself.

Depending on the circumstances, a construction project can range from a small renovation of an existing facility to construction of a new facility. The sport professionals who understand how to design and have constructed a facility within budgetary parameters meeting the programmatic goals with concern for user-efficiency, energy efficiency, and long-term maintenance will be far ahead of their colleagues. More than likely, they will have building opportunities come their way more frequently. Often the burden of developing a facility falls on the shoulders of the director, who many times has little or no experience nor training in designing a state-of-the-art facility.

This chapter has been developed to assist the sport professional in planning a comprehensive state-of-the-art facility. The intent, however, is not to provide an all-inclusive document but rather to provide a conceptual approach to the overall construction process. Yet, there will be provided some detailed information about specific areas within and without the facility.

Survey and Evaluation of Existing Facilities

Before deciding that a new facility is needed, it is important for the "building committee" to evaluate the current facility and its potential for renewal. Sport professionals must ensure that sport facilities can adequately support the programs and the enrollment loads for each program.

The initial step is to survey existing facility spaces and compare usage and adequacy of location. This data must be compared to accepted standards for the specific areas. The purpose for the evaluation is to reveal adequacies and inadequacies, and to recommend changes in the existing facilities to better facilitate the programs offered. Without such an evaluation and analysis, it is impossible to make decision(s) to modify existing facilities or to construct new ones, and to seek funding. The final report must prove conclusively to the owner(s) or park and recreation board or school board or financial institution that the improvements are needed to maintain current programming, provide future services, and maintain safety standards. The data collected must be sound and unbiased in order to support and illustrate the case.

The survey and evaluation should be conducted by the most knowledgeable and experienced members of the professional staff. These people must consult with the people most directly involved with use of each space or area. Further, inside or outside engineers familiar with electrical, mechanical, and structural aspects of the building must be consulted. Finally, a facilities analysis chart (Table 12-1) should be utilized to gather the appropriate data.

After completing the facilities analysis chart (Table 12-1), it is easy to determine current and future needs for a sport facility. The example indicates that the current facility is inadequate for present programming and grossly inadequate, based on estimated growth figures, for the future membership of the sport facility.

The Facility Planning Process

The first step in constructing a new facility or remodeling an old building is outlining the planning process. The planning process is the most fundamental and important phase in developing facilities.

The process includes a: (1) program analysis (a study to determine programmatic needs), (2) feasibility study (a study to ascertain what is possible), (3) master plan (this is the "road map" for the project), (4) cost analysis (a determination of project cost), (5) site selection (a study to determine site location options), and (6) design development (the architect designs a building based on the master plan), and financial plan (the steps to be followed to raise the necessary funds to construct the facility).

Table 12-1
Facilities Analysis Chart
Sport Center

A Space/ area	B Standard Current sf	B Standard Future sf	C Quantity/ sf	D Need Current sf	D Need Future sf	E Conclusions Adq. CF	E Conclusions Inadq. CF
Strength training	4,800	9,600	2,400	2,400	7,200		XX
Cardiovascular	960	3,000	800	160	2,200		XX
Aerobic Dance	2,500	7,500	2,400	100	5,100		XX
Games	1,250	2,500	1,500	0	1,000		XX
Multipurpose	4,800	9,600	0	4,800	9,600		XX
Swimming Pool	10,000	10,000	0	10,000	10,000		XX
Pro Shop	250	250	0	250	250		XX
Laundry	400	600	300	100	300		XX
Storage	250	500	800	0	0		XX
Lounge	900	900	1,100	0	0		XX
Lobby/Entrance	900	900	1,200	0	0		XX
Administration	800	800	600	200	200		XX
Men's lockers	1,500	5,000	1,200	300	3,800		XX
Women's lockers	1,800	5,700	1,200	600	4,500		XX
Tennis court	3	8	2	1	5		XX
Racquetball court	3	8	5	0	3		XX
Total	**32,410**	**58,650**	**13,500**	**18,910**	**45,150**		

Directions: After filling in **column A** using Table 1 move **column B** and complete it. Subtract **column B** from **column A** and fill in **column C** and then complete **column D**. Key: adq = adequate; inadq. = inadequate; C = current; F = future; sf = square foot

Planning is essential in making the building project a success. It can be time-consuming, frustrating, and in the end rewarding, particularly when the end result is pleasing and functional. No matter how much planning is completed there will always be something you would like to change after the project has been completed. This is not a failure in the process, just a fact of life. Most building projects from start to finish take between one and 10 years. A private concern can move much faster on a building project than a governmental or nonprofit agency. Thus, the range is from one to two years (private concern) and three to 10 years or longer with a governmental or nonprofit agency.

The key to successful planning is involving all the interested parties in the project. A team approach (participatory planning) is the best way to approach a building project, no matter how large or small. Participation of those affected is important to the overall success of the plan. Participation provides much needed information and a greater acceptance of a plan and its results. The team should include such persons as program specialists, administrators, clientele, local government officials, local financing representatives, and representatives from other policy-making bodies (e.g., representatives from local educational institutions, and the building consultant, architect, and/or engineer). However, if you are the owner of a small sport or fitness club, it is suggested you select a good architect and sport facility consultant and begin the process without a committee structure.

The advantages of participatory planning include:

- working together (administrators, program specialists, clients, and others) to develop common goals,
- involving the client from beginning to end,
- participating in decision-making rather than reacting to decisions made,
- limiting duplication of services, programs, and facilities,
- improving cooperation among communities and agencies rather than road blocks,
- improving communication, and
- improving support, credibility, and understanding is achieved.

The development of a participatory planning team and process can be done by following the steps below:

1. Establish a "building committee" that includes those persons listed earlier. This group should be diversified to ensure representation of as many segments and opinions of the community as possible, see Figure 12-1.
2. Develop procedures for identifying the needs and desires of the customers and the community, as well as what the community is willing to support.
3. Prepare a data base of demographic, programmatic, facility, financial, and other related information dealing with the aging population.
4. Compare survey results and statistical information to determine program and facility priorities.
5. Conduct public hearing(s) (public projects only) to obtain community input to supplement needs assessment results.
6. Appoint subcommittees to work in-depth on various aspects of the project, such as financial package, development of space and floor plans, programmatic needs, site selection, etc.
7. The building committee, after reviewing the results of the subcommittee work, should develop alternative solutions for meeting the needs.
8. The building committee should prioritize all solutions.
9. The building committee should decide the final direction(s) for the building project.

Figure 12-1
Building Committee Composition

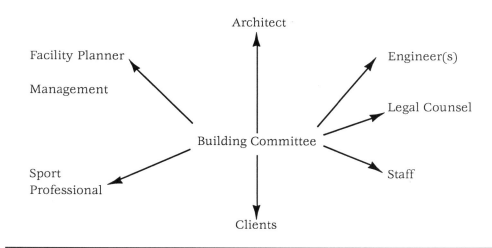

The Construction Opportunity

The initial task of the building committee is to prepare the building program or master plan. It is a statement that will be used to communicate the needs of the organization to the consultant(s), architect(s), and/or engineer(s). Further, this document will be used to sell the new building or major renovation to those who must agree to finance the project.

The building program is a written description of purpose/mission, objectives and timelines; organizational structure and function; programmatic needs; interrelationships of health/fitness activities; other program activities; and the proposed future use of the facility. This document must be written well in advance of selecting site(s), consultant(s), architect(s), and/or engineer(s). It is important that this statement be written in a concise and organized manner.

The program writer(s) (facility manager or building committee) should employ the following guidelines in preparing the building program:

- Write clearly and concisely,
- Outline program needs in a "blue sky" fashion as well as minimally,
- Root the project in fiscal reality,
- Evaluate current programs to determine if new programs should be emphasized, old ones should be eliminated or modified, or old and new combined,
- Consider all indoor and outdoor facility needs,
- Be aware that location of facilities will affect the program offered, and
- Distribute all draft copies of the document to all contributors for review and comment.

Sample Outline of a Building Program
for a Sport Center

1. Health/fitness center program objectives
   a. health promotion,
   b. health programming,
   c. fitness screening and prescription,
   d. fitness programming,
   e. recreational programming, and
   f. other.
2. Basic assumptions to be addressed
   a. facilities will provide for a broad health/fitness program,
   b. facilities will provide easy access for handicapped,
   c. facilities will provide for easy use by older men and women,
   d. existing facilities will be programmed for use,
   e. facility expansion will be provided for in the planning, and
   f. outdoor facilities will be located adjacent to the indoor facilities.
3. Trends which affect health/fitness planning for all ages/levels
   a. emphasis on individual exercise programs,
   b. a surge in walking programs,
   c. the strength training movement,
   d. the cardiovascular concern,
   e. new health promotion programs for aging people,
   f. introduction of functional fitness testing,
   g. increase in Federal and state funding for health/fitness programming, and
   h. new products.
4. Explanation of current and proposed programming
   a. health promotion,
   b. health programming,
   c. fitness programming,
   d. fitness screening,
   e. health screening, and
   f. recreational programming.
5. Preliminary data relative to the proposed new facilities
   a. existing indoor facilities square footage consisting of program areas, equipment, storage, and administrative areas,
   b. a priority listing for the proposed new indoor area with square footage,
   c. existing outdoor facilities broken down by area, and
   d. a priority listing for the proposed new outdoor facilities.
6. Space needs and allocations in the proposed new facilities
   a. multipurpose area,
   b. strength training,
   c. cardiovascular,
   d. fitness testing,
   e. swimming pool,

  f. racquetball and tennis courts,
  g. walking/jogging trails,
  h. lobby-lounge,
  i. administrative complex,
  j. conference/class rooms,
  k. game room, and
  l. others.
7. Service areas
  a. locker, shower, and drying rooms,
  b. toilets,
  c. equipment and storage,
  d. custodial,
  e. sauna, steam room, hydrotherapy pool area,
  f. laundry,
  g. mechanical,
  h. staff lounge/kitchen, and
  i. others.
8. Projected use for present facility(ies)
9. Space relationships—the relationships each space has with another, and
10. Equipment list—all movable and fixed items identified in the document
  a. weight equipment,
  b. cardiovascular,
  c. fitness testing,
  d. lounge/office furniture,
  e. audio,
  f. visual,
  g. kitchen, and
  h. other.

Selecting an Architect/Engineer/Consultant

After the building program and facility analysis chart have been completed, the building committee's next task is to select a consultant, architect, and/or engineer. This may be the most critical aspect of the committee's task. Before the committee can begin, this task must decide what type(s) of professional(s) it needs to complete the project.

Many architectural firms have either their own engineering department in-house or a working relationship with an engineering firm. It is best to allow the architectural firm to arrange for the most compatible engineering relationship.

However, it is advisable to employ a consultant who is experienced in the area of health/fitness facility planning to assist the committee and the chosen architect. Many times the consultant can be very helpful in this team effort because of expertise in designing the specific spaces with which the architect and committee may not be familiar. The consultant, if experienced, may be a very valuable asset when selecting an architectural and engineering firm.

What should the committee consider when selecting a consultant? The basic considerations in selecting the consultant are:

1.   educational background,
2.   work experience,
3.   planning experience,
4.   proximity to project,
5.   reputation,
6.   ability to work with architects and engineers,
7.   ability to understand and read blueprints and specification documents, and
8.   ability to understand the organization's programs and the future of such programs and others.

The committee can develop a list of consultants by contacting the American Alliance for Health, Physical Education, Recreation and Dance (AAHPERD, Reston, VA), American Association for Fitness and Business (AFB, Indianapolis, IN), other health/fitness facilities, or a local college or university that has a department of physical education, exercise science, kinesiology, recreation, or sport management. The selection process should be similar to that process used to select an architect.

What should the committee consider when selecting an architect? The basic considerations for selecting an architect are the following:

- membership in the American Institute of Architects (AIA),
- a license to practice in the state where the facility is to be built,
- a good reputation,
- good references,
- examples of work on similar projects,
- close enough proximity to the project to provide weekly visitations,
- ability to work with the "building committee,"
- ability to recommend reliable and respected contractors and subcontractors, and
- ability to provide strong competent supervision for the project.

The committee should develop a list of prospective architectural firms experienced in this area. A list can be solicited from the American Institute of Architects (AIA, Washington, D.C.) or the American Association for Fitness in Business (AFB, Indianapolis, IN) or by contacting other sport facilities that have just been completed or are under construction. After the list is completed, contact each firm and request a proposal outlining what the firm can do for the committee. Once the proposals have been gathered, reviewed, and ranked, select the top five firms for interview. Interview these firms and select the firm that can provide the best service and work cooperatively with the committee. After selection of the architectural firm, a contractual agreement will be completed and signed. This legally binding contract will be the official AIA document B141, a standard form of agreement between the client and architect. The responsibilities of the architectural team include reviewing the building program, evaluating the site for the proposed building, schematic design, design development, construction documents, bidding for the contractor, and construction supervision.

There are three types of engineers who will be working on the building, they are civil, structural, and mechanical/electrical. The *civil engineer* is responsible for the following tasks: grading and land movement plans, geometric layout of new improvements, plans for new roads and street pavements, utility plans, and plans for water collection system and sanitary sewers. The *structural engineer* is concerned about determining possible structural systems and materials, providing cost of preferred systems and materials, and designing the final structure to meet architectural requirements. Finally, the *mechanical/electrical engineer* will provide such information as: specifications for heating and air conditioning equipment, drawings and specifications for power and lighting, determinations of plumbing requirements, and the design of any communication system (security, PA, music, closed circuit TV, etc.).

Site Selection

The committee will have selected the building site prior to the completion of the building program. The considerations for site selection include:

1. access to the site,
2. circulation within the site,
3. parking,
4. water supply,
5. sewage disposal,
6. electrical supply,
7. telephone service,
8. other utilities including oil/natural gas transmission lines, or cable TV,
9. structures to be constructed,
10. on-site sources of pollution,
11. easements and other legal restrictions,
12. zoning requirements must be obtained and clearly understood. Changing the zoning is usually time consuming and expensive and frequently not possible,
13. record any existing (activities) uses on the site,
14. climatic conditions that are prevalent in the area,
15. the economic impact of a site location is a key factor in deciding where to locate,
16. the important land characteristics, and
17. there are a variety of local and regional factors that need to be considered when selecting a site (Fogg, 1986).

The most important aspect of site selection is—location, location, location. If the site is not in the most accessible location with a high profile for people to recognize, it will have a negative effect on the success of the venture.

Designing the Facility

After completing many of its major tasks, including writing the building program, completing the Facility Analysis Chart, recommending a site selection, and employing a sport facility planner/consultant, an architectural firm, and an engineering firm, the committee is ready to have some real fun. The next phase is to begin the facility design for either new construction, renovation, or a combination. This starts with a schematic design prepared by the architect.

Schematic Design

The architect takes the written building program developed by the committee and places it into a conceptual drawing of the new facility. The architect begins with rough drawings of the interrelationships of requested facilities and space allocation. Sketch plans are then prepared showing the overall arrangement of areas and how they connect.

The *schematic drawings* include a site plan, which denotes the new building and how it coordinates with an existing or new site, and preliminary drawings of various floor plans showing the projected scope of the design layout. At this stage all drawings are in sketch form so that the committee and consultant with the architect can make modifications. It is *important* to take the time to *understand* every aspect of the initial design. *It is the committee's obligation to ask questions and consider every facet before approving the initial schematic drawings.*

After the schematic drawings have been approved, a preliminary estimate can be made of construction costs. If the estimate is beyond the committee's budget, another series of meetings will be required with the consultant and architect to reduce the building project. Once the building project is in line with the proposed budget, then the next step can commence, designing the floor plans.

Floor Plans

The floor plans indicate all rooms drawn to scale and in their designed shape. As each room is designed, the architect's considerations include: intended users and uses for each space, physical requirements, relationship with other spaces, and equipment.

Once a floor plan has been completed, it is reviewed for traffic flow, crowd control, entrances and exits, city/county/state codes, space utilization, storage, and potential safety and security problems. Now the architect will meet with the "building committee" and consultant to evaluate every step that a given member would experience on a daily basis, including parking, facility entrance, check-in, locker room entrance, access to all activity areas, and facility exit. The layout will be further reviewed for safety, security, and emergency response. It is important to consider each type of member that will be using the center, including older populations, the handicapped, and children. After the committee, consultant and architect have completed this review, select current members, including older people, men, women, and the handicapped, to perform a similar "walk-through." These two reviews, although they take time to complete, can and have reduced to a minimum and alleviated many major design errors and problems.

Construction Phase

Before construction can commence, the architect must prepare a number of final documents, including: construction drawings, a specification manual, and bid documents. The construction drawings are broken down into trades, such as A-1 for architectural drawings, S-1 for structural drawings, P-1 for plumbing drawings, M-1 for mechanical drawings, E-1 for electrical drawings, and C-1 for communication drawings.

The specification manual contains a detailed verbal description of the project. The contractor uses the manual and the graphic designs to build the building. Think of the construction drawings as a road map and the specification manual as a tour guide book.

After the construction documents (construction drawings and specification manual) are completed, the architect or owners announce that the building project is ready to be bid upon. A *bid* is a contractor's best estimate of construction costs for a project. The announcement will be published in the newspaper and sent to a list of contractors in the local and regional area. The bidders are given 4-6 weeks to complete and submit their bids. It is recommended that the project be bid in three parts as follows: general, electrical, and mechanical. This way of bidding will reduce the costs of construction and allow more contractors to be involved in the project.

In competitive bidding, the contractors are asked to provide information including experience, financial condition, and ability to be bonded and to submit references. They further submit their bids, providing the price of the main project (guaranteed for specific time period) and any add or delete alternatives. An *add alternate* is part of the project that could be added if money is available; whereas, a *delete alternate* is the amount of money saved if this part of the project is deleted. Traditionally, the lowest bidder is selected for the project. However, it is not always advisable to go with the lowest bidder. Considerations should be given to references, previous work completed, personnel involved, and the overall construction market before such a decision is made. The key to competitive bidding is starting with reputable construction firms until you eventually select one considered acceptable.

The architect assists the owner, the owner's lawyer, and the insurance advisor in the preparation of the contract. The AIA has published forms that cover most types of contractual agreements. Because these forms have been approved by the Associated General Contractors of America, it is best to use these forms wherever possible. These contracts include payment schedules, procedures for change-of-orders, project time table and completion date, and penalties for late completion.

The owner may wish to hire his own construction manager who reports directly to the owner and not the architect or contractors. However, the architectural firm may provide this service to the owner. In any case it is *important* that there is a construction manager to represent the owner or owner and architect.

The construction manager should be hired during the design phase. The expertise the construction manager has in regard to all aspects of construction will be very helpful during the design phase. Generally, construction managers are hired on a cost-plus-fee basis, because their services vary from project to project. The fixed cost is usually between 5 and 8% of the total construction cost, whereas the additional fees include reimbursable expenses and services not covered in the general agreement.

Change-orders

Change-orders are a fact of life in construction projects. They are also very expensive for the owner and should be avoided like the "plague". Many times change-orders are necessary, but they should be kept to a minimum. All construction project budgets should have included a contingency line item between 10 and 15% of the total project.

General Facility Planning Considerations

When designing a facility, planners need to consider many details from traffic patterns to electrical systems to climate control. The pages that follow outline many details that are necessary for planners to consider.

Traffic Patterns within Building

1. The location of locker and shower areas is a key to the smooth operation of the facility and ease of programming. These areas need to be easily accessible to indoor and outdoor facilities.
2. Locker and shower areas need to be given special consideration because of the wet and confined areas. Make sure there is a separate drying area large enough to accommodate 25 percent of the shower room capacity and located between the shower and locker areas. The exit from the locker room should not be through wet or drying areas.
3. The placement of service, activity, instructional, and spectator areas should provide for efficient means of supervising those using the facilities.
4. Careful consideration must be given to the relationships between activity, instructional, and service areas so that the placement and size of corridors, lobbies, stairs, and doors are efficient and adequate to meet the traffic needs.
5. Spectator areas should be separated from activity space and the spectators should enter directly into the spectator spaces from the outside or lobby without going through other activity or service areas.
6. Areas of the building that will require truck delivery or pickup should be grouped together to reduce the number of delivery points, loading docks, and large overhead or double wide doors.
7. The public restrooms and entrances to these areas must be adequate in size to service the expected population.

8. The entrance foyer to the facility must be large enough to accommodate the anticipated population and uses including membership sales, member check-in, public telephone(s), cloakroom, information area, and entrance to public restrooms.

9. Stairways need to be given careful consideration. There should be at least two located at the extremes of the building. They should be wide enough to handle anticipated peak loads, but should be two-lane stairways. They should be well lighted with railings. The risers should not exceed 6 1/2 inches, and treads should be at least 10 1/2 inches measured from riser to riser. Circular or winding stairs should not be used.

10. City, county, and state building codes will dictate where exit doors need to be placed; however, the following is a good rule of thumb: an exit will be located within 100 feet of a doorway of every room designed for occupancy and every floor should have a minimum of two exits remote from one another. All exits should be lighted appropriately.

11. All doors should open outward, with the entire door swinging free of the door opening. Double doors should be provided with a removable center mullion so that each door will operate independently with one such opening at least 36 inches wide. Doors leading to and from wet areas (i.e., showers, pools, or laundry), should be heavy-duty and moisture-resistant. Finally, exterior doors should be recessed to protect them from the elements. If not recessed they need to be protected from the weather by projections, overheads, or soffits.

Surface Materials

There are various surfaces suggested for floors, walls, and ceilings for the different areas in the facility. The specific considerations include:

1. In the facility there will probably be only one space with a wooden floor, that being the dance area. They remainder of the areas will be carpeted, tiled, or a roll-out resilient synthetic flooring. In choosing the floor surface, the following must be considered in regard to the surface: flexibility, durability, initial cost, and long-term maintenance costs. There are two synthetic flooring systems. The first is a plasticized polyvinyl chloride (PVC) which is primarily prefabricated and sent to the site in either rolls (like rugs) or sheets and glued to the floor. The second system, polyurethane, is either poured in place or produced in factory prefabricated sheets. Either system can be used; however, the roll-out or sheet systems glued to the floor are far superior in resiliency because of their uniform thickness versus the poured floor, which is self-leveling in nature, and the thickness can vary from thin to thick throughout the floor. Further, it is easier to repair sheet materials than poured.

2. Walls should not only be considered as barriers to segregate, but also as barriers to sound, light, heat, cold, and moisture. Other considerations for walls should include acoustical, moisture-resistance, heat/cold loss, and texture properties.

3.   Serious consideration should be given to the roof for the facility. It should not be flat, but rather sloped or pitched to shed moisture rather than retain it.
4.   Ceilings considerations should include insulation, acoustics, aesthetics, and maintenance. False ceilings with catwalks above them are effective for maintenance and repair of lighting and ventilating systems, particularly in racquetball and pool areas.

Sound and Acoustics (see appendix for specifics)

1.   The most troublesome aspect of any project is the acoustical environment. It is *important* that an acoustical engineer is consulated about the project.
2.   Hard surfaces reflect sound and produce reverberations, and soft surfaces absorb sound and produce dead areas. Therefore, most surfaces have some materials with sound-absorbing qualities in order to balance the sonic environment for good hearing conditions.
3.   Unwanted sound can be reduced by using insulation in walls, using sound baffles, and lining or covering ducts with sound-absorbent, fire-resistant materials. Further, double-wall construction can be used to reduce the transmission of sound. This is done by alternating studs in such a manner that there is no through connection from one wall surface to another.
4.   Machinery vibration or impact sounds can be reduced by use of the proper floor covering and/or by installing the machinery on floating or resilient mountings. Sound locks, such as double walls or doors, are needed between noisy areas and adjoining quiet areas. Improper location of doors can create noise problems.

Electrical Systems

An electrical engineer should be consulted for the design of the electrical, lighting, fire-alarm, security, program-signal, audiovisual, computer, and PA systems. Electrical considerations should include:

Illumination

1.   Full consideration should be given to current and future program plans. The increasing use of electrically operated equipment, higher standards for illumination, and special audiovisual equipment should be anticipated.
2.   There are two considerations relating to illumination. The first is the amount of light needed followed by the quality of light. You may want to secure an illuminating engineer to assist in this task.
3.   The measurement of light intensity at a given point is called a footcandle. Table 12-2 presents suggested levels of illumination for specific areas.

Table 12-2
Illumination Requirements

Area	Foot Candles on Task
Testing Area	100
Corridors/stairwells	20
Dance/exercise	50 (with rheostats)
Multipurpose	80
Strength training/cardiovascular	50
Locker/shower	30
Racquetball	70
Tennis	70
Lobby/lounge/foyer	50-70
Offices	70-100
Storage/custodial	30-50
Swimming pools	50
Toilets	30

*Adopted from *Planning Facilities for Athletics, Physical Education, and Recreation* by Richard B. Flynn (1985).

4. Make sure the lighting system can be easily maintained, repaired, replaced, and cleaned.
5. The lighting system for all areas, except large multipurpose rooms, racquetball courts and swimming pools, should be fluorescent. The multipurpose rooms, racquetball courts, and swimming pools should have metal halide lighting rather than mercury or sodium vapor.
6. Each area should have night lights installed that burn continually. These lights are extremely important for safety and security purposes and should have separate controls.
7. Provisions for outside lighting, emergency and exit lights, are important and should be given proper consideration.
8. Consider the use of natural lighting using skylights and glass-enclosed corridors and stairwells. There should be light sensors installed for each skylight area to automatically control the artificial light.

Fire-alarms

The fire-alarm system is a separate system that operates independently from all other electrical systems. The system must meet all state and local fire laws and regulations. It should be an audible and visual system (strobe lights) and have an indicator board to pinpoint the fire's location.

Program-signal System and Other Systems

The program-signal system is one that is controlled by a master clock including buzzers, chimes, gongs, and an automatic security system. There are other systems that need to be considered, including audiovisual security, public address, and emergency assistance.

Electrical Service Controls

There are many electrical controls that need to be considered for a health/fitness center including:

1. All light controls for the various program areas should be centralized in the control area.
2. The controls for the basketball backboards and room dividers should be located in the central control area.
3. The central control area should have a bank of security monitors that scan all program areas, corridors, stairwells, and lobby/lounge.
4. The electrical service to the building should be underground to ensure safety of all clients.
5. Main service panels with main service switches, meters, and main light and power panels should be located so as to prevent entrance by anyone except those authorized.
6. The controls for the different program-signal systems should be centralized in the control area.
7. Three-way switches should be provided at the foot and head of stairs, near each end of corridors, and near doorways of large activity spaces.

Services for Electrical Equipment

Every facility has numerous pieces of specialized equipment that need electrical wiring and connections. Careful planning is needed when developing the electrical system. Consideration must be given to the following:

1. Motors that operate wenches for backboards and overhead curtains and doors; exhaust fans; blowers for heating, cooling, and ventilating.
2. Strategically located receptacles for heavy-duty cleaning equipment.
3. Wiring for hand and hair dryers.
4. Wiring for kitchen and laundry areas.
5. Wiring for computers, floor fans, treadmills, etc.
6. Ground fault interrupters for receptacles in wet areas, such as swimming pools.
7. Special wiring for pools such as pumps, underwater vacuum cleaners, and special lighting.

Climate Control

The selection of climate control systems should be made with special consideration for economy of operation, flexibility of control, quietness of operation, and capacity to provide desirable thermal conditions. The design and location of all climate control equipment should provide for possible future expansions. The climate control system consists of heating, ventilating, and air-conditioning. In designing the climate control system the services of a mechanical engineer will be essential and the engineer's considerations should include:

1. The peak loads a space will endure,
2. The provision of variable controls to supply the proper amount of fresh air and total circulation for maximum occupancy in any one area,
3. The provision of humidity control for wet areas and the swimming areas,
4. The noise level of the system during operating periods,
5. Maintaining separate temperature and humidity controls for swimming areas,
6. Insulating all steam, hot water, and cold water,
7. Color coding all pipes for safety,
8. Exhausting dry air through the locker rooms and damp air from the shower room to the outside,
9. Providing at least four air changes per hour without drafts,
10. Installing locking type thermostats in all areas, with guards to protect then from damage,
11. Locating thermostats for the highest efficiency,
12. Zoning the areas for night use,
13. Eliminating drafts on participants, and
14. The selection of the most cost-effective climate control system.

Security and Safety

The sport facility presents unique security and safety problems. Security is accomplished in two ways: constructing the facilities according to a plan that allows for maximum security, and adopting an administrative plan for the direction and control of all persons using the building.

The following are some design considerations for security:

1. Avoid open and descending stairways, walled entries, and deep-set entrances,
2. All entrances and exits should be well lighted from dusk until dawn,
3. The exterior of the building should be well lighted,
4. All corridors should be continuous and straight and lined up with entrance doors, providing a commanding view of the doorway and the corridor,
5. Avoid angular corridors, and eliminate cubbyholes,
6. Night lighting should be installed in the building using separate wiring and control switches that are key operated,

An example of outdoor lighting for sidewalks or parking areas at Indiana State University, Terre Haute, Indiana. (Photo: Tom Sawyer)

7. Good door framing, substantial doors, and heavy-duty hardware and locks should be provided that will hold up against wear and abuse,

8. Lock/key system should be developed featuring:
    • building master lock/key plan,
    • lock with lock-tumbler adjustments so that an area may have its own control and authorization, and
    • the building should be divided into areas with area master keys,

9. An annunciator system in which outside or other doors (swimming pool) may be connected to an electrically controlled detection system (if the door is opened illegally or tampered with an audible signal will sound at the site and a light will flash and an audible signal will sound at the central control panel),

10. A sonar detection system or a sound amplication system can be installed in the pool area that will announce illegal use or entry, and

11. A closed-circuit television system, inside and outside the building, should be installed to monitor all entrances, exits, and activity areas.

The designers must also consider the safety of the users of the building. The safety considerations should include the following:

1. A visual and audible emergency alarm system installed in the swimming pool, sauna, steam room, and whirlpool/hot tub area to alert all personnel to any emergency,

2. A similar system as outlined above for the fitness testing area,

3. All activity spaces should be free of objects or floor plates which set up above the floor level,

4. Shower and dressing room floors should be kept free of objects and obstruction that may cause foot injury,

5. Shower space should be equipped with towel bars, nonslip floors, and hot water controls that will not allow the water temperature to exceed 120 degrees,

6. Areas for vigorous activity, where combative or competitive sports are engaged in should have floor and/or wall covering to protect participants, and

7. Doors to steam rooms and dry-heat rooms (sauna) should be capable of being locked from the outside when the area is unsupervised. Steam room controls should be set not to exceed a maximum room temperature of 130 degrees. This control should be tamper proof.

Handicapped Access

The Americans with Disabilities Act (ADA) was signed into law July 26, 1990, by President Bush. The ADA became effective July 26, 1992. The ADA makes it illegal for employers who are covered to discriminate in employment against qualified individuals who have disabilities. Further, reasonable accommodation must be made for the disabled person, unless such an accommodation would impose undue hardship on the employer. Sport facilities and employee recreation organizations, need to review the Act in its entirety (Public Law 101-336; 42 U.S.C. 12101-12213 [1991]).

An example of a handicap shower area. (Photo: Tom Sawyer)

Under the law certain protections are extended to those with statutory disabilities in the areas of: employment; government services; places of public accommodation; public transportation; and telecommunications. Health clubs, fitness and exercise facilities, health care provider offices, day care or other social service establishments, as well as gymnasiums, health spas and other places of exercise or recreation are all covered under the ADA. Most of these facilities will be required to comply with the provisions of the law when dealing with members of the public. The remainder of this section will deal with the ADA's Title III: Public Accommodations and Commercial Facilities.

It is important that facility planners become familiar with the ADA requirements. The following list will assist the planner in gaining more information about the ADA and its impact on public facilities:

- Sports Complex for the Handicapped
  The 52 Association, Ossining, N.Y. 10562

- The John H. Cole Recreation Center
  31st and G Streets, S.E.
  Washington, D.C. 20019

- Broken Bowl Picnic Ground
  Willamette National Forest
  USDA-Forest Service
  210 East 11th Avenue
  Eugene, OR 97401

- The Widener Trail
  Schuylkill Valley Nature Center
  Hagyps Mill Road
  Philadelphia, PA 19128

- Chapter VIII-Planning for the Handicapped Planning
  Facilities for Athletics, Physical Education and Athletics
  The Athletic Institute & American Alliance
  for Health, Physical Education, Recreation, and Dance 1985
  1900 Association Drive
  Reston, VA 20191

- Office on the Americans with Disabilities Act
  Civil Rights Division
  U.S. Department of Justice
  P.O. Box 66118
  Washington, D.C. 20035-6118
  (202)514-0301 [voice]
  (202)514-0383 [TDD]
  (202)514-6193 [Electronic Bulletin Board]

- Mr. John McGovern
  Executive Director
  Americans with Disabilities Consultants, Inc
  St. Charles, IL 60174

Finally, it is recommended that people with disabilities be involved in the planning of the facility, especially if it is a public facility. (See appendix for specific guidelines for construction).

Indoor Facilities

Planners must take into consideration a variety of indoor activity areas when designing a facility. These areas need to be designed to meet the needs of all age groups. Further, for information about specific game line layout, consult with the governing body (interscholastic athletics—National Federation for High School Activities Associations; intercollegiate athletics—National Collegiate Athletic Association) for the activity. After reading the following pages, the student will have an understanding of indoor facility needs.

Multipurpose Area

Description: A multipurpose area is a space that can be used for a variety of activities from basketball to badminton to jogging/walking to volleyball, and others. Years ago they were called gymnasiums, and in many instances they are still recognized as gymnasiums by many people.

Before beginning serious planning of this space, numerous questions need to be answered, including the following:

1. How will the area be used by the professional staff and participants?
2. What kinds of health, fitness, recreational, and other activities are planned to be held in the space?
3. How will participants enter and exit the space?
4. Is there a need for spectator seating?
5. Is there a need for a large entrance door for receiving equipment?
6. How much storage is needed in the area?
7. Is there a need for overhead doors?
8. Is there to be a custodial space in the area?
9. What type of flooring is most appropriate for activities planned and ease of maintenance and operations?
10. Should the running area be ground level or elevated?
11. How high should the ceiling be?
12. Are dividers needed when multiple activities are scheduled for the space?
13. Will there be spectator space?

A good example of a graphic that has been painted on a wall of a multipurpose area. Multipurpose areas have four tall walls that are usually blank, graphics such as the one in the picture can put life into a very blah environment. (Photo: Tom Sawyer)

Size: The size of the multipurpose space needed for a given facility will depend on the following factors:

•   estimated peak participation periods,
•   activities planned for the area, and
•   number of spectators.

Wall(s): The walls should be of masonry blocks painted with an epoxy paint in a bright, cheerful color covered with appropriate graphics depicting the use(s) of the space. The masonry blocks on the interior walls should be filled with insulation to deaden the sound(s). The surface of the walls should be smooth to reduce dirt collection and allow uses such as rebounding.

Floor: The floor should be a multipurpose surface that is easy to maintain. The most appropriate surface for this area is resilient synthetic material. This can be plasticized polyvinyl chlorides (PVC's) or polyurethanes. Whichever is chosen it should be factory prefabricated sheets rather than poured surfaces. A wood surface can be inserted for use as a competition basketball/volleyball court or a portable wooden floor can be purchased.

Ceiling: The roof should be designed with a pitch rather than flat to reduce leakage problems in the future. The interior ceiling will be constructed of exposed steel painted beams with sound buffers added to reduce acoustical problems. The beams will be strong enough to support climbing ropes, basketball frames, and a suspended jogging track.

Electrical: There will be numerous outlets around the perimeter at just above floor level, others on the steel ceiling beams which can be lowered to floor level, stationary outlets on the steel beams for the basketball and curtain wenches, at least four 220 volt outlets on the perimeter for cleaning machines, outlets in the storage and custodial spaces, exit signs on all exit doors, and outlets for clocks on the four walls.

The lighting system for the area needs to be able to produce 70 footcandles of illumination, achieving a brightness balance and eliminating extremes in brightness and glare. The recommended lighting fixture is metal halide. The lighting should be designed for ease of maintenance.

There should be a control center at the front desk to control all lights and raising and lowering of basketballs and curtains.

Sound: Large rectangular spaces like this are hard to design for a total audible environment. Therefore, it is imperative that an acoustical engineer is consulted during the design phase of this space. Sound-absorbing materials must be used in order to balance the sonic environment for good hearing conditions.

Climate Control: This area must be designed for appropriate heating, cooling, and humidity control. The space is large and efforts must be made for the economy of operation, flexibility of control, quietness of operation, and capacity to provide desirable thermal conditions. Do not forget humidity control (55%), or your participants will be complaining of dry mouths and throats during the winter months.

Security: All exterior doors should be alarmed with silent and audible alarms. There should be emergency lighting provided for times when the power fails or in case of fire. There should also be at least four lights provided.

Special Considerations:

- The running/walking track should have a coarse, synthetic covering to absorb short spikes. If the running/walking track is overlaid on the basketball courts, it is recommended that the space be enlarged to accommodate a track that does not compromise the basketball courts or install a suspended running/walking track.
- The custodial space will have a dyed concrete floor, industrial sink, shelves and cabinets, an overhead door and a regular door.
- The storage space will have a dyed concrete floor, shelves, pegs for nets, cabinets, and an overhead door.
- The basketball backboards should be pulled to the ceiling for storage using a powerized wench as will the divider curtains, which are 1/3 vinyl and 2/3s mesh.
- There should be a public address system and scoreboards.

Strength Training Area

Description: This area will be one of the most popular spaces in the facility. You should expect a mixture of dedicated bodybuilders, recreational weight lifters, dedicated fitness and body tone people, and novices who are just getting interested in strength training. There will be an equal number of men and women involved in strength training programs. Further, this area needs to include space for free weights, strength training machines, and cardiorespiratory equipment. The designer must consider all these variables and create a room that will fit the needs of all groups.

The designer needs to define the use of the space. This is done by responding to the following questions:

- What programs will be offered (i.e., circuit training, free weights, cardiorespiratory)?
- What is the size of the total membership or the membership registered to use the strength training area?
- What is the approximate peak demand for the area?
- What are the equipment preferences (i.e., a mixture of free weights and machines, free weights only, machines only)?
- Is there a high demand for separate or coed areas?
- What type of flooring would be most appropriate?
- Has the equipment been chosen? If yes, who is the vendor and what are the specific dimensions of the equipment and what is the proposed layout?

Size: The strength training area will include coed free weight, strength training, and cardiorespiratory areas. A minimum of 9,000 sf is recommended for this space with at least a 10' ceiling. Many new strength training areas are inadequate when they open, because the designer did not perceive the popularity of the activity during the design stage.

A neat way to store personal articles while in the strength training area. (Photo: Tom Sawyer)

Walls: Three of the walls should be solidly covered with materials that will reduce sound internally as well as externally. The walls should be painted with an epoxy for ease of cleaning. There should be graphics provided to make the walls come alive. Further, there should be numerous mirrors placed around the walls. The fourth wall should be constructed of durable glass and face into the lobby/lounge area (with drapes) to further encourage greater use of the area. There should be at least one bulletin board for each area (i.e., cardiorespiratory, weight machines, and free weight) in the strength training space.

Floor: The floor should be carpeted with a good quality commercial carpet brightly colored in the cardiorespiratory and machine areas. In the free weight area, the floor should be covered with a rubberized flooring material that is glued to the sub floor or one of the new portable rubberized floors. Further, in the free weight area there should be a 10' x 10' x 6" platform constructed of sturdy materials covered with a rubberized flooring material to be used for heavy weight activities. This platform should be recessed into the concrete slab.

Ceiling: The ceiling clearance needs to be at least 10'. The ceiling should be constructed with acoustical ceiling materials. A drop ceiling can be installed for these spaces; however, the ceiling panels are more susceptible to damage by objects or individuals, requiring considerable maintenance. Therefore, it is recommended that a permanent ceiling be considered rather than a drop ceiling.

Electrical: The electrical needs of the equipment (i.e., treadmills, stairclimbers, computerized bicycles, etc.) to be used in the facility must be considered as well as the equipment layout. There should be numerous receptacles around the perimeter of the room. The designer will need to provide for audio and video needs in the room as well as for computer access.

The lighting in the area should provide at least 50 footcandles of illumination. The ideal lighting system has both an indirect and a direct component, throwing surface light on the ceiling to give it about the same brightness as the lighting unit itself. It is recommended that fluorescent lamps be installed because they have the advantage of long life and give at least two and one-half times the amount of light that incandescent lamps give for the same amount of current used.

Sound: The strength training space by its nature and the equipment in use is noisy. Therefore, it is necessary to design the room to accommodate the noise generated. The use of materials in the walls, on the floor, and in the ceiling should have good acoustical qualities.

Climate Control: When people use weights they generate lots of heat, perspiration, and odor. The designer must consider these problems when designing the mechanical aspects of the room. The three most critical concerns are cooling, humidity control (55%), and ventilation. Unfortunately, designers and/or owners neglect these concerns and are extremely disappointed after the facility opens due to poor climate control. Climate control can make or break a strength training program.

Security: The room should have provisions for emergency and night lighting.

Special Considerations:

- There should be at least two 220-volt electrical outlets to service heavy-duty cleaning equipment.
- There should be a provision for a large (40-50") TV with VCR in the cardio-respiratory area.
- Commercial structures typically have a 60-pound-per-square-foot load-bearing capacity, but exercise areas need at least 100-pound-per-square-foot capacity.
- The appearance of the room is important. The right ambience entices members to exercise while enjoying their surroundings. Special consideration should be given to the use of mirrors, lighting, carpeting, rubberized flooring, graphics, and skylights.
- Carpeting that extends on a side to wainscoting height serves as an excellent acoustical buffer as well as protective surface for the free weight area.
- The color schemes of walls, equipment upholstery, flooring, and ceiling must all be coordinated to appeal to the user.

Testing Area

Description: A testing area is a must in any health/fitness facility. The testing area should include equipment and space to perform fitness appraisals such as body composition, functional capacity, strength, flexibility, and/or exercise stress test analysis. The room should be designed according to the testing that will be accomplished. The testing protocol will facilitate the determination of the specific space needs.

Size: The testing area will be 20" x 40" or 800 sf with an 8' ceiling. There will be adequate space in this area to house two chairs, a desk, a file cabinet, a storage cabinet, a computer station, a bicycle ergometer, a flexibility tester, a treadmill, control console, crash cart, metabolic cart, 12 lead ECG, cholesterol analyzer, examination table, double sink, and a storage cabinet for equipment such as skin fold calipers, stop watches, and stethoscope(s).

Walls: Simple dry wall construction, epoxy painted with a pleasing color(s), appropriate graphics for the area, and a bulletin board.

Floor: The floor will be carpeted with a commercial grade carpet color coordinated with the walls and equipment in the room.

Ceiling: A suspended acoustical panel ceiling is appropriate.

Electrical: The electrical needs of the equipment in the room should be considered as well as the eventual location of the equipment within the room. There should be numerous electrical outlets around the perimeter of the room. The outlets near the sink should be Ground Fault Interrupters (GFI). The recommended lighting for this area is fluorescent units that will produce at least 50 footcandles of illumination.

Climate Control: The mechanical considerations for this space include cooling, heating, humidity control (55%). The public restrooms and entrances to these areas must be adequate in size to service the expected population.

Security: There should be emergency lighting and an audible emergency alarm to alert other personnel to a medical emergency in the testing area.

Dance Exercise Area

Description: Another high-interest area in a health/fitness/recreation center is the dance exercise area. This space will be used by men and women who will perform various dance routines to music. It will also be used for stretch and tone classes. The designer's concerns include room size, floor surface, lighting, ventilation, climate control, and a sound and video system.

Size: The size of the room will be dictated by the peak load for classes to be held at the center. After the peak load or maximum class size is determined, then that number is multiplied by 50 sf the minimum recommended space that should be allowed per participant. Ideally the multiplier should be closer to 100 sf per participant. In the sample facility it has been determined that the maximum class size will be 50. Therefore, the room will be 50' x 75'= 3750 sf. The most prevalent and popular room designs are rectangular.

Walls: The walls should be constructed of wall board and painted with brightly colored epoxy paint. At least one wall, preferably the front wall, should be covered with mirrors. However, it would be nice to have the front and rear walls covered with mirrors. The painted walls should also have appropriate graphics and at least one bulletin board.

Floor: The International Dance Exercise Association (IDEA), dance instructors, flooring specialists, and the American College of Sports Medicine (ACSM) have identified essential criteria for the selection of a safe dance exercise flooring system including the following:

Here is an example of a dance exercise instructor's elevated platform. This one is permanently located in one position, whereas, in some facilities they are portable and can be moved to another location. Further, some facilities roll them under the wall when not in use so the area can be used for other activities. (Photo: Tom Sawyer)

An example of how floor covers can be stored. (Photo: Tom Sawyer)

- Shock absorption—the flooring system must provide for adequate shock absorption generated by the dancers during exercise.
- Foot stability—the system must provide a stable base for foot impact.
- Surface traction—the system must allow for ease of sliding movements and reduce side-to-side stresses during a horizontal glide or slide movement(s).
- Resiliency—the floor must have energy return qualities and capabilities to rebound or spring back into shape after impact.

The most widely used flooring systems are carpet and wood. The carpet systems used are a good commercial grade carpet with a high-density foam pad. The wood floors are most often spring-loaded systems. However, another approach that should be considered is a four-layer system as follows: first layer, 4' x 8' x 1" high-density foam sheets on top of the concrete, followed by a course of 4' x 8' x 3/4" plywood, third layer, a second course of plywood run diagonally across the first course, then followed by hardwood flooring (either maple or oak). The recommended flooring is wood.

Ceiling: The ceiling will be 9' to 10' in height. Most likely a drop ceiling with acoustical tiles to minimize sound conduction.

Electrical: There should be numerous outlets on each wall. The electrical engineer will need to provide wiring for a built-in audio system including speakers located around the room to provide adequate sound penetration. The lighting system designed should be able to provide a minimum of five footcandles and as much as 50. This type of variable system is necessary if the health/fitness/recreation center plans to use this area for more than aerobic/dance exercise. However, if the area is only to be used for aerobic/dance exercise, then a variable lighting system is not warranted. Incandescent lights are preferred over fluorescent lights, and natural lighting, such as skylights or windows, is preferred in combination with the incandescent lights.

Sound: The room should be designed to be as soundproof as possible. It should also be a space that provides ideal sound for the dancers participating.

Climate Control: This area will be a sparsely used space if proper considerations for climate control are not made. The space should be provided with heating, cooling, and humidity controls. The humidity should not exceed 55%. Do not forget to provide proper ventilation to the area. The planner should be aware that cooling this room will be more difficult than heating due to the body heat generated by the participants. The climate control mechanisms must be quiet so as not to interfere with the music.

Security: The basic security needs for this room include emergency lighting, a night security light, and a means to directly call the control center for help in an emergency.

Special Considerations:

- The selection of an appropriate stereo sound system is very important.
- Seek the assistance of an acoustical engineer when designing and selecting the stereo system. The system should include numerous speakers, instructor microphone system (including an instructor-mounted remote unit, microphone backups, tape deck with playing and recording capabilities, record player, disk player, and control unit.
- Ceiling fans may be necessary as a backup for the ventilation system. A good rule of thumb is one fan for every 300 sf of room space. Do not use fans unless there is at least a 10' ceiling, preferably 12'.
- The instructor should have a small stage that is at least 6" high. It should have the same surface as the dance floor.
- If the room is to be a multipurpose dance space, than an oak ballet bar, 42" high, 1.5-2" in diameter, and 6-7" from the wall, should be mounted on at least one wall (preferably the mirrored wall), but preferably two.

Racquetball/Handball Courts

The fastest growing racquet sport in America is racquetball. Many sport club members enjoy playing racquetball. Some may also like an older game, handball. Both activities are played in the same size court. The recommended number of courts is one per 1000 general memberships.

Size: The dimensions of a racquetball/handball court are 40' long x 20' wide (800 sf), with a front wall and ceiling height of 20', and a back wall that is at least 12-15' high.

Walls: The best system on the market today is a panel system constructed of compressed wood with a hard lament surface similar to formica. These 4' x 8' panels are grooved and slide into metal spines on metal framing. Before the panels are slid into place the steel frame is covered with glue to fasten the panel in place. These panels are easy to clean with mild soap and water. The resiliency of the panel system is the key to selecting the best panel. The best panel is the most resilient. The top 3' of the rear wall will be open for viewing and instruction. The last 2' before the opening at the top will be covered with carpet to reduce sound conduction in the room. If walleyball, a modified volleyball game, is to be played in the courts, the net fasteners should be secured to the metal framework during the construction of the wall. Other acceptable materials for wall use are plexiglass and/or reinforced fiberglass concrete. The planner should consider the following before selecting the wall material: material cost, moisture and stability concerns, overall appearance, maintenance, ball action, and acoustics.

Ceiling: The ceiling is constructed of the same material as the walls. The last 15' of the ceiling should be constructed with durable acoustical tile to help reduce sound in the racquetball/handball room.

Floors: The most frequently used floor system is wood. The following is the newest wood system on the market and provides the greatest resiliency for the players. The system is constructed in this manner:

• Treated 2" x 4" pine studding are placed on 1/2" blocks across the width of the floor at 16" intervals (the blocks are 12" apart) and fastened to the concrete floor;
• Roofing tar is then poured onto the floor to a depth of 1' and allowed to setup;
• Two courses of 1/2", 4' x 8' sheets of plywood are fastened to the 2" x 4" floor joists, the first course is laid lengthwise and the second course runs at a diagonal to the first; and
• The maple flooring is laid on this surface to complete the job.

Lighting: The favored lighting is metal halide that is recessed with a protective coating. Access to the lighting fixtures should be from the court using suspended walkways above the ceiling. The light switches should be located in the central control area at the main entrance. A racquetball/handball court should be provided with 75 footcandles. The fixtures should be easy to install and maintain, and energy efficient.

Sound: A racquetball/handball court is a large rectangular box that when closed produces dangerous levels of sound that can and has damaged ears due to extremely high decibel levels. It is important to design the courts with the assistance of an acoustical engineer in order to reduce the decibel levels. Suggestions have already been made in relation to the walls and ceiling. Further, on the second floor in the observation/instruction space, a series of sound baffles can be hung to deflect the sounds exiting the court through the observation/instruction openings.

Climate Control: This area even though it has a high ceiling needs cooling considerations. The space needs to have adequate ventilation and humidity control. The humidity should be held at 55% and the air exchanged completely every 10 to 15 minutes.

Security: All courts should provide a place for valuables either recessed into the door or into the wall.

Special Considerations:

• A full-height, solid-core court door that has the same ball action characteristics as the front and side walls is ideal.

- The door should be flush with the back wall and have no protruding edges.
- All hinges and door handles should also be flush with the door.
- A small viewing window of shatterproof glass, mounted into the door at approximately the height of an average adult.
- The window should no larger than 4" x 6".
- If glassed courts are planned, then the planners should consider a viewing area for instruction and tournament play.

Swimming Pools (Gabrielson, 1987)

Swimming pools require considerable planning to make them energy efficient and safe.

Walls and Pool Shell: The pool shell should be of poured concrete with a tile finish. The tile finish is the most expensive finish, but it requires the least maintenance and will save the owner in the long run many dollars. Another finish is an epoxy coating that requires regular expensive maintenance. There are also steel and aluminum pools that must be painted regularly.

The deck should be finished with tile to match or complement the tile in the pool. The deck space should be large enough to provide adequate space for instruction. It is suggested that there be at least a 15' deck surrounding the pool. The pool room walls should be constructed of concrete block that is finished with an epoxy paint. The color scheme should be bright with appropriate graphics.

Ceiling: The ceiling in a pool must be moisture resistant, be able to tolerate high humidity conditions, and be corrosive resistant. The most appropriate material for the ceiling is metal that has been painted with a corrosive resistant paint.

An example of signage found in most swimming areas, which displays the depth of the water and a reminder not to dive. (Photo: Tom Sawyer)

Electrical: It is recommended that 50 footcandles be used for lighting. The lighting system should be designed for easy maintenance and not directly over the edge of the pool. All electrical outlets must be GFI rated and should be covered when not in use. There will be special needs in the pump room including power for various chemical pumps, the main pump for the filter system, and the automated chemical control system.

Sound: The pool room is a difficult acoustical problem and needs the attention of a qualified acoustical engineer. There are many surfaces that have to be softened to improve the acoustical quality of the area. It is a challenge and many times one that is not properly considered.

Climate Control: The climate control requirements of a pool area are demanding and challenging. The water must be heated at one temperature and the air at yet another (usually two degrees higher than the water). The average water temperature ranges from 80 to 86 degrees. The average air temperature ranges from 82 to 89. The humidity must be held at 55%. This can be accomplished with a separate exhaust system. It is important that the mechanical engineers understand the humidity problem and design an air movement system that is adequate to solve the problem. The problem involves control of the humidity over the pool and also over the deck areas. Ask the architect and engineers to review the European approach to two-zone humidity control.

The mechanical engineers should consider heat recovery and appropriate energy management to save the owner energy dollars during the winter months.

Gutter/Overflow Systems: There are three common overflow systems used by pool designers; they include the following:

- perimeter overflow systems,
- roll-out overflow systems, and
- recessed overflow systems.

The designers of the pool will determine which system is preferable in light of cost, storage space, and pool use.

Pump/Filter Systems: The hydraulic system consists of a pump and filter. This system circulates the pool water through a filter before returning it to the pool. The turnover rates can range from four to six hours depending upon the use of the pool, the state health department will dictate the appropriate turnover rate. There are three filter systems that are used by the pool designers, they include the following:

- cartridge filter systems,
- sand filter systems, and
- diatomaceous earth filter systems.

The sand filter is the most efficient mechanically and financially for the use in most swimming facilities.

Security: The pool area should always be lighted when it is not in use. Security lights should be located in the four corners of the room. An alarm system should be installed to alert the front desk of aquatic problems.

An example of graphics used in a swimming area at Terre Haute YMCA, Terre Haute, Indiana. (Photo: Tom Sawyer).

Special Considerations:

- Provide an adequate slope for drains and gutter system.
- Provide the proper number of inlets and outlets to circulate water effectively in the pool.
- Construct pool deck that prevents slipping and is not uncomfortable to the feet.
- Provide for guard stands.
- Design handicapped access to the pool.
- Provide for lane markers.
- Design an office space that overlooks the pool area.
- Include an automated chemical control system.
- Provide for moisture barrier in exterior walls so that condensation does not compromise the wall.
- Insulate the walls of the pool with 1" to 2" of foam before back filling around the pool shell.
- Provide for an adequate pool cleaning system.

Locker Room(s)

The locker room should be spacious, comfortable, functional, and aesthetically pleasing to the participants. The image of a locker room plays a major role in selling prospective individuals and retaining current members. As competition for the membership revenue and member approval increases, attractive locker rooms become a necessity. Do not let this space become an afterthought in the design process nor an area that suffers when budgetary cutbacks are required.

Size: The size is based on the number of individuals using the area. A general rule of thumb recommends a minimum of 20 sf per person. The designers should always consider space needs based on peak usage times. The planners need to ask the following questions before developing the layout and design of the locker room:

- How many participants will the locker room serve?
- What size of lockers will be used?
- What specific amenities will be provided ... sauna, whirlpool, steam room, massage, toiletries, etc.?
- Where will the locker room be placed in relation to activity areas?
- What will the budget be for the locker room?

Walls: The walls should be constructed of concrete block with an epoxy finish. Tile in many cases is the recommended wall covering. There should be a planned total color scheme for the area. The colors should be bright and relaxing.

Floor: The floor can be painted concrete, tile, or commercial indoor/outdoor carpeting. It should be a nonskid surface. The floor should be pitched away from the dressing areas and toward adequately-sized drains. The best floor for the shower and drying areas is tile, and the locker area should be concrete painted with a sand mix. Carpet is nice but causes various health problems because it holds moisture and bacteria for long periods of time. This retention of moisture and bacteria develops an irritating odor in the area, which becomes a marketing problem.

Ceiling: The ceiling should be light in color, acoustically treated, and built with materials that are impervious to moisture. The recommended height is 9'.

This is an example of one way to store valuables for clients while they are using the facility: a simple coin-operated locker system. After inserting a quarter, the key is released and can be affixed to clothing by using the attached safety pin. (Photo: Tom Sawyer)

Electrical: The lights have vapor-proof fixtures and should be centered directly over the locker aisles for maximum efficiency. The lights in the shower and drying areas should be recessed into the ceiling and covered with plexiglass or translucent plastic. All electric outlets should be approximately 3' above the floor level and be GFI rated. Emergency lighting should be available at all times.

Climate Control: The locker room must have a great ventilation system. Taking short cuts with the ventilation system will spell disaster. Locker rooms contain hot and humid air which needs to be converted into dry inside air. An improper ventilation system affects mechanical systems, the structural system, electrical fixtures, and floor and wall finishes. The humidity level should not be greater than 55%.

Do not forget to plan for air conditioning in this space. The lack of air conditioning in this area will immediately affect your membership. Comfort is a key to any locker room complex. Most participants spend 20-30% of their time in this space while at the health/fitness center.

Security: Security problems in locker rooms range from theft to rape. The security for this area must be well planned. The questions planners need to answer include, but are not limited to:

- How much security does the locker need to provide?
- How will entry and exit from the locker area be controlled?
- What kind of emergency system needs to be designed for the interior of the locker area?

Special Considerations:

- All doors should be of heavy-duty moisture-resistant material and when open form a natural sight barrier.
- All corners in rooms should be rounded.
- Mirrors should be placed in strategic locations; full-length mirrors should be placed at least 12" from the floor and be available for individuals as they leave the room.
- Hair-drying facilities are encouraged; ratio 1:5 for females and 1:3 for males.
- Refrigerated drinking fountains of stainless steel or noncorrosive material should be located near traffic flow.
- A swimsuit dryer should be located near the drying area.
- There should be 10 shower heads for the first 30 patrons and an additional head for every additional four persons.
- Locker rooms must be handicap accessible.
- The most economical shower arrangement in terms of space is installations on the outside of the wall. However there are other systems available such as center post and privacy cubes.
- The shower system must have a master control to regulate hot and cold water mixing.
- The toilet and lavatory area must be large enough for the expected usage.
- The designers need to consider the following questions before selecting lockers:

- What must the user store in the locker?
- Is a laundry system available or planned?
- Will the lockers be day lockers only?
- Will the lockers be rented by the year?
- Are personnel available to administer a basket system?
- Who are the patrons?

There are several locker systems available and selection should be made carefully considering the following requirements:

- security of street clothing,
- efficient use of space,
- control of odors,
- economy of operation, and
- flexibility for use by different groups.

Service Area(s)

There are a number of service areas that need to be planned for and understood. These areas are described in the following pages.

Administrative Area. This area should include offices for the following personnel: director of the center, director's secretary, program coordinator, etc. The offices, except for the director's, should be no larger than 120 sf and the director's should be no larger than 300 sf.

There should be a control center or check-in desk located near the entrance of the facility. The design considerations for this area include the following:

- high visibility for security and easy access,
- control for lights in various areas, public address system, exterior doors, emergency systems (fire alarm and burglar alarm),
- central phone system,
- storage area for rental and other equipment,
- central computer location, and
- central security station and facility monitoring system.

Storage lockers are a necessity and need to be designed around these guidelines:

- located near control area,
- lockers must be large enough to store patrons equipment or heavy coats, etc.,
- a locker system similar to an airport or bus terminal should be considered,
- provide good ventilation for the lockers,
- design adequate lighting around the location,
- recess lockers into the wall, and
- these lockers are to be used mainly for valuables.

Day Care Area. Immediately one thinks of youngsters when day care is mentioned but do not forget older adults need attention as well. The day care area should be designed for both young children and older adults in mind. This may require two separate rooms. Considerations for the young people include a rest room, toys that are designed for the child's safety, games for them to play, and a television with VCR and appropriate children's tapes. The area for the older adults should have comfortable chairs, magazines, a television with VCR and appropriate tapes for the older adult, and a restroom. Both areas need to be painted and decorated appropriately for each set of patrons.

Laundry. The health/fitness/physical activity/recreation/sport facility needs to have a laundry located near the control area, locker rooms, and pool. The designer's considerations for this area should include the following:

- space for the area will be determined by equipment chosen,
- use nonskid concrete floors,
- provide for storage and folding areas,
- provide for drains in the floor,
- design proper ventilation for the area,
- treat walls and ceiling acoustically,
- allow for sufficient hot and cold water supplies,
- provide for an adequate exhaust system to eliminate odors, and
- design the electrical system to adequately supply the purchased.

Therapeutic Areas

The health/fitness centers should provide certain therapeutic amenities. This area, if not properly designed, can turn into an owner's nightmare. Patrons will expect to find the following therapeutic amenities: massage area, sauna, steam room, whirlpool/hot tubs, and beauty salon. These amenities can be placed in one large area so that activities can easily be monitored. This area will be located adjacent to the locker rooms.

Massage area. The massage space should be a minimum of 8' x 10' with a tiled floor; acoustical ceiling; cabinets for storage of lotions, linens, and towels; a sink; a mirror; and standard massage table. Clients should not have to go from a locker room through a shower room to get to the massage area.

Sauna. This unit can either be built from preassembled packages or constructed by a carpenter. The walls, ceiling, and floor should be constructed of redwood; however, cedar, spruce, kiln-dried pine or clear pine can be used. The thicker the walls, ceiling, and floor, the better the heat retention. It is recommended that the minimum thickness be 1 1/2". All benches should be screwed from underneath rather than nailed or stapled from the top, because nails and staples will transmit heat and work loose due to expansion and contraction of the wood.

The sauna unit needs to be ventilated for proper operation. The openings for ventilation can be located either under or near the heater and between the upper and lower benches. There should be a complete air exchange made six to seven times per hour.

The sauna should have a window so it can be monitored on a regular basis. The unit should be large enough to accommodate at least 12 people at a time. There should be adequate lighting (at least two). The heater units are designed to fit in the sauna room. Regulated temperature controls should be placed in a lockbox for liability purposes. An accurately functioning thermostat, properly positioned, is a high priority. The thermostat should be designed to be read internally as well as externally. The heating element should be Underwriters Laboratories-approved and designed appropriately for the room size.

Steam Room. The steam room should have concrete walls, ceiling, and floor with a tile finish. The floor tile should be textured. There should be at least two floor drains and the floor pitched to the drains. The hot steam should be piped into the steam room from a steam generator located outside the area. The generator is thermostatically controlled and maintains an environment of approximately 120 degrees Fahrenheit and 98% humidity.

The steam room is free standing and no other walls should be attached to them. There should be a space between the steam room walls and any other room walls. There should be a floor pan placed in this space sloped to a drain to remove moisture that will collect on the exterior of the steam room walls.

The door frame should be constructed of anodized aluminum. The remaining part of the door should be insulated glass for observation purposes. The door enclosure should be strong enough to keep a tight fit, even with heavy usage.

Whirlpool/Hot Tub. A whirlpool/hot tub is nothing but a small swimming pool. Whirlpools come in a wide variety of shapes, sizes, and materials. Most whirlpool shells and linings are acrylic, fiberglass, or high-impact plaster. An insulation layer is recommended around the inside shell before the lining is installed. The best material for the whirlpool is concrete with a tile lining. The floor tile should be textured. Additional safety features are a handrail and steps that are easily seen.

The mechanical system of a whirlpool consists of a filter, motor, pump, and heater. Additional elements include an air blower to increase water pressure and a heater that will easily heat the water to 104 degrees Fahrenheit. The mechanical room should be designed so it is close to the whirlpool with easy access for maintenance.

The pipes to the body of the whirlpool should be accessible for maintenance purposes. An assortment of whirlpool jets provides varied airflow rates and nozzle adjustments. The jets should be placed strategically to hit important areas of the body, including knees, lower back, and shoulder regions.

The floor around the whirlpool should be tiled with textured tile. The room in which the whirlpool is placed should have proper ventilation, air-conditioning, and humidity control. A change of air at least eight to 10 times per hour is recommended.

Beauty Salon. The size of the beauty salon should be between 200 and 500 sf. The minimum requirements for a salon include appropriate electrical power, water supply, styling station(s), shampoo sink(s), storage space(s), and hair dryer(s).

Outdoor Facilities

The planners need to take into consideration what outdoor facilities will be needed. The planning for these facilities is as important as the indoor spaces. The student will understand what the outdoor needs are after reading this section.

Tennis Courts

Tennis is a very popular activity and the health/fitness center should plan for both indoor and outdoor courts. There should be one court per 1000 general membership. The following information will pertain to outside courts except for the general dimensions.

Size: A single, doubles court is 36' x 78'. There should be 12' of clearance on each side of the court and 21' of clearance between the baseline and the fence or wall. This would mean that there will be an area of 60' x 120' for each court. The baseline fence will remain constant regardless of the number of courts. If there are several courts, they should be placed so that there are 12' between adjacent sidelines. Considering a bank of four tennis courts, an area of 23,780 sf would be required (120' x 198').

The layout in most private club installations is two courts for each battery. This reduces drainage problems and reduces traffic. The courts should drain from side to side. The slope for porous courts should be 1" in 20' and 1" in 10' for nonporous courts.

Surfaces: There are over 100 different court surface finishes suitable for tennis courts. The United States Tennis Association (USTA) in their booklet *Tennis Courts* outlines the various classification of surfaces by type and characteristics. This booklet is available from the USTA Education and Research Center, 729 Alexander Road, Princeton, NJ 08540.

The planners' considerations should include the following:

* long-term maintenance costs,
* initial construction cost,
* player preference,
* player safety—sliding characteristics,
* ease and cost of resurfacing,
* resiliency of the surface,
* surface speed,
* uniformity of ball bounce,
* effect of color on glare and heat absorption,
* drying time after rain,
* availability of service from court builder, (it is *important* to contract with a tennis court builder and not a driveway/roadway contractor.)
* colorfastness of surfaces and its effect on ball discoloration,
* effect of abrasive surfaces on balls, rackets, shoes, and falling players,
* effect of lines on ball bounce, tripping hazards, and maintenance of lines,
* durability, and
* adaptability for other uses.

USTA Classification of Tennis Court Surfaces standards include the following:

- pervious construction (one which permits water to filter through the surface)
- fast dry (fine crushed aggregate),
- clay,
- grass, and
- others ... dirt, grit, etc.
- impervious construction (one which water does not penetrate, but runs off the surface)
- non-cushioned,
- concrete,
- asphalt,
- hot plant mix,
- emulsified asphalt mix,
- combination hot and emulsified,
- penetration macadam,
- asphalt job mix, and
- others ... wood, etc.
- cushioned construction,
- asphalt bound systems,
- hot leveling course and hot cushion course,
- hot leveling course and cold cushion courses, and
- cold leveling course and cold cushion course
- synthetic
- elastomer
- textile

Lighting. The recommended lighting for tennis courts is metal halide. The intensity of the lighting system should be at least 30 footcandles. Each light should be covered with a safety grill. The current trend is to extend the lights and poles over the fence to the court clearance area, so more direct light is positioned over the court. This system prevents light pollution from occurring around a multi-court layout.

Site Considerations. The planner's considerations for a site for the tennis complex should include:

- A site on high ground,
- A natural wind protection,
- A study of the prevailing winds,
- An engineer's soil compaction tests, and
- Soil base with an adequate slope to assist in water drainage.

Electrical. There should be at least two electrical outlets on each courts.

Plumbing. There should be at least one drinking fountain for each four tennis courts with a hose bib.

An example of a typical indoor tennis court arrangement with indirect lighting located between and at the ends of the court. (Photo: Tom Sawyer)

Special considerations:

• There needs to be a chain-linked fence constructed around the perimeter of the courts. This fence should be 10' to 12' high. The fencing material should be made of anodized aluminum. The most popular color is black. The poles for the fence should be deep enough to support the windscreen that will be used to reduce the flow of wind. The poles should be placed in concrete-filled holes that have a depth of 25-40% of the length of the pole above ground.

• Each court will be surrounded with a windscreen. The windscreen should be dark-colored (black, dark blue or green). The dark coloring provides a good background against which players can follow the ball that is in play.

• Vented screens and open mesh curtains are also suggested, so the wind escapes through the screens and doesn't cause heavy tension against the frame of the fence.

Shuffleboard

The shuffleboard court is 52' long and 10' wide. However, the actual playing area is only 39' x 6'. The court(s) should be oriented north and south. A level, smooth surface is essential. The painted lines (white) will be 1" in width. The base lines shall be extended to adjoining courts, or to 24" beyond sides of the court.

The area around and under the court(s) must be well drained. The court is constructed of reinforced concrete with a burnished finish. A depressed alley must be constructed between and at the sides of the court. The alley should be at least 24" deep at mid-court, where a suitable drain shall be installed. The alley, from both extensions of the base lines, should slope down toward the center of the court. The downward fall shall begin with a 1" drop in the first 6", and then gradually slope down to mid-court.

The scoreboard and benches are located at the base of the court. Many courts have 2" x 2" backstops installed (loosely) to prevent discs from rebounding back into the court. The courts many be lighted from poles overhead with metal halide lamps.

Exercise Trail

Exercise trails are marketed under various commercial names, such as Fitness Trail, Fit-Trail, Lifecourse, and Parcourse. These trails combine cardiovascular development, agility, flexibility, strength, and endurance. The exercise trail consists of a number of exercise stations located at various lengths along a jogging or walking course. A typical trail could have a 1.5 mile distance with 10-14 exercise stations. The jogging or walking intervals and exercises are designed for flexibility, agility, strength, all the while developing the participant's cardiovascular system.

Horseshoes

A regulation horseshoe court is 9' wide and 46' long. In the middle of this strip are two steel stakes exactly 40' apart at the base of the stakes. It is preferable to have a north-to-south orientation for the court. This will eliminate pitching into the sun at anytime.

The stake should be of one-inch rolled steel and 24" in length. The stake should stand 14" above the level of the ground. The stake is best secured by driving it into a piece of cross tie, and burying it in the clay. The cross tie should be treated with creosote or some other substance that will protect it against rot. The hole into which the stake is to be driven should be a 15/16 inch hole, and the bottom of the stake should be dipped in motor oil before being driven. This will insure a snug fit. There are ready-built boxes that have a stake on a welded base. This is more expensive, but it saves a lot of work. The box can be made easily by a local welder.

The hard surface the throwers stand on may be of concrete, asphalt, lumber, or any other hard material. Concrete is the preferred material by most throwers. The frame should be constructed of 2" thick lumber by 4" wide. The area within the frame should be filled with clay, preferably blue clay. The clay should be kept moist so it maintains a putty-like consistency. Therefore, a source of water needs to be in close proximity. The area should be covered with either metal, plywood, or hard rubber with a hole for the stake, when not in use.

The backstops should be constructed of durable materials such as wire mesh, 2" diameter wood, or heavy belting. The backboard should be 2' high and 6' wide. The horseshoe area should be lighted like the tennis court. Each court will need a scoreboard constructed of plywood (marine) with a plastic cover attached to be used during inclement weather.

An outdoor roller blade hockey rink used for recreational sports adjacent to the Recreational Sports Center at Miami University of Ohio. (Photo: Tom Sawyer)

Outdoor Field or Court Areas

Safety Factors for the Site

The primary consideration for planning any facility must be the safety of the participants and spectators. Safety considerations for outdoor fields include the following:

- adequate space for the specific field away from open water, power lines, highways, railroad tracks, parking lots, and driveways,
- appropriate traffic control in parking areas, entrances and exits to parking areas, and highways leading to the parking areas,
- acceptable location of walkways to provide direct access between areas and facilities which prevents any interference with activities or the creation of a safety hazard,
- appropriate landscape design to be effective barriers or separations because different age groups play different games at different levels of intensity;
- adequate consideration of environmental conditions, such as locating near areas adjacent to an industrial site,
- appropriate set back from utility poles and wires, and
- adequate consideration given to locating facilities and storage areas in places well lighted and easily observed.

Orientation of the Fields or Courts

Outdoor fields and courts should be oriented so players will not have to face into the late-afternoon or early-morning sun. It may not be possible to get the best orientation of a particular field or court, the long axis should generally be at right angles to the late-afternoon sun's rays. Locate the sunset position at mid-season of the sport and orient the field or court accordingly.

The general pattern of the ball's flight, on baseball, softball, and similar fields, covers an arc of more than 90 degrees. Since the field cannot be oriented to give equal protection to all players and spectators, a choice must be made. Because the batter, pitcher and catcher are in the most hazardous positions, they should be given first consideration. A line through these positions should be the axis for orienting the field.

Site Development Considerations

The sport manager with the facility planner and designers must consider the following when developing the site for an outdoor field or court: (1) grading—the area should be as level as possible for each field or court site; however, the topography of available sites may require some terracing between fields or courts; (2) drainage—the biggest mistake made by planners is not providing adequate drainage of a field or court area; therefore the planners need to consider the following recommendations: (a) 1% slope is the maximum for turf areas, (b) for stadium football field, a 12" crown down the longitudinal axis on the middle of the field, (c) for baseball, the pitcher's box should be elevated 10" above the base lines and home plate, the slope from the pitcher's box to home plate and to all base lines should be gradual, and a 1% slope drainage grade for the outfield, (d) large, hard-surface multipurpose areas are generally sloped (1" in 8') so that surface water is directed toward specific collection points (e.g., for net games the slope should be from one side of the court to the other), and (e) subsurface drainage can be a problem and the planners should consult with a competent soils engineer, (3) fencing—is frequently required for outdoor fields and courts for security, safety, isolation, enclosure, separation, noise abatement, wind screening, sun screening, traffic control, and for protection of participants, the general public, spectators, and the public, therefore the following recommendations are offered for the planners consideration: (a) perimeter fencing for baseball and softball should be 8' high, for football, lacrosse, field hockey, soccer, and rugby should be 4' high and at least 5' beyond the playing field, for tennis at least 10'-12' high, (b) some good characteristics to look for in fencing are stability, durability, economy of maintenance, attractiveness, and effectiveness, (c) suitable fencing could be woven wire (chain-link, 11-gauge, available in galvanized steel, aluminum-coated steel, plastic-coated steel, and aluminum alloy mesh, the plastic-coated steel in forest green requires the least amount of maintenance) using H-type or circular-line posts and a hard-surface mowing strip placed under the fence for maintenance, (d) fencing less than 8' surrounding baseball or softball fields should be covered with a plastic material (painted drainage tile) to protect the participants, and (e) the minimum height for fencing protecting spectators should be seven feet, (4) walkways—all-weather walks should be confined to a minimum in open play areas and should be provided only where foot traffic is heavy, (5) utilities and electricity—no turf playing can be properly developed or maintained without an adequate water supply and sprinkler system, an electrical supply should be available at all field locations for lights, concession areas, public-address system, scoreboards, and maintenance equipment, (6) parking—off-street parking is a necessity for outdoor facilities for both participants and spectators, (7) surfacing—There is no one surface which will satisfactorily meet the needs of all outdoor activities. Each activity surface has its own surface requirements, which will dictate what type or types of material can be used, however, certain qualities should be sought, including multiplicity of use, durability, dustless and stainless, reasonable initial cost and economy, ease of maintenance, pleasing appearance, non-abrasiveness, resiliency, and year-round usage (see Table 12-3 for a summary of available surfaces), (8) service facilities—all outdoor facilities need to consider the provision of the following services to participants and spectators: restrooms, storage for equipment and machinery, locker room facilities, press box, and concessions area, (9) outdoor lighting—lighting for field and court facilities must be placed outside of the playing areas (see Table 12-4 for specific levels of illumination) (Flynn, 1992).

Table 12-3
Types of Surfacing Materials

Group	Type
Earth	Loams, sand, sand-clay, clay-gravel, fuller's earth, stabilized earth, soil-cement
Turf	Bluegrass mixtures, bent, fescue, Bermuda
Aggregates	Gravel, graded stone, graded slag, shell, cinders
Asphalt	Penetration-macadam, asphaltic concrete (cold and hot-laid), sheet asphalt, natural asphalt, sawdust asphalt, vermiculite asphalt, rubber asphalt, cork asphalt, other patented asphalt mixes
Synthetics	Rubber, synthetics resins, rubber asphalt, chlorinated butyl-rubber, mineral fiber, plastics, vinyls
Concrete	Monolithic, terrazzo, precast
Masonry	Flagstone, (sandstone, limestone, granite, etc), brick, etc.
Miscellaneous	Tanbark, sawdust, shavings, cotton-seed hulls

Table 12-4
Levels of Illumination Currently Recommended for
Outdoor Sports Areas

Sport Area	Footcandles on Task
Archery	30 infield
Badminton	10
Baseball	20 outfield
Basketball	30
Field Hockey	30
Football	30
Horseshoes	10
Ice Hockey	20
Lacrosse	30
Rugby	30
Soccer	30
Tennis	30
Volleyball	20

Field Sports

Sport fields in general require the greatest quantities of space in the outdoor facilities area. The activities are conducted on large playing areas, and additional acreage is required for spectators. The specifics for field design can be found in Appendix D. Further specifics are found in the rule books for the specific sport.

Stadiums

Stadiums are built more specifically for exhibition purposes with mass seating. In addition to competetive athletic events, these structures are often used for such purposes as convocations, concerts, mass meetings, and rallies. Too often, single-purpose facilities are not cost efficient and they become liabilities rather than assets. However, the trend currently is to develop single-purpose professional stadiums with luxury boxes and other amenities.

A stadium is a spectator structure, seating structure, and a money "machine." The designers of a stadium are concerned about the following features:

- seating capacity,
- lines of sight,
- restrooms,
- concession areas,
- decks,
- railings,

- lighting,
- communication facilities,
- media facilities,
- space utilization beneath stadium,
- field surface,
- scoreboards,
- luxury seating,
- deluxe seating,
- field illumination,
- merchandise centers,
- child-care centers,
- playgrounds,
- picnic areas,
- dry cleaners,
- movie theaters,
- fitness clubs,
- locker rooms, and
- medical facilities for players and spectators

Summary

This chapter was designed to assist the health/fitness/recreation/sport professional to develop a plan for a sport facility. An exciting facet of the sport professional's career is the opportunity to be involved in a building or remodeling project. After completing this chapter, the professional should feel more competent in attacking such a project.

Learning Objective 1: Understand the planning process for facility development.

Planning is extremely important when developing a state-of-the-art sport facility. The facility must meet the needs of the spectator, player, participant, community, and staff. The planning team should be diverse. The team should gather information from many sources and groups of users. Planning is not a luxury, it is a necessity.

As the project goes beyond the building program and site selection phases, it enters into the schematic design phase. After the design is accepted, construction documents are prepared and the bidding process begins. The construction begins and the design is brought to reality. If planning was successful, there will be very few change orders.

Learning Objective 2: Develop spaces and floor plans.

There are many spaces that need to be designed in a modern-day sport facility. The spaces are both indoor and outdoor. Spaces are developed using available standards, sport rules, customer needs, staff needs, and available funds.

Learning Objective 3: Selection of architect, consultant, contractors, and engineers.

The selection of a facility consultant early in the planning stages is very useful. The consultant assists in developing the building program, site selection, and selection of the architect. The architect is the most important person in the project, and is a very critical selection. The architect will assist in the selection of the most appropriate engineers and contractors.

Case Study

You have recently accepted a position as chairperson of a large department of physical education. This department is the result of a hostile merger of the men's and women's physical education departments a few years ago. The resulting new department is split by philosophy as well as gender. You currently are residing 1,700 miles from your new work site. You are not to report to work until August 15. It is mid-July and you receive a phone call from your new supervisor informing you that the women's gymnasium was engulfed in flames. This facility included the following spaces: exercise physiology laboratory, sports medicine laboratory, two dance studios, 16 offices, one lounge, two gymnasiums, one gymnastics practice facility for women, and locker rooms. This represents better than 50% of the physical education and athletic facilities on campus. The displaced faculty have been relocated in offices spread across campus. The men's facility has been designed for men, not women.

The fire insurance will reimburse the institution approximately $4.5 million. Your new supervisor has charged you with the task of bringing the men and women together to develop a plan for a new facility to replace the destroyed facility and modernize the men's gymnasium. You are given four years to complete the task.

1.   What will be your first steps?
2.   How will you appoint a planning team?
3.   Once the team is appointed, what will be the planning strategy?
4.   How will the team prioritize spaces?
5.   How will the team gather the state-of-the-art information?
6.   What steps will be taken in selecting an architect?
7.   How will the team determine whether or not a consultant is needed?
8.   How will the site be determined?
9.   What steps will be taken to guarantee easy access by the handicapped?
10. What will the committee do to provide adequate security for the users?

References

Flynn, R.B. (1985). *Planning facilities for athletics, physical education, and recreation.* (2nd ed.). Miami/Reston, VA: The Athletic Institute and American Alliance for Health, Physical Education, Recreation, and Dance.

Fogg, G.E. (1986). *A site design process.* Chicago: National Recreation and Parks Association.

Gabrielson, A.M. (1987). *Swimming pools: A guide to their planning, design, and operation.* (4th ed.). Champaign, IL: Human Kinetics Publishers.

Public Law 101-336: The American Disabilities Act [July 26, 1991], 42 U.S.C.A. 12101-12213 (1991).

Suggested Readings

Journals

Athletic Business. Circulation director, *Athletic Business*, 1842 Hoffman Street, Suite 201, Madison, WI 53704. Subscription rate: $36 for 12 issues.

Club Industry. Sportscape, Inc., 1415 Beacon Street, Brookline, MA 02146. Subscription rate: $36 for 12 issues.

Employee Services Management. National Employee Services and Recreation Association, 2400 S. Downing, Winchester, IL 60154. Subscription rate: $30 for 8 issues.

Fitness Management. Fitness Management, 3923 W. 6th Street, Los Angeles, CA 90020. Subscription rate: $24 for 12 issues.

Idea Today. Idea, Inc., 6190 Cornerstone Court East, Suite 204, San Diego, CA 92121-3773. Subscription rate: $36 for 12 issues.

National Aquatics Journal. Council for National Cooperation in Aquatics, 901 West New York Street, Indianapolis, IN 46223. Subscription rate: $24 for 8 issues.

National Strength and Conditioning Association Journal. National Strength and Conditioning Association, 300 Old City Hall Landmark, 916 O Street, Lincoln, NE 68508. Subscription rate: $18 for 6 issues.

Recreation Sports and Leisure. Lakewood Publication, 50 South Ninth Street, Minneapolis, MN 55402. Subscription rate: $24 for 9 issues.

13

FACILITIES AND EVENTS MANAGEMENT

◆ ———————————— ◆

Instructional Objectives

After reading this chapter the student should:

- be able to define the role of booking, the box office, concession, merchandising, and scheduling,

- understand how to develop a facility/event policy and procedure manual,

- be able to develop an appropriate communication plan,

- be able to develop a security, crowd control, and emergency plan, and

- understand the role signage plays in facility/event management.

Introduction

Facility management is critical in keeping any organization operating smoothly and efficiently. A facility that is well-maintained and managed is one of the best public and consumer relations tools in an organization's arsenal. Further, event management is intimately related to facility management. They go hand-in-hand with each other and cannot be easily separated. An organization's facility and event manager must become involved in many tasks, including, but not limited to facility and event admission access control, crowd control, directing, emergency operations, facility maintenance, operation policies and procedures, scheduling, and security.

Scheduling the Facility or Event

A standard procedure should be established for requesting use of facilities. The organization should create and adhere to a standard request form and establish priority guidelines for authorizing use. Figure 13-1 is an example of a priority list used by a major university. Strict adherence to priority guidelines and request protocol should be stressed to all groups using facilities. In smaller organizations, scheduling may be less complicated, but there is still a need for protocol and proper authorization for facility use. Computer programs for facility management are available to assist in scheduling.

Figure 13-1
XYZ University
Priority Listing for Facility Usage

1. Scheduled academic classes
2. Scheduled nonacademic classes
3. Recreational sports
4. Athletic practices and contests
5. Other campus groups—academic
6. Other campus groups—nonacademic
7. Off-campus groups

Fundamentals of Booking Events

A facility without a schedule of events has little purpose. A public facility has an obligation to provide for scheduling community events. A private facility may limit charitable and nonprofit activities. Regardless of the facility's purpose and mission, its manager is encouraged to book a well-rounded schedule of events geared to satisfy the desires of the market. Because rental income is such a major portion of annual operating revenue, this is an extremely important process.

Booking is the act of engaging and contracting an event or attraction to be held at the facility on a specific date. *Scheduling* is the reservation process and coordination of all events to fit the facility's annual calendar. There are two types of reservations: *tentative* indicates that an organization requested a specific date and time on a tentative-hold basis; *confirmed* refers to an organization that has placed a deposit for the agreed upon date and time (contracted reservation).

Facilities that are successful in scheduling events have made a good first impression on the tenants and the ticket-buying public. These facilities are clean, well-maintained, well-lit, environmentally comfortable, and staffed by friendly, courteous, and professional people.

There are a number of fundamentals to be considered when attracting, booking and scheduling a facility, including, but not limited to:

- Developing a level of confidence others have in the quality of services available at the facility;
- Establishing trust on the part of the promoter and the ticket-buying public in the professionalism of the facility manager and staff;
- Advertising the facility in various trade publications such as *Amusement Business, Variety*, and *Performance*;
- Attending appropriate trade and convention functions and networking with other facilities;
- Maintaining visibility with local and national promoters;
- Producing a facility informational brochure detailing the specifications of the building, staff, types of events, and event suitability;
- Preparing and making available a current financial report for the facility;
- Assigning responsibility of booking and scheduling to one person; and
- Preparing contracts for the event and follow up to make sure the contracts are executed and returned with the necessary deposits and certificates of insurance (Lewis & Appenzeller, 1985).

Managing the Box Office

The box office is an important operation and contributes to a facility's revenue and public and consumer relations efforts. It is the public's initial contact with the facility.

The box office area (see Larry Karasz's book, *A Complete Guide to Box Office Management* [1982] which is considered the authoritative source in this area) should be able to accommodate the sale, pickup and distribution of tickets. There should be an adequate number of windows available to handle an unexpected number of walk-up sales. Each window should be capable of selling all price ranges of tickets. The window areas should be computerized. The main entrance to the facility should contain 40% of the ticket-selling windows with the remainder distributed among the other entry areas of the arena. Finally, all box office windows should be located outside the turnstiles and in an area that is easily accessible to the public.

The primary product of the box office is the ticket. A number of factors must be considered before selecting the appropriate tickets, such as: (1) physical characteristics of the facility; (2) seating plans; (3) pricing structure; (4) sales incentive plans; (5) type of ticket system (e.g., preprinted, computer generated); (6) reserved seating, and (7) general admission.

The box office will have established policies and procedures including the following:

- telephone credit card service,
- group sales,
- remote ticket outlets,
- season ticketing services,

A good example of a wide-open airy entrance lobby with an information counter. Recreational Sports Complex, Miami of Ohio University. (Photo: Tom Sawyer)

- sales policies,
- refunds/exchanges,
- mail orders,
- will call,
- lost tickets,
- scalping, and
- reporting and auditing (Lewis & Appenzeller, 1985).

Communication Technology Necessary for Facility/Event Management

Communication is a key to successful facility/event management. The communication must be total and instant for it to be of any value. All facilities should have the following tools for enhanced communication: a radio system; mobile phones; beepers/pagers; a telephone system with automatic busy redial, automatic call return, call forwarding, special call forwarding, call waiting, special call waiting, speed calling, three-way calling, VIP alert, dial datalink service, and calling number ID; fax machine; and computer capabilities such as electronic mail, the Internet, and the World Wide Web. If the facility sells a large number of tickets for numerous events, then 800 service needs to be installed.

Radios and beepers/pagers should be for business only. The Federal Communications Commission (FCC) regulations govern all language on the air, use of profane and/or obscene language and derogatory remarks should be strictly forbidden. A code system to communicate critical information should be developed and all security personnel should be required to memorize and use it.

Controlling Admission and Access
for Facility/Event Management

Facilities should have controlled access. Only people who have purchased a ticket or have been given authorized passes should gain entry into the facility. Most facilities do not allow entry unless the person is a member or has an authorized visitor pass.

Admission control begins in the box office with the ticket itself. Tickets must be clearly printed on a safety stock to prevent counterfeiting. The ticket must be designed for easy recognition (i.e., event, date, performance time, section, row, seat) by the admissions-control staff (ticket-takers, users). Tickets should be published by a reputable and bonded ticketing company that ships them with the audited manifestation directly to the box office to be counted, racked, and distributed under direct control. An alternative to this process is computerized ticketing, which offers the greatest control.

There are two basic categories for admission-type events: (1) "general admission" which permits a person to sit in any available seat on a first-come, first-serve basis, and (2) "reserved seating," which provides patrons with a specific seating location (Jensen, 1988).

It is advisable to open the doors to the facility approximately 75 minutes prior to the scheduled starting time. This allows patrons adequate time to locate seats, use the rest rooms, visit the concession stand, socialize, and get settled before the event begins. It is important to constantly monitor the size and mood of a crowd in the lobby and outside the facility before the doors are opened.

There should be a system for admitting people to the facility who do not have tickets. Many facilities use a photo identification system which provides one of the best means of identifying persons with legitimate business (i.e., employees, media, show personnel, security, and service contractors).

Entrance into facilities that are not spectator venues requires proper identification. In large facilities that is most often accomplished with the issuance of photo identification (ID) cards that can be scanned by computers. Cards do have many uses for fitness, physical activity, recreation, and sport facilities that relate in some way to security. They are most often used to ensure that a person coming to use the facility is an actual member/customer/client, which can be verified visually or by swiping the card through an electronic reader (scanner), and then the user is admitted into the facility. This can be done (1) manually by a member of the staff who reads the display of relevant information that pops up on the screen and then buzzes users through the door or turnstile, or (2) the card can automatically allow entry to users by buzzing the door latch or freeing the turnstile mechanism.

Current software has many uses such as: (1) storing information about the user's past medical history, purchasing records, rental records, fitness program progress, results of last workout or stress test; (2) alerting the user to messages, (3) informing staff of certain user restrictions; (4) flagging unpaid accounts; and (5) alerting staff to special announcements for users such as birthdays or anniversaries (Railey & Tschauner, 1993).

274 The Management of Clubs, Recreation, and Sport: Concepts and Applications

The main entrance area at the Recreation Sports Center at Miami University of Ohio. (Photo: Tom Sawyer)

There are a number of small facilities that cannot afford a computer card ID system. The "low-key" solution is simple. It involves the use of fluorescent, plastic ID wristbands, free to all users. They are numbered sequentially, and each user is expected to wear the band. The bands can be clipped to a gym bag or sneakers, so "I do not have it with me" no longer works as an excuse. A replacement band costs the user $5.

Facility/Event Manager Role in Controlling Crowds

Facility/event managers are responsible for crowd control and are liable for injuries that happen caused by crowd violence. No facility/event manager can anticipate all the situations that might lead to disorder. Cooperation between the facility management staff and promoters, agents, performers, admission control staff, security, police, fire, and government officials will do a great deal to minimize risks and is a key to crowd control.

The International Association of Auditorium Managers (IAAM) recommends the following in regard to crowd control:

- There should be clearly defined and published house policies that should be implemented for each event. The facility management staff should be clearly in charge and ensure compliance with all laws, house rules and regulations, health standards, and common sense practices.
- Carefully evaluate the effects of the sale of alcohol.
- Clearly define the chain of command and the duties and responsibilities for the facility/event manager, as well as all policemen, security guards, ushers and usherettes, ticket takers and first-aid personnel. Be sure they are constantly trained on how to properly react in an emergency situation.

- Encourage patrons to report dangerous and threatening situations.
- Avoid general admission ticketing and seating if at all possible.
- Carefully plan the sale of tickets, especially when the demand will greatly exceed the supply. Develop a fair and equitable distribution system, mechanisms to control lines, and policies requiring personnel to treat the crowds well and courteously.
- Conduct search and seizure to confiscate bottles, cans, and other items which may be used to injure others.
- Establish legal attendance capacities for each event set up, and obtain the written approval of the fire marshal and building inspector.
- Pay close attention to the architectural plans and designs of the facility. Do not allow illegal or dangerous obstructions. Make sure the graphics system works to the facility's advantage and to the crowd's advantage by helping them get to their seats and other conveniences and exits as quickly and safely as possible.
- Develop an emergency evacuation plan.
- Make sure the public address system works and that its volume and clarity are adequate.
- Keep aisles clear.
- Keep people without floor tickets off the floor.
- Do not turn the lights off completely; maintain at least three footcandles of light to illuminate aisles and emergency exits.
- Play soft, soothing music before and after an event and during intermission.
- Control the stage and the attraction and do not allow the attraction to overly or dangerously excite the crowd.
- Insist on a clean, well-maintained building and a hassle-free atmosphere (see additional approaches to crowd control in appendix).

How are Traffic and Parking Best Handled?

Traffic can be a major problem if not controlled by facility security in the parking lots and local police on the public streets. It is vital that the facility management provide training for security and parking lot attendants including first aid, C.P.R., traffic control, security procedures, and crowd control procedures. Further, the management must develop a strong relationship with the local police in order to assist in controlling traffic entering and exiting parking facilities.

Parking is always a problem, but if handled properly it can be a very lucrative source of revenue that should not be ignored. Virtually everyone who attends an event arrives by car. Careful attention must be given when creating parking areas, including: (1) handicapped parking spaces, (2) appropriate curb cuts, (3) bus entrances and parking areas, (4) tractor-trailer entrances and parking, (5) paving, (6) lighting, (7) drainage, (8) sidewalks, (9) landscaping, (10) reserved parking areas, and (11) security controls, such as sensors or loops buried in each entrance lane; single pass lane; video surveillance of entrances, exits, and cashier booths; and appropriate signage (Olson, Hirsch, Breitenbach, & Saunders, 1987).

Procedures for Security and Emergencies

There is no substitute for well-trained security and emergency medical personnel. This personnel can be off-duty police, deputies or EMTs. The most basic training tool for security and emergency medical personnel is a security and emergency medical handbook. The handbook can be used to orient and indoctrinate the security and emergency medical personnel. The main function of this personnel is to provide professional service on behalf of the facility for the patrons' health and safety. The handbook should provide personnel with guidelines for providing appropriate service, and assist them in becoming aware of potential trouble and increasing their safety awareness. Further, the handbook should contain a clear written outline of the appropriate chain of command in the facility. (see Appendix I for contents of handbook).

Importance of Proper Signage

Signs are easy to take for granted and many people do just that. But a lot of thought goes into determining the need for signage, the vital messages to be provided, and where signs need to be posted. Signs affect everyone in a facility; therefore, their messages, sizes, shapes, colors, and locations should be determined during the initial development stages of a project.

There are warning, danger, caution, notice, emergency, rules and regulations, and standard operating procedure signs. All these, in one way or another, aim to inform. Signs, in order to have a purpose, need to attract the facility user's attention. Careful and conspicuous placement of signs in the appropriate areas and at the right heights is key.

The contents of particular signs have different meanings for different clientele. Signs must be designed to meet the educational levels of the users for which they are intended. A YMCA's signs, for example, will tend to read differently than signs posted in a fitness center or health club.

The simplest form of communication on a sign does not involve text, but rather a graphic or distinctive shape (i.e., octagonal stop sign) or color. Signs do not have to be one color or square. A recent international trend is the use of pictorial signs with no text. This is important because facility signs must take on and convey a universal message to many ethnic populations.

The purpose of posting a safety sign for users should be threefold: (1) to identify an immediate or hidden hazard to the observer; (2) to convey an urgent message of danger or caution to the observer; and (3) to attempt to modify the behavior of the observer in such a way as to prevent injury (Berry, 1993).

Role of Concessions

A well-operated concession operation is more often than not the determining factor in the financial status of a facility. Rarely is an auditorium successful without a sound concessions operation. The importance of a good concessions operation to the average facility cannot be overemphasized. The role of the con-

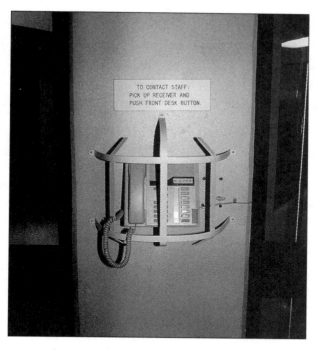

A good example of signage and protection for the telephone in a multipurpose facility. (Photo: Tom Sawyer)

A good example of a sign that is easy to read and undersand that is displayed so that it can be seen easily. (Photo: Tom Sawyer)

An example of signage directing participants to walk in the inside lane and pass on the outside lane. You could also direct the runners to run in the outer lane. (Photo: Tom Sawyer)

cessions operation is to generate revenue and provide good food and drink to the consumers.

The concessions operation requires managers to understand the following: (1) how to serve good food at a reasonable price, (2) development of marketing strategy, (3) financial management, (4) business planning, (5) purchasing, (6) inventory management, (7) business law, (8) health codes, (9) OSHA regulations, (10) selection of insurance, (11) how to advertise, (12) selection of personnel, (13) stocking the concession area, (14) maintaining the equipment, (15) housekeeping requirements, (16) how to establish price, and (17) convenience foods (Lewis & Appenzeller, 1985).

The location and configuration of concession operations is extremely important to their success. There are four sources of good information about concessions operation: (1) International Association of Auditorium Managers [IAAM], (2) National Association of Concessionaires [NAC], (3) Don Jewell's book, *Public Assembly Facilities Planning and Management* (1981), and (4) Steve Rogers' article, "Avoiding Concession Design Problems in Managing the Leisure Facility" (1980).

Olson et al., (1987) listed the major shortcomings as: (1) not enough concession stands to serve the number of seats; (2) inadequate kitchen location and space; (3) no installation of floor drains in kitchen and stand areas; (4) no provision for a commissary for hawking (vending) operations; (5) service elevators on the opposite side of the building from storage areas; (6) no provisions for exhaust; (7) loading docks and storerooms on different floors than needed; (8) inadequate ventilation; (9) insufficient energy and water availability; and (10) lack of wide concourse areas to facilitate traffic flow.

Concession stands should be (1) conveniently located to all seats (a patron should be able to reach a stand in 40 to 60 seconds); (2) well-organized with clear indications of where the patrons should line up for service; (3) bright, colorful, well-lit, and decorated with attractive pictures of food and beverage being served; (4) able to generate the aroma of food such as popcorn into the concourse; (5) designed so equipment, food, and cash registers are located so that items can be quickly served by a single person in each selling station; (6) constructed so that menu boards are appropriately placed indicating the products and prices; and (7) attention grabbers (Bucher & Krotee, 1993).

The National Association of Concessionaires (NAC) in conjunction with Coca-Cola USA, and Cornell University published a study (1982) for NAC members entitle, "Creating and Handling Buying Fever," which discussed the basic elements of a successful concession operation, the key points of the NAC's "Buying Fever Check List (Table 13-2)."

Table 13-2
Buying Fever Check List

- Review merchandising and menu boards for clarity. Communicate and make it easier to order.
- Cut down on inquiry time through effective menu board layout.
- Use of combinations of menu items to reduce the number of customer decisions.
- Keep your equipment in good repair. Perform preventative maintenance checks regularly.
- Locate equipment and supplies for soft drinks and popcorn adjacent to the dispensers.
- Place the menu board so that it is easily visible to all customers.
- Ensure that employees check supplies during slack time and that additional supplies are easily accessible.
- Make lettering on the menu boards large enough so that it is easily readable for all customers. List all brands of soft drinks carried in their logo script and all the names of sizes and prices for all items.
- Provide containers or boxes for customers to carry large orders.
- If you do not have a cash register, place an adding machine or table of prices for popular combinations for the employees to use.
- Design the stand with promotions in mind. Build in space to handle premiums such as plastic cups and posters.
- Location must be accessible with the right products, packages, and price.
- The stand should be very neat and clean.
- The personnel shall be well-trained and pleasant.

All facilities should consider having "vendors" or "hawkers" take food and beverages to the people in the seating are who are a reluctant to get up and risk missing part of the event. Another contribution made by "vendors" or "hawkers" is that they relieve the pressure placed upon permanent concession stands during the intermission, when customers literally swarm the concession facilities.

Finally, all facilities should have portable concession stands to be used during special events. These usually are attractive wagons that everyone has seen in shopping malls and airports.

Role of Merchandising

The term "merchandising" describes the process of selling programs, novelties, T-shirts, and other event-related souvenirs. This business has changed dramatically in the last decade. There are literally thousands of T-shirts, jerseys, and painters caps commemorating each touring group or event from rock acts to country-western shows to ice shows to circuses. The revenue generated from these sales has increased from $1.08 per capita in 1982 to over $8.90 per capita in 1995.

A typical souvenir store or stand will offer many licensed products for the customer. A licensed product is one that has a "mark" and belongs to the organization. Every time the "mark" appears on a piece of merchandise, a percentage of the sale, approximately 8-10%, is returned to the "mark" owner. Licensed products have been very profitable for sporting organizations as well as a great source of "free" advertisement. The sport manager should seriously consider licensing opportunities if they arise.

Establishing an Effective Maintenance and Housekeeping Program

In establishing an effective maintenance and housekeeping program, it must be realized that each organization has problems and needs unique to the organization. The maintenance and housekeeping operation of any two organizations will not be exactly alike. The following principles should be used as guidance in the development of a maintenance and housekeeping program:

- establishing objectives and standards, such as all facilities should: (1) have a clean, orderly appearance at all times, (2) be maintained to create a safe and healthful environment, and (3) promote good public relations by providing facilities where people have an opportunity for an enjoyable experience,
- performing all tasks with economy of time, personnel, equipment, and materials,
- implementing operations based on a sound, written maintenance plan,
- scheduling maintenance and housekeeping based on sound policies and priorities,
- placing a high emphasis on preventive maintenance,
- developing a sound organizational plan for the maintenance and housekeeping department,

- providing adequate fiscal resources to support the program,
- furnishing adequate personnel to implement the maintenance and house-keeping functions,
- designing the program to protect the natural environment,
- assuming the responsibility for both customers, visitors, and staff,
- designing renovation or new construction projects with maintenance and housekeeping in mind, and
- accepting responsibility for the public image of the facility.

A "clean" facility will encourage greater member retention. The most important people in the organization are the maintenance and cleaning personnel. However, often they are also the lowest paid employees in the organization.

Maintenance of the facility and equipment should be done on a regular schedule. Some areas will need more frequent attention (e.g., swimming pools or spas) then others (e.g., lobby or offices). The maintenance personnel in some cases will need to be certified (e.g., swimming pools).

The cleaning personnel should be scheduled to work during off hours, but at least one should be on duty while the facility is open. There should be a clearly planned cleaning schedule developed by the sport manager. The sport manager should also consider recycling paper products and soda cans. If the facility is large enough, recycling could become a profit center.

Finally, the sport manager will need to assign personnel to maintain the outside grounds (e.g., grass cutting, planting flowers, watering, snow removal, etc). These tasks can either be assigned to employees or outsourced to an independent contractor. The latter would be more convenient. The organization will not have to purchase, store, or maintain lawn and yard maintenance and snow removal equipment. But make certain a dependable service is selected. A member's first impression begins at the approach to the facility. If the organization fails to respect its facility and adjoining grounds, the member will not either.

Developing a Policies and Procedures Manual

There are any number of reasons why it is important to have written policies and procedures for governing facility/event management. The primary reasons are to: (1) provide a formal policy that guides administrative decisions, (2) reduce the organization's vulnerability to litigation, and (3) clearly communicate to staff and customers/clients a set of uniform and standard practices to guide decisions and behaviors.

A well-designed policy and procedure manual for facility/event management can assist in answering questions such as:

- What type of reports, records, or documentation are staff required to file and keep?
- What are the due process procedures?
- What are the staff's legal responsibilities and procedures for implementing them?

- What is the policy regarding requisitioning, purchasing, inventorying, servicing, maintaining, and inspecting equipment?
- What is the recruiting, hiring, and evaluating process?
- What are the emergency procedures?
- What are the crowd control procedures?
- What process is utilized for inspecting and maintaining the facilities?
- What procedures are employed for program evaluation?
- What process is implemented to control admission?
- How is the facility scheduled?
- What are the procedures for evaluating whether or not a person can return to activity after injury or illness?

Contents for a Policies and Procedures Manual for Facility/Event Management

A facilities/event policies and procedures manual delineates general as well as specific program guidelines. The kind of information that should be contained in the policies and procedures manual will vary from one organization to another. In general, the policies should reflect: (1) the rights of all participants, (2) the philosophy of the organization and the rationale for the existence of the program, (3) such legislative dictates as Title VII (sexual harassment), Title IX (gender equity), and the Americans with Disabilities Act (equal access for disabilities participants) (Conn & Malloy, 1989).

Steps in Developing a Policy and Procedure Manual

Conn (1991), Conn and Malloy, (1989) suggested that the following steps should be used when developing policies and procedures:

Step 1: Developing a policy and procedure manual is a long, arduous task that requires management's complete involvement and support. It is important that all personnel (management as well as staff) are involved in the development of the policies and procedures for the organization. The typical approach is to appoint a committee to carefully research and ultimately recommend policies and procedures. Management must be prepared to allocate resources (i.e., time and funds) and encourage the involvement of all staff members. Policies and procedures must be carefully researched and synthesized before being written. Therefore, it is extremely important to involve people who look at policies and procedures from many different angles. The more widespread the involvement, the greater the chances are that the manual will be used and maintained after completion.

Several factors should be considered when deciding who will be appointed to the committee:

- Size of the staff—every member of a small staff will have intimate involvement on the committee, however, larger staffs should be divided into subcommittees that will prepare specific sets of policies and procedures;

Management Tip
Possible Contents for the Manual

- Accountability: annual financial audits, facility and equipment maintenance audits, facility and equipment inspection audits, inventory control, personnel evaluation, program evaluation, risk assessment survey, and ticket inventory control and sales audits.
- Sport/Athletic Council: purpose, function, structure, and operating rules.
- Governance structures/authorities.
- Equipment: acceptable supplier or vendor list, requisition process, purchasing process, bidding procedures, inventory process, inspection audits, and maintenance procedures.
- Budgeting, formulation, accountability, and control.
- Events: staging, concessions, entertainment, scheduling, traffic, and parking.
- Computer operations.
- Conduct and ethics: staff and participants.
- Courtesy Car Program.
- Disbursements: goods and services, payroll, travel expenses.
- Employment conditions: educational benefits, hiring, holidays and vacations, leaves of absences, parking, performance evaluation.
- Expansion and curtailment of programs.
- Expansion/renovation of facilities.
- Facilities: maintenance, inspection, risk assessment, usage, key distribution.
- Film office: equipment, operations.
- Fundraising and booster organizations.
- Advertising, marketing, and promotion.
- Media relations: events, news releases, publicity materials, television and radio programs, printed media.
- Philosophy, mission, goals, objectives.
- Printing.
- Receipt, deposit, and custody.
- Scheduling: events, practices, sport officials, personnel (e.g., ushers, ticket sellers and takers, program sellers, concession workers, police, emergency personnel).
- Summer camps.
- Telephones: Fax, mobile phones, beepers.
- Ticket Office: distribution, operations, sales, complimentary tickets, auditing.
- Concessions: sales, inventory, licenses.
- Alcohol: sales, inventory, licenses.
- Leasing and Contractual agreements: advertising, signs and posters, ticket office service, program development and distribution, staging, traffic, parking, concessions, alcohol, security, insurance, emergency management.

- Administration and board—the manual must be approved by management and the board (if one exists); therefore, it is important that management and the board are represented on the committee;
- Customer/client/student-athlete—it is important to involve those most affected by the policies and procedures on the committee that develops them;
- Community interest—most organizations have links with the community and community representation could be very useful in future activities; therefore, it is important to involve community members on the committee; and
- Diversity or inclusiveness—the committee should be a mirror image of the organization and the community as a whole.

Step 2: The format of the manual must be flexible. It is suggested that (1) a three-ring binder be used to store the information, (2) the information be divided into logical sections and subsections with appropriate paginations (i.e. section one—1.1, 1.2, 1.3; section two—2.1, 2.2, 2.3), (3) a table of contents, definition section for acronyms and terms, and an index be included, and (4) the various sections be color-coded.

Step 3: The committee should assign one person to write the manual after collecting the appropriate data from the various task groups. The committee needs to adopt an outline and structure for the manual as well as a timeline for completion of the various sections. The writer should use a computer and appropriate word processing software.

Step 4: The completed manual is dynamic in nature and must be reviewed periodically. A procedure for reviewing the manual must be established. All staff members should be encouraged to periodically review the policies and procedures within their domain and then recommend any changes to the appropriate authorities. Making policy and procedure changes a regular agenda item at staff meetings sensitizes the staff to the importance of the manual and maintains its currency.

The sport manager needs to spend time developing a policy and procedures manual. The above four steps will assist the sport manager in efficiently developing the manual. The manual should be reviewed and revised annually after implementation.

Summary

Facility management is critical in keeping any organization operating smoothly and efficiently. A facility that is well-maintained and managed is one of the best public and consumer relations tools in an organization's arsenal. Further, event management is intimately related to facility management.

Learning Objective 1: Describe the roles of booking, the box office, concessions, merchandising, and scheduling.

There are a number of critical areas in facility/event management that generate revenue. These areas are scheduling and booking appropriate activities at optimal times of the year, selling tickets through an efficient box office, meeting the refreshment needs of spectators, and selling appealing merchandise as souvenirs of the event.

Learning Objective 2: Development of a facility/event policy and procedure manual.

All facilities need to have a policy and procedures manual. The policy and procedures manual is the guide to overall operation of the facility and the events held within. This guide will enable personnel to maintain efficient operations with very little supervision.

Learning Objective 3: Development of an appropriate communication plan.

When an event is underway, communication within the facility with employees is a critical component of efficient operations. A well-designed communication plan assists in crowd management, security, and emergency operations. Every facility must have a well-planned and financed communication plan in order to protect spectators, participants, and staff.

Learning Objective 4: Development of security, crowd control, and emergency management plan.

Major concerns for facility managers are security, crowd control, and emergency management. All facilities should have a detailed plan to adequately manage these very critical areas that impact spectator, participant, and employee safety. Facility managers should never underestimate the importance of security, crowd control, and emergency management.

Learning Objective 5: Understanding the role of signage in facility and event management.

Signs are important for a number of reasons, including safety, crowd management, warnings, traffic control, identification of area, emergency management, and more. Facility managers need to be very careful in the development of the signage plan for the facility. The signage throughout a facility needs to be maintained and kept current.

Case Study

A.   John was recently hired as the director of a medium-sized town (75,000) civic center. He has been given the task by the city council to make the civic center self-sufficient within four years. The civic center can seat 10,500 for basketball games. There are two large high schools in town, four others within 25 miles, and one medium-sized university and one small college in town as well. The state high school athletic association a few years ago used the facility for sectional and regional basketball games but has not renewed the contract for the past three years. The facility has fallen into disrepair from neglect and lack of appropriate funding. The staff has suffered from a lack of leadership and displays low morale. The civic center director reports to the mayor. The center does not have an advisory board. The town is within two to three hours from major cities with populations exceeding one million.

The center does not have a policies and procedures manual in place. Security, crowd control, and emergency management is handled by the chief of police and fire departments, respectively. Maintenance and housekeeping has been contracted out to a local firm.

The center does not control the concessions for events. The concession function has been farmed out to local civic groups for fund-raising. The center does not sell any kind of nonfood merchandise. Finally, the center relies on two national ticket-selling organizations to sell its tickets to all events.

1.   What should John do first?
2.   How should the staff be organized?
3.   What should be done regarding ticket sales, concessions, and merchandise sales?
4.   How should security, crowd control, and emergency management be handled?
5.   What should be done about maintenance and housekeeping?
6.   How should John handle the scheduling and booking of events?
7.   What should be done regarding communication within the facility and in the parking areas?
8.   How should admission and access to the facility be controlled?
9.   What type of signage should John request?

B.   The World Wide Wrestle Mania is underway with a capacity crowd (10,500). The event is a minimum of three hours. The main event of the evening has just gotten underway. Suddenly a tile floats down from the ceiling and lands in the front rows on the north of the arena. Then another, and another, and another. It appears to be snowing tiles from the ceiling.

1.   What should be done?
2.   How have the employees been trained to deal with such an emergency situation?
3.   What should the announcer say over the loud speaker?
4.   What should the emergency management team do in this situation?

References

Berry, Dennis W. (1990). Maryland study shows simple signage works. *Aquatics, (2)*6, 16-20.

Bucher, Charles A., & Krotee, March I. (1993). *Management of physical education and sport* (10th ed.). St. Louis, MO: C.V. Mosby Year Book.

Cohen, Andrew. (1993). Security check. *Athletic Business, (17)*3, 41-44.

Conn, James H. (1991). An open-book policy. *Athletic Business, (15)*2, 57-60.

Conn, James H., & Malloy, B.P. (1989). *Organizing policy for interscholastic athletic programs*. Carmel, IN: Benchmark Publishing.

Jensen, C.R. (1988). *Administrative management of physical education and athletic programs* (2nd ed.). Philadelphia: Lea Febiger.

Jewell, D. (1981). *Public assembly facilities planning and management.* Chicago: International Association of Auditorim Managers.

Lewis, Guy, & Appenzeller, Herb. (1985). *Successful sport management.* Charlottesville, VA: The Michie Company.

Olson, J., Hirsch, E., Breitenbach, O., & Saunders, K. (1987). *Administration of high school and collegiate athletic programs*. Philadelphia: Saunders College Publishing.

Railey, Jim H., & Tschauner, Peggy Railey. (1993). *Managing physical education, fitness, and sports programs* (2nd ed.). Mountain View, CA: Mayfield Publishing Company.

Rogers, S. (1980, November/December). Avoiding concession design problems. *Managing the Leisure Facility, 4*(3), 36-38.

Turner, Edward T. (1994). Vital signs. *Athletic Business, 17*:8, 65-67.

Suggested Readings

American Sport Education Program. (1996). *Event management for sport directors.* Champaign, IL: Human Kinetics Publishers.

Karasz, L. (1982). *A complete guide to box office management*. New York: Ticket Craft.

Parkhouse, Bonnie L. (1995). *The management of sport: Its foundation and application* (2nd ed.). St. Louis, MO: C.V. Mosby Year Book.

14

LEGAL ISSUES IN
SPORT MANAGEMENT

◆ ———————————— ◆

Instructional Objectives

After reading this chapter the student should be able to:

- understand what role a tort plays in sport management,

- describe what negligent conduct is,

- outline the various defenses for negligence,

- describe the eight legal duties of a sport management professional,

- define the legal responsibilities in regard to supervision and planning,

- describe the purpose of an exculpatory agreement and use of warnings,

- outline the different type of users, and ways to provide notice of inherent danger,

- define the uses of a contract in sport management,

- describe the impact of the ADA on employment and facilities, and

- outline the relationship held by an organization with an independent contractor.

Introduction

The threat of malpractice suits against sport professionals is a real one. The chances of physical activity accidents and death are widely recognized. These risks are often misunderstood and, even if recognized, not always appreciated. Legal risks to the professional are genuine and ever changing. As more people participate and as the number of accidents increases, the legal system will become involved to resolve the problems that arise from exercise programs.

Since the early sixties, our society has become increasingly predisposed to solving problems through the courts. Today medical malpractice is a common thing, but 20 years ago it was virtually unknown in this country. Just a decade ago, lawyers were rarely, if ever, sued for their own negligence. Today, verdicts rendered by judges and juries in lawsuits against physicians, attorneys, and other professionals have dramatically increased. It is clear that our society has become legally sophisticated and its members more knowledgeable about the legal process (Baley & Matthews, 1989; Anderson & Kumpf, 1990).

It is only a matter of time before this "litigation epidemic" affects the sport professional. The importance of preparing for this eventuality must be obvious. The first exercise-related death to an older American in a program supervised by a health/fitness/recreation/sport professional that results in suit and national media attention may very well open the flood gates to a major increase in litigation (Dougherty, et al., 1994; Wong, 1993). One must anticipate this development unless it is assumed that negligence in this field is highly unlikely. Such an assumption has no basis in experience, especially given the relative infancy of the sport field, as related to the older population, with its rapidly changing knowledge base and technical content. Operating on such an assumption promotes a false sense of security and renders personnel insensitive to operational conditions that are susceptible to legal challenge and perhaps liability.

The sport professional who provides physical activity services needs to understand the legal risks attendant to facilities and equipment as well as to the operating policies and procedures utilized for various clientele. The risks obviously increase with the number and severity of the special medical considerations inherent in the clientele. Therefore, the precautions and safety measures utilized must grow in complexity to maximize safety for those categories with the poorest health status. Moreover, the support facilities and equipment, the expertise of the staff, and the environmental setting are linked to clientele health status and program practices.

In any case, policies and procedures should be developed and implemented only after consultation with a legal advisor. Proceeding without careful legal advice is foolhardy. Attention to this matter should be regarded as no less important than the medical advice needed to specify the participant screening requirements or clinical contraindications to be utilized in a given program. What follows can serve as a useful guide for such individualized professional advice.

The Law of Torts

The law of torts is a body of legal principles which govern "wrongs" done by one individual to another. Tortious acts can be: *intentional,* or assault and battery; *negligent,* or personal injury/malpractice; or, governed by standards of *strict li-*

ability, or injuries arising out of fact for which there will be absolute liability (van der Smissen, 1990).

At the dawn of common law, crime and tort covered much the same ground, both stemming from a common desire for vengeance, distinguishable only by the nature of the respective sanctions. Tort liability, unlike crime, provided a means whereby the victim could be "bribed" into abstaining from retaliation by the prospect of being able to compel the wrongdoer to render him monetary compensation for the wrong done.

A *tort* is an act or omission producing injury to another. It is a civil wrong for which the remedy is a common law action for damages. Put another way, it is a wrong done to a plaintiff or injured party. The act of the defendant (tortfeasant, or wrongdoer) may not have been intentional, but could have been the result of negligence.

What is Negligence?

Liability in ordinary *negligence* is the failure to do what a reasonably careful and prudent person would have done under the same or like circumstances, or the doing of something that a reasonably careful and prudent person would not have done under the same or like circumstances. This will be determined by the court based on the evidence presented in each case (van der Smissen, 1990).

What is Negligent Behavior?

Negligence is any conduct that falls below the standard established by the courts and professional associations for the protection of others against unreasonable risk of harm. The various levels of negligence important to sport professionals are:

1. *Malfeasance, or a commission of an unlawful act.*

Example:
You own a fitness center and indicate in your advertisements that you will prescribe and design exercise programs; but you are not certified by the ACSM or any other established certifying agency that certifies your competency to prescribe or design exercise programs.

2. *Misfeasance, or an improper performance of some lawful act.*

Example:
You are certified by ACSM to prescribe and design exercise programs. You prescribe an exercise program for a client that is deemed inappropriate and it caused injury to your client when it was implemented.

3. Nonfeasance, or failure of a person to act.

Example:

You are certified to perform C.P.R. but failed to do so when your client was in need.

4. Reckless misconduct, or intent to commit an act, but no intention to harm anyone.

Example:

You received your C.P.R. training a few years ago when the precordial thumb was part of the procedure. You were leading an exercise session when one of the clients had a cardiac arrest, you performed C.P.R. including the precordial thumb and caused damage to the sternum. The client sued you because of the damage caused by an inappropriate procedure.

5. Willful/wanton conduct, or intentional act of an unreasonable char- acter in to- tal disregard for human safety.

Example:

You are a certified exercise leader and know you are not trained to prescribe or design exercise programs for clients. You are an exercise instructor and can implement programs for clients. Yet you decide the program prescribed for this client is inappropriate and needs major modification. You modify the program and implement it. The client has a cardiac relapse caused by the modified exercise program.

6. Gross negligence, or failure to use even slight care or the omission to use ordinary care and diligence to avoid a discovered or apparent danger.

Example:

You purchased new exercise equipment and in the manufacturer's warranty information was a section regarding regular systematic equipment inspection and maintenance procedures including a maintenance reporting form that could be duplicated for future use. You totally and willfully ignore the manufacturer's suggestions and fail to inspect regularly or provide necessary maintenance for the equipment. A few months later a client is injured on the new equipment due to faulty equipment maintenance.

7. Slight negligence, or the failure to exercise great care or an absence of that degree of care and vigilance to which persons of extraordinary prudence and foresight are accustomed.

Example:

Using the equipment example above, the owner decides to modify the manufacturer's suggested maintenance procedure and allows for a longer period time between inspections and actual performance of necessary maintenance. A client is injured on the equipment and the maintenance procedures established by the owner are found to be inappropriate.

What are the Components of Negligence?

Damage is essential in negligence. In the first place, it has to be shown that the damage was caused by the defendant's carelessness. The question is not "whose act", but "whose carelessness caused the damage?" Secondly, the damage has to be legally attributable to the defendant. The predominant test used to determine this is "foreseeability of damage". The test is foreseeability in the sense of hindsight, not foresight; it is what a court, reviewing an event later, considers to have been foreseeable in order to do justice in the case before it (Baley & Matthews, 1989; van der Smissen, 1990; Wong, 1993).

Liability in negligence requires affirmative answers to four questions: (1) Does the law recognize liability in this kind of situation? The law must recognize that a *duty* to conform to the requisite standard of care to protect another against the kind of harm in question existed. (2) Was the defendant careless, i.e., did his conduct fall short of the requisite standard of care and come within the scope set by the law? Once a *duty* has been determined, then a *breach of duty* must be established. (3) Did the defendant's carelessness in fact cause the damage or injury? The court must recognize that the defendant's action or lack of action was the *proximate cause* of the injury. (4) To what extent should the damage in suit to the particular plaintiff be ascribed in law to the defendant? In other words, is there a reasonably *proximate casual* link between the *breach of duty* and the harm? (Koehler, 1988; Nygaard & Boone, 1989; Jennings & Skipper, 1989).

A Sport Professional's Duties

Once the injured participant or those persons responsible for the injured party believe that the injury suffered is related to the professional's negligence, the situation is taken into court for resolution. A goal of all professionals is to prevent situations that provide the basis for legal action from occurring. All sport professionals have duties. Specific responsibilities are imposed upon sport management professionals from several sources: federal and/or state constitutions, legislation, the common law that evolves through precedents established in cases decided by the various courts, and the various professional standards established by national professional organizations (Nygaard & Boone, 1988). Of these four, common law is usually more important in resolving liability or negligence issues resulting from injuries during participation.

A *duty* is a legal obligation to another. As early as 1977, duties for sport professionals were considered important. Langerman & Fidel (1977) in *Trial* magazine listed seven duties as common focal points of participant injury litigation, and later Nygaard and Boone (1989) outlined eight. Every sport management professional should consider the following as their legal duties to:

1. Provide adequate supervision for all participants;
2. Warn participants of the inherent risks in an activity;
3. Provide safe facilities for participation;
4. Evaluate for injury or incapacity prior to participation;
5. Provide adequate and proper equipment for activities;
6. Match participants to appropriate activities based on their age and physical condition;
7. Provide good, sound planning for all lessons and programs; and
8. Provide proper first aid, and establish and implement an emergency medical plan" (Nygaard & Boone, 1989).

The Establishment of a Standard of Care

Negligence is conduct that fails to conform to the standard required by law for safeguarding others or oneself against unreasonable risk of injury. Common law developed the *"reasonable man (person) test"* as the model against which to evaluate a particular defendant's conduct for conformity with what is required at any given time and/or place in order to avoid unnecessary danger. The test prefers an objective standard of judging behavior. It avoids the perplexing task of having to scrutinize each specific defendant's subjective capacity; instead, it judges external manifestations of conduct by whether or not it measures up to the normal set by the reasonable man.

As a sport management professional you will be held to a standard of care established by case law using standards developed by such professional organizations as the American College of Sports Medicine (ACSM), American Alliance for Health, Physical Education, Recreation, and Dance (AAHPERD), National Association for Sport and Physical Education (NASPE), North American Society for Sport Management (NASSM), International Dance-Exercise Association (IDEA), Institute for Aerobic Research (IAR), Aerobic and Fitness Association of America (AFAA), Council on Facilities and Equipment (CFE), and Young Men's Christian Association (YMCA). These organizations have established guidelines for exercise testing and prescription protocol(s). Health and exercise professionals need to be very concerned about testing and prescription guidelines developed by recognized national and international professional organizations.

What is Breach of Duty?

Once a duty has been established, it is the task of the plaintiff's lawyer to prove you breached or failed to perform your duty as prescribed by case law or professional organizations. Breach means to *improperly* or *fail* to perform a duty.

What is Proximate Cause?

This concept is based on the relationship between the cause of the injury and the professional's breach of duty. If the plaintiff's lawyer can show a proximate causal relationship between the professional's breach of duty and the injury, then the court might very well find the defendant guilty of negligence. The attorneys often call this the "*BUT FOR*" test; the injury would have occurred "*BUT FOR*" this breach of duty.

In the practical situation, the determination of liability and one's duty will depend upon all the facts and circumstances surrounding the injury. In reviewing many cases it becomes evident that the court usually weighs the following factors in making its final judgement:

1.   The value of that which is exposed to the risk; in our case, participants are given the highest value in the formula.

     - For example, did the participant perform the activity knowingly and voluntarily with an understanding of all possible consequences or did the participant act because the professional said to perform?

2.   The reason for the conduct of the person taking the risk.
3.   The magnitude of the risk; is the potential injury a bruised ego or broken bones ?
4.   The utility of the risk.
5.   The necessity of the risk; is there some other activity that would produce the same result without the risk?

What Does the Extent of Injuries/Damage Have to Do with Negligence?

What is the extent of actual injury or damage? Is there a presence of actual injury or damage? If a young quadriplegic girl is wheeled into the courtroom or the grief-stricken family of an elderly patient who died while participating in a prescribed exercise program, you can imagine the dramatic effect on a judge and jury. However, if the damage is emotional strain or harassment, the damage will not be as apparent, but still can be determined to be present.

What Are the Defenses for Negligence?

Carelessness is a fact of life. We all make mistakes in our professional capacities and sometimes those careless errors cause injury to others. It is helpful to understand the appropriate defenses for negligence just in case you are sued. There are four common defenses for negligence: assumption of risk, contributory negligence, comparative negligence, and governmental immunity.

What is Assumption of Risk?

The doctrine of "assumption of risk" has been recognized as a defense against liability in activities such as competitive sports and exercise testing and prescription. It is based on the theory that people who know, understand, and appreciate the danger involved in an activity and voluntarily engage in it, willingly expose themselves to certain predictable inherent risks. The defense of assumption of risk

Risk Management Considerations

In developing a risk management plan for a Baby Boomers Sport Club, the writers must consider the following relating to tort liability and negligence:

1. Try to perceive reasonableness in the situation from the standpoint of the other person or people;
2. When asked to accept a new challenge, do not hold yourself up to be something you are not. There is a fine line between what you really are and what you think you are. Stay within the parameters of what you are qualified and competent to accomplish;
3. Do not assume any duty(ies) beyond your level of competence;
4. Realize and recognize that the standard of care may change in the same activity, within the same time frame, as the risk increases;
5. Record all changes in planning, policies, and procedures within your organization that affects clientele;
6. Familiarize yourself and/or staff with policies and procedures that will result in the establishment of an appropriate amount of prudence in actions to be taken, for example:
    a. conduct regular inspection of facilities and equipment;
    b. insist on prompt and full repair of faulty equipment;
    c. treat all injured clients using proper first aid and emergency procedures and properly trained personnel; and
    d. properly train and certify personnel assigned instructional, testing, or supervisory duties;
7. Learn to recognize the following situations:
    a. behavior that could be negligent;
    b. an act not properly done;
    c. appropriate care not provided; or
    d. circumstance under which it is done creates risk or creates situations that are unreasonably dangerous to others;
8. Conduct seminars or inservice programs to inform and educate staff of the legal issues that surround their profession; and
9. Show reasonable care in the performance of voluntarily assumed duties.

is in fact quite narrowly confined and restricted by two requirements: first, that the plaintiff must know, understand, and appreciate the risk being incurred, and second, that the choice to incur it must be entirely free and voluntary. Because in the ordinary case there is no conclusive evidence against the plaintiff on these issues, they normally go to the jury; and because juries are notoriously unfavorable to the defense, the percentage of cases in which the plaintiff has actually been barred from recovery by his assumption of the risk is quite small (van der Smissen, 1990).

Assumption of risk is a rule existing either by itself or in conjunction with contributory or comparative negligence. There are several categories of assumption of risk. ***Expressed* assumption of risk** is related to waivers and release of liability where one contracts or expressly agrees to accept a risk. ***Implied* assumption of risk** is present when a participant agrees to accept inherent risks in an activity, but does not contract to release another from liability. ***Primary* assumption of risk** is the assumption of the inherent risks of an activity, that is, those risks that are the result of the normal action within the activity. ***Secondary* assumption of risk** is present when one agrees to accept the risk of an activity performed in a facility that is less than ideal for that activity (Wong, 1993).

"Knowledge of the risk" is the watchword of assumption of risk. Under ordinary circumstances the plaintiff will not be taken to assume any risk of either activities or conditions of which he/she is ignorant. Furthermore, the plaintiff must not only know of the facts that create the danger, but must comprehend and appreciate the danger itself. If because of age or lack of information or experience, he does not comprehend the risk involved in a known situation, he will not be taken to consent to assume it. The standard to be applied is, in theory at least, a subjective one, geared to a particular plaintiff and situation.

At the same time, it is evident that a purely subjective standard opens a very wide door for the plaintiff who is willing to testify that he did not know or understand the risk. It is imperative the health/fitness/recreation/sport professional take the time to educate the clientele of all inherent risks involved in testing procedures and exercise prescriptive programs.

Even where there is knowledge and appreciation of a risk, the plaintiff may not be barred from recovery where the situation changes to introduce a new element, such as increasing the intensity in a prescribed exercise program without informing the client. The fact that the plaintiff is fully aware of one risk does not mean that he/she assumes another of which he/she is unaware (van der Smissen, 1990).

The second limitation for the defense of assumption of risk is that the plaintiff is not barred from recovery unless the choice is a free and voluntary one. There must first of all, of course, be some manifestation of consent to relieve the defendant of obligation of reasonable conduct. But even though the conduct may indicate consent, the risk will not be taken to be assumed if it appears from his/her words, or from the facts of the situation, that he does not in fact consent to relieve the defendant of the obligation to protect the client. It is clear that the sport management professional must make sure the client consents beyond a shadow of a doubt to participate in exercise testing and a prescriptive exercise program (Weiler & Roberts, 1993).

What is Contributory Negligence?

Contributory negligence is conduct on the part of the plaintiff contributing as a legal cause to the harm suffered. It is conduct that falls below the standard to which the plaintiff is required to conform for his/her own protection. Unlike assumption of risk, the defense does not rest upon the idea that the defendant is relieved of any duty toward the plaintiff. Rather, the plaintiff is denied recovery because his/her own conduct disentitles him/her to maintain the action; even though the defendant has breached his/her duty, has been negligent, and would otherwise be liable. In the eyes of the law, both parties are at fault; and the defense is one of the plaintiff's error, rather then the defendant's innocence (Moriarty, et al., 1994).

What is Comparative Negligence?

The hardship of the doctrine of contributory negligence upon the plaintiff is readily apparent. It places upon one party the entire burden of a loss for which two are, by hypothesis, responsible. The negligence of the defendant has played no less a part in causing the damage; the plaintiff's deviation from the community standard of conduct may even be relatively slight, and the defendant's more extreme. Recently, however, some states have modified these harsh interpretations and have adopted *comparative negligence laws.* In these states the negligence of the parties is compared on a percentage basis. Although there are exceptions, generally, under a comparative negligence statute, a player cannot recover if his or her negligence contributes 50% or more to the accident (Wong, 1993).

What is Governmental Immunity?

Governmental immunity is a common-law theory that holds that because the state and its agencies are sovereign, they cannot be sued without their consent and should not be held liable for the negligence of their employees. In recent years this doctrine has been widely condemned by legal writers, and an increasing number of state courts or legislatures have abolished governmental immunity. In other states that support the concept, the courts or legislature have found that the purchase of liability insurance eliminates the defense to the extent of the insurance coverage, or they have created exceptions to the doctrine by adding the concepts of discretionary duties (those duties that are not prescribed by law but are discretionary in nature) and ministerial duties (those duties that are prescribed by law). In the latter concept a governmental official or employee can be sued, but not in the former (van der Smissen, 1990).

What is Meant by Supervision?

Supervision is viewed by the courts as an important and essential legal duty for the sport management professional. However, many times this duty is given the least amount of attention by the professional. It is important to document what one does relating to supervision of clients. If the professional can show he/she is concerned about the client and has a reasonable supervision plan, the courts will look favorably upon the professional as one who cares for the well-being and safety of the client (Nygaard & Boone, 1988). *Supervision* means you are in charge of others as they perform some activity. As a sport management professional, it means you are in charge of your clients and possibly other sport management personnel. Supervision means you also have responsibilities to your clients.

Your responsibility to supervise involves two different but related forms of supervision, general and specific. *General supervision* is the supervision of all areas and activities related to the activity at hand. For example, if you are in charge of the testing, strength training, and cardiovascular training areas that are on the same floor, you are responsible for all clients, activities and equipment in these areas, not just in your immediate area or vicinity. *Specific supervision* is the close supervision of an activity when your client is performing a specific activity. For example, you have specific supervisory duties to your client when performing a treadmill test; however, you also have general responsibilities to other clients exercising in the strength and cardiovascular training areas (Nygaard & Boone, 1988).

What is a Qualified Supervisor?

A *qualified supervisor* is a person who has adequate education and certification to perform the specific task(s) assigned. For example, the person assigned to perform exercise testing should have American College of Sports Medicine certification (ACSM) at the appropriate level (Exercise Test Technologist) or others, such as The Institute for Aerobics Research (IAR) or The Young Men's Christian Association (YMCA), before they should be allowed to perform such task(s).

A competent supervisor is a person who knows how to do the following:

1. Supervise exercise testing and/or exercise;
2. Plan appropriate exercise programs;
3. Present clear warnings of inherent risks within exercise testing and/or exercise programs;
4. Assist in providing a safe testing and exercise environment;
5. Be able to evaluate injury or incapacity;
6. Properly match participants to appropriate exercise programs; and
7. Administer first aid, C.P.R., and activate the emergency medical system (Nygaard & Boone, 1988).

What is Considered Proper Supervision?

Supervision is a learned skill. Sport professionals must be trained to supervise properly. The work site must have a developed written procedure for supervision for all personnel. When providing inservice training and developing a supervisory plan the professional must take into consideration the following aspects:

1. What should the supervisor look for?
2. What should the supervisor listen for?
3. Where should the supervisor stand?
4. How should the supervisor move around?
5. What should the supervisor do if a problem arises?
6. Identify all potential dangerous activities.
7. How close should the supervisor be to the activity?
8. Understand the warning signs of impending trouble during an activity or in a client.
9. Establish a "stop signal" that can be used when the supervisor must immediately suspend activity (Nygaard & Boone, 1988).

Sample Supervision Plan for a Strength Training Area

The strength training area supervisor has the following responsibilities while on duty in the strength training area:

1.   Check to see that all weight bars, collars, and plates are functional and safe for use.
2.   Check all pulleys, cables, and pins in every weight machine.
3.   Check to make sure that treadmills are set on 0% incline and 0 MPH.
4.   Check to see that all weight racks (squat, etc.) are secured to the floor and wall for greatest stability for lifters.
5.   Be prepared to provide spotting assistance when needed.
6.   Be prepared to provide emergency assistance.
7.   Assist all clients in proper lifting techniques.
8.   Watch all lifters and correct improper lifting techniques when possible.
9.   Help the clients establish their maximum and target heart rates.
10. Instruct all free weight lifters to use collars and replace weights when finished lifting.
11. Instruct all machine users to secure selector pin before lifting the weight selected.
12. Instruct treadmill users to resent treadmill at 0% incline and 0 MPH.
13. Instruct treadmill users to place feet on both sides of treadmill before starting the treadmill, then step on the treadmill.
14. Recommend to all free lifters that a spotter be present when using heavy weight— weights greater than body weight.
15. Instruct all free lifters to use weight racks (squat, etc.) when lifting heavy weights.

Risk Management Considerations

A supervision plan should include the following considerations relating to supervision:

1.   Develop a very detailed general and specific supervision plan to be utilized by all personnel involved with clientele such as:
2.   Make sure that all supervisors are qualified, competent, and have the appropriate certifications necessary to supervise the activity;
3.   Never leave a testing or exercise area unattended;
4.   Make sure that every supervisor understands all aspects of the exercise programs being performed; and
5.   Don't be too close to the activity nor too far away.

Planning for Safety

Planning should and must precede everything a sport management professional does with a client. Plans must be reasonable, well thought out, and based on the past experiences, tests results, and readiness of the client. All plans should be updated continuously. Further, testing procedures, exercise prescriptions, and exercise plans should be written and retained. The plan should be adequate, contain properly written performance objectives, and document a logical sequence and progression.

Components for an Adequate Exercise Plan

In developing an adequate exercise plan there are a few key points to be considered, including the following:

1. Are your goals realistic and attainable?
2. Have you considered such things as
    a. client's medical background?
    b. client's ability level?
    c. client's interest?
    d. client's attitude(s) toward health/fitness/recreation/sport and you? and
    e. your own interest and enthusiasm for the plan?
3. Does your plan provide for
    a. an initial level of difficulty with an appropriate sequence of increasing difficulty?
    b. did you make allowances for variety in the program? and
    c. is the program interesting and meaningful for the client?
4. Did you consider the following organization and administrative aspects for implementing the program?
    a. were your explanations and directions clear and concise?
    b. did the client understand exactly what was expected?
    c. do you have emergency plans in case of a medical emergency?, and
    d. is all equipment ready and in good repair when needed?

Performance Objectives for an Exercise Plan

No exercise plan is complete without well written performance objectives. Many exercise professionals do not write good performance objectives. Which of the following is a performance objective, A or B ?

a. "I will teach you how to monitor your heart rate."
b. "During this exercise session each participant will take his/her heart rate at rest, after the warm-up session, every five minutes during the cardio session, every minute during the cool down, and at two and five minutes after the exercise session has concluded. This experience will be repeated during each

exercise session so that the participant understands the role of heart rate in exercise intensity."

The latter statement is written as a performance objective. However, statement B, can be improved as illustrated below:

"During exercise session, participants shall:

1.   Take their heart rate at the following intervals: at rest; after the five minute warm-up; every five minutes during the cardio session; every minute during the cool down; and at two and five minutes after the exercise session is concluded.
2.   The instructor shall explain the importance of heart rate in establishing exercise intensity. The importance of heart rate monitoring will be discussed as well as target heart rate and the training zone.
3.   Before the participants leave, the instructor will discuss warning signs of heart distress and what to do if these symptoms appear."

Performance objectives are a critical component of any adequate plan. The writing of the performance objectives should not be taken lightly. The objectives should be reviewed and modified on an annual basis (Nygaard & Boone, 1988).

Sequence and Progression are Important Elements for an Exercise Plan

Every exercise plan must have an appropriate sequence and progression. If a plan does contain such information it will be deemed an adequate plan. Exercise planners should consider and understand the "Law of Readiness" (Nygaard & Boone, 1988). This law basically says a plan is not ready for implementation until it affirmatively answers the following queries:

1.   Are the participant(s) able to perform this activity safely?
2.   What lead-up activities are necessary?
3.   Who can perform safely under what conditions?
4.   When may the 22-year-olds participate with the 55-year-olds?
5.   What about new participants —those who join the class after it has begun?

The following are recommendations for sequence and progression that should be considered when developing the exercise plan:

1.   Find out what the typical, usual, or recommended sequence and progression of an activity is.
2.   Be sure to review the pertinent literature, especially books and periodical literature concerned with a given activity.
3.   Be sure to consult any existing plans, and if changes in those plans are made, the changes should be approved by your immediate supervisor.
4.   Have the plan for sequence and progression approved by your supervisor.

Exculpatory Agreement

Operators of sport-related businesses often use exculpatory agreements to protect themselves against financial liability resulting from negligence. An ***exculpatory agreement*** is an agreement signed by a participant in an activity in which the participant agrees not to hold the people in charge of the activity responsible for any injury that might result from participation in the activity. The common type of exculpatory agreements are waivers and informed consent (van der Smissen, 1990).

What is a waiver?

A ***waiver*** is a form of an exculpatory or fault-free agreement between parties. The purpose of an exculpatory clause is to relieve one party of all or a part of its responsibility to another. It is considered a contract and as such is in conflict with the fundamental principle of negligence law that states that one should be responsible for negligent acts which cause injury to others. Contract law states that all persons with contractual capacity should have the freedom to contract as they wish. A sport professional should not rely too heavily, however, on these waivers for protection (van der Smissen, 1990; Wong, 1993). A well-written waiver, signed voluntarily by an adult, cannot serve as a complete bar to liability for *injuries caused by the negligence of the business or its employees*. These agreements are often challenged in court and rendered ineffective, either because of deiciencies in the agreement or the circumstances under which the agreement was signed (Cotten, 1996).

The basic effect of a waiver is to relieve one party of all or a part of its responsibility to another. Courts, in general, have tended to carefully scrutinize these agreements. The agreements tend to create dangerous conditions. While some exculpatory clauses have been upheld, they have usually been upheld in cases involving experienced adult performers participating in a hazardous activity.

There are a number of factors that make the value of an exculpatory clause questionable or even nonexistent, including the following:

- a strong public policy which prohibits such a clause,
- one party being in a clearly dominant position, such as an employer-employee relationship,
- the presence of any fraud or misrepresentation in the clause,
- any agreement which is signed under duress,
- the clause or the conditions it creates are unreasonable,
- the agreement is ambiguous,
- the signature for such an agreement does not immediately follow the agreement, and
- presence of wanton, intentional, or reckless misconduct (Dougherty, Auxter, Goldberger & Heinzmann, 1993; Moriarty, Holman, Brown, & Moriarty, 1994).

For all these reasons, exculpatory agreements, waivers and releases of liability must be used with great care. In the event of negligence, do not rely totally on them as a defense. The following questions (Cotten, 1996) must be answered in a positive fashion for a waiver to be considered valid in most states. After each question is a sample phrase that should be included in the waiver. Sample waivers can be found in Appendix I.

Requirements for a legal contract (Cotten, 1996) include the following:

1. Is the wording of the waiver such that it is clear and easily understandable by the patrons signing it? "I hereby release XYZ sport organization from any and all present and future claims resulting from ordinary negligence on the part of ....."
2. Is consideration denoted within the contract? "In consideration of my participation, I agree to relinquish my right to file suit."
3. If the signer of the waiver is a minor, does the waiver include a space for a parent's signature? In this case the agreement becomes an "Agreement to Participate" and lays the foundation for an assumption of risk defense.
4. Does the waiver specify parties other than the signer who are relinquishing claims by virtue of the waiver? "I relinquish, on behalf of myself, spouse, heirs, estate and assigns, the right to recover for injury or death." This phrase will not be effective in all states.
5. Is the waiver specific as to who is protected by the waiver? "and all others who are involved."
6. Does the language broaden the interpretation of what was meant by the waiver? "As a result of engaging in or receiving instruction in or any activities incidental thereto wherever or however the same may occur."
7. Is the agreement free of any untrue or fraudulent statements? If any statement in the agreement is false the entire agreement is invalid.

Format and Exculpatory Language

1. Is the title of the waiver descriptive? Cotten (1996) indicates that these titles— waiver, release of liability, or indemnity—agreement can be used; however, titles such as sign-up sheet, roster, application for membership, entry blank, receipt, or sign-in sheet can be deceptive and affect the validity of the waiver.
2. Is the print size large enough to be easily read? Using 10- and 12-point type size can eliminate the problem.
3. Is the exculpatory language conspicuous in the agreement? This can be done by using bold lettering, underlining, or using all capital letters, and using notices such as "Caution: Read Before Signing."
4. Is the signature near the exculpatory language? Make sure the exculpatory language is on the same page and near the signature line.
5. Is there a statement by which the signer affirms having read the agreement? "I have read and understand this waiver."
6. Does the agreement refer specifically to the ordinary negligence of the business or its employees? According to recent case law it would be safer to include the phrase "ordinary negligence."

7. Does the agreement include of any risks that are unique to your business? The following are examples of risks that are unique to a specific business: Aquatic Centers—Scuba Diving and the absence of a recompression chamber; Fitness Clubs—Fitness Testing and the absence of a Cardio Crash Cart; or Bar—requiring patrons to sign a waiver that includes an assertion that the signer was not under influence of alcohol before the patron was allowed to ride the mechanical bull.

8. Does the agreement specify the duration of the waiver? "For injuries now or in the future," "which may hereinafter occur," "forever release and discharge," or "I forever release."

9. Does the agreement contain a severability clause? "The undersigned hereby expressly agrees that the release and waiver is intended to be as broad and inclusive as permitted by the laws of the and that if any portion hereof is held invalid, it is agreed that the balance shall, notwithstanding, continue in full legal force and effect."

Other Protective Language Within The Waiver

1. Does the waiver include a statement of disclaimer by the business? The organization asserts lack of responsibility for injury resulting from the provisions of the service.

2. Does the waiver include a "covenant not-to-sue"? The agreement must have a phrase indicating that the participant will not sue.

3. Does the waiver include language by which the signer promises to indemnify or repay the business for financial loss caused by injury to the patron? "agrees to indemnify," or "reimburse," or "hold harmless," or "save harmless."

4. Does the waiver include a selection of venue? This means the instrument specifies in which state and county any legal proceeding will take place.

5. Does the waiver clearly describe the nature of the activity? The details of the description will depend upon the level of experience of the patron.

6. Does the waiver clearly warn of the risks involved in the activity? "Including, but not limited to," with a list of a few minor, common injuries and more serious ones, including death, should be included.

7. Does the waiver include an affirmation of voluntary participation? "I understand the risks involved in this activity and am voluntarily participating in [activity]."

8. Does the waiver contain a statement by which the signer assumes the risk of the activity? " I recognize that scuba diving is a dangerous activity and agree to accept any and all risks."

What is Informed Consent?

Informed consent has been basically associated with research and human subjects in research, and is a fundamental part of health education and welfare research guidelines. *Informed consent* is a contractual agreement, usually an agreement to participate in some research, procedure or experimentation (Koehler, 1988). (see sample informed consent form in Appendix [])

It is best defined by the *Code of Federal Regulations* (CFR):

> "Informed Consent means that knowing consent of an individual or his legal authorized representative, so situated as to be able to exercise free power of choice without undue inducement or any element of force, fraud, deceit or other forms of constraint or coercion" (45 CFR 46.103C)

For the informed consent to be valid, the participant must know, understand, and appreciate many of the aspects of the total experience they are about to be involved in. The question of knowing, understanding, and appreciating will be one for the court to resolve at a later date. However, it should be recognized that it is the individual or legal, authorized representative who may exercise the consent.

The essential components of an informed consent document are explained as follows from the Code of Federal Regulations:

> "... no investigator may involve a human being as a subject in research covered by these regulations unless the investigator has obtained informed consent of the subject or the subject's legal authorized representative. An investigator shall seek consent only under circumstances that provide the prospective subject or the representative sufficient opportunity to consider whether or not to participate and that minimize the possibility of coercion or undue influence. The information that is given to the subject or representative shall be in language understandable to the subject or representative.
>
> No informed consent, whether oral or written, may include any exculpatory language through which the subject or the representative is made to waiver or appear to waive or appear to waive any of the subject's legal rights, or releases or appears to release the investigator, the sponsor, the institution or its agents from liability or negligence." (45 CFR 46:103C)

The American College of Sports Medicine (ACSM) (Herbert & Herbert, 1993) has recommended that the following items be included in an informed consent form as appropriate to a particular project:

1.   A general statement of the background of the project and the project objectives.
2.   A fair explanation of the procedures to be followed and their purposes, identification of any procedures that are experimental, and description of any and all risks attendant to the procedures.

3.   A description of any benefits reasonably to be expected and, in the case of treatment, disclosure of any appropriate alternative procedures that might be advantageous to the subject.
4.   An offer to answer any queries of the subject concerning procedures or other aspects of the project.
5.   An instruction that the subject is free to withdraw consent and to discontinue participation in the project or activity at any time without prejudice to the subject.
6.   An instruction that in the case of questionnaires and interviews, the subject is free to deny answers to specific items or questions.
7.   An instruction that if services and treatment are involved in the setting or context of the project, they will be neither enhanced nor diminished as a result of the subject's decision to volunteer participation in the project.
8.   An explanation of the procedures to be taken to ensure the confidentiality of the data and information to be derived from the subject. If subjects are to be identified by name in written documentation, permission should be included in the informed consent form or obtained in writing at a later date.

What is a Warning?

A *warning* is any device that informs one in advance of impending or possible harm/risk (see sample warnings in Appendix I). Before a person can assume a risk, he/she must be made aware of that inherent risk. The person must be aware that improper, dangerous techniques, if used, increase the risk of injury.

There are three levels of comprehension: knowing, understanding, and appreciating the risk (Baley & Matthews, 1989). Each of the three levels of comprehension must be clarified. A one-time brief summary of the inherent risks within an activity is not sufficient warning for your clients. Your warning should be thorough, clear, and repeated. Remember, a beginner does not have the same comprehension or appreciation as does an intermediate or advanced participant. Comprehension or appreciation only comes with a great deal of experience.

Generally, an *inherent risk* is a risk incurred participating in a normal exercise testing and/or exercise program in a safe facility under the supervision of a qualified professional working with clients who have had qualified instruction and who know, understand, and appreciate the risks of the activity (Jennings & Skipper, 1989). It is possible for the clients to assume the risk of a sprained ankle in an aerobic dance class, but they should not assume the risk of running into an open door or support post. However, inherent risks sometimes do change, depending on improvement in different exercise standards, testing protocols, facilities, and equipment. You should remember your clients can only assume those risks which are an inherent part of the activities, and you must do whatever you can to assure they know, understand, and appreciate those risks.

A warning should:

1.   specify the risks presented by the activity or test,
2.   be consistent with the activity or test,
3.   provide a reason(s) for the warning,

4.   attempt to reach foreseeable participants,
5.   be specific and clear so that it creates knowledge, understanding, and appreciation in the participants' minds,
6.   be written, and explained orally if possible.

An adequate warning is:

1.   *conspicuous*, so it attracts the user's eye;
2.   *specific*, so it is understood by the user; and
3.   *forceful*, so it convinces the user of the range and magnitude of the potential harm.

When developing a warning, the sport professional needs to take into consideration the following points:

1.   estimate the physiological demands,
2.   request medical certification,
3.   encourage safe performance,
4.   emphasize any major standard warning(s), if present,
5.   emphasize any major unique inherent risk(s),
6.   emphasize other common risks ranging from major to minor, and frequent to rare,
7.   explain any inherent safety rule(s)/protocol(s),
8.   explain equipment recommendations and use,
9.   explain necessary etiquette,
10.   solicit and encourage questions,
11.   summarize the know, understand, and appreciate statement,
12.   request that the warning statement be signed and dated
       (do not require that the form be signed), and
13.   file the warning statement.

Making Facilities and Equipment Safe

Many lawsuits in the sport areas contain an allegation of an unsafe or hazardous area or facility. The common causes for facility lawsuits are improper design, improper maintenance, and defective products associated with the facility (Nygaard & Boone, 1988; van der Smissen, 1990; Wong, 1993). All facility owners or operators should be aware of the standard of care they owe to participants. The standard is based on whether the participant is an invitee (a person who goes onto another's premises by the specific or implied invitation of the owner or operator) or licensee (a person who comes on the premises for his own purpose, but with the owner's or operator's consent) or trespasser (a person who intentionally and without consent or privilege enters another's property).

Risk Management Considerations

It is necessary for the sport manager to draft and use warnings, waivers, and informed consent. The guidelines provided below should assist the health/fitness professional in developing sound warnings, waivers, and informed consent, which in turn will reduce risk.

1. The utilization of accident/injury reports will assist in identification of high-risk areas where the use of a waiver or informed consent would be feasible.
2. Health/fitness programs involving the adult and/or senior citizen are potential areas for the waiver and release format depending upon the risk factor or condition of the participant.
3. All activity programs are suitable target areas for using informed consent or waivers.
4. Prior to beginning any programming, an assessment of potential risk areas, nature of involved populations, insurance, and medical compensation should be made to ascertain if, when and how a waiver or informed consent instrument will be used.
5. Warn all exercise testing and/or exercise program participants of all inherent risks. Be sure your warning enables your clients to know, understand, and appreciate the risks involved.
6. Put the warnings in written form and be sure they are carefully read and signed. Retain a copy of this signed form for the files.
7. After presenting the warnings, be sure to ask for questions, giving thorough and unbiased answers to these questions.
8. It is strongly recommended that none of the sample warning, waiver, or informed consent forms be adopted for any program until they have first been reviewed by legal counsel and the medical advisor for the program. To be acceptable, each form must be written in accordance with prevailing state laws and should simply state to the participant the reasons for the procedure, the risks and benefits, etc., in a manner specific to the program activities for which consent is being considered.

What is an Invitee?

A person is an *invitee* on land of another if he/she enters by invitation, expressed or implied, his/her entry is connected with the owner's business or with an activity the owner conducts or permits to be conducted on his/her land, and there is mutuality of benefit or benefit to the owner (Koehler, 1988). The standard of care owed an invitee is the highest. This means that the owner must exercise reasonable care in providing a safe place for invitees. This means the premises must be inspected regularly and thoroughly, with foreseeability, or professional anticipation. Any hazards, especially hidden hazards or conditions that have changed since the last time the invitees were present, must be noticed and removed or repaired, or else the invitees must be warned of them and protected from them. It is important that the owner or operator of a facility anticipate foreseeable users and uses.

What is a Licensee?

A *licensee* is permitted, due to a lease agreement, to use the premises of another. The owner or operator of a facility owes a licensee the duty of keeping the premises in a reasonably safe condition, and warning of hidden hazards or changed conditions. The duties of inspection, notice, and foreseeability mentioned above apply, but it is also assumed that the licensee will be more observant, especially for any known dangerous condition or any dangerous condition that is obvious (Moriarty, et al., 1994).

What is a Trespasser?

A *trespasser* is a person who enters on the property of another without right, lawful authority, or an expressed or implied invitation or license (Jennings & Skipper, 1989). An owner or operator of a facility owes no duty of care to a trespasser. However, a child trespasser is considered different, in that children are immature and lack the experience and judgement of adults. They may be incapable of understanding and appreciating the possible dangers that might occur during the trespass. As a consequence, the owner/operator has a greater burden of care toward a child trespasser than toward an adult trespasser.

Why is It Important to Provide Notice, Actual Notice, and Constructive Notice?

The term *notice* is defined as the knowledge of a fact or state of affairs that would naturally lead an honest and prudent person to make inquiry. A person has notice of a fact if he or she knows the fact, has reason to know it, should know it, or has been given notification of it.

Actual notice is notice expressly and actually given to a supervisor or a person who has the authority to correct the problem (Koehler, 1988). Actual notices that cannot be handled at a lower administrative level of responsibility should be transmitted to the next level in written form with copy placed in a file and a verbal follow-up to confirm receipt of the written notice.

Constructive notice is information or knowledge of a fact that a person could have discovered by proper diligence (Koehler, 1988). Or put another way, the health/fitness/recreation/sport professional is responsible for all knowledge that encompasses that specialty area.

What are Other Duties Relating to Safe Facilities and Equipment?

As an owner and/or operator of a sport facility, the sport manager will be required to perform the following duties in relation to providing a safe facility and equipment:

Risk Management Considerations

The sport manager needs to develop an efficient and functional emergency medical plan for the facility. The following risk considerations should be included in the plan:

1. Regular training seminars in first aid and C.P.R. for all personnel;
2. A listing of all emergency phone numbers placed near every telephone in priority order;
3. Steps to be taken in each of the following situations:
   a. heart attack,
   b. heat exhaustion/stroke,
   c. muscle strain,
   d. stroke,
   e. diabetic reactions, and
   f. joint sprain.
4. Follow-up procedures;
5. Development of accident reports and procedures for completing and filing the report;
6. All medical records should be retained on file;
7. All fitness testing records should be retained on file;
8. Accident reports should contain a statement of the first aid and emergency treatment provided, the activity in progress at the time of the accident, the specific location of the instructor and the proximity of other members in the activity environment; and
9. All accident reports should be retained over the time frame recommended by legal counsel (usually seven years).

1. Conduct regular and thorough facility and equipment inspections and record the results in written form and file for future reference.
2. Maintain current standards for the appropriateness of facility and equipment for the activities being implemented.
3. Develop a regular preventive maintenance schedule for the facility and equipment.
4. Advise all personnel of the "shared responsibility doctrine" that states that all parties share in the responsibility for conducting programs safely by fulfilling their shared responsibilities in a manner that is consistent with preventative maintenance.
5. Purchase the best equipment affordable for the activity.
6. Be aware of changes in equipment and standards of safety relating to equipment.
7. Take care when adjusting, fitting, or repairing equipment.
8. Be wary of new untested equipment.
9. Avoid "illegal" equipment.
10. Present necessary warnings for equipment as specified by the manufacturer.

11. Avoid "homemade" equipment.
12. Teach proper technique for using equipment.
13. Avoid hand-me-downs.
14. Be sure insurance reflects the current status of equipment.
15. Include equipment in the sport center's safety program.
16. If equipment is not used, keep it inaccessible (Nygaard & Boone, 1988).

First Aid and Emergency Medical Procedures

The need to provide appropriate emergency care by well-educated and competent personnel is one of the most important of the legal duties of the sport management professional. This duty is always present. The supervisor has two specific supervisory duties when an injury occurs. The first is to render emergency care, and the second is to continue to supervise the activity.

The basic duties are the following four:

1. Protect the individual from further harm;
2. Attempt to maintain or restore life to the injured party;
3. Comfort and reassure the party; and
4. Immediately activate the emergency medical system (Nygaard & Boone, 1988).

What is the Americans with Disabilities Act?

The Americans with Disabilities Act (ADA), which was signed by President Bush (July 26, 1990), gives to individuals with disabilities civil rights protection with respect to discrimination that are parallel to those that are already available to individuals on the basis of race, color, national origin, sex, and religion. It combines in its own unique formula elements drawn principally from two key civil rights statutes—the Civil Rights Act of 1964 and Title V of the Rehabilitation Act of 1973 (Bartlett & Rabinoff, 1991; Scanlin, 1992; Herbert, 1992). The ADA generally employs the framework of Titles II (42 U.S.C. 2000a to 2000a-6) and VII (42 U.S.C. 2000e to 2000e-16) of the Civil Rights Act of 1964 for coverage and enforcement, and the terms and concepts of section 504 of the Rehabilitation Act of 1973 (29 U.S.C. 794) for what constitutes discrimination.

What are the Pitfalls to Avoid with the ADA?

Bartlett and Rabinoff (1991) in an article under the legal section of *Employee Services Management*, outline the following pitfalls to avoid in administering the ADA:

- Each person must be treated as an individual and must not be treated based upon some general stereotype or concept concerning type of apparent disability.

- An employer cannot avoid responsibility by contracting or otherwise have a third party provide a service. (For example, if an employer contracts with a health club to supervise and operate a health/fitness/recreation/sport program, the same restrictions apply against the employer; and the employer may well be held liable for any actions by the health/fitness/recreation/sport club in violation of the ADA.)
- A disabled person does not need to prove intentional discrimination. An honest, unintentional mistake that is discriminatory and prohibited by the ADA can result in sanctions provided by the law.
- The ADA, in general, prohibits preemployment medical examinations as well as questions about disabilities, but specifically permits voluntary medical examinations in wellness programs.
- Any information gathered through voluntary medical examinations must be confidential and the medical examination requirements must apply to all employees.
- The ADA does not supersede or preempt any other federal or state law. Therefore, it is theoretically possible for an employer to subject itself to liability under another law or laws.
- The greatest pitfall of all would be to do nothing.

What is a Contract?

A *contract* is an agreement (or promise) between two or more persons that creates an obligation to do or not do a particular action (see sample contract in Appendix []). A contract is a promise or set of promises for the breach of which the law gives a remedy, or the performance of which the law in some way recognizes as a duty (Berry & Wong, 1986). In other words, a legal relationship consisting of the rights and duties of the contracting parties or a promise or set of promises constituting an agreement between the parties that gives each a legal duty to the other and also the right to seek remedy for the breach of those duties.

There are five major legal concepts involved in the formation of a contract (Berry & Wong, 1986). The first is *offer*. An offer is a conditional promise made by the party offering (offeror) to the party accepting (offeree). Most often an offer is in writing outlining a few essential bits of information including, but not limited to: (1) the involved parties' names, addresses, and phone numbers; (2) the subject matter; (3) the time, day, and place for the subject matter to be performed, and (4) the agreed upon price to be paid.

The second concept is *acceptance*. The only person who can accept an offer is the party (offeree) it was offered to by the offeror. No one else can accept the offer made unless the offer was made to more than one party. In that case, all parties involved must accept the offer.

The third is *consideration*. Consideration involves an exchange of value wherein one party agrees through a bargaining process to give up or do something in return for another party's doing the same. The courts most often view consideration as the glue in the agreement. Consideration makes the contract legally enforceable. Without consideration, there may be a promise to do something, but it may not be legally enforceable as a contract in court.

The fourth concept is *legality*. Legality means that the underlying bargain of the contract is for a legal action(s). The courts will not enforce contracts for illegal actions such as prostitution, gambling, drug deals, loan sharks, and so forth.

The final concept is *capacity*. Capacity is the ability to comprehend the nature and effects of one's acts. Generally speaking, anyone who has reached the age of eighteen (sometimes referred to as the age of majority in many states) has the capacity to enter into a contract. There are conditions that invalidate a contract including intoxication, mental incompetence, fraud, and illegal acts.

Generally a contract is valid, whether it is written or oral. By statute, however, some contracts must be evidenced by a writing. Such statutes are designed to prevent the use of the courts for the purpose of enforcing certain oral agreements or alleged oral agreements. They do not apply when an oral agreement has been voluntarily performed by both parties (van der Smissen, 1990).

Apart from statute, the parties may agree that their oral agreement is not to be binding until a formal written contract is executed, or the circumstances of the transition may show that such was their intention. Conversely, they may agree that their oral contract is binding even though a written contract is to be executed later.

Similarly, the failure to sign and return a written contract does not establish that there is no contract as there may have been an earlier oral contract. If one of the parties, with the knowledge or approval of the other contracting party, undertakes performance of the contract before it is reduced to writing, it is generally held that the parties intended to be bound from the moment the oral contract was made (Weiler & Roberts, 1993).

Contracts should be used as preventive mechanisms for a specific purpose with appropriate safeguards and limitations drafted into the written document. Contracts that must be evidenced by a writing (i.e., the contract itself must be writing and signed by both parties, or there be a sufficient written memorandum of the oral contract signed by the person being sued for breach of contract) include: (a) an agreement that cannot be performed within one year after the contract is made; (b) an agreement to sell or a sale of any interest in real property; (c) a promise to answer for the debt or default of another; (d) a promise by the executor or administrator of a decedent's estate to pay claim against the estate from his personal funds; (e) a promise made in consideration of marriage; and (f) a sale of goods for $500 or more (Weiler & Roberts, 1993).

What Kinds of Contracts Are There?

Contracts are classified in terms of their forms as (a) contracts under seal, (b) contracts of record, and (c) simple contracts (Berry & Wong, 1986; Anderson & Kumpf, 1990). The first two classes are considered formal contracts. A *contract under seal* is executed by affixing a seal or by making an impression upon the paper or upon some tenacious substance, such as wax, attached to the instrument. The modern courts treat various signs or marks to be equivalent of a seal. A contract under seal is binding at common law solely because of its formality.

Contracts of record arise when one acknowledges before a proper court that he/she is obligated to pay a certain sum unless a specified thing is done or not done. For example, a party who has been arrested may be released on his promise to appear in court and may bind himself to pay a certain sum in the event that he fails to do so.

A *simple contract* is a contract that is not under seal or of record. Simple contracts include express, implied, valid, voidable, void, executed, executory, bilateral, and unilateral contracts. An *expressed contract* is one in which the parties have made oral or written declarations of their intentions and of the terms of the transaction; while an *implied contract* is one in which the evidence of the agreement is not shown by words, written or spoken, but by the acts and conduct of the parties. Such a contract arises when one person, without being requested to do so, renders services under circumstances indicating that he expects to be paid for them, and the other person, knowing such circumstances, accepts the benefit of those services.

A *valid contract* is an agreement that is binding and enforceable. A *voidable contract* is an agreement that is otherwise binding and enforceable but, because of the circumstances surrounding its execution or the capacity of one of the parties, may be rejected as the option of one of the parties; whereas, a *void* agreement is without legal effect.

An *executed contract* is one that has been completely performed; while an *executory* contract has something remaining to be completed. A *bilateral* contract is where the offeror extends a promise and asks for a promise in return and if the offeree accepts the offer by making the promise, then each party is bound by the obligation to perform his promise. In contrast, in a *unilateral* contract, the offeror may agree to obligate himself only when something is done by the offeree.

Remedies for Broken Promises

Contract law provides for remedies in broken promises. Generally the remedies are called damages. The purpose of damages in contract law is "to place the aggrieved party in the same economic position he/she would have had if the contract (promise) had been performed" (Anderson & Kumpf, 1990). Contract law provides for compensatory (recovery of actual losses due to nonperformance of the contract) not punitive (punishment) damages. There is an exception to this rule and that is when fraud or other illegal actions are involved.

Damages must be proven with reasonable certainty before the court will make any monetary awards. It is imperative that the plaintiff be able to document all losses caused by the nonperformance of a contract. There are four remedies used by the courts—monetary damages (most common), specific performance, rescission and restitution, and restoration/reformation (Berry & Wong, 1986). The usual type of award in a contract action is *monetary damages*. For example, in a contract for sale of goods the usual measure of difference between the contract price and the market price. Health/Fitness/Racquetball Club A contracts with Supplier A to purchase a certain brand and model of racquetball racket at $47 per unit. The supplier sells out of that model and substitutes another cheaper model, which breaches the contract. Supplier is unable to provide the contracted brand and model as promised. Now, after six weeks, Club A locates another Supplier who ships the brand and model requested but at a higher price—$59. Therefore, the damages incurred by Club A are $12 times the number of rackets to be purchased.

The second remedy is *specific performance.* This provides that the breaching party must perform the act as promised in the contract. It is limited to cases in which a sales contract for a unique item is breached. For example, a person contracts to purchase the only original copy of Mark Twain's *Tom Sawyer* and the seller refuses to convey the book. This is a breach of the contract. Monetary damages cannot cure the breach since the person cannot purchase another book anywhere for any amount of money. There is only one book in existence. The most appropriate remedy is specific performance. However, it may not be used in a personal service contract.

Recession and restitution, a third remedy, is an action to cancel a contract and restore the parties to the status occupied prior to the contract. This is used most frequently in case involving fraud, duress, or mistake.

The final remedy is *restoration/reformation.* The court allows the parties to rewrite a contract to conform to their true intentions. This is most appropriate in case of mutual error or where through oversight all of the contract terms were not specified.

How Can a Contract Be Discharged?

A contract is usually discharged by the performance of the terms of the agreement, but termination may also occur by later agreement, impossibility of performance, operation of law, or acceptance of breach. Contracts are commonly discharged by performance.

A contract *discharged by performance* includes when (a) *payment* is required by the contract, performance consists of the payment of money or, if accepted by the other party, the delivery of property or the rendering of services; (b) the date or *period of time* (time of performance) for performance is stipulated, performance should be made on that date or in that time period; and (c) a *tender* (an offer to perform is a tender) has been completed or refused (Anderson & Kumpf, 1990).

What Makes a Contract Void?

An offer gives the offeree power to bind the offeror by contract. This power does not last forever, and the law specifies that under certain circumstances the power shall be terminated. Offers may be terminated in any of the following ways: (1) revocation (offeror revokes the offer before it is accepted), (2) counteroffer by offeree, (3) rejection of offer by offeree, (4) lapse of time, (5) death or disability of either party, and (6) subsequent illegality (Anderson & Kumpf, 1990).

What Type of Business Transactions Will Require Contracts?

The sport management professional must realize that a business transaction is involved when dealing with outside suppliers. A supplier is any person or organization that contracts for supplies, services, or events. Some of the primary areas of involvement with suppliers are merchandise, services, concessions, medical and emergency medical, agreements with other organizations or schools, joint facilities, and leases.

Merchandise. When purchasing merchandise it is important to understand the terms of delivery and payment as contained on the order form or other agreement. When merchandise is delivered it should be carefully examined for defects. Check the terms of payment to see if: (1) discounts for early payment are available, (2) merchandise may be returned, and (3) time limits have been established on returns.

Services. When contracting for services, obtain a list of references and check them to ascertain if the contractor is capable of adequately performing the task(s). Be careful of service contractors who use standard contracts. Generally, a standard form contract is unfavorable to the purchaser.

Concessions. Concessions can be a "cash cow." It is important to consider the following before deciding what to do about concessions:

1. How will the concessions be handled at events?
2. Are they provided by the organization or an outside concessionaire?
3. Should the outside concessionaire be under contract?
4. Who is liable for injuries caused by the concessionaire's personnel or equipment or food poisoning?
5. What financial agreement should be entered into with concessionaire?
6. Who provides the personnel?
7. Who provides the equipment?
8. Who secures the alcohol license?
9. Who is responsible for the restaurant license?

If it is decided to secure an outside organization to provide concessions, there should be a contract for this service. The contract should contain the following covenants and conditions:

1. type of products to be sold,
2. financial considerations for both parties,
3. proof of liability insurance up to $1 million and indemnification,
4. alcohol and restaurant licenses,
5. security,
6. equipment,
7. length of contract,
8. option to renew,
9. termination, and
10. duties and responsibilities of each party (Berry & Wong, 1986).

Medical and emergency care services. It is extremely important to provide medical and emergency care services for employees, customers, clients, and/or student-athletes. The following questions need to be answered before a contract can be drafted (Anderson & Kumpf, 1990):

1. Do you have a doctor present at all of your events or only for major undertakings (e.g., road races, contact sport activities, racquetball or tennis tournament)?
2. Are you required by law to have a doctor present at events?
3. When should you have a doctor present?
4. When do you have an emergency vehicle present?
5. Should you contract for these services?

The following are the components that should be in a contract for medical or emergency care services:

1. Type of doctor desired (e.g., cardiologist, internist, orthopedic),
2. Retained for what purpose(s) and service(s),
3. Consult with who (e.g., management, trainers, coaches, athletes, clients),
4. Time commitment,
5. Rate of compensation, and payment schedule,
6. Physicians' recommendations, include prescriptions, prescribing treatment, recommendations for surgery, recommendations for rehabilitation,
7. Proof of liability insurance (i.e., at least $1 million),
8. Understanding that the physician or emergency medical service is an independent contractor and is not acting as the organization's agent, employee, or servant,
9. Option to renew contract, and
10. Termination clause.

Agreements with other organizations. When should you have agreements with other organizations? The following are suggested as contractable:

1. Activity schedules (i.e., in school/college/professional sports a standard agreement should be developed for scheduling contests),
2. Fundraising events (e.g., a nonprofit agency requests to use your facilities for a fundraising event that will involve not only your facilities but also clients as well as other people — you had better have a contract to cover liability as well as expenses),
3. For services (e.g., cleaning, laundry, food), and
4. Education (e.g., local college or public schools do not have racquetball facilities and elect to teach the classes at your facility) (Berry & Wong, 1986).

Joint facilities. If you share ownership or use a facility with another organization (i.e., public school or college), do you have a written agreement defining the rights and responsibilities of each owner or user? Does the agreement adequately protect you if an accident occurs while the other party is using the facility? A carefully drafted agreement defining the terms of use, supervision required during use, and the specific responsibilities of each party could be very important in the event of an injury at the jointly operated facility.

Leases. For *each* facility that you lease for your use, or that you lease to others, you should have a written lease agreement. That lease agreement should have the following components:

1.   definition of lessor and lessee,
2.   consideration, and
3.   terms and conditions, such as (a) commencing and terminating the lease, (b) rights to the facility, rent, insurance (copy of binder to be attached), security, concessions, maintenance, catastrophe, additional facilities, special terms or conditions, construction, option to renew, termination clause, affirmative action clause, signature by appropriate personnel, and notarized if appropriate.

Contracts with staff. It is important for both the employer and employee to enter into an employment contract which describes the responsibilities of both, rate of compensation, fringe benefit package, evaluation, length of contract, option to renew, and a termination clause.

Contracts with clients, customers, or participants. Many health and fitness facilities require members to sign a membership contract. Contracts with users and particpants (e.g., membership, fitness/health, scholarships, injuries, club sports) are common. The membership contract obligates the member to pay dues for services rendered.

Do You Need an Attorney?

An attorney is an extremely valuable and necessary member of the management team. Those organizations that do not consult with a lawyer are asking for serious management problems that will lead to large legal expenses in the future.

The attorney you select must understand the needs of the organization, be experienced in dealing with matters that affect the organization's programs (e.g., contracts, bonding, insurance, affirmative action, and much more), and be willing to assist in planning events/programs and other transactions. You should develop a list of legal needs before you try to select an attorney. The attorney's expertise must parallel the needs of the organization. You should enter into a contract for the legal services. Do not select the least expensive but rather the most experienced.

The Game Contract

The components of a game contract consist of (1) teams involved; (2) location, date, and time; (3) game officials; (4) guarantees, (5) complimentary tickets; (6) broadcast rights; (7) termination provision; (8) option for renewal; and (9) locker room arrangements.

Further, use the attorney in the planning stages of a proposed event or transaction. Frequently, the attorney's advice at the planning or negotiation levels may lead to better results, and she can make suggestions that may be beneficial to both parties and save the organization money in the long run.

Independent Contractor

An independent contractor is one who renders service in the course of an occupation representing the will of his employer only as to the result of the work. Independent contractors include: attorneys, concessionaires, dance exercise instructors, physicians, professional trainers, sport officials, and companies (e.g., insurance companies, custodial service companies, fitness equipment maintenance companies). The general rule, relating to independent contractors, has been that liability can be shifted from the employer to the independent contractor (van der Smissen, 1990). However, the employer must exercise reasonable care to select a competent, experienced, certified, and careful contractor with proper equipment and who follows appropriate safety precautions to protect employees and the invited public.

The courts are holding the employer liable because he remains the primary beneficiary of the work, selects the independent contractor, and maintains financial responsibility, and can demand indemnity from the independent contractor. There are four situations that most frequently cause legal problems for the employer-independent contractor relationship in court: (1) negligence of the employer in hiring and supervising the contractor, (2) failure to prevent activities or conditions that are dangerous to clients, (3) nondelegable duties, such as keeping premises reasonably safe for business invitees, and to provide employees with a safe place to work, and (4) peculiar risks, such as construction of pools or reservoirs, use or keeping of vicious animals, and the exhibition of fireworks, wherein injurious consequences can be expected unless special efforts are made to protect (van der Smissen, 1990).

Finally, an independent contractor who is servicing an organization is not covered under workers' compensation. Whether a person is an independent contractor or not usually is determined by who has the right to control the manner in which the work is done, the method of payment, the right to discharge, the skill required in the work to be done, and who furnishes the tools, equipment, or materials needed to accomplish the work.

Risk Management Consideration

Do not attempt to be a lawyer. Do not assume that because a situation was handled one way last year, that a similar situation will be handled exactly the same this year. If the law has changed, or if the circumstances are not exactly the same, then last year's solution will not work. **Never** simply retype an agreement that you have previously used and substitute names and dates.

What is a Lease?

A lease exists whenever one person holds possession of the real property of another under an express or implied agreement. The person who owns the real property and permits the occupation of the premises is known as the *lessor* or *landlord*. The *lessee* or *tenant* is the one who occupies the property. A *lease* establishes the relationship of landlord and tenant (Anderson & Kumpf, 1990).

The essential elements of a lease include: (1) the occupying of the land must be with the express or implied consent of the landlord; (2) the tenant must occupy the premises in subordination to the rights of the landlord; (3) a reversionary interest in the land must remain with the landlord (i.e., the landlord must be entitled to retake the possession of the land upon the expiration of the lease); and (4) the tenant must have an estate of present possession in the land (i.e., must have a right that entitles him to be in possession of the land now) (Anderson & Kumpf, 1990).

Summary

Learning Objective 1: Role of torts in sport management.

Torts are wrongs done by one individual to another. In the world of sport many wrongs are committed daily by practitioners either carelessly or intentionally. The bulk of torts fall under the heading of ordinary negligence. Ordinary negligence is defined as when someone carelessly does something wrong in completing his/her duty (commission) or carelessly forgets to do something that causes an injury (omission). In either case the key word is "carelessly." Legal intervention over the past decade has reduced the number of injuries attributed to ordinary negligence. Lawsuits, a negative aspect of business, have forced the sport industry and others to become safety conscious.

Learning Objective 2: What is negligent conduct?

Negligent conduct is characterized by careless commissions or omissions by practitioners while applying their skills to a particular activity. All practitioners have duties to perform as well as responsibilities to their patrons. They are required to maintain their professional knowledge and skill base. But everyone makes mistakes and careless mistakes are considered ordinary negligence. The action or lack of action will be determined to be either careless or intentional by the court. The key to the seriousness of the negligent conduct is the intent of the practitioner at the time of the event in question.

Learning Objective 3: Defenses for negligence.

The commonly used defenses for negligence actions are: practitioner was not negligent, the practitioner's action was not the cause of the injury, the practitioner did not have a duty to protect or warn the participant, assumption of risk, contributory negligence, comparative negligence, or Act of God.

Learning Objective 4: Legal duties of sport professionals.

Every practitioner working in the health, fitness, physical activity, recreation, and sport fields has the responsibility to make the environment within which they work safe for themselves and participants. Over the past two decades case law has developed a series of legal duties that have been accepted by the various professional organizations under the umbrella of sport. These duties must be understood and put into practice in order to continue to reduce injuries caused by ordinary negligence.

Learning Objective 5: Supervision and planning responsibilities.

The two areas of greatest risk for sport managers are supervision and planning. The courts have been very clear that as a profession we must do a better job of planning and supervising activities. The key to eliminating careless mistakes is by providing adequate time to plan carefully and develop appropriate supervision plans. If a solid plan has been developed accompanied by a well-designed supervision strategy, the courts are more apt to rule in the organization's favor.

Learning Objective 6: The use of exculpatory agreements and warnings.

A key component of planning is designing exculpatory agreements and appropriate warnings for the activities being developed. An exculpatory agreement is used to protect the organization against financial liability resulting from negligence and develop a foundation for assumption of risk. The warnings should be designed to alert patrons of all risks and develop a foundation for assumption of risk.

Learning Objective 7: Facility users and inherent risk.

The sport manager is responsible for four types of facility users. The facility user whom the manager has the greatest responsibility for is the business invitee, followed by the invitee, licensee, and trespasser. The manager is responsible to all users to warn them of inherent risks in the facility and with the equipment used in the facility.

Learning Objective 8: Contract uses.

Contracts are a very important part of any sport managers' job. Contracts are used for many aspects of business from employment to food and cleaning services to accounting and legal services. All sport managers should understand clearly what their responsibilities are with regard to each contract entered into for the organization. Contracts should be prepared to protect the organization and its financial integrity.

Learning Objective 9: Impact of ADA of employment and facilities.

The Americans with Disabilities Act has and will continue to have a major impact on society as did the Civil Rights Act of 1964.The ADA opens the door for the handicapped for equal opportunities for employment in all areas of the American economy. Handicapped accommodations have become an integral part in the planning of all sport facilities. Sport managers of the future must make sure that greater gains are made for the handicapped in the areas of employment and facility friendliness.

Learning Objective 10: Independent contractor relationship.

An independent contractor is a necessary component of all sport businesses. The independent contractor completes tasks for the organization that do not require full-time personnel. The independent contractor is not an employee; therefore, the organization is not responsible for taxes, medical insurance, liability insurance, retirement, disability insurance, and so on. The relationship is simply based on a contract to do a specific task for a specific amount of money.

Self-testing Exercise

1. You are the new YMCA executive director. You have been charged to develop an overall supervisory plan for all activities operated by the YMCA. How would you go about developing such a plan?
2. You are in charge of developing an in-service program for the staff regarding their legal duties. Outline the in-service program you intend to implement.
3. Visit a local YMCA, YWCA, Boys Club, or Health and Fitness Club and ask for a copy of their supervisory plan, exculpatory agreement, and warnings. Carefully review these documents and determine their strengths and weaknesses.
4. Prepare waiver forms for youth soccer and football programs.
5. Prepare appropriate warnings for youth soccer and football programs.
6. As the personnel manager, how would you guarantee ADA compliance when hiring new personnel?
7. Develop an ADA checklist for use when designing facilities.
8. Develop a checklist for evaluating contracts.
9. Develop a checklist for preparing a contract for an independent contractor.

References

Anderson, Roland A., & Kumpf, Walter A. (1990) *Business law.* (15th ed.). Cincinnati, OH: South-Western Publishing Co..

Baley, J.A., & Matthews, D.L. (1989). *Law and liability in athletics, physical education, and recreation* (2nd ed.). Dubuque, IA: W.C. Brown Publishing.

Bartlett, C.B., & Rabinoff M. (1991). Americans with Disabilities Act. *Employee Services Management, 13*:2.

Berry, R.C., & Wong, G.M. (1986). *Law and business of the sports industries.* Boston: Auburn House.

Code of Federal Regulations: 45 CFR 46.103c56 Federal Register 144, 35402-35786

Cotten, Doyice J. (1996). Before the Fall. *Athletic Business, (20)*5.

Dougherty, Neil J., Auxter, David, Goldberger, Alan, & Heizmann, Gregg. (1993). *Sport, physical activity, and the law.* Champaign, IL: Human Kinetics Publishers.

Herbert, D.L., & Herbert, W.G. (1993). *Legal aspects of preventive and rehabilitative exercise programs.* (3rd ed.). Canton, OH: Professional & Executive Reports & Publications.

Herbert, D.L. (1992). *The Americans with Disabilities Act: A guide for health clubs and exercise facilities.* Canton, OH: Professional Reports Corporation.

Jennings, M.M., & Skipper, F. (1989). *Avoiding and surviving lawsuits.* San Francisco: Jossey-Bass Publishers.

Koehler, R.W. (1988). *Law: Sport activity and risk management.* Champaign, IL: Stipes Publishing Company.

Langerman, S., & Fidel, N. (1977). Responsibility is also part of the game. *Trial 13*:1.

Moriarty, Dick, Holman, Marge, Brown, Ray, & Moriarty, Mary. (1993). *Canadian/American sport, fitness and the law.* Toronto: Canadian Scholars' Press Inc.

Nygaard, G., & Boone, T.H. (1989). *Law for physical educators and coaches* (2nd ed.). Columbus, OH: Horizon Publishing Company.

Scanlin, M.S. (1992). Better camping for all: A beginning look at the Americans with Disabilities Act. *Camping Magazine, 26*: 1.

van der Smissen, Betty. (1990) *Legal liability and risk management for public and private entities.* Cincinnati, OH: Anderson Publishing.

Wong, G.M. (1993). *Essentials of amateur sports law.* (3rd ed.). Boston: Auburn House.

Weiler, Paul C., & Roberts, Gary R. (1993). *Sports and the law: Cases, materials, and problems.* St. Paul, MN: West Publishing Company.

Suggested Readings

Reporters

> *The Sports Medicine Standards and Malpractice Reporter*
> *The Exercise Standards and Malpractice Reporter*
> *The Sports, Parks, and Recreation Law Reporter*

(Subscriptions to these reporters can be obtained by calling 1-800-336-0083, Professional Reporters Corporation, 4571 Stephen Circle, NW, Canton, OH 44718-3629; each $39.95 per year, quarterly)

Newsletters

Recreation and Parks Law Reporter (RPLR), National Recreation and Park Association, 2775 S. Quincy Street, Suite 300 Arlington, VA 22206, 703/820-4960, $100, quarterly

Legal Issues in Recreation Administration (LIRA), National Recreation and Park Association 2775 S. Quincy Street, Suite 300, Arlington, VA 22206, 703/820-4960 $100, quarterly

Sports Law Monthly, 1964 Laughing Gull Lane, Suite 1311, Clearwater, FL 34622, 813/573-0576, $30

Legal Aspects of Sport & Physical Activity Newsletter, SSLASPA, 5840 South Ernest Street, Terre Haute, IN 47802, 812/237-2186, Fax 812/ 237-4338, $40, quarterly

Community Risk Management Insurance, Nonprofit Risk Management Center, 1001 Connecticut Avenue, NW, Suite 900, Washington, D.C. 20036, 202/785-3891, Fax 202/833-5747

Books

Gallup, Elizabeth. (1995). *Law and the team physician.* Champaign, IL: Human Kinetics Publishers.

Herbert, David. (1993). *The Americans with Disabilities Act: A guide for health clubs and exercise facilities.* Canton, OH: Professional Reports Corporation.

Herbert, David. (1993). *The standards book for exercise programs.* Canton, OH: Professional Reports Corporation.

Herbert, David, & Herbert, William (1995). *Legal aspects of sports medicine.* (2nd ed.). Canton, OH: Professional Reports Corporation.

Landrum, John. (1991). *Out of court: How to protect your business from litigation.* New Orleans, LA: The Headwaters Press.

15

RISK MANAGEMENT

◆ ———————————— ◆

Instructional Objectives

After reading this chapter the student should be able to:

• define risk management,

• describe the components of risk management,

• outline the benefits of risk management,

• describe risk treatment,

• discuss various tools of risk management,

• describe risk implementation and evaluation,

• outline what makes personnel important to the effectiveness of risk management, and

• discuss the value of insurance.

Introduction

In 1885, there were less than 2,000 civil cases filed in the United States. This increased to over 112,000 in 1980, and to nearly 250,000 in 1990. This represents a doubling of law cases in the United States in 10 years. A similar trend has been seen in the total number of appeal cases in the last 10 years from 24,122 in 1980 to 50,982 in 1990. In 1990, there was an average of 408 civil filings for each judgeship. The United States has less than 6% of the world's population and 51% of the world's practicing attorneys (United States Courts, 1995).

As a result of Americans' propensity to sue and the high cost of effective insurance, many small providers of health and fitness, recreation, and sport, both public and private, are either underinsured or have no insurance coverage at all (Peterson & Hronek, 1992). However, a solid risk management program can change "odds" in favor of the provider. Finally, the sport manager needs to be aware of the top 20 most common claims in lawsuits against the professionals (see Risk Management Appendix).

Wong (1987) suggests there are three reasons for the increase in litigation: (1) sport is a reflection of society, and we have resorted to the courts system as a means of resolving our disputes; (2) when the stakes are higher, people and sport organizations are more willing to pursue litigation; and (3) sport organizations are being run as businesses, and wherever business is involved, people are aware of their rights and consequently will protect those rights in a court of law.

Risk Management

Risk management is a total program that analyzes where and why accidents occur and how the hazards might be controlled. At the same time, a good program will determine which calculated risks are acceptable. A risk management program is a proactive approach to establishing safe activities, facilities, and equipment. Once the program is established, it should prevent most accidents. However, if an accident should occur and a lawsuit is initiated, the risk management program will be evidence of having acted responsibly.

Components of a Risk Management Program

A risk management program consists of (1) program feasibility, (2) risk identification, (3) risk treatment, (4) risk implementation, and (5) risk evaluation. The risk management program should be developed by a risk management committee with representation from management or owners, supervisors, employees, volunteers, and participants. The committee should also have legal and insurance consultants. The committee needs to complete the following tasks: (1) develop a philosophy and policy statement, (2) complete a needs assessment identifying the strengths and weaknesses of the organization, and (3) establish objectives that are Specific, Measurable, Attainable, Realistic, and Time-framed (SMART).

After completion of the tasks, the committee should be retained to implement the risk management program. One employee should be designated as the risk program manager for the organization. The risk program manager would become the chair of the committee.

The risk management committee should be concerned with the follow aspects of program and facility management (Peterson & Hronek, 1993; Peterson, 1987): (1) site and facility development, (2) program development, (3) supervision,

(4) personnel policies, (5) testing procedures, (6) establishment of rules, regulations, and procedures, (7) facility and equipment inspection procedures, (8) facility and equipment maintenance procedures, (9) accident reporting and analysis, (10) first aid and emergency procedures, (11) releases, waivers, agreements to participate, (12) methods of insuring against risk, (13) in-service training, (14) public relations, (15) contract procedures, (16) outside specialists, legal/insurance/CPA/ Medical, (17) signage, (18) risk management audit, and (19) periodic review (see Appendix I for a sample Risk Assessment tool). This can be used as a checklist to evaluate an organization's risk management program.

A risk management program should be distinguished from a legal audit. A legal audit reviews all aspects of the organization which have a legal element. A legal audit should include at least these categories: general information, governance, organizational purposes, financial information, books and records, property information, employee and labor relations, personnel, licenses and other regulatory requirements, tax-exempt status, charitable solicitation, antitrust, and copyright and trademarks (van der Smissen, 1990).

Benefits of a Risk Management Program

A risk management program is valuable in the event of legal action against any organization. A strong risk management program shows intent. A risk management program serves as a deterrent to being sued and, if sued, as evidence of intent to act as a reasonable and prudent person. Other benefits include the following (Peterson & Hronek, 1993):

- increased safety for the customers,
- reduced losses to the organization,
- more effective use of available funds,

Risk Identification

The purpose of risk identification is to ascertain probability of loss. The risk program manager will develop a list of all risks, large or small, for every program, facility and piece of equipment, as well as business functions. Once the list is completed, a determination is made for each risk as to the **frequency** of exposure (rank 1 [infrequently] to 5 [very frequent]), and the **magnitude** (severity) of the risk (rank 1 [minor concern] to 5 [very serious concern]). Frequency is equal to the number of injuries divided by the total number of program days. Magnitude is equal the number of lost days divided by the number of program days. After each risk is classified (a score between 2 and 10—frequency + magnitude), it is time to prioritize the risks from very serious to minor (see sample risk chart, Table 15-1). Those risks that score the highest should be dealt with immediately.

number of injuries divided by the total number of program days. Magnitude is equal the number of lost days divided by the number of program days. After each risk is classified (a score between 2 and 10 - frequency + magnitude).

Table 15-1
Risk Chart

Risk	Frequency	Severity	Classified	Priority
Trampoline	5	5	10	1
Climbing Wall	4	4	8	2
Swing	3	3	6	3

Risk Treatment

Once a risk has been identified it can be treated one of four ways (Moriarty, Holman, Brown, & Moriarty, 1993):

1. Avoid making a conscious decision not to accept the specific risk present at that time, and therefore not run the program.
2. Transfer—informing participants of high-risk activity situations and having them assume the risk of participation, and seeking appropriate liability insurance coverage.
3. Reduce—the use of additional safety equipment and/or procedures that are designed to reduce potential accidents.
4. Retain or modification—intentional continuation of the program with planned consideration of the risk.

The risk program manager needs to seriously consider the most appropriate and safe path to take when deciding how to treat a particular risk. Many risks can be avoided with careful planning and good supervision. Do not eliminate programs without first attempting every possible way to make the activity safe for the participants.

Risk Management Tools

There are a number of tools to assist in reducing risk. These include a rules, regulations, and procedures manual, safety inspections, regular maintenance, accident reporting, and waivers and agreements to participate.

Rules, Regulations, and Procedures Manual

The establishment of a rules, regulations, and procedures manual is a key step to making programs, facilities, and equipment safe, and personnel more safety-conscious. The organization should compile all the safety rules and regulations for each facility and activity site. Further, there should be a standard procedure for reporting and keeping records as a means of monitoring the system.

Safety Inspections and Investigations, and Regular Maintenance

The regular use of safety checklists (see Appendix I) can aid the risk program manager. All facilities and equipment should have a safety inspection completed. The length of time between inspections will be determined based on usage. The important factor in inspections is that they be regular and that a pattern of inspection is developed.

Regular maintenance is as important as safety inspections. Most equipment purchased today outlines very specifically within the warranty what the customer must do to maintain the warranty. When you purchase a car, it comes with an owner's manual as well as a schedule for regular maintenance. If you fail to maintain the car as suggested by the manufacturer, the manufacturer is not liable for any damages that occur because of your failure to comply with the maintenance schedule. It is important to establish a clear pattern of maintenance for facilities and equipment.

An example of how to protect participants from injury from permanent structures in an activity area at Body Heat Fitness Center in Terre Haute, Indiana. The support beams are padded and covered with rugs. (Photo: Tom Sawyer)

Accident Reporting

Accident reporting is a system of recording all the facts from an accident in an objective and unbiased manner. All staff should be trained in the completion and follow-up of such reports. An accident report form should include the following:

1.   date of accident,
2.   time of accident,
3.   date of the report,
4.   facility or area where injury occurred (exact location),
5.   name of activity involved in,
6.   weather conditions,
7.   cause and manner of accident,
8.   specific nature and extent of accident (diagram of human body useful here with lines to check specific areas of the injury),
9.   name of the injured,
10. gender,
11. age,
12. date of birth,
13. address,
14. names and addresses and phone numbers of witnesses; information to glean from witnesses includes—did you witness the accident? was first aid administered? by whom? what kind of first aid was administered? was assistance summoned? what type of assistance was summoned? how was assistance summoned? who requested the assistance?
15. name of officer in charge,
16. removed to hospital— which hospital? what time? by whom?
17. if minor, were parents contacted at what time? who contacted the parents?
18. were police photographs taken?
19. was property damage involved?
20. are there extra pages attached? if yes, number of pages,
21. have other reports been submitted? if yes, how many and type(s)?
22. who made the final report?

The final report format should be reviewed by legal, medical, and insurance consultants.

Waivers and Agreements to Participate

There is considerable debate regarding the efficacy of waivers (as was discussed in the previous chapter) and other such documents. If the waiver is (1) worded properly and not too broad, and (2) brings the danger present to the attention of the person who has signed it, it is likely that the waiver will be upheld in a court of law (Moriarty, Holman, Brown, & Moriarty, 1993). Waivers and/or release forms should have four parts: (1) nature of the activity, (2) possible injuries that may occur, (3) the expectations of the participant, and (4) the condition of the participant (van der Smissen, 1990). Before the organization uses a waiver or release to participate form, have counsel review the forms carefully (see Appendix for Sample Waivers).

A perfect example of what not to do with cords that operate treadmills. These can be easily tripped over, which can cause other problems for the client on the treadmill. (Photo: Tom Sawyer)

Participation forms have the value of (1) documenting the nature of the activity and possible consequences of participation, (2) providing a valid exculpatory agreement, and (3) establishing public relations (van der Smissen, 1990). Participation forms are not only for reduction of risks, but also can be a transfer of financial risk.

Risk Implementation

Risk implementation consists of emergency procedures, methods of insuring against risk, in-service training, and public relations. Risk implementation is a critical part of the risk management program.

Emergency Procedures

There are two types of emergencies for which one must prepare: (1) emergencies that occur due to an accident and cause primarily physical injury to one person, sometimes more than one, and (2) emergencies that occur due to natural phenomena (e.g., tornado, flood, lightning, strong winds) (van der Smissen, 1990).

The risk program manager should seek medical consultation when developing the emergency procedures to be implemented by program staff. The emergency procedure should be a step-by-step outline of how to handle emergencies that will adapt to all settings and programs. Once the emergency procedures are

All basketball backboards should have padding along the lower portion of the board that goes up each side by two or three feet as seen in the picture above. (Photo: Tom Sawyer)

written, then staff must be familiarized with the procedures and trained in first aid and CPR on a regular basis.

In-service Training

There are three important steps to be taken in developing a comprehensive in-service training program. This program should be available to all staff and volunteers. The steps are (Peterson, 1987):

1. Identify who will be trained and placed in similar groupings based on job classifications;
2. Develop objectives of each group identified to encourage the overall safety of the facility or organization; and
3. Establish training sessions within the organization for in-house information distribution. Utilize outside training opportunities by sending staff to seminars, workshops, specialty courses, regional, state, or national conventions.

Public Relations

Once you have completed the development of a strong risk management program, it benefits the organization to share it with others. Good public relations will include providing information about the risk management program in news releases, program brochures, conference presentations, and at staff meetings. Another aspect of good public relations would be showing genuine concern for an injured participant with a follow-up call to ascertain how he/she is and what you can do for him/her.

Risk Evaluation

There is no replacement for good legal and insurance consultants on the risk management program committee. Ideally, these counselors would be an active part of the committee; however, as long as each consultant is available for inquiries, planning, and general advice, the same purpose would be served.

An annual review of the risk management program and procedures can become documented evidence that your organization has good intentions in the prevention of accidents. Establish a timetable to review the program and procedures. Once the program and procedures is reviewed, it is important to submit a dated report. The report should outline the good aspects and document any changes or adjustments made to the program and procedures.

Competence of Personnel

There are three aspects related to personnel of critical importance to the effectiveness of risk management: (1) communication of responsibilities (i.e., the key to any reduction program is the personnel of the organization, both employees and volunteers, and the internal communication with them), (2) professional judgement and decision making (i.e., the standard to be maintained is that of a reasonable and prudent professional for that specific situation), and (3) credentials/expertise (i.e., credentials encompass education, experience, certifications, and general expertise in a given area; e.g., gymnastics safety instructor, NATA certified athletic trainer, ACSM certified fitness specialist or program director, or EMT certificate) (van der Smissen, 1990).

Insurance

Are you worried that bad weather will cancel the event you have spent days planning for, or that the star athlete will suffer a career-ending injury, or a patron will slip on a spilled soft drink or ice on the sidewalk and break a leg? Today's litigious environment and tight budgets mean managers and owners must take a closer look at insurance and risk-management strategies. In the past 10 years, there has been a dramatic increase in the number of companies specializing in insurance for the fitness, physical activity, recreation, and sport industries.

The risk management program manager should be prepared to cover injuries arising from four main areas of possible liability (van der Smissen, 1990): (1) building and premises, (2) motor vehicles, (3) activities (i.e., from incidents due to the nature of the activity engaged in), and (4) employee conduct (i.e., out of actions of employees).

At this point, the legal and insurance consultants can be very helpful to the risk management program manager. The risk program manager should become familiar with some basic insurance jargon before trying to engage an insurance consultant. Further, the risk program manager should know what insurance the organization currently has and its limits. A survey of companies specializing in this type of insurance shows a wide variety of coverages available, including (Schmid, 1993):

1. *Professional teams, athletes, and events*—liability and accident medical coverage, high-limit accidental death and disability insurance, contractual bonus and performance incentive programs;
2. *Amateur athletes and events* (e.g., Olympic Festivals, USOC, National Governing Bodies, Pan American Games, World Games);
3. *College and high school teams, athletes, athletic associations, club/recreational sport activities, sports camps, facilities*—sports liability and accident medical coverage, disability insurance, play-practice coverage, transportation insurance, catastrophic injury coverage;
4. *Youth/adult recreational teams and leagues*—liability and accident coverage;
5. *Health clubs, fitness centers, and sports clubs*—property, accident and liability insurance for participants/members and staff, day-care facilities, tanning beds, diving boards, whirlpools, weight rooms, trampolines, food and liquor services;
6. *Venues* (stadiums, arenas, recreational facilities, water parks)—spectator and participant liability, property insurance, casualty insurance; and
7. *Promotions and special events*—event cancellation, sponsorship/prize guarantee, special events liability, weather and nonappearance insurance.
8. *General public liability*—products liability, watercraft liability, saddle animal liability, liquor liability, personal injury liability, independent contractor's liability, advertiser's liability, and adventure and tripping program liability.
9. *Liability coverage protecting employees, directors and officers.*
10. *Vehicle insurance*—bodily injury liability, property damage liability, business auto policy, user of other autos, employers non-owned and hired autos, camp bus coverage, medical payments, comprehensive, and collision insurance.
11. *Protection of finances and operations*—loss of income, discrimination or civil liberties violations, advertising liability, or contractual liability by endorsement (hold harmless agreement or indemnification).

The most necessary coverage is catastrophic injury insurance for fitness, physical activity, recreational activity, and sports. Beyond this coverage, the manager should add liability insurance that includes participant legal liability. It is important to choose a carrier that has a stable, long-term knowledge of this industry. Investigate the insurance company, because there are companies out there that are not experienced in the fitness/sport/recreation field.

What do insurance companies consider before determining if a facility or event is insurable? The insurer reviews information regarding five basic areas: (Schmid, 1993) (1) security, (2) maintenance and housekeeping, (3) emergency services, (4) parking and traffic control, and (5) concessions. The company is concerned as to how these areas are managed. Premiums are based on how these areas are managed. The only thing that makes insurance inexpensive is good loss experience, and if year after year a facility or event or team has good loss experience, then all the insurance company needs to collect the premium for is the inevitable "what if?" If the experience is consistently good, the insurance company does not have to build in premiums to pay losses and take care of routine claims.

The cost of premiums can be reduced by opting for higher deductibles or taking the initiative of hiring a risk management expert to survey the facilities and programs for unsafe conditions. Some insurance companies offer on-site safety inspections as a value-added service, which can help facilities develop ongoing risk management strategies.

Insurance Checklist

The following checklist contains recommendations for managers, instructors, coaches, volunteers, and staff when securing insurance (Moriarty, Holman, Brown, & Moriarty, 1993):

- never assume you are covered; always check your insurance coverage,
- check insurance policy at least twice a year for changes and to be sure you still have adequate coverage,
- file a report on an incident as soon as it happens and submit a proper claim to the insurance company,
- anyone involved in an activity outside their job jurisdiction or areas of control may seek to secure more personal liability coverage,
- be aware of potential hazards and report them to the necessary people or group,
- secure a short-term group accident policy to cover special activities when risk is foreseeable,
- analyze the liability aspects of your program or area and ensure adequate coverage in these areas,
- have release forms; they may solve small liability problems because the participants acknowledge the risk they are assuming and their voluntary participation in the program, but do not rely on them to solve any negligent actions, and
- have participants in events obtain medicals.

Self-insurance

This option is not appropriate for small organizations but is quite practical for large and governmental organizations. Self-insurance usually means retaining financial risks to a substantial level through establishing a reserve fund to insure availability of cash when needed. The amount of such a fund and its management may be controlled by state regulations or statutes. Taxable profit-making organizations rarely establish such a reserve because of the tax structure and usually the working capital is adequate, at least for larger corporations. Some corporations have established trust funds to maintain such funds (van der Smissen, 1990).

What Should You Ask a Prospective Insurer?

Buying insurance for a sporting organization or club can be a difficult task. It is difficult for managers and owners to assess what type of coverage to buy, how much coverage is adequate and from which agent they should purchase. Before a policy is purchased, ask the prospective agent the following questions. The answers can help you sort out what type of coverage and which amount is best for your facility, and can help you determine whether the agent is sufficiently schooled in insurance for sporting organizations or clubs (Handley, 1997).

1. *Does the agent write many policies for sporting organizations and clubs?* It is critical in a specialty industry that the agent be familiar with the industry. The manager should request a list of current customers who can provide a reference. An agent who knows and understands sporting organizations and clubs will better know which carriers to approach and how to negotiate with them. The agent should currently write policies for the same kind of facilities.

2. *What is included in a basic policy?* At a minimum, a basic property and casualty policy should cover a facility and its contents, loss-of-income insurance, general liability coverage, crime (by outsiders or dishonest employees), boiler and machinery, and extra-expense insurance. All businesses should have an umbrella liability policy to cover losses that exceed the limits of the basic policy.

3. *What other types of coverage should be considered?* The agent should know the exclusions and extensions of the basic policy and advise you what additional coverage is needed for the business. Often, the following are excluded from sporting organizations and club policies: glass, summer camps, childcare facilities, sexual harassment, professional liability, computer hardware and/or software, and spas.

4. *How much insurance can the organization afford?* The agent should easily be able to determine how much of a deductible is reasonable for the organization. Further, the agent should be familiar with the formulas used to determine the premium. Finally, he/she should explain all warranties that apply.

5. *Can the agent provide you with a list of all claims and losses?* The agent should be able to provide a list of claims and the status of the claims. This will assist the manager in ascertaining the efficiency of the insurance company. What is included in a basic policy?

6. *What is the carrier's rating?* The agent should be able to provide the insurance carrier's rating, which ranks a carrier's financial strength and service. The highest rating is A+ 15. Avoid nonrated carriers. A high rating can offer an indication of how long a carrier is likely to continue in the industry.

7. ***Can the agent coach the manager on loss control and safety issues?***
The agent should perform this prevention service at no charge. He/she should be able to help check all the organization's contracts such as leasing and equipment. Periodically, the agent should tour the facilities with the manager, flagging possible problem areas. The agent should not just write the policy and disappear. The manager should expect the agent to service the account.

How Should the Sport Manager Choose the Appropriate Deductible?

Choosing the right deductible requires a thorough analysis by the sport manager. A higher deductible can reduce the premium, but at the same time increase out-of-pocket expenditures for care that doesn't meet the deductible amount. On the other hand, decreasing the cost of coverage can allow for more liquid funds and provide the option of building a reserve if funds can carry over from year to year (Cole, 1996). The following are a few recommendations that should be considered when choosing a deductible:

1. Access student-athletes' or patrons primary insurance first and once it has been exhausted the organization pays until its deductible is reached, then the secondary insurer, the organization's carrier, pays the remaining amount. This is called a straight-deductible policy.
2. Select a higher deductible since it will mandate a more aggressive management of insurance claims. However, if the organization has a large number of student-athletes or patrons who lack primary insurance coverage, a lower deductible should be chosen.
3. The manager should base the deductible on the physical activity involved and gender of the participants. For example, lower deductible for contact activities, and higher for non-contact.
4. The sport manager should coordinate all medical care through an HMO or a special arrangement with a local hospital. This will assist the sport manager in controlling losses and take advantage of a higher deductible.
5. The sport manager should consider placing a physician on a stipend which will reduce overall costs and allow for a higher deductible.
6. The sport manager should establish a referral policy to maximize in-house medical services. This will also allow for the selection of a higher deductible.

Summary

The sport manager who provides physical activity services needs to understand the legal risks attendant to facilities and equipment as well as to the operating policies and procedures utilized for various clientele. The risks obviously increase with the number and severity of the special medical considerations inherent in the clientele. Therefore, the precautions and safety measures utilized must grow in complexity to maximize safety for those categories with the poorest health status. Moreover, the support facilities and equipment, the expertise of the staff, and the environmental setting are linked to clientele health status and program practices.

In any case, policy and procedure should be developed and implemented only after consultation with a legal advisor. Proceeding without careful legal advice is foolhardy. Attention to this matter should be regarded as no less important than the medical advice needed to specify the participant screening requirements or clinical contradictions to be utilized in a given program.

Risk management is (1) inversely related to the ability to predict an outcome, (2) the planned and thoughtful practice of eliminating or minimizing risk in order to maximize the predicted outcome, (3) an active way of attempting to avoid potentially dangerous situations, and (4) not just identification of potential physical environmental problems. There can be problems with contracts of personnel, property, vehicles, equipment, and buildings. The losses in these areas can affect the strength of the organization.

Learning Objective 1: Define risk management.

All organizations need to be very conscious of their liabilities or risks to reduce the opportunities of being sued. Risk management is a total program that analyzes where and why accidents occur and how the hazards can be controlled.

Learning Objective 2: Describe the components of risk management.

A risk management plan must be feasible. It must identify risks and suggest appropriate treatments. After the treatments are accepted they must be implemented and then evaluated.

Learning Objective 3: Outline the benefits of risk management.

An organization that has implemented a sound risk management program will have a valuable defense in a lawsuit. Further, the program will increase safety, reduce injury, reduce losses to the organization, increase effective usage of funds, identify risk, increase attractiveness of the organization to insurance companies, monitor claims and losses, and reduce uncertainties associated with future projects.

Learning Objective 4: Describe risk treatment.

Once a risk is identified, the risk manager must decide the best method(s) that need to be implemented to reduce the risk of injury to participants. There are four basic methods for treating risks: avoidance, transfer, reduction, or modification.

Learning Objective 5: Discuss the various tools of risk management.

There are a number of tools used in reducing risks. A key step in making equipment, facilities and programs safe is the development of a rules, regulations, and procedures manual. All facilities should have in place procedures for conducting regular safety inspections as well as regular maintenance protocols. Further, all accidents should be reported thoroughly. Finally, no program should be implemented without the development and use of appropriate waiver or agreement to participate forms.

Learning Objective 6: Describe risk implementation and evaluation.

All risk management programs must have prepared emergency procedures and appropriate staff in-service training workshops. Further, no risk management program should be implemented without the establishment of an effective evaluation plan for the program.

Learning Objective 7: What makes personnel important to the effectiveness of a risk management program?

A risk management plan is as good as the personnel implementing the plan. The staff must communicate effectively, provide sound professional judgement and decision making, and maintain credentials and appropriate certifications.

Learning Objective 8: Discuss the value of insurance.

Every program manager needs to seriously consider whether or not to transfer risk through an appropriate insurance policy. Insurance is a necessary luxury that needs to be planned for each program.

Self-Testing Exercise

1. Audit and evaluate the risk management program of a local facility using the 19-item checklist.
2. Develop a facility and equipment checklist to evaluate a sport facility of your choice.
3. You have been hired as a risk manager for a large civic center. Your first task is to develop a "risk management program" for use by management. List the major headings and at least three (3) subheadings you would include. Make sure you cover areas such as personnel, facilities and equipment, management and supervision, policies and procedures for insurance, transportation, accidents, special populations, evaluation and others as you see fit.
4. What are four general areas of insurance that businesses should have? Visit a local agency and see if and to what extent they are covered.
5. The Director of the local YMCA has hired you as a consultant to determine appropriate insurance for the agency. List the types of insurance you would recommend and the purpose of each. Remember resources are scarce, so cost must be restrained.

References

Administrative Office of the United States Courts, 1995 Report.

Cole, Steven L. (1996). Deductible reasoning. *Athletic Business. (20)*5, 56-60.

Handley, Ann. (1997). Management notebook: Questions to ask a prospective insurer. *Club Industry. (13)*8, 48- 50.

Moriarty, Dick, Holman, Marge, Brown, Ray; & Moriarty, Mary. (1993). *Canadian/American sport, fitness, and the law*. Toronto: Canadian Scholars' Press Inc.

Peterson, James A., & Hronek, Bruce B. (1992). *Risk management for park, recreation, and leisure services.* (2nd ed.). Champaign, IL: Sagamore Publishing, Inc.

Peterson, James A. (1987). *Risk management for park, recreation, and leisure services*. Champaign, IL: Management Learning Laboratories.

Schmid, Sue. (1993). Premium coverage. *Athletic Business, 16*:4, 39-42.

van der Smissen, Betty. (1990). *Legal liability and risk management for public and private entities.* Cincinnati, OH: Anderson Publishing Company.

Wong, Glenn M. (1987). Legal issues permeate administrators' work. *Athletic Business, 11*:12, 18.

Suggested Readings

Camp Fire. (1993). *Management of risks and emergencies, a workbook for program administrators*. Kansas City, KS: Camp Fire.

Coalition of Americans to Protect Sports. (1992). *Sports injury risk management and keys to safety.* North Florida, FL: CAPS (1-800-338-8678).

McGregor, Ian, & MacDonald, Joseph. (1990). *Risk management manual for sport and recreation organizations*. Corvalis, OR: NIRSA.

Minor, Jacqeline, & Minor, Vern B. (1991). *Risk management in schools.* Newbury Park, CA: Corwin Press, Inc.

APPENDIX A

ACOUSTICAL GUIDELINES FOR CLUB, RECREATION, AND SPORT FACILITIES

♦ ———————————— ♦

Owners and managers of club, recreation, or sport facilities should incorporate the following noise guidelines into the design and operation of the club, recreation, or sport facility.

Area	STC Rating	Measured Reverberation Time
Aerobic studio	45 to 55	.8 to 1.4s
Control desk	45 to 50	.8 to 1.4s
Cardiovascular training area	40 to 50	.8 to 1.4s
Resistance training area	40 to 50	.8 to 1.4s
Free-weight area	40 to 50	.8 to 1.4s
Gymnasium	45 to 55	.8 to 1.4s
Racquetball court	45 to 55	.8 to 1.4s
Squash court	45 to 55	.8 to 1.4s
Indoor pool	45 to 55	.8 to 1.4s
Locker rooms	45 to 50	.8 to 1.4s
Pro shop area	60 minimum	.8 to 1.4s
Massage	45 to 55	.8 to 1.4s
Sports/physical therapy	45 to 55	.8 to 1.4s
Playroom	50 to 55	.8 to 1.4s
Offices	50 to 55	.8 to 1.4s
Storage	40 to 45	.8 to 1.4s
Indoor tennis courts	45 to 55	.8 to 1.4s
Laundry area	50 to 60	.8 to 1.4s
Indoor track area	45 to 55	.8 to 1.4s

Sound Control Objectives

The primary reasons for attempting to control noise within the health/fitness facility involve either increasing the comfort level for facility employees and users or improving communications between occupants of the facility. Although little or no threat of hearing loss from sound abuses exists within the health/fitness facility, high noise levels do cause other problems. Noise can be disruptive and is usually irritating. Noise also hinders an individual's sense of privacy. Perhaps most importantly, noise can have negative effects on task performance.

Noise Standards

Noise is generally measured with sound-pressure meters that record sound in decibels (dB). Minimal acceptable standard for safe noise levels have been established by two federal regulatory agencies—the Occupational Safety and Health Administration (OSHA) and the Environmental Protection Agency.

Noise Solutions

Excessive noise levels can be reduced to acceptable levels by specific actions depending upon the cause of the noise. The two primary sources of unwanted sound—high noise levels and excessive reverberation—can be dampened by adding acoustical absorbents in the affected areas. The degree of insulation of airborne sound provided by a given material is indicated by its sound transmission class (SIC) rating. The higher the rating, the better the level of sound absorption. Other methods for diminishing unwanted sound include changing the shape of layout of an area, using background sound to mask the noise, directly eliminating the cause of the noise (e.g., the stereo system may be too loud), and isolating either the sound or the vibration.

APPENDIX B

THE AMERICANS WITH DISABILITIES ACT (ADA) AS IT APPLIES TO CLUB, RECREATION, AND SPORT FACILITIES

◆ ————————————— ◆

On July 26, 1990, the Americans With Disabilities Act (ADA) was signed and enacted into law. The ADA is a landmark civil rights law that was designed to further the goal of full participation in American society by people with disabilities. A critical part of the ADA involves the fact that places of public accommodation must provide access to their facilities and programs to all persons, including those with disabilities, unless exclusion or limitation of activity is necessary for safety considerations. Therefore, the ADA mandates that most health/fitness facilities must provide equal access to both non-disabled and disabled individuals.

In 1991, the issue of how public places of accommodation (including club, recreation, and sport facilities) must afford disabled individuals access to and egress from all areas in a building, including all public accommodations such as drinking fountains, bathrooms, telephones, and so on, was greatly clarified with the enactment and publication of ADA Accessibility Guidelines for Buildings and Facilities (ADA-AGBF). These guidelines provide specific information regarding how health/ fitness facilities must be designed and constructed (and, in some instances, existing buildings modified) so that they are readily accessible to individuals with disabilities.

Because by law all club, recreation, and sport facilities must conform to applicable local, state, and federal codes of design and access/admissions regarding access for individuals with disabilities, as specified by the ADA-AGBF, facilities must take every reasonable step to ensure that they are in full compliance with applicable laws. One of the first steps that a facility can undertake to conform to the law is to obtain information on the ADA-AGBF. Such information is readily available from both governmental agencies and private concerns. Among the most commonly recommended sources are the following:

Governmental Agencies

Architectural and Transportation Barriers Compliance Board
1111-18th St. NW, Ste. 501
Washington, D.C. 20036-3894
800-USA-ABLE (voice/TDD)

This agency sets guidelines adopted as accessibility standards under Titles II and III of the ADA. Provides information on technical and scoping requirements for accessibility and offers general technical assistance on the removal of architectural, transportation, communication, and attitudinal barriers affecting people with disabilities.

Accessibility Guidelines for Buildings and Facilities; ADA Accessibility Guidelines for Transportation Vehicles; ADA Accessibility Guidelines for Transportation Facilities; manuals on ADA accessibility guidelines for transportation vehicles; ADA Accessibility Guidelines Checklist for buildings and facilities; Uniform Federal Accessibility Standards Accessibility Checklist; design bulletin series explaining various provisions of ADA Accessibility Guidelines for Buildings and Facilities; booklets and guides on barrier-free design, accessible rest rooms, wheelchair lifts and slip-resistant surfaces, transit facility designs, assisted listening devices, visual alarms, airport TDD access, and air carrier policies affecting people with disabilities.

Centers for Independent Living Program
Rehabilitation Services Administration
U.S. Department of Education
Mary E. Switzer Building
330 C St. SW
Washington, D.C. 20202

Approximately 400 Independent Living Centers, most funded by this program, provide local services and programs to enable individuals with severe disabilities to live and function independently. Centers offer individuals with disabilities a variety of services, including independent living skills training, counseling and advocacy services on income benefits and legal rights, information and referral, peer counseling, education and training, housing assistance, transportation, equipment and adaptive aid loans, personal care attendants, and vocational and employment services. Assistance available to employers includes accessibility surveys; job analyses; advice on job accommodations, job modifications, and assisted devices; recruitment; job training; job placement and support services; and information and referral to specialized technical assistance resources.

Private Organizations

Barrier Free Environments, Inc.
P.O. Box 30634
Highway 70 West-Watergarden
Raleigh, NC 27622
919-782-7823 (voice/TDD)

Provides consultation and technical assistance on accessibility design at all stages of construction planning or product development. Conducts on-site accessibility surveys, product evaluations, and work-site modifications and provides cost-effective accommodation and barrier removal solutions. Offers seminars, workshops, and publications on accessible and universal design and information on design standards for all national and federal legislation mandating building and program accessibility.

> Mainstream, Inc.
> 3 Bethesda Metro Center, Ste. 830
> Bethesda, MD 20814
> 301-654-2400 (voice/TDD) or 301-654-2401 (voice/TDD)

Provides on-site accessibility surveys and job analyses and offers advice on cost-effective accommodations for people with disabilities. Offers publications on several relevant topics, including accessibility checklists, architectural barriers, and workplace accommodations.

> National Center for Access Unlimited
> 155 N. Wacker Dr., Ste. 315
> Chicago, IL 60606
> 312-368-0380 ext. 49 (voice) or 312-368-0179 (TDD)

Provides consultation, education, information, training, and technical assistance to business, industry, and nonprofit agencies on meeting ADA requirements for accessible work environments for people with disabilities. Develops accessibility checklists, inspects existing and future work sites, and conducts plan reviews for identifying physical and structural barriers. Offers practical ideas for immediate, low-cost accessibility improvements. Offers consultation on overcoming communication and transportation barriers. Provides training on ADA requirements, accessibility solutions, and attitudinal training.

Once a health/fitness facility has obtained sufficient information on the ADA-AGBF, the next step is to identify how these guidelines apply to the facility. For discussion purposes, at least seven facility-related factors are affected by the requirements of the ADA-AGBF: entrances and exterior areas; floor surfaces; stairs, ramps, and elevators; wall fixtures; toilets, lockers, and showers; emergency warning systems; and assisted learning systems. A number of examples of how the ADA-AGBF can apply to each of these factors follow:

- A facility must provide free and unobstructed access to and egress from a particular area or location for pedestrians and wheelchair users. This requirement refers to all pathways, which may consist of internal walkways and external sidewalks, curb ramps, pedestrian ramps, lobbies, corridors, elevators, activity areas, restroom facilities, or any combination of these.
- At least one accessible route must be provided within the boundaries of the facility's property that connects parking and public transportation stops with the facility's entrance.
- If the access entrance for individuals with disabilities is located out of the major path of travel, the access door should be automatic. Automatic doors with independent and separate two-level push plates are recommended.

- At least one door at each accessible entrance to the facility must be designed in accordance with the ADA-AGBF. In addition, at least one door at each accessible space within the facility must comply with this act.
- All doors must have a minimum width of 32 inches for accessibility.
- Lever hardware must be provided on all accessible doors.
- All hardware on doors must be mounted at 36 inches maximum to the centerline from the floor.
- A wheelchair access symbol must be mounted on all accessible doors.
- Door-mounted door stops or panic bolts must not be installed in the toe-strike zone.
- Doors with closures must be set with 8 1/2 pounds or less of pressure for exterior doors and 5 pounds or less for interior doors.
- Fire doors must not exceed 15 pounds of pressure.
- The appropriate signage denoting accessible parking spaces and building entrances must be provided. This requirement includes signage located at the facility's main entrance that provides directions to all accessible entrances for people with disabilities.
- If passenger loading zones are provided, they must have an access pathway that is 60 inches wide and 20 feet long, adjacent and parallel to the vehicle space.

Floor Surfaces

- All parking spaces for people with disabilities must be located as near as possible to entrances that are accessible to these people.
- A minimum of one parking space per 25 of the total number of spaces available must be for individuals with disabilities. Each parking space set aside for people with disabilities must be at least 96 inches wide and provide an adjacent 60-inch-wide access pathway.
- The slope of any parking space for people with disabilities must not exceed one quarter inch per foot of parking space in any direction.
- All parking structures must have ceiling clearances of a least eight feet for parking spaces for people with disabilities.
- Signage indicating which parking spaces are for the exclusive use of people with disabilities must be posted.
- Floors within a facility must be at a common level throughout (no more than one quarter inch variance) or must be accessible (connected) by pedestrian ramps, passenger elevators, or special access lifts.
- The maximum height for carpet tile or carpet is one-half inch. In addition, all carpet edges must be fastened to the floor.

Stairs, Ramps, and Elevators

- All activity areas (e.g., weight rooms, exercise classrooms, gymnasiums, courts, and swimming pools) and support areas (e.g., pro shop, food and beverage areas, offices, and sports medicine areas) must be accessible to people with disabilities. An accessible pathway at least 36 inches wide must be provided in all activity areas.

- All steps, stairs, and ramps must be stable, firm, and slip resistant. For interior stairs, the top and bottom stairstep (tread) must be marked by a strip of contrasting color. For exterior steps, every step should be marked with a strip of contrasting color.

- Stairs must have continuous-grasp (1 1/4 to 2 inches in diameter) handrails located on both sides of the stairs. These handrails must be 30 to 34 inches in height. If handrails are not continuous, they must extend 12 inches at the top of the stairs and 12 inches plus a tread width (the width of a stairstep) at the bottom of the stairs.

- Stairs must have uniform riser heights and tread widths.

- Access ramps must be designed to accommodate individuals with disabilities.

- Ramps must be provided on external and internal pathways where there is more than a one-half-inch vertical change in floor elevation.

- Ramps must have slip-resistant surfaces that are stable and firm.

- Ramps must have landing areas of at least 60 inches by 60 inches.

- Ramps must not have slopes greater than 1:12, although a slope of 1:16 may be the most appropriate slope for a club environment.

- Ramp handrails must be continuous grasp, 1 1/4 to 2 inches in diameter, and 30 to 34 inches in height and must be provided wherever the ramp has a rise greater than 6 inches.

- Whenever possible, ramps should be installed instead of wheelchair lifts. Ramps are usable by everyone, whereas lifts are not. If alternate means of access are not otherwise available, a wheelchair lift should be put in a facility.

- If installed, a wheelchair lift should be located on major paths of travel.

- If wheelchair lifts are installed, they should have automatic doors and buttons that don't require constant pressure.

- Button heights for any wheelchair lift should be the same as for elevators.

- A wheelchair lift should not go higher than five feet.

- Keys should be required on all unenclosed wheelchair lifts.

- Appropriate signage should be posted for all wheelchair lifts. For example, a sign explaining the location of the key for a lift should be posted in a conspicuous location.

- One passenger elevator must be provided in facilities with more than one floor, and the elevator must serve all floors.

- All elevators in a facility must accommodate wheelchair users.

- Call buttons in the hallway or in elevator lobbies must be mounted at 42 inches above the floor and must be located away from corners.

- All floor buttons inside the elevator must be located away from the corners. These buttons must be mounted horizontally (instead of vertically) on the side panels at the lowest allowable height (35 inches to the lowest button and 48 inches at the highest point is required). All buttons must be raised and at least three-quarters inch in diameter.

- Elevator key locations must be designated by signage.
- The entrance to the elevator must have a minimum width of 36 inches.

Wall Fixtures

- At least 50 percent of all drinking fountains or water coolers provided on each floor of facility must be in accordance with the ADA-AGBF regarding access for people with disabilities.
- Electrical-cooler water fountains should be installed in the facility as opposed to manual drinking fountains. In the electrical type, a person applies pressure to a button or similar element, whereas in the manual type, a person must turn a handle, which is a more difficult task.
- Telephones must be accessible to people with disabilities. This can be facilitated by mounting the telephones at a height of 48 inches from the center of the coin slot to the finished floor. At least one public phone in the facility must provide a telecommunications device for the deaf (TDD).
- All light and control switches must be located at a maximum height of 36 inches above the finished floor.
- All objects protruding from walls (e.g., cabinets and shelves) must comply with the AGBF.

Toilets, Lockers, and Showers

- Single-accommodation toilet facilities must have sufficient space in the toilet area (room) for a wheelchair (measuring 30 inches wide by 48 inches long) to enter the room and permit the door to close. A minimum turning radius of five feet in the toilet area must be provided for adequate wheelchair maneuverability.
- Designated toilet facilities must be user-friendly for individuals with disabilities.
- At least one water closet must be 60 inches wide for wheelchair access and another must be at least 36 inches wide with grab bars.
- Accessibility signage must be posted on doors.
- Bathroom doors must swing outward to a minimum of 32 inches of clear opening.
- Lever hardware must be placed on both sides of the door.
- Urinals must be 17 inches high.
- Flush valves must be located on the open side of toilet walls for people with disabilities.
- Lavatories must have space for maneuverability to permit access by people with disabilities.
- Lavoratories must be 34 inches maximum in height, 29 inches maximum height to the bottom of the apron form the finished door.
- All hot water and drain pipes must be insulated.
- The faucet-control mixing valve must be operable with one hand. Lever-operated, push-type, and electronically controlled mechanisms are the recommended, acceptable designs for lavatory valves.

- The force to operate the controls of lavatories must require no more than five pounds of pressure.
- The faucet controls and operating mechanisms of lavatories must not require grasping, pinching, or twisting to operate.
- Towel and soap dispensers must be located on a side wall or clear area, not above or between sinks, and should be placed at a height no greater than 36 inches from the floor.
- Lockers must be made accessible to people with disabilities. A path of access not less than 36 inches wide should be provided to these lockers.
- Appropriate signage indicating which lockers are accessible to people with disabilities should be posted in a conspicuous location in the locker room.
- Showers must be made accessible to people with disabilities. Following are design considerations.
  - Showers must be at least 36 inches wide and 36 inches deep and must provide an outside clearance of at least 36 by 48 inches.
  - Grab bars must be strategically placed adjacent to a reasonable number of showers.
  - At least one shower unit must have a handheld apparatus consisting of a hose 60 inches long mounted 48 inches above the floor, or at least one unit must have two shower heads, one 40 inches above the shower floor and the other set at standard height.
  - If the unit includes two shower heads, both shower heads must operate independently and have both vertical and horizontal swivel angle adjustments.
  - If the unit includes two shower heads, the lower shower head must have a mixing valve operable with one hand.
  - Appropriate signage must be posted.

Emergency Warning Systems

- Emergency warning system, if provided, must include both audible alarms and visual alarms, in accordance with the ADA-AGBF (1991).
- The center of the alarm-initiating device (box) on manual alarm stations must be located at a height not greater than 48 inches above the level of the floor or other surface.

Assisted Listening Systems

- A facility must provide a permanent assisted listening system in any facility area that will be used for meeting or banquets where more than 50 people are present.

APPENDIX C

CRITERIA AND PROCEDURES FOR NEWS RELEASES

◆ ———————————————————— ◆

The news media must sort through daily stacks of news releases in order to select those stories they believe to be of most interest or benefit to their clients. The quality of presentation has a bearing upon whether or not a release is used and competition is intense. One method of improving the chances that a release will be used is to meet the standards expected in preparing and delivering the story. Some of the most critical areas in meeting these standards are the following:

- The essential facts will be included in the first paragraph.
- Use full names, correct initials, and addresses.
- Be accurate in purported facts-correct spelling, correct grammar, and good sentence structure are minimal expectations.
- Short sentences are more readable and understandable. Depending upon the classification of words used, the length of the sentence should seldom exceed 17 words. Sentences that incorporate technical terms, figures, or unusual name places should be shower for clarity and understanding.
- Paragraphs should be short; use new paragraphs for each separate point.
- Arrange paragraphs in descending order of importance; include all material that you consider important. The newspaper will cut the story to meet their needs.
- Select a main point for your story and state it in the first paragraph.
- State the facts pertaining to the story; if opinions are included, cite the sources and use quotations.
- All news releases should be double- or triple-spaced on white paper; use 8 $\frac{1}{2}$ by 11 inches paper. Use only one side of each sheet of paper; allow a minimum of one inch on sides and bottom and four inches at the top of first page. The sender's name, address, and telephone number should appear on the upper right-hand corner; the release date or for immediate release should appear on the upper right-hand corner of the first page. Use a black type-writer ribbon; use unwatermarked white typewriter paper. If a letterhead is used on the first page, make certain that it is clearly indicated as such by some form of separation or by using a divider-line. At the bottom of every

page except the last one, use the word "More." Number pages and mark the end of the story by the word "End" or a series of circled ### marks.

9.   Do not write a headline for the story; identification of the story can be stated in a brief phrase or sentence appearing on the margins that must be increased in width to accommodate this method.

10.   Use clear, dark photo copies; use of mimeograph or duplicator copies is generally unacceptable.

11.   Do not mislead the editor or anyone else that the story is exclusive if, in fact, it is not.

12.   Fasten pages together with paper clips unless you are advised that the use of a staple is acceptable.

13.   Do not use all capital letters or some rare form of type.

14.   Address mailing pieces to the sports editor as well as the individual's name so that it will be opened by anyone occupying that desk if the individual to whom it was addressed is not in or is not in the office.

15.   Know your mail distribution time systems and the deadline of the receiver; generally allow for the story to arrive two days before its release date for daily papers and at least six days for a Sunday edition. Delivery by mail, messenger, or self must be selected to meet specific needs. If you deliver the story, hand it to the proper person; use civility and depart without attempting to influence the use of the story.

16.   Determine which day or days are best for particular stories. These days may change according to other activities, particularity nationwide interest in some sporting event, local professional results, or some other influences. Chart the calender for appropriate and inappropriate days and plan accordingly.

17.   Sunday papers are able to devote more space to stories as a rule. However, there is much more general material for the reader, so the impact may be dulled. Saturday papers are not usually read in full.

18.   In preparing advance stories, hold essential materials or follow-up purposes; do not expend everything in an early advance story.

19.   Provide photographs whenever possible. A glossy-finish still-picture is preferred; avoid the use of more than two or three persons in one picture. Attempt to employ some form of action in the picture. Be certain that all subjects in the picture are property identified, names fully used and spelled correctly. Usually, the less descriptive material required to understand the significance of the picture, the better the picture. When people are posing for a picture, they become conscious of their hands and feet; to assist them in relaxing, have them hold some item, point to something, or shake hands. Place something in front of their feet, if possible.

20.   For television, a matte-finish still-picture or a one- to two-minute film clip is preferred.

21.   Identify photographs by typing the information on the lower half of a standard sheet of paper, then paste the upper half to the photograph so that the caption material will drop down below the picture when it is withdrawn from the envelope. Do not write on the back of the picture.

Modified from Bronzan, Robert T., & Stotlar, David K. (1992). *Public Relation and Promotions in Sport.* Daphne, AL: United States Sports Academy.

APPENDIX D

FACILITY DEVELOPMENT

◆ ——————————————— ◆

Approaches to Crowd Control

The sixth National Conference of City and County Directors of AAHPERD spent considerable time on the subject of crowd control at sport contests. A summary of their discussion follows.

Approaches to Crowd Control — A Summary of Reports from Small Group Discussions

The nature and seriousness of the problems in crowd control have recently become more drastic and bizarre as they have occurred with increasing frequency. They take on the collective character of a deliberate attempt to either ignore or confront the system. This social problem may be impossible to eliminate completely, but an attempt must be made to cope with the immediate symptoms. Our only hope is for imaginative and coordinated efforts by the school and sport management, the majority of the students, and community authorities to promote standards of conduct conducive to continuing spectator sports in comparative tranquility. The alternatives are to allow a disruptive element to completely negate the nature of school sport, to play with no spectators, or to abandon the activity.

The following will present some causes of crowd control problems and some approaches to solutions.

Some Causes of Problems

- lack of anticipation of, and preventative planning for, possible trouble
- lack of proper facilities
- poor communication resulting in lack of information
- lack of involvement of one or more of the following: school administration, faculty, student body, parents, community, press, and law enforcement agencies

- lack of respect for authority and property
- attendance at games of youth under the influence of illegal substances
- increased attitude of permissiveness
- school dropouts, recent graduates, and outsiders

Some Approaches to Solutions

Develop written policy statements, guidelines, and regulations for crowd control:

1. Consult the following before writing policy statements or promulgating regulations: school administration, athletic director, coaches, faculty members involved in the school sports program, school youth organizations, local police departments, and community leaders.
2. Properly and efficiently administer regulations and provide for good communications.
3. Constantly evaluate regulations and guidelines for their relevance and effectiveness.
4. Make guidelines and regulations so effective that the director of athletics who follows them is secure in knowing he or she has planned with the staff for any eventuality and has sufficient help to cope with any situation that may arise.

Provide Adequate Facilities

1. Plan and design stadiums, fieldhouses, and gymnasiums for effective crowd control.
2. Provide for adequate restroom facilities.
3. Establish a no smoking and drug-free school and promote these during contests.
4. Provide for complete preparation of facilities before game time.

Teach Good Sponsorship Throughout the School and the Community

1. Begin education in good sportsmanship in the earliest grades and continue it throughout the school life.
2. Make frequent approving references to be constructive and commendable behavior.
3. Arrange for program appearances by faculty members and students jointly to discuss the true values of sport competition including good sportspersonship.
4. Make use of all news media through frequent and effective television, radio, and press presentations and interviews, commentaries, and frequent announcement of good sportspersonship slogans and awards.
5. Distribute a printed Code of Ethics for Good Sportspersonship.

6. Include the good sportsmanship slogan in all printed programs at sports events.

7. Urge the use of sports events as an example in elementary school citizenship classes, stressing positive values of good conduct at games, during the raising of the flag, and singing of the national anthem. Also emphasize courtesy toward visitors.

8. Involve teachers in school athletic associations, provide them with passes to all sports events, and stress the positive value of their setting an example of good sportsmanship.

Intensify Communications Before Scheduled Games

1. Arrange an exchange of speakers at school assembly programs—the principals, coaches, or team captains could visit the opposing school.

2. Discuss with appropriate personnel of the competing school the procedures for the game, including method and location of team entry and departure.

3. Provide superintendent or principal, athletic director, and coach with a copy of the written policy statement, guidelines, and regulations.

4. Meet all game officials and request them to stress good sportspersonship before, during, and after all contests.

5. Meet with coaches and instruct them not to question officials during a contest; stress the importance of good sportspersonship and that their conduct sets the tone for spectator reaction to game incidents.

6. Instruct students about what to expect and what is expected of them.

7. Schedule preventative planning conferences with local police to be assured of their full cooperation and effectiveness in spectator management.

Inform the Community

1. Request coaches and athletic directors to talk to service groups and other community groups.

2. Invite community leaders (nonschool people) to attend sports events on a regular basis.

3. Post on all available notice boards around town, in businesses, factories, and other public places, posters showing the Sportspersonship Code of Ethics and Guidelines in brief.

4. Release constructive information and positive statements to news media and request publication of brief guidelines on sports pages.

5. Provide news media with pertinent information as to ways in which the community may directly and indirectly render assistance in the crowd control problem.

Involve Law Enforcement Personnel

1. Police and other security personnel should be strategically located so as to afford the best possible control.

2.   Law enforcement professionals should handle all enforcement and disciplining of spectators.
3.   Strength in force may be shown by appearance of several police officers, motorcycles, police car, etc., at and near the site of the game.
4.   Police may be stationed in restrooms.
5.   Civil Defense organizations could patrol parking areas.
6.   A faculty member from the visiting school may be used as a liaison with police and local faculty in identifying visiting students.
7.   Attendants, police, county sheriffs, and deputies should be in uniform. Uniformed authority figures command greater respect.

Use Supervisory Personnel Other Than Police

1.   Carefully select teacher supervisors who are attentive and alert to signs of possible trouble.
2.   Identify faculty members by armbands, t-shirts, or other means.
3.   Provide for communication by means of walkie–talkie systems.
4.   Assign some faculty members to sit behind the visiting fans—this reduces verbal harassment of visitors.
5.   Employ paid ticket takers and paid chaperones to mingle strategically among the crowd and to remain on duty throughout the game, including half-time.
6.   Issue passes to elementary and junior high physical education teachers and coaches to provide more adult supervision.

Plan for Ticket Sales and Concession Stands

1.   Arrange for advance sale of student tickets to avoid congestion at the gate.
2.   Sell tickets in advance only to students in their own schools, and avoid non-students.
3.   Provide for a close check at the gate or entrance.
4.   Arrange for concession stands to be open before the game, during half-time, and after the game.
5.   Channel traffic to and from concession stands using ropes or other means—keep traffic moving and away from the playing area.

Prepare Spectators

1.   Encourage as many students as possible to be in the uniforms of the athletic club, pep club, booster club, band, majorettes, cheerleaders.
2.   Bus participants to and from the game.
3.   Have participants dressed to play leaving for a game or contest.
4.   Adhere to established seating capacity of stadiums and gymnasiums.
5.   Request home team fans to remain in their own stands until visiting team fans have left.

6. Try to arrange for a statewide athletic association regulation prohibiting all noise makers, including musical instruments except for the school band or orchestra under professional supervision.
7. Request assistance of visiting clubs.
8. Educate cheerleaders, student leaders, band captains, pep squads, and faculty supervisors by means of a one-day conference program.
9. Keep spectators buffered from the playing area as much as practical.
10. Request that elementary school children be accompanied by an adult.

Miscellaneous

1. Inform and involve school superintendents when problems arise in connection with sports events.
2. Impose appropriate penalties on faculty, coaches, and students guilty of poor conduct.
3. Publish the identity of offenders at games and notify parents if possible; any penalties inflicted should also be noted (Note: If the offense leads to juvenile court action, care should be taken not to contravene laws about publishing names of juvenile offenders).
4. Consistently enforce rules and regulations; this is a necessity.
5. Work toward the assumption of responsibility for strong regulation and enforcement of team behavior on the part of the state athletic associations.
6. Attempt to work with the courts toward greater cooperation.
7. Avoid overstressing the winning of games.
8. Discontinue double and triple headers.
9. After-game incidents away from the proximity of the stadium or gymnasium are out of the control of school officials, but they do cause bad public relations.

Keep in mind what is expected of security and emergency medical personnel, such as (Cohen, 1993; Turner, 1994):

- Knowing where and how to get help when necessary;
- Being alert at all times on duty;
- Watching for activities, conditions, or hazards which could result in injury or damage to person or property;
- Having an attitude that supports good public relations;
- Being helpful;
- Being courteous but firm at all times;
- Obeying and executing all directives from management;
- Taking pride in their duties;
- Maintaining a keen interest in their job;
- Acting without haste or undue emotion;
- Avoiding arguments with visitors, customers, employees, or management;
- Reporting on time and ready for work;
- Wearing a proper, complete, and neat uniform;

- Following instructions by reading and implementing posted directives;
- Remaining at an assigned post until relieved;
- Refraining from eating, drinking, or smoking while on duty;
- Assessing injuries appropriately;
- Administering immediate and temporary care;
- Implementing the appropriate emergency medical procedures necessary;
- Activating the emergency medical response plan; and
- Completing all necessary reporting forms.

Characteristics of good signage include:

- Must be easily understood,
- Should never cause confusion in the reader's mind,
- Be as brief as possible and plainly worded,
- Establish a consistent shape that informs by its shape (i.e. rectangular denotes information, diamond = caution, and octagonal = danger or stop),
- Contain graphics (icon) and text or pictorial without text,
- Establish signs that are either single-concept signs (i.e. single-concept text or single-concept-graphic sign) or multiple-concept text (a multiple-concept text sign, such as pool rules signs, are difficult to read and remember),
- Should be of a size that can be read easily,
- Contain braille when appropriate,
- Be either freestanding or mounted,
- Constructed of a variety of available materials (e.g., plastic, wood, metal, cardboard, paper),
- Have a non-gloss finish to reduce glare,
- Could be illuminated or not,
- Might be electronic,
- Meets all fire and building codes as well as Americans with Disabilities Act (ADA) requirements, and
- Attempts to make the facility safer and user friendly for the user. (Berry, 1990)

Summary

Safety and crowd controls at school sport functions are imperative! Greater concentration on treating the causes of the problem is essential. Preliminary groundwork is the key to good crowd control. Coordination and cooperation of school, community, and law enforcement agencies are keys to success.

Youths should be taught to know what to expect and what is expected to them. Consistent enforcement of rules and regulations is a necessity if youth are to respect authority. Adult behavior should be such that it may be advantageously and admirably emulated by youth whose actions may result in deserving praise instead of negative criticism and disapproval.

The sport program is a constructive and valuable school activity. It should be permitted to function in a favorable, healthful, and friendly environment.

FACILITY
SPECIFICATION
GUIDE

The information contained in this guide, based on information provided by various associations and governing organizations, is intended merely as a guide and is not applicable to all situations. Contact the appropriate organization for further information.

BASEBALL

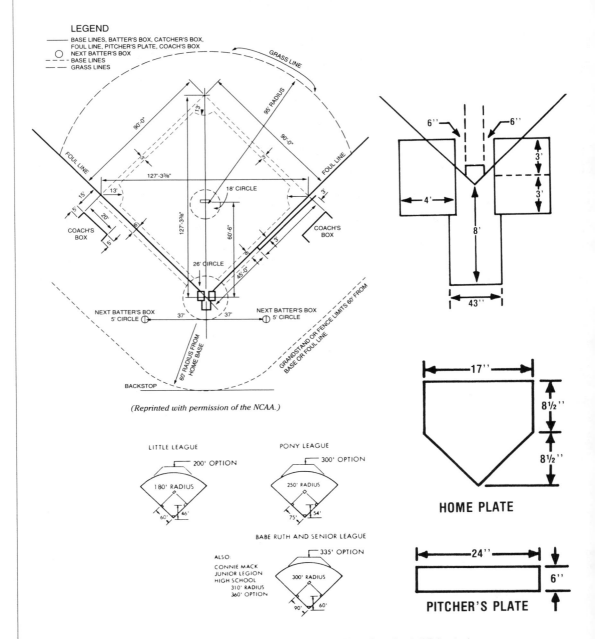

(Reprinted with permission of the NCAA.)

(Diagrams courtesy of the United States Baseball Federation.)

For more information contact:

United States Baseball Federation
2160 Greenwood Ave.
Trenton, NJ 08609
(609) 586-2381

American Amateur Baseball Congress
118 Redfield Plaza
P.O. Box 467
Marshall, MI 49068
(616) 781-2002

National Collegiate Athletic Association
6201 College Blvd.
Overland Park, KS 66211-2422
(913) 339-1906

BASKETBALL

PROFESSIONAL COURT

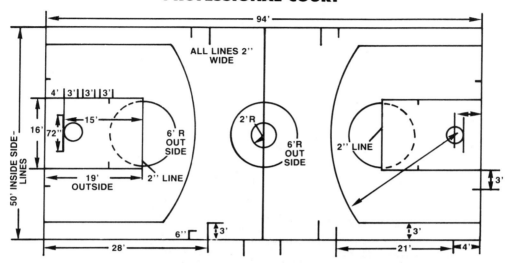

HIGH SCHOOL & COLLEGE COURT

Note: The optimum length of the high school court is 84 feet. If court is less than 74 feet long, it should be divided by two lines, each parallel to and 40 feet from the farther end line.

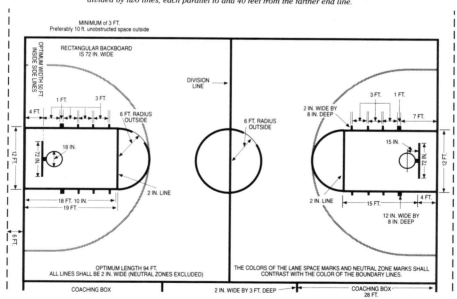

(Reprinted with permission of the NCAA.)

For more information contact:

National Basketball Association
Olympic Tower
645 Fifth Ave.
New York, NY 10022
(212) 826-7000

National Collegiate Athletic Association
6201 College Blvd.
Overland Park, KS 66211-2422
(913) 339-1906

FOOTBALL

PROFESSIONAL

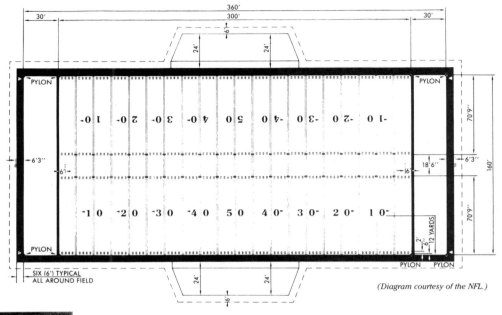

(Diagram courtesy of the NFL.)

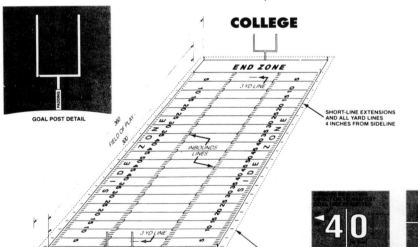

COLLEGE

(Diagrams courtesy of the NCAA.)

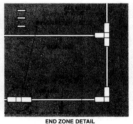

For more information contact:

National Football League
410 Park Ave.
New York, NY 10022
(212) 758-1500

National Collegiate Athletic Association
6201 College Blvd.
Overland Park, KS 66211-2422
(913) 339-1906

FOOTBALL

HIGH SCHOOL

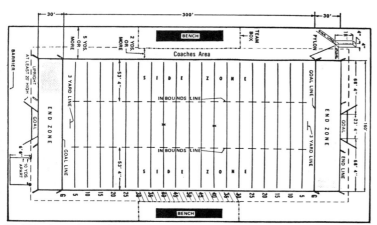

(Diagram courtesy of the NFSHSA.)

Note: Both team boxes may be on one side between the two 45- and 20-yard lines. End lines and sidelines should be at least 4 inches wide. Other field dimensions should be 4 inches wide.

Note: Recommend the area between team boxes and sidelines be solid white or marked with diagonal lines.

Note: Inbounds lines should be 24'' long and 4'' wide.

Note: Recommend the field slope from center to each sideline at 1/4-inch per foot.

Note: A 4-inch wide broken restraining line may be put around the entire field, 2 or more yards from boundaries.

For more information contact:

National Federation of State High School Associations
P.O. Box 20626
Kansas City, MO 64195
(816) 464-5400

VOLLEYBALL

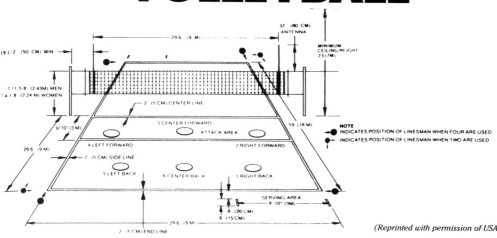

(Reprinted with permission of USA Volleyball.)

The following net heights are currently in practice for the below indicated age groups and scholastic levels of competition:

AGE GROUPS	GIRLS	BOYS/COED
18 years and under	2.24m (7'4⅛")	2.43m (7'11⅝")
16 years and under	2.24m (7'4⅛")	2.43m (7'11⅝")
14 years and under	2.24m (7'4⅛") or 7'0"	2.24m (7'4⅛")
12 years and under	2.10m (7'0") or 6'6"	2.10m (7'0") or 6'6"

SCHOLASTIC LEVELS	GIRLS	BOYS/COED
Grades 1 thru 6 (Elementary School):	1.85m (6'1")	1.85m (6'1")
Grades 7 and 8 (Middle School):	2.24m (7'4⅛")	2.24m(7'4⅛")
Grades 9 thru 12 (Sr. High School):	2.24m (7'4⅛")	2.43m (7'11⅝")

In the interest of safety for age group and scholastic competition, the height of the net shall be that specified for male competition. This height requirement shall not be modified.

For more information contact:

USA Volleyball
3595 E. Fountain Blvd.
Colorado Springs, CO 80910-1740
(719) 637-8300

HOCKEY

PROFESSIONAL

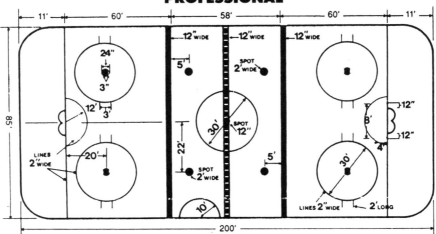

COLLEGE AND HIGH SCHOOL

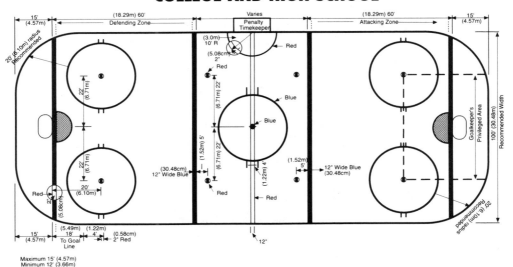

(Diagram courtesy of the NCAA.)

For more information contact:

National Hockey League
1800 McGill College, Suite 2600
Montreal, Quebec H3A 3J6
(514) 288-9220
Fax: (514) 284-3667

**National Federation of State High
School Associations**
P.O. Box 20626
Kansas City, MO 64195
(816) 464-5400

**National Collegiate Athletic
Association**
6201 College Blvd.
Overland Park, KS 66211-2422
(913) 339-1906

RACQUETBALL/ HANDBALL

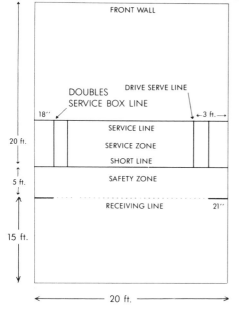

FRONT WALL

FRONT AND
SIDE WALL
HEIGHT: 20'0"

REAR WALL
HEIGHT:
AT LEAST 14'0"

DOUBLES
SERVICE BOX LINE

DRIVE SERVE LINE

18"

←3 ft.→

SERVICE LINE

20 ft.

SERVICE ZONE

5 ft.

SHORT LINE

5 ft.

SAFETY ZONE

RECEIVING LINE   21"

15 ft.

←———— 20 ft. ————→

For more information contact:

**American Amateur Racquetball
Association**
1685 W. Uintah
Colorado Springs, CO 80904-2921
(719) 635-5396
Fax: (719) 635-0685

SQUASH

NORTH AMERICAN COURT   ## INTERNATIONAL COURT   ## DOUBLES COURT

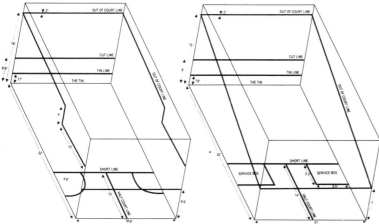

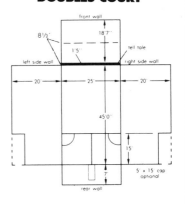

For more information contact:

**United States Squash Racquets
Association**
23 Cynwyd Road, P.O. Box 1216
Bala-Cynwyd, PA 19004
(610) 667-4006

SOCCER

LAW I. — THE FIELD OF PLAY
The Field of Play and appurtenances shall be as shown in the following plan:

Note: For players under 16 years of age, the size of the playing pitch, as well as the width of the goal posts and the height of the cross-bar may be modified.

OUTDOOR FIELD

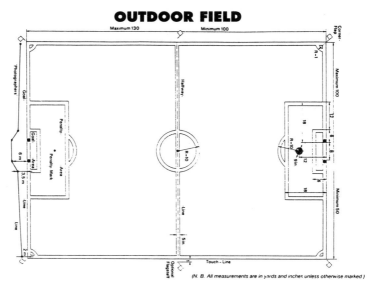

(N. B. All measurements are in yards and inches unless otherwise marked.)

Note: The soccer field cannot be square.

INDOOR FIELD

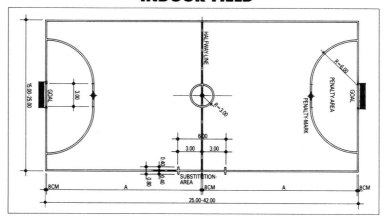

For more information contact:

United States Soccer Federation
1801-1811 S. Prairie Ave.
Chicago, IL 60616
(312) 808-1300

American Youth Soccer Organization
5403 W. 138th St.
Hawthorne, CA 90250
(310) 643-6455

SOFTBALL

OFFICIAL DIMENSIONS FOR SOFTBALL DIAMONDS

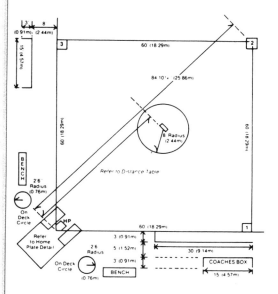

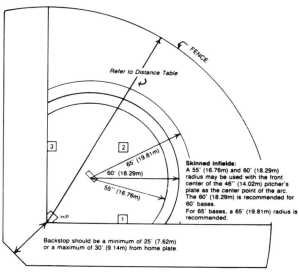

(Diagrams courtesy of the Amateur Softball Association of America.)

Skinned infields:
A 55' (16.76m) and 60' (18.29m) radius may be used with the front center of the 46'' (14.02m) pitcher's plate as the center point of the arc. The 60' (18.29m) is recommended for 60' bases.
For 65' bases, a 65' (19.81m) radius is recommended.

Backstop should be a minimum of 25' (7.62m) or a maximum of 30' (9.14m) from home plate.

DISTANCE TABLE

ADULT

GAME	DIVISION	BASES	PITCHING	FENCES Minimum	FENCES Maximum
Fast Pitch	Women	60' (18.29 m)	40' (12.19 m)	200' (60.96 m)	250' (76.20 m)*
	Men	60' (18.29 m)	46' (14.02 m)	225' (68.58 m)	250' (76.20 m)
	Jr. Men	60' (18.29 m)	46' (14.02 m)	225' (68.58 m)	250' (76.20 m)
Modified	Women	60' (18.29 m)	40' (12.19 m)	200' (60.96 m)	
	Men	60' (18.29 m)	46' (14.02 m)	265' (80.80 m)	
Slow Pitch	Women	65' (19.81 m)	50' (15.24 m)	265' (80.80 m)	275' (83.82 m)
	Men	65' (19.81 m)	50' (15.24 m)	275' (83.82 m)	315' (96.01 m)*
	Co-Ed	65' (19.81 m)	50' (15.24 m)	275' (83.82 m)	300' (91.44 m)
	Super	65' (19.81 m)	50' (15.24 m)	300' (91.44 m)	325' (99.06 m)
16 Inch Slow Pitch	Women	55' (16.76 m)	38' (11.58 m)	200' (60.96 m)	
	Men	55' (16.76 m)	38' (11.58 m)	250' (76.20 m)	
14 Inch Slow Pitch	Women	60' (18.29 m)	46' (14.02 m)		
	Men	60' (18.29 m)	46' (14.02 m)		*Effective 1996

YOUTH

GAME	DIVISION	BASES	PITCHING	FENCES Minimum	FENCES Maximum
Slow Pitch	Girls 10-under	55' (16.76 m)	35' (10.67 m)	150' (45.72 m)	175' (53.34 m)
	Boys 10-under	55' (16.76 m)	35' (10.67 m)	150' (45.72 m)	175' (53.34 m)
	Girls 12-under	60' (18.29 m)	40' (12.19 m)	175' (53.34 m)	200' (60.96 m)
	Boys 12-under	60' (18.29 m)	40' (12.19 m)	175' (53.34 m)	200' (60.96 m)
	Girls 14-under	65' (19.81 m)	46' (14.02 m)	225' (68.58 m)	250' (76.20 m)
	Boys 14-under	65' (19.81 m)	46' (14.02 m)	250' (76.20 m)	275' (83.82 m)
	Girls 16-under	65' (19.81 m)	50' (15.24 m)	225' (68.58 m)	250' (76.02 m)
	Boys 16-under	65' (19.81 m)	50' (15.24 m)	275' (83.82 m)	300' (91.44 m)
	Girls 18-under	65' (19.81 m)	50' (15.24 m)	225' (68.58 m)	250' (76.02 m)
	Boys 18-under	65' (19.81 m)	50' (15.24 m)	275' (83.82 m)	300' (91.44 m)
Fast Pitch	Girls 10-under	55' (16.76 m)	35' (10.67 m)	150' (45.72 m)	175' (53.34 m)
	Boys 10-under	55' (16.76 m)	35' (10.67 m)	150' (45.72 m)	175' (53.34 m)
	Girls 12-under	60' (18.29 m)	35' (10.67 m)	175' (53.34 m)	200' (60.96 m)
	Boys 12-under	60' (18.29 m)	40' (12.19 m)	175' (53.34 m)	200' (60.96 m)
	Girls 14-under	60' (18.29 m)	40' (12.19 m)	175' (53.34 m)	200' (60.96 m)
	Boys 14-under	60' (18.29 m)	46' (14.02 m)	175' (53.34 m)	200' (60.96 m)
	Girls 16-under	60' (18.29 m)	40' (12.19 m)	200' (60.96 m)	225' (68.58 m)
	Boys 16-under	60' (18.29 m)	46' (14.02 m)	200' (60.96 m)	225' (68.58 m)
	Girls 18-under	60' (18.29 m)	40' (12.19 m)	200' (60.96 m)	225' (68.58 m)
	Boys 18-under	60' (18.29 m)	46' (14.02 m)	200' (60.96 m)	225' (68.58 m)

Note: The only difference between college and high school is the pitching distance.

high school	fast pitch male	...........46'
	slow pitch male	...........46'
	slow pitch female	..........46'
	fast pitch female	..........40'
college	............................43'	

For more information contact:

Amateur Softball Association of America
2801 N.E. 50th St.
Oklahoma City, OK 73111
(405) 424-5266

SWIMMING & DIVING

INTERNATIONAL AND NATIONAL COMPETITION

There are a number of sanctioning organizations for national and international amateur competition. Included here are the facility standards of FINA (the Federation Internationale de Natation Amateur) and one of its U.S. affiliates, United States Swimming Inc.

FINA STANDARDS
• Length—50m. When touch panels or electronic timing devices are used, the pool must be of such length that ensures the required distance between the panels.
• Width—21m.
• Depth—1.8m.
• Number of lanes—8.
• Width of lanes—2.5m, with spaces of 50cm outside of lanes 1 and 8. A lane rope must separate these spaces from lanes 1 and 8.

U.S. SWIMMING STANDARDS
• Length—Long course, 164'½" (50m); short course, 82'¼" (25m) or 25 yds.
• Width—Eight lanes, 9' (2.75m) in width (centerline to centerline), with

approximately 1½' (0.43m) outside lanes 1 and 8.
• Water depth—For national championships and international competition, 6'7" (2m) throughout the course. Minimum water depth for racing starts during competition and practice shall be measured for a distance 3'3½" (1m) to 16'5" (5m) from the end wall. Starting requirements and height of starting blocks shall be as follows: (1) In pools with water depth less than 3'6" (1.07m) at the starting end, the swimmer must start from the deck or from within the water; (2) In pools with water depth 3'6" (1.07m) to less than 4' (1.22m) at the starting end, starting platforms shall be no more than 18" (0.46m) above the water surface; (3) In pools with water

depth 4' (1.22m) or more at the starting end, starting platforms shall meet the following height requirements: A. Long course: The front edge of the starting platforms shall be no less than 1'8" (0.50m) nor more than 2'5½" (0.75m) above the surface of the water. B. Short Course: The front edge of the starting platforms shall be not higher than 2'6" (0.762m) above the surface of the water.

NOTE: Local, state and municipal statutes, ordinances, rules and regulations may have depth limitations in conflict with the above. The LSC and all member clubs should check for this at all times.

STANDARD DIMENSIONS FOR PUBLIC SWIMMING POOLS

The following are the currently recommended standard dimensions for Class B and Class C public swimming pools, not designed for sanctioned competition.

MINIMUM DIMENSIONS FOR DIVING PORTION OF CLASS B AND C POOLS
(This drawing does not show the shallow portion of the pool)

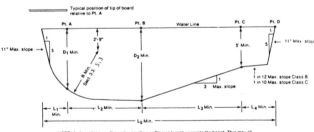

NOTE: L₄ is a minimum dimension to allow sufficient length opposite the board. This may of course be lengthened to form the shallow portion of the pool

POOL TYPE	RELATED DIVING EQUIPMENT		MINIMUM DIMENSIONS								MINIMUM WIDTH OF POOL AT:		
	MAX. DIVING BOARD LENGTH	MAX. BOARD HGT. OVER WATER	D₁	D₂	R	L₁	L₂	L₃	L₄	L₅	PT. A	PT. B	PT. C
VI	10'	26" (¾ meter)	7'-0"	8'-6"	5'-6"	2'-6"	8'-0"	10'-6"	7'-0"	28'-0"	16'-0"	18'-0"	18'-0"
VII	12'	30"(¾ meter)	7'-6"	9'-0"	6'-0"	3'-0"	9'-0"	12'-0"	4'-0"	28'-0"	18'-0"	20'-0"	20'-0
VIII	16'	1 Meter	8'-6"	10'-0"	7'-0"	4'-0"	10'-0"	15'-0"	2'-0"	31'-0"	20'-0"	22'-0"	22'-0"
IX	16'	3 Meter	11'-0"	12'-0"	8'-6"	6'-0"	10'-6"	21'-0"	0	37'-6"	22'-0"	24'-0"	24'-0"

L2, L3 and L4 combined represent the minimum distance from the tip of the board to pool wall opposite diving equipment.

For board heights exceeding 3 meters, see Article 3.5.4.

* NOTE: Placement of boards shall observe the following minimum dimensions. With multiple board installations minimum pool widths must be increased accordingly.

Deck level board to pool side . . . . .8'
1 meter board to pool side . . . . .10'
3 meter board to pool side . . . . .11'
1 meter or deck level board to 3 meter board . . . . .10'
1 meter or deck level to another 1 meter or deck level board . . . . .8'
3 meter to another 3 meter board . . . . .10'

DEPTH
• Swimming—In Class B and C pools, water depths at the shallow end of the swimming area shall be 3' minimum with 3'6" minimum for racing pools. Exceptions may be made in a recessed area of the main swimming pool, outside of the competitive and/or swimming course, when the pool is of an irregular shape with the permission of the state or local authority.
• Diving—Class B and C pools intended for diving shall conform to the minimum water depths, areas, slopes and other dimensions shown in Article 4.7 and shall be located in the diving area of the pool so as to provide the minimum dimensions as shown in Article 3.6.1. Competitive diving equipment shall not be installed in Class B and C pools.

There shall be a completely unobstructed clear vertical distance of 13' above any diving board, measured from the center of the front end of the board. This area shall extend horizontally at least 8' behind, 8' to each side and 16' ahead of point A. (See diagram.)

According to a spokesperson for the National Spa and Pool Institute (NSPI), this standard has been approved by the American National Standards Institute. American National Standards, once approved, may be revised at any time. Make sure that you have the latest edition of this standard by ordering the NSPI-1 Standard for Public Swimming Pools from the NSPI.

For more information contact:

National Spa and Pool Institute
2111 Eisenhower Ave.
Alexandria, VA 22314-4678
(703) 838-0083

SWIMMING & DIVING

The following are NCAA standard pool dimensions. These are recommended dimensions for collegiate competition only, and specifications are subject to annual review and change.

POOL CROSS-SECTION

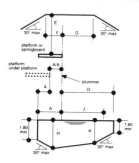

LONGITUDINAL SECTION
DIAGRAMMATIC ONLY

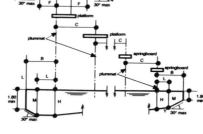

CROSS SECTION
DIAGRAMMATIC ONLY

DIVING CHART

NCAA Recommended Dimensions for Diving Facilities	Dimensions are in Feet	SPRINGBOARD		PLATFORM		
		1 Meter	3 meters	5 meters	7.5 Meters	10 Meters
Revised to March 3, 1991	LENGTH	16'	16'	20'	20'	20'
	WIDTH	1'8"	1'8"	5'	5'	6'7"
	HEIGHT	3'4"	10'	16'5"	24'8"	32'10"
		Horiz. / Vert.	Horiz. / Vert.	Horiz. / Vert.	Horiz. / Verth.	Horiz. / Vert.
A — From plummet BACK TO POOL WALL	Designation	A-1	A-3	A-5	A-7.5	A-10
	Minimum	5'	5'	4'2"	5'	5'
	Preferred	6'1"	6'1"	4'2"	5'	5'
A/A — From plummet BACK TO PLATFORM plummet directly below	Designation			A/A5	A/A7.5	A/A10
	Minimum			2'6"	2'6"	2'6"
	Preferred			4'2"	4'2"	4'2"
B — From plummet to POOL WALL AT SIDE	Designation	B-1	B-3	B-5	B-75	B-10
	Minimum	8'3"	11'6"	10'8"	14'	17'3"
	Preferred	8'3"	11'6"	12'4"	14'10"	17'3"
C — From plummet to ADJACENT PLUMMET	Designation	C-11	C-331	C-531	C-7.5531	C-107.55531
	Minimum	6'7"	7'3"	7'5"	8'3"	9'1"
	Preferred	7'1"	8'3"	8'3"	8'3"	9'1"
D — From plummet to POOL WALL AHEAD	Designation	D-1	D-3	D-5	D-7.5	D-10
	Minimum	29'7"	33'8"	33'8"	36'2"	44'4
	Preferred	29'7"	33'8"	33'8"	36'2"	44'4"
E — On plummet from BOARD TO CEILING	Designation	E-1	E-3	E-5	E-75	E-10
	Minimum	16'5"	16'5"	10'8"	10'8"	13'2"
	Preferred	16'5"	16'5"	11'6"	11'6"	16'5"
F — CLEAR OVERHEAD behind and each side of plummet	Designation	F-1 / E-1	F-3 / E-3	F-5 / E-5	F-7.5 / E-7.5	F-10 / E-10
	Minimum	8'3" / 16'5"	8'3" / 16'5"	9'1" / 10'8"	9'1" / 10'9"	9'1" / 13'2"
	Preferred	8'3" / 16'5"	8'3" / 16'5"	9'1" / 11'6"	9'1" / 11'6"	9'1" / 16'5"
G — CLEAR OVERHEAD ahead of plummet	Designation	G-1 / E-1	G-3 / E-3	G-5 / E-5	G-7.5 / E-7.5	G-10 / E-10
	Minimum	16'5" / 16'5"	16'5" / 16'5"	16'5" / 10'8"	16'5" / 10'8"	19'9" / 13'2"
	Preferred	16'5" / 16'5"	16'5" / 16'5"	16'5" / 11'6"	16'5" / 11'6"	19'9" / 16'5"
H — DEPTH OF WATER at plummet (minimum required)	Designation	H-1	H-3	H-5	H-7.5	H-10
	Minimum	11'	12'	12'2"	13'6"	14'10"
	Preferred	11'6"	12'6"	12'6"	14'10"	16'5"
J-K — DISTANCE AND DEPTH ahead of plummet	Designation	J-1 / K-1	J-3 / K-3	J-5 / K-5	J-7.5 / K-7.5	J-10 / K-10
	Minimum	16'5" / 10'10"	16'5" / 11'10"	19'9" / 11'10"	26'3" / 13'2"	36'2" / 14'
	Preferred	16'5" / 11'2"	19'9" / 12'2"	19'9" / 12'2"	26'3" / 14'6"	36'2" / 15'7"
L-M — DISTANCE AND DEPTH each side of plummet	Designation	L-1 / M-1	L-3 / M-3	L-5 / M-5	L-7.5 / M-7.5	L-10 / M-10
	Minimum	5' / 10'10"	6'7" / 11'10"	19'11" / 11'10"	12'4" / 13'2"	14'10" / 14'
	Preferred	9'11" / 11'2"	8'3" / 12'2"	12'2" / 11'6"	12'4" / 14'10"	14'6" / 17'3" / 15'7"
N — MAXIMUM SLOPE OF REDUCE DIMENSIONS beyond full requirements	Pool depth / Ceiling Ht.	30 degrees / 30 degrees		Note 1: Dimensions C (plummet to adjacent plummet) apply for Platforms with widths as detailed. For wider Platforms increase C by half the additional width(s). Note 2: All dimensions rounded up, even if only fractionally greater than the enxt lowest inch.		

LONG COURSE SWIMMING POOL

• Preferred—The racing course should be 164'1½" (50m, 2.54cm) in length by 75'1" (22.89m) in width, providing for eight 9' (2.74m) lanes with additional width outside lanes 1 and 8. A minimum water depth of 7' (2.13m) is desirable for competition. Optional markings: nine 8' (2.44m) lanes or ten 7' (2.13m) lanes.

• Acceptable—The racing course may be 164'1½" (50m, 2.54cm) in length by 60' (18.29m) in width, providing for eight 7' (2.13m) lanes with additional width outside lanes 1 and 8. The water depth may be no less than 4' (1.22m) at the starting end of the racing course and no less than 3'6" (1.07m) at the opposite end. However, a water depth of no less than 4' (1.22m) is recommended throughout the entire length of the racing course.

SHORT COURSE SWIMMING POOL

• Preferred—The racing course should be 75'1" (22.89m) in length by at least 60' (18.29m) in width, providing for not less than eight 7' (2.13m) lanes with additional width outside lanes 1 and 8. A minimum water depth of 7' (2.13m) is desirable for competition.

• Acceptable—The racing course may be 82'1¼" (25m, 2.54cm) in length by at least 45' (13.72m) in width, providing for six 7' (2.13m) lanes with additional width outside lanes 1 and 6. The water depth may be no less than 4' (1.22m) at the starting end of the racing course and no less than 3'6" (1.07m) at the opposite end. However, a water depth of no less than 4' (1.22m) is recommended throughout the entire length of the racing course.

DIVING POOL

• Preferred—The diving facility should be 60' (18.29m) in length by 75'1" (22.89m) in width. It should be equipped with two 1-meter and two 3-meter springboards and a diving tower, providing takeoff platforms at 5, 7.5 and 10 meters. Recommended dimensions for diving facilities are specified in the table on the left.

• Acceptable—The diving facility may be separated from or incorporated with the swimming pool. Recommended dimensions for diving facilities are specified in the table on the left.

Note: The above dimensions may be incorporated in "L," "T," "Z," and "U" shaped pools.

For more information contact:

National Collegiate Athletic Association
6201 College Blvd.
Overland Park, KS 66211-2422
(913) 339-1906

Reprinted by permission of the NCAA from the 1994 NCAA Men's and Women's Swimming and Diving Rules.

TEAM HANDBALL

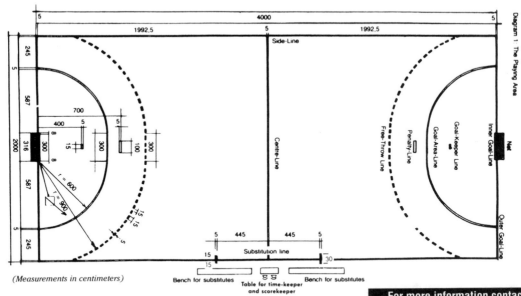

(Measurements in centimeters)

For more information contact:

United States Team Handball Federation
One Olympic Plaza
Colorado Springs, CO 80909
(719) 578-4582 or (800) 468-8666
FAX:(719) 475-1240

FIELD HOCKEY

FIELD DIMENSIONS

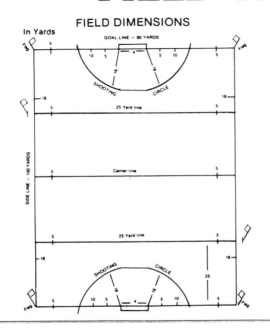

For more information contact:

U.S. Field Hockey Association
One Olympic Plaza
Colorado Springs, CO 80909-5773
(719) 578-4567
Fax: (719) 632-0979

TENNIS

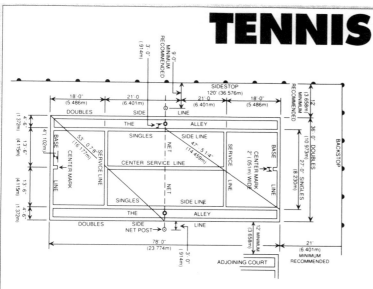

(Reprinted with permission of the USTC&TBA.)

For more information contact:

**U.S. Tennis Court and
Track Builders Association**
720 Light St.
Baltimore, MD 21230-3816
(410) 752-3500

United States Tennis Association
70 W. Red Oak Lane
White Plains, NY 10604
914/696-7000

BADMINTON

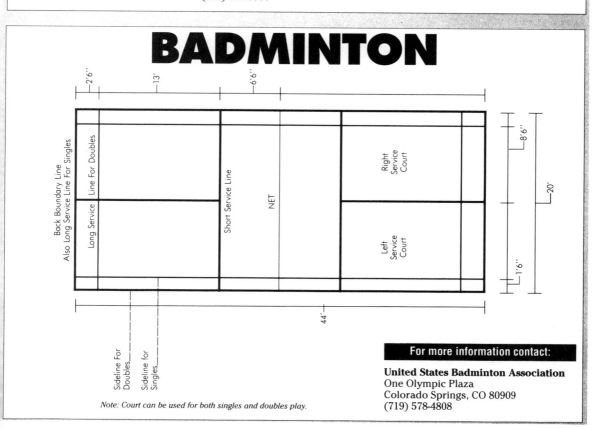

Note: Court can be used for both singles and doubles play.

For more information contact:

United States Badminton Association
One Olympic Plaza
Colorado Springs, CO 80909
(719) 578-4808

TRACK & FIELD

Dimensions for track and field events appearing in the following diagrams are set forth by the International Amateur Athletic Foundation (IAAF). Variations for the National Collegiate Athletic Association (NCAA) are also stated below each diagram.

OVERALL DIAGRAM OF FIELD EVENTS

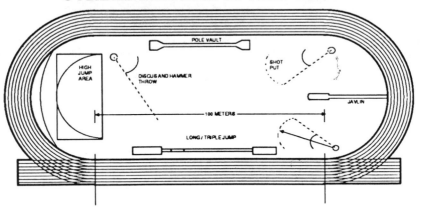

STANDARD 400M TRACK

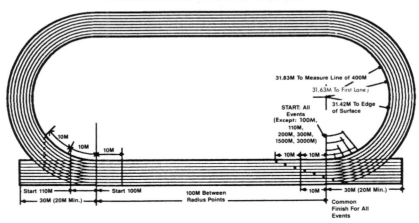

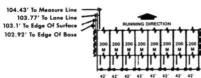

INSET

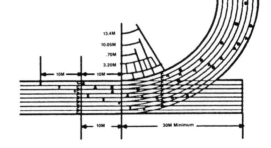

Variations:
Track Width:
NCAA—6.40m (6 min. width lanes) minimum

Lane Width:
NCAA—1.07m (42") recommended

Curb Dimensions:
NCAA—5.08cm (2") minimum height

TRACK & FIELD

STEEPLECHASE HURDLES

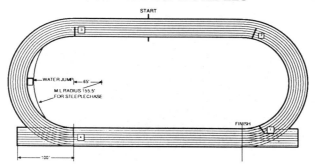

Variations:
Distance for Junior
Events—2,000m
No variation for
NCAA

SHOT PUT, DISCUS AND HAMMER THROWS

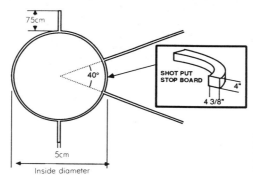

Circle measurements:
Shot put: 2.135m
Discus: 2.500m
Hammer 2.135m
(Inside Diameter)

JAVELIN THROW

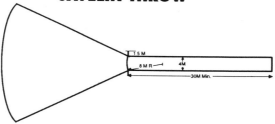

Variations:
Runway:
NCAA — 36.5m (120') minimum length. 70' shall be 4' wide and 50'
     shall be 13.12' wide.

Foul Line:
NCAA — 8m (26'3") radius arc; 4m between extremities.
     It shall be made of wood or other suitable materials 7cm
     (2.75") wide, painted white and sunk flush with the surface.

For more information contact:

U.S. Tennis Court and Track
Builders Association
720 Light St.
Baltimore, MD 21230-3816
(410) 752-3500

TRACK & FIELD

POLE VAULT

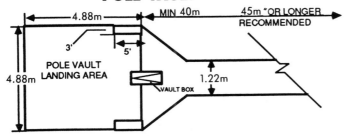

4.88m

MIN 40m

45m *OR LONGER RECOMMENDED

3'

5'

POLE VAULT LANDING AREA

4.88m

1.22m

VAULT BOX

Variations:
Runway:
NCAA—Same as IAAF except minimum length 38.1m (125')

Landing Pit Area:
NCAA—4.88m (16')

VAULT BOX

6"

9"

3' 6"

3' 3"

2' 7"

2'

LONG JUMP

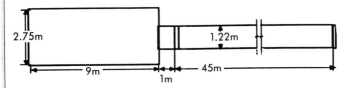

2.75m

1.22m

9m

1m

45m

TRIPLE JUMP

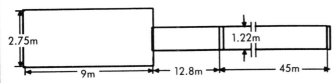

2.75m

1.22m

9m

12.8m

45m

Recommended width 1.22m

Variations:
Runway:
NCAA — Minimum length 39.62m (130')
        Recommended width 1.22m (4')

Landing Pit:
NCAA — Minimum length 7.92m (26')

HIGH JUMP

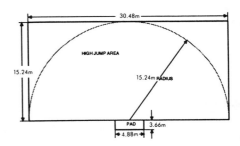

30.48m

HIGH JUMP AREA

15.24m

15.24m RADIUS

PAD

3.66m

4.88m

Variations:
NCAA—Minimum run-up 15m (49.21')
Recommended run-up 21m (68.90')

WOMEN'S LACROSSE

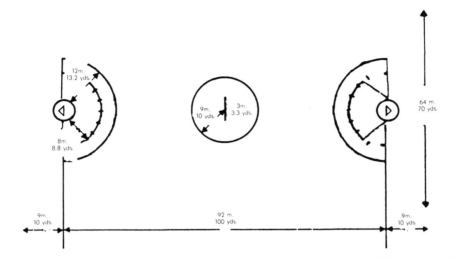

(Diagram courtesy of the U.S. Women's Lacrosse Association.)

For more information contact:

U.S. Women's Lacrosse Association
45 Maple Ave.
Hamilton, NY 13346
(315) 824-2480
Fax: (315) 824-4533

MEN'S LACROSSE

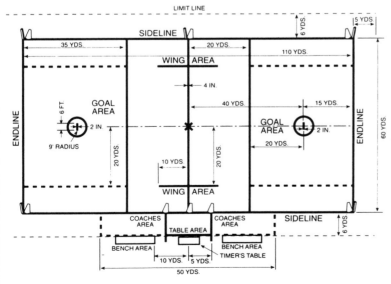

(Diagram courtesy of the NCAA.)

For more information contact:

The Lacrosse Foundation
113 W. University Pkwy.
Baltimore, MD 21210
(410) 235-6882
Fax: (410) 366-6735

or

National Collegiate Athletic Association
6201 College Blvd.
Overland Park, KS 66211-2422
(913) 339-1906

APPENDIX E

FUND-RAISING SUPPORT GROUP CONSTITUTION

The components of a constitution include, but are not limited to:

Article I	Organization
Article II	Purpose
Article III	Membership
Article IV	Officer Elections
Article V	Duties of Officers
Article VI	Executive Committee
Article VII	Board of Directors
Article VIII	Meetings
Article IX	Standing and Special Committees
Article X	Property Rights
Article XI	Constitutional Amendments
Article XII	Relationship with Principal/Athletic Director/School Board

APPENDIX F

MANAGING HUMAN RESOURCES

◆ ──────────────── ◆

Mark Twain Fitness Center
Employment Application

1. Personal Data: Date _____
    Name _____

    Address _____
                Street   City   State   Zip

    _____   _____
    Telephone   Social Security#

    Person to notify in case of an emergency:
    Name _____

    _____
    Address   Street   City   State   Zip

    _____
    Telephone

2. Education:

    _____
    Type of School   School Name   Degree   Major

    _____
    High School

College

_____

Post Graduate

_____

Business/trade

_____

Other

3.   Employment Record:

_____

Date

_____

Name & Address

_____

Supervisor

_____

Reason for Leaving

From   To
From   To

4.   Professional References

        List three, not relatives or former employers, who are well acquainted
with you.

Name	Address	Phone

Name	Address	Phone

Name	Address	Phone

5.   Remarks

Use this space to record any explanations or supplementary information you may wish to submit.

6.   I authorize Mark Twain Fitness Center, Inc. to investigate all statements in this application and to contact all employers and references. I understand that false or misleading statements in this application will be sufficient cause for dismissal if employed.

Date   Signature of Applicant

Sample Letter of Appointment

July 1, 1995

Ms. Becky Thatcher
1321 Indian Joe Lane
Hannibal, MO 42317

Dear Ms. Thatcher:

I am pleased to advise you of your appointment as Day Care Director at Mark Twain Fitness Center. The conditions of your employment, which were discussed with you are now confirmed as follows:

- You will assume your position as a member of staff on 7/15/95.
- Your annual salary will be $18,000, payable in twelve monthly installments on the 1st of each month. Your performance will be reviewed annually to determine annually salary adjustments.
- Six months after commencing employment you will be eligible to participate in the group health insurance plan, and at the conclusion of the first year you can begin participating in the group retirement plan.
- You will be allowed two weeks vacation with pay each year for the first three years.
- You will earn sick leave at the rate of one day per month of employment which can be accumulated. At termination (voluntary or forced) you will be paid for up to 100 days of sick leave at the rate of pay at termination.
- You will be expected to take part in regularly-scheduled staff meetings, in-service education programs, and any other programs deemed advisable for your professional growth.
- You will appear, as scheduled, at the Hannibal Medical Center for a physical examination.

On behalf of the staff of the Mark Twain Fitness Center, I welcome you to our team. We look forward to a happy and rewarding association and one long in duration.

Sincerely,

Mark Twain Fitness Center
Performance Appraisal

Work Plan Form

Employee	Manager	Date
Job requirements (e.g., projects, goals, specific tasks to be accomplished, timelines)	Assessments measures (e.g., timelines, expected outcomes	Priorities

Progress Review Form

Employee: _____ Manager: _____ Date: _____

Progress to date _____

Problems/Concerns_____

Suggested Actions_____

Employee: _____ Supervisor: _____ Date: _____

Period under review: _____

I. Review of Accomplishments

Job Requirements:	Achievement Measures:	Results Achieved:
Describe the major duties or goals of this job	Indicate specific results you and employee expected to be accomplished during the review period	Assess results of each requirement

1. Administration
   (job requirement)

Duties:

Goals:

II. Overall Evaluation of Performance:

III. Highlights of Performance

    A. What are the employee's most outstanding qualifications?

    B. How does the employee need to improve within the present job?

IV. Training and Development Plans:

To what extent or educational activities should this employee be exposed during the coming year to assist him or her in improving individual performance?

V. Potential:

What is the employee's capacity to handle increased responsibilities outside present type or sphere of work? Specify:

VI. Discussion of Review:

    A. Employee's Reaction to this performance review:

    B. Employee's Acknowledgement: The contents of this form have been reviewed with me.

_____

Employee's Signature   Date

    C.

_____

Reviewer's Signature   Date

(Attach separate sheet if additional space is required)

APPENDIX G

MANAGING THE MARKETPLACE

◆ ———————————————— ◆

Market Characteristics

The following information must be gathered in order to define the characteristics of a market:

1. Population

- total # males and # females
- urban, rural, suburban, interurban
- singles, married, one-parent families, size of families
- regional distribution
- age groups (Baby Boomers 30-49; Baby bust 18-29; Generation X 0-17)
- education levels
- occupations
- race, national origin
- religion

2. Economic Factors

- average personal income
- average disposable income
- average discretionary income
- inflation rate
- unemployment rate
- expenditure patterns

3. Competition

Scope of Marketing Research Activities

1. Research on products and services

- determining customer acceptance of proposed new products/services,
- making comparative studies of competitive products/services,
- evaluating new competitive products/services,
- determining current or new uses of present products/services,
- evaluating and market testing proposed new products/services,
- determining sources of customer dissatisfaction with products/services,
- simplifying product/service line, and
- making packaging and design studies.

2. Research on markets

- analyzing size of market for existing product/service,
- estimating demand for new products/services,
- forecasting sales and general business,
- determining characteristics of markets and products/services,
- analyzing sales potentials and relative profitability of region, and
- studying trends in market size and composition.

3. Research on sales methods and policies

- establishing and revising sales areas,
- evaluating present and proposed sales methods,
- studying competitive pricing, and
- studying distribution costs.

4. Research on advertising

- evaluating advertising effectiveness,
- analyzing competitive advertising and selling practices, and
- selecting advertising media.

5. Research on miscellaneous activities

- analyzing opinions of employees, customers, stockholders, or owners regarding the organization, its products/services, or its policies.

APPENDIX H

REVENUE GENERATION

◆ ———————————————— ◆

Suggested Components for Concessionaire Agreement

- name of parties
- appropriate dates
- term (i.e., from when to when)
- exclusions (i.e., community activities, religious conventions, circuses, Disney on Ice, luxury suites, etc.)
- definitions (i.e., gross sales, net sales, gratuities, off-premise sales, subcontracted sales, novelty sales)
- product control (i.e., brand, variety, quality, portion, pricing)
- marketing, advertising, and promotion
- management control (i.e., interviews with mangement candidates, authority to dismiss management, staffing levels, training involvement)
- investment (i.e., leasehold, equipment, smallware [pots and pans], approval of all investments, approval of depreciation/amortization, buyout provisions)
- insurance (i.e., hold harmless, product liability)
- audit controls (i.e., daily event summaries, monthly and profit loss, annual audit, unannounced audits)
- commission or managment fee
- computerization/cash registers
- operational audits
- repairs and renovation
- utilities
- default, bankruptcy, and mechanic's lien(s)
- quality assurance (i.e., management, staffing, product, and service)
- records
- controlling law(s) (i.e., health codes, OSHA)
- notice
- termination upon breach
- assignment
- renewal option
- final execution

(Modified, Wong, 1986).

APPENDIX I

RISK MANAGEMENT

♦ ——————————————— ♦

CAUTION: It is strongly recommended that no form be adopted by a program until it has been reviewed by legal counsel. An acceptable form must be written in accordance with prevailing state laws by independent legal counsel and should simply state to the participant the reasons for the procedure or activity, the risks and benefits, etc., in a manner specific to the program's activities for which consent is being obtained.

Sample Warnings

Strength Training Warning

Serious injuries can occur if struck by falling weights, moving parts of machines, using improper technique, or using improper equipment. You assume a risk of injury every time you use free weights or machines. This risk can be reduced by following these guidelines:

1. Do not use any equipment without QUALIFIED SUPERVISION.
2. Before using, INSPECT EQUIPMENT for loose, frayed, or worn parts. If in doubt, do not use until parts are repaired or replaced. Using damaged equipment can cause injury.
3. When using free weights, ALWAYS HAVE A SPOTTER. Use two spotters when lifting maximum poundages in overhead lifts.
4. The use of weight belts is highly recommended to prevent lower back strain or injury.
5. Rely on leg power rather than back strength in lifting weights from the floor by keeping the hips low and the back as vertical as possible.
6. Use and tighten clamps/collars on bars at all times. Keep the floor area clear to avoid falling over other weights. NEVER LEAVE WEIGHTS ON A BAR! ALWAYS return weights to the weight tree of the same color when finished.

8. Always warm up properly before lifting heavy weights. This consists of exercising large muscle groups as well as practicing the lift or activity with minimum poundage.

9. If weights, pulleys, or other parts become jammed, DO NOT attempt to FREE BY YOURSELF because weights might fall unexpectedly. Obtain spotter's, supervisor's, or instructor's assistance immediately.

10. When machines are in use, selector keys must be FULLY INSERTED AND LOCKED. Do not allow the plates to drop—set them down gently.

11. To reduce chance of injury, KEEP HEAD AND LIMBS CLEAR of weights and moving parts at all times. Don't be careless. STAY ALERT!

12. The weight room is not a play room. Concentrate on completing your workout and avoid "playing around."

Violation of these guidelines and rules may result in suspension from the weight room.

Thank you for your cooperation!

Sample Weight Room Warning #2

Warning

Serious injuries can occur if one is struck by falling weights or moving parts of machines and by improper technique or use of equipment. One assumes a risk of injury every time he uses free weights and machines. This risk can be reduced by always following these guidelines and rules:

1. Do not use any equipment without QUALIFIED SUPERVISION. When in doubt about proper use or technique, ASK!

2. Always warm up properly before lifting heavy weights. This consists of exercising large muscle groups as well as practicing the lift or activity with minimum poundage.

3. When using free weights, ALWAYS HAVE A SPOTTER. Use two spotters when lifting maximum poundages in overhead lifts.

4. The use of weight belts is highly recommended to prevent lower back strain or injury.

5. Rely on leg power rather than back strength in lifting weights from the floor by keeping the hips low and the back as vertical as possible.

6. Use and tighten clamps/collars on bars at all times.

7. Keep the floor area clear to avoid falling over other weights. NEVER LEAVE WEIGHTS ON A BAR! ALWAYS return weights to the weight tree of the same color when finished.

8. Before using, INSPECT EQUIPMENT for loose, frayed, or worn parts. If in dorbt, do not use until parts are repaired or replaced. Using damaged equipment can cause injury.

9.   If weights, pulleys, or other parts become jammed, DO NOT attempt to FREE THEM BY YOURSELF because weights might fall unexpectedly. Obtain spotter's, supervisor's, or instructor's assistance immediately.

10. When machines are in use, selector keys must be FULLY INSERTED AND LOCKED. Do not allow the plates to drop; set them down gently.

11. To reduce chance of injury, KEEP HEAD AND LIMBS CLEAR of weights and moving parts at all times. Don't be careless. STAY ALERT.

12. Remember—the weight room is not a play room. Concentrate on completing your workout and avoid "playing around."

Violation of these guidelines and rules may result in suspension from the weight room.

Sample Warning Sign Designed for a Facility Where a Trampoline is in Use

WARNING! CRIPPLING INJURIES CAN OCCUR DURING SOMERSAULTS.

Somersaulting should never be attempted without an overhead safety harness operated by a trained instructor. Refer to instruction manual. Almost all benefits and enjoyment of the trampoline can be obtained by learning the non-somersaulting, twisting skills, and routines provided in the manual furnished with this trampoline.

Any activity involving motion or height creates the possibility of accidental injury. This equipment is intended for use ONLY by properly trained and qualified participants under supervised conditions. Use without proper supervision could be DANGEROUS and should NOT be undertaken or permitted. Before using, KNOW YOUR LIMITATIONS and the limitations of this equipment. If in doubt, always consult your instructor.

Always inspect for loose fittings or damage and test stability before each use.

Sample Health Questionnaire

I. Medical information

Name _____

Address (W) _____

Address (H) _____

Gender _____ Male   _____ Female

Ethnicity: _____

Phone (W) _____ (H) _____ Fax _____
    E-Mail _____

Is your mother living: _____ Yes   _____ No

Age at death: _____ Cause: _____

Is your father living: _____ Yes   _____ No

Age at death: _____ Cause: _____

Are you on any medications now? _____

If yes, please list: _____
_____

Do you have allergies: _____ Yes   _____ No

If yes, please list: _____

Physical injuries: _____

Limitations: _____

Contact in case of emergency: _____

Phone: _____

Have you been seen by a physician in the past year? _____ Yes _____ No

Have you ever been diagnosed as having any cardiovascular abnormalities?
_____ Yes   _____ No

Have you ever experienced any adverse effects during or after exercise (such as fainting, vomiting, shock, palpitations, hyperventilation? _____ Yes _____ No
If yes, what was the diagnosis: _____

Have you ever had any of the following cardiovascular problems?

Myocardial infarction _____   Bypass surgery _____
Arrythmias _____   Heart murmur _____
Chest _____   Palpitations _____
Valve problems _____   Chest pressure _____
Shortness of breath _____   Heart attack _____

II. Lifestyle Information

Do you use tobacco? _____ Yes _____ No

If yes, how many years did you use tobacco: _____
Amount per day: _____
How many years? _____
How much per day:? _____
Number of years since you quit: _____

Have you had any of the following?

Rheumatic fever _____   High blood pressure _____
Kidney/liver disease _____   Obesity _____
Diabetes _____   High cholesterol _____

Do you currently have respiratory (breathing) ailments? _____ Yes _____ No

If yes, type (circle):

Asthma   COPD
Common cold   Emphysema
Bronchitis

Does anyone in your family have any of the conditions listed above? _____
If yes, please list family member and problem: _____
_____

How often do you drink the following?
Coffee: _____ oz./day   Wine: _____ oz./day
Tea: _____ oz./day   Beer: _____ oz./day
Caffeinated cola: _____ oz./day   Hard alcohol: _____ oz./day

III. Physical Activity

What do you do for physical activity?

Please check if you would like information about the following:
How often do you exercise? _____ days per week/month
How long each session? _____ minutes

Estimate your intensity level: Circle one or list your target exercise heart rate:
Easy, Medium, Hard or THR = per minute

Please describe your knowledge of exercise and fitness.
Circle one: Good, Fair, Poor

What is your occupation (Circle one)?
Inactive work (e.g., desk job)
Light work (e.g., light carpentry)
Heavy work (e.g., heavy carpentry, farming, lifting)

Which do you eat regularly?
Breakfast _____   midafternoon snack _____
Midmorning snack _____ dinner _____
Lunch _____   after-dinner snack _____

How often do you eat out each week? _____ times

Current weight? _____ What would you like to weigh? _____

What weight loss method(s) have you tried? _____

How long does it usually take you to eat a meal? _____

Do you eat while doing other activities (watching TV, reading, etc.)? _____

When you snack, how many times per week do you eat the following?

____ cookies, cake, & pies   ____ soft drinks
____ fruit   ____ milk (skim, low fat, whole)
____ fried bread   ____ veggies
____ cheese and crackers   ____ candy
____ doughnuts   ____ potato chips, etc.
____ ice cream   ____ Other (identify)

How often do you eat fried foods? _____ times a week
Do you salt your food at the table? _____
Circle one: Never, Seldom, Sometimes, Always)

How would you characterize your life? Circle one:
Highly stressful, Moderately stressful, Minimally stressful

Please check if you would like information about:
_____ muscular strength and endurance
_____ flexibility
_____ cardiovascular fitness
_____ percentage of body fat
_____ diet and eating habits
_____ management of stress
_____ how to quit smoking or drinking
_____ how to rehabilitate after an injury

IV. Physical Activity Readiness Information

For most people, physical activity should not pose a problem and hazard. This questionnaire has been designed to identify individuals in which physical activity may be inappropriate.

Comments:

Yes   No

____ ____ Has your doctor ever said that you have a heart condition and that you should only do physical activity recommended by a doctor?

____ ____ Do you feel pain in your chest when you do physical activity?

____ ____ In the past month, have you had chest pain while not doing physical activity?

____ ____ Do you lose your balance because of dizziness or do you ever lose consciousness?

____ ____ Do you have bone or joint problems that could be made worse by a change in your physical activity?

____ ____ Is your doctor currently currently prescribing drugs (e.g., water pills) for your blood pressure or heart condition?

____ ____ Do you know of any other reason that you should not do physical activity?

Client's name: _____   Date: _____
Client's signature: _____
Wellness consultant: _____

Source: Based on the ACSM's Guidelines, Fig 2-1, 5th ed. 1995.

Sample Waiver

DISCLAIMER: INDIANA STATE UNIVERSITY IS NOT RESPONSIBLE FOR ANY INJURY (OR LOSS OF PROPERTY) TO ANY PERSON SUFFERED WHILE PLAYING, PRACTICING, OR IN ANY OTHER WAY INVOLVED IN THE RUGBY CLUB FOR ANY REASON WHATSOEVER, INCLUDING ORDINARY NEGLIGENCE ON THE PART OF INDIANA STATE UNIVERSITY, ITS AGENTS, OR EMPLOYEES.

In consideration of my participation, I hereby release and covenant not-to-sue Indiana State University, Indiana State University Board of Trustees, Indiana State University Student Government Association, Indiana State University's Department of Recreational Sports, the Rugby Club, and any of their employees, instructors, or agents, from any and all present and future claims resulting from ordinary negligence on the part of Indiana State University or others listed for property damage, personal injury or wrongful death, arising as a result of my engaging in or receiving instruction in Rugby Club activities or any activities incidental thereto, wherever, whenever, or however the same may occur. I hereby voluntarily waive any and all claims resulting from ordinary negligence, both present and future, that may be made by me, my family, estate, heirs, or assigns.

Further, I am aware that rugby is a vigorous team sport involving severe cardiovascular stress and violent physical contact. I understand that rugby involves certain risks, including, but not limited to, death, serious neck and spinal injuries resulting in complete or partial paralysis, brain damage, and serious injury to virtually all bones, joints, muscles, and internal organs, and that equipment provided for my protection may be inadequate to prevent serious injury. I further understand that rugby involves a particularly high risk of knee, head, and neck injury. In addition, I understand that participation in the rugby club involves activities incidental thereto, including, but not limited to, travel to and from the site of the activity, participation at sites that may be remote from available medical assistance, and the possible reckless conduct of other participants. I am voluntarily participating in this activity with knowledge of the danger involved and hereby agree to accept any and all inherent risks of property damage, personal injury, or death.

I further agree to indemnify and hold harmless Indiana State University and others listed for any and all claims arising as a result of my engaging in or receiving instruction in rugby club activities or any activities incidental thereto, wherever, whenever, or however the same may occur.

I understand that this waiver is intended to be as broad and inclusive as permitted by the laws of Indiana, and agree that if any portion is held invalid, the remainder of the waiver will continue in full legal force and effect. I further agree that the venue for any legal proceedings shall be in Indiana.

I affirm that I am of legal age and am freely signing this agreement. I have read this form and fully understand that by signing this form, I am relinquishing legal rights and/or remedies that may be available to me for the ordinary negligence of Indiana State University or any of the parties listed above.

_____   _____

(Signature of Participant)   Date

_____   _____

(Signature of Parent if Participant is Under 18)   Date

Sample Informed Consent Form

Note:The following form has been modified.The original form is presented in Herbert & Herbert, 1993. If you are interested in other informed consent forms for clients with known or suspected heart disease, for participation in an exercise program for apparently healthy adults, or clients with known or suspected heart disease; release from liability; or medical approval forms—call (800)336-0083 or (216)492-6063 or write PRC Publishing, Inc., 4418 Belden Village Street, NW, Canton, Ohio 44718-2516 [ISBN # 0944183-18-2].

Informed Consent for Exercise Testing Procedures (Apparently Healthy Adults)

Note: The phrases in bold are key links to gaining acceptance of the form during a legal action.

1. Purpose and Explanation of Test

It is my understanding that I will undergo a test to be performed on a motor driven treadmill or bicycle ergometer with the amount of effort gradually increasing. As I understand it, this increase in effort will continue until I feel and verbally report to the operator any symptoms such as fatigue, shortness of breath, or chest discomfort which may appear, or until the test is completed, or otherwise terminated. It is my understanding and I have been clearly advised that it is my right to request that a test be stopped at any point if I feel unusual discomfort or fatigue. I have been advised that I should immediately stop upon experiencing any such symptoms or if I so choose, inform the operator that I wish to stop the test at that or any other point. My stated wishes in this regard shall be carried out. **IF CORRECT AND YOU AGREE AND UNDERSTAND, INITIAL HERE _____.**

It is further my understanding that prior to beginning the test, I will be connected by electrodes and cables to an electrocardiographic recorder which will enable the program personnel to monitor my cardiac (heart) activity. During the test itself, it is my understanding that a trained observer will monitor my responses continuously and take frequent readings of blood pressure, the electrocardiogram and my expressed feelings of effort. I realize that a true determination of my exercise capacity depends on progressing the test to a point of my fatigue. Once the test has been completed, but before I am released from the test area, I will be given special instructions about showering and recognition of certain symptoms that may appear within the first 24 hours after the test. I agree to follow these instructions and promptly contact the program personnel or medical providers if such symptoms develop. **IF CORRECT AND YOU AGREE AND UNDERSTAND, INITIAL HERE _____.**

Before I undergo the test, I certify to the program that I am in good health and have had a physical examination conducted by a licensed medical physician within the last six months. Further, I hereby represent and inform the program that I have accurately completed the pre-test history interview presented to me by the program staff and have provided correct responses to the questions as indicated on the history form or as supplied to the interviewer. It is my understanding that I will be interviewed by a physician or other person prior to my undergoing the test who will, in the course of interviewing me, determine if there are any reasons that would make it undesirable or unsafe for me to take the test. Consequently, I understand that it is important that I provide complete and accurate responses to the interviewer and recognize that my failure to do so could lead to possible unnecessary injury to myself during the test. **IF CORRECT, AND YOU AGREE, INITIAL HERE _____.**

2. Risks

It is my understanding, and I have been informed, that there exists the possibility of adverse changes during the actual test. I have been informed that these changes could include abnormal blood pressure, fainting, disorders of heart rhythm, stroke, and very rare instances of heart attack or even death. I have also been informed that aside from the foregoing, other risks exist. These risks include, but are not necessarily limited to the possibility of stroke, or other cerebrovascular or cardiovascular incident or occurrence; mental, physiological, motor, visual or hearing injuries, deficiencies, difficulties, or disturbances; partial or total paralysis, slips, falls, or other unintended loss of balance or bodily movement related to the exercise treadmill (or bicycle ergometer) that may cause muscular, neurological, orthopedic, or other bodily injury as well as a variety of other possible occurrences, any one of which could conceivably, however remotely, cause bodily injury, impairment, disability, or death. Any procedure such as this one carries with it some risk, however, unlikely or remote. THERE ARE ALSO OTHER RISKS OF INJURY, IMPAIRMENT, DISABILITY, DISFIGUREMENT, AND EVEN DEATH. I ACKNOWLEDGE AND AGREE TO ASSUME ALL RISKS. **IF YOU UNDERSTAND AND AGREE, INITIAL HERE ____.**

Every effort, I have been told, will be made to minimize these occurrences by preliminary examination and by precautions and observations taken during the test. I have also been informed that emergency equipment and personnel are readily available to deal with these unusual situations should they occur. Knowing and understanding all risks, it is my desire to proceed to take the test as herein described. **IF CORRECT, AND YOU AGREE AND UNDERSTAND, INITIAL HERE ____.**

3. Benefits to be Expected and Alternatives Available to the Exercise Testing Procedure

I understand and have been told that the results of this test may or may not benefit me. Potential benefits relate mainly to my personal motives for taking the test, i.e., knowing my exercise capacity in relation to the general population, understanding my fitness for certain sports and recreational activities, planning my physical conditioning program, or evaluating the effects of my recent physical activity habits. Although my fitness might also be evaluated by alternative means, e.g., a bench step test or an outdoor running test, such tests do not provide as accurate a fitness assessment as the treadmill or bike test, nor do those options allow equally effective monitoring of my responses. **IF YOU UNDERSTAND, INITIAL HERE _____.**

4. Consent

I hereby consent to voluntarily engage in an exercise test to determine my circulatory and respiratory fitness. I also consent to the taking of samples of my exhaled air during exercise to properly measure my oxygen consumption. I also consent, if necessary, to have a small blood sample drawn by needle from my arm for blood chemistry analysis and to the performance of lung function and body fat (skinfold pinch) tests. It is my understanding that the information obtained will help me evaluate future physical fitness and sports activities in which I may engage. **IF CORRECT AND YOU AGREE, INITIAL HERE _____.**

5. Confidentiality And Use Of Information

I have been informed that the information that is obtained in this exercise test will be treated as privileged and confidential information and will consequently not be released or revealed to any person without my express written consent. I do, however, agree to the use of any information for research or statistical purposes, so long as same does not provide facts that could lead to the identification of my person. Any other information obtained, however, will be used only by the program staff to evaluate my exercise status or needs. **IF YOU AGREE, INITIAL HERE _____.**

6. Inquiries and Freedom of Consent

I have been given an opportunity to ask questions as to the procedures. Generally, these requests that have been noted by the testing staff and their responses are as follows:

IF THIS NOTATION IS COMPLETE AND CORRECT, INITIAL HERE _____.

I acknowledge that I have read this document in its entirety or that it has been read to me if I have been unable to read same.

I consent to the rendition of all services and procedures as explained herein by all program personnel.
Date: _____

Witness' Signature Participant's Signature _____

Witness' Signature Spouse's Consent _____

Test Supervisor's Signature _____

Sample Report of an Accident or Injury

Date of accident or injury _____

Witnesses (include phone numbers and addresses) _____
_____

Time of incident _____

Participant's name _____
    Home phone _____
    Address _____

Staff person reporting _____
    Work phone _____
    Address _____

Director's name _____

Description of accident _____
_____
_____

Action taken by the staff member(s) _____
_____

File this accident/injury report in the participant's file and give a copy to the director.

Sample Contracts—Facility Contract

A sport manager must be well versed in negotiating a facility's lease agreement. Therefore, he must consider various issues before signing such an agreement with an outside organization or agency. Some of these issues include the following outline.

I. Know the Client

A. Can the facility meet all league rules for competition?

B. Can the facility meet all the mechanical needs of the event (e.g., electric, sound, stage, playing surfaces) as well as repairs, fixed operations costs, and administrative expenses as agreed upon?

C. Can your facility meet the revenue requirements of the user for the event?

1. Advertising—What type of advertising will be appropriate for the client?

2. Scoreboards—What type and how many scoreboards will be needed for the event?

3. Seats—What type of seating pattern will be required for the client's needs?

4. Ticket sales—Who will be responsible for the sale of the tickets and what type of tickets will require—general or reserved seating?

5. Concessions—Who will be responsible for organizing the concession operations?

    a. Food—Who will be responsible for the sale of food and drink?

    b. Merchandising—Who will be responsible for the sale of non-food items:? Will the merchandise be licensed products. Who is responsible for monitoring the sale of licensed products?

    c. Parking—Who will be responsible for the parking concession?

6. Sponsorships—What special arrangements will be necessary for sponsors of the event?

II. Know the Politics

A. Can the organization support the specific event given the established purpose of the facility and intended usages?

B. Can the facility withstand potential damage to its areas while still supporting other events, activities, and programs?

III. Know the Media and Community

A. Can the facility and management work with the media in presenting the events that are to take place?

B. Can the community assist with the event or support it?

IV. Know the Legal Issues

A. Can you provide complete access to the facility for minority or disabled persons?

B. Can the facility conduct business with other organizations without affecting the agreement with existing organizations?

C. Will the entity wanting to use the facility sign an indemnity clause?

V. Know the Security Requirements

A. Security

1. How many police will be needed?
2. How many ushers will be needed?

B. Fire

1. How many fire marshals are needed?

C. Emergency medical

1. How many EMTs are needed?
2. How many emergency vehicles are needed?

VI. Know Necessary Safety Precautions

A. Appropriate facility inspection has been completed.

B. Appropriate maintenance has been completed.

C. Appropriate warning signs have been installed.

Employment Contract

A typical employment contract should contain the following (Walker & Stotlar, 1997; Wong, 1994; Schubert et al., 1989) elements:

1. Clause describing the job responsibilities and duties
2. Provisions for salary
3. Fringe benefits
4. Duration of the contract
5. Evaluation process and causes for termination
6. Method of reimbursement for expenses
7. Any non-compete clauses
8. Any rights for new products or research while in the employ of the company

The most critical aspect of an employment contract from the sport manager's perspective is that of responsibilities and duties the professional is to perform according to standards in the industry. Therefore, it requires that the sport manager be available to supervise and assist professional staff, especially when the staff are in direct contact with participants.

Sport Contracts

In commercial settings, the courts have been active since the late 1980s. As a result, many states have enacted legislation governing and regulating the commercial fitness center or health club or spa industry. Van der Smissen (1990) states that:

> the focus of the laws is upon the rights of the buyers, specifically upon provisions of the contract for services, which must be written and have very specific rights related to cancellation of the contract (p. 148).

Mark Twain Risk Management Service
Health, Fitness, Physical Activity, Recreation, and Sport Facility Survey

Facility Name: _____

Address: _____

Person(s) Interviewed: _____

Person Completing This Survey: _____

Date: _____

THE ONLY PURPOSE OF THIS DOCUMENT IS TO PROVIDE INFORMATION RELEVANT TO THE SUBJECT PROPERTY. IT IS PUBLISHED WITH THE UNDERSTANDING THAT MARK TWAIN RISK MANAGEMENT SERVICE (MTRMS) IS NOT ENGAGED IN RENDERING LEGAL, MEDICAL, OR OTHER PROFESSIONAL SERVICES BY REASON OF THE DOCUMENTATION OF THIS SURVEY.

Copyright © by Indiana Center for Sport Education, Inc., 1995.

Thomas H. Sawyer, Ed.D., President
5840 South Ernest Street
Terre Haute, IN 47802
812/237-2186; FAX 812/237-4338; E-Mail pmsawyr@scifac.indstate.edu

I. Instructions

With this checklist the attempt is to be simple, while being as comprehensive as possible in the time given. The checklist items are written so one may simply check "yes," "no," or "not available" ("N/A"). Attach: 1) membership agreement/contract, 2) brochures, if available, 3) equipment inventory, if available, 4) inside and outside photos (especially any hazardous areas), and 5) other pertinent material, if available.

In "comments" following each section, provide comments where further explanation is necessary and write the appropriate number and/or letter for the section that is applicable for the comment. If additional or general comments are appropriate, provide them at the end of the document in the space provided. While observing the facility, take slide photos or a videotape, including all different types of activities offered by the facility. Finally, on the last two pages, list (1) *suggestions* (changes that *should* be made), and (2) the *recommendations* (changes that *must* be made) which are essential to this facility and include relevant slides or video, where applicable.

The checklist must be *signed and dated* by person completing this survey.

Signature: _____ Date: _____

II. General Introduction

Full organization name: _____
CEO name and title: _____

Years in this type of business: _____
CEO's experience and background: _____

List person(s) responsible for making and implementing business decisions, i.e., hiring, supervision, training:

1. _____
2. _____
3. _____

Current number of members/students (Male to female): _____
Minimum age required: _____
Current number of student athletes (Male to female): _____

Types of memberships available: ___ Individual ___ Family ___ Corporate ___ Other

New member orientation given: _____ Yes _____ No

Describe: _____

Number [#] of full-time employees/Coaches: _____ Number certified: _____

Number of full-time coaches who have completed either a coaching en dorsement _____ coaching minor _____ or coaching education course (either Indiana PACE _____ or ACEP/NFCEP _____).

Subjects taught by coaches: _____

Number of part-time employees/Coaches: _____ Number certified: _____

Number of part-time coaches who have completed either a coaching en-dorsement _____, coaching minor _____, or coaching education course (either Indiana PACE _____ or ACEP/NFCEP _____).

What sports coached: _____

_____ # male coaches   _____ # female coaches   _____ # male coaches
who coach girls   _____what sports

Check certifications held: _____ ACSM   _____Dance Exercise
_____ NFI _____ NSCA _____ CPR _____ First Aid _____WSI _____ LG
_____ NATA _____ Other

Number of boys' sports: _____ Number of girls' sports: _____
Number of ticket personnel: _____ Are sellers bonded? ___ Yes ___ No
Is athletic director bonded? ___ Yes ___ No
Business manager? ___ Yes ___ No

Are there employees handling money who are not bonded (paid volunteer)?
___ Yes   ___ No

Annual gross receipts: _____

Circle the following:

Football   Gymnastics
Soccer [B]   Swimming [B]
Basketball [B]   Swimming [G]
Basketball [G]   Concessions
Volleyball   Proshop
Soccer [G]   Donations
Baseball   Fundraising
Softball   Sponsorship
Wrestling   Licensing

Do you hold any gambling activities to raise money (e.g., 50/50 draws)?
What are your days and hours of operation?
   M-F   _____ a.m.   _____ p.m.
   Saturday _____a.m.   _____ p.m.
   Sunday _____ a.m.   _____ p.m.

Check the following which are offered at this location:

Aerobic classes—how many per day? _____
Free weights (including barbells and dumbbells) _____
Square footage of area _____
Cardiovascular machines—how many? _____
Specify type: _____
Sauna _____   Steam room _____   Showers _____   Hot tub _____

Locker rooms _____   Cold plunge _____   Whirlpool _____

Body toning machines—how many? _____

Tanning beds—how many? _____

Racquetball or handball courts—how many? _____

Tennis Courts—Number indoor _____ Number outdoor _____

Basketball courts—Number indoor _____   Number outdoor ____

Jogging track: _____Indoor, size _____ Outdoor, size:

Swimming pool(s) _____Indoor, size: _____Outdoor, size:
   Is the depth? _____ ft. shallow _____ ft. deep _____ Is there a diving area? ____Yes _____ No If yes what size diving boards:___1 m ___3m
   ___ 5m platform   ___ 7m platform   ____ 1m platform

Is scuba diving offered? ____Yes ____No   If yes, do you provide any of the
following? _____ snorkel____ mask _____ tanks _____ air

Wrestling area, size: _____

Sport medicine/training room _____

Child care offered _____

Masseuse _____

Beauty salon _____

Dance studio _____

Gymnastics _____

Trampolines _____

Martial arts _____

Pro shop _____

Restaurant _____

Bar/lounge _____

Alcoholic beverages (sold or permitted) _____

Nutrition center or food supplements _____

Special events, i.e., camps, adventure excursions, dances, picnics, etc. _____
Specify _____

Do you sublease any space to others? _____ yes _____ no
   If yes, please describe:_____

III. Screening for Physical Activity Readiness

A. Profile on medical history
   1. Any health questionnaire used
   2. Physician release required for special participants
   3. Records maintained with health screening information

B. Any consent/waiver/release/assumption of risk form used
   [Attach copy(ies)]

C. Qualified staff to do exercise screening tests
   [Describe certifications held]

D. Exercise testing equipment properly maintained
   [Document procedures and forms used]

E. Emergency procedure in place for testing
   [Attach copy of procedures]

F. Program and membership information include: ___   ___   ___
    1. Description of services [Attach a copy]   ___   ___   ___
    2. Hazards/risks [Attach a copy]   ___   ___   ___
    3. Disclaimer [Attach a copy]   ___   ___   ___
    4. Minor consent (parent or guardian) [Attach a copy] ___   ___   ___
    5. Membership agreement [Attach a copy]   ___   ___   ___
    6. Guests   ___   ___   ___
G. Percentage of participants over 50 years of age: _____
H. Orientation for new members [Attach a copy]   ___   ___   ___
I. Waiver/consent/medical forms used other than
    those provided by the IHSAA [Attach copies]   ___   ___   ___
J. Do participants purchase injury insurance?
    [Cost: _____]   ___   ___   ___

Comments: _____

_____

_____

IV. Emergency Plan

	Yes	No	N/A
A. Are procedures in place for emergencies?			
1. Is there a written emergency evacuation plan?	___	___	___
B. Is at least one CPR certified person on duty during operating hours or on the field/court/track/pool?	___	___	___
C. Are emergency telephone numbers posted by each telephone (e.g., police, fire, EMS)? [Attach a copy]	___	___	___
D. Are staff members trained in emergency procedures? [Document the training provided]	___	___	___
E. Is the expected response time less than 15 minutes?	___	___	___
F. Is there a manager/coach on duty at all times?	___	___	___
G. Are emergency equipment and supplies accessible, such as fire extinguishers, stretchers, sprinkle systems?	___	___	___
H. Is a first aid kit available and well-stocked?	___	___	___
I. Practice, drills and education			
1. Are drills documented?	___	___	___
2. Are mock drills varied to match the most common and most serious potential emergencies the specific facility may encounter?	___	___	___
3. Are all shift personnel involved in drills and emergency training?	___	___	___
4. Are staff reviews of actual facility incidents done that involve injured patrons?	___	___	___
5. Any emergency education training information given to staff? [Attach copies]	___	___	___

J. Is documentation of accidents incidents made?
  (e.g., form completed) [Attach copies]   —   —   —

COMMENTS: _____

_____

V. Subleasing

A. Contracts executed with all independent contractors
  [Attach sample copies]   —   —   —
B. Are subcontractors managed and supervised?
C. Are subcontractors required to carry liability
  insurance coverage? [How much:_____]   —   —   —
D. Any leasing by outside organizations for meetings?
  [Provide a list of organizations]   —   —   —
E. Do you employ independent contratcors (e.g., dance
  exercise instructors)?   —   —   —

Comments: _____

_____

VI. Staffing And Personnel

A. Academic course work, degrees, or certification required for any staff?
  ____Yes ____ No
B. Experience required for any staff?
  ____ Yes ____ No   [Attach detailed listing & job descriptions]
C. Background and employment records checked on all prospective
  employees prior to hiring? ____ Yes ____ No
D. Special staff preparation requirements
  1. Nutritionist   —   —   —
  2. Physical therapist   —   —   —
  3. Athletic trainer
  4. Personal trainer   —   —   —
  5. Health promotion and/or special
    populations staff   —   —   —
  6. Massage therapist   —   —   —
  7. Babysitting / child care   —   —   —
  8. Beautician   —   —   —
  9. Other: _____

Comments: _____

_____

VII. Facility Checklist

A. General overall facility

1. Floors free of debris, standing liquid, and undamaged ___ ___ ___
2. Entry/exits visible, marked ___ ___ ___
3. At least two entry/exits present ___ ___ ___
4. Floor coverings properly secured ___ ___ ___
5. Partitions functioning/undamaged ___ ___ ___
6. "No Smoking" signs visible undamaged in hallways ___ ___ ___
7. Are storage areas properly secured? ___ ___ ___
8. Smoking areas specified ___ ___ ___
9. Flammable or combustible materials properly stored ___ ___ ___
10. [List and describe controls for these materials] ___ ___ ___
11. Emergency power available ___ ___ ___
12. Housekeeping satisfactory ___ ___ ___

B. Handball/racquetball/squash courts

1. Entry/exits visible, marked unobstructed ___ ___ ___
2. Walls clean, free of debris, and undamaged ___ ___ ___
3. Walls smooth and undamaged ___ ___ ___
4. Floors smooth (no cracks or warps) ___ ___ ___
5. Lights functioning ___ ___ ___
6. Eyeguard and safety rule signage visible, undamaged, and enforced ___ ___ ___
7. Light switches undamaged and functioning ___ ___ ___
8. Doors flush with walls ___ ___ ___
9. Doors in good condition ___ ___ ___
10. Movable walls ___ ___ ___
11. Viewing window ___ ___ ___
12. Valuable storage ___ ___ ___
13. Glass walls on blank sides ___ ___ ___
14. Second floor viewing area ___ ___ ___
15. Acoustically sound ___ ___ ___

Comments: _____

_____

C. AUXILIARY COURTS (e.g., basketball, volleyball, badminton)

1. Entry/exits visible, marked and unobstructed ___ ___ ___
2. Signs visible and undamaged (safety, no smoking, exit) ___ ___ ___
3. Floor free of debris and standing liquid ___ ___ ___
4. Floors smooth (no cracks or warps) ___ ___ ___
5. Backboards padded ___ ___ ___
6. Gorilla rims ___ ___ ___

7. Walls padded under baskets   ____ ____ ____
8. Scorers area wiring safe and secured   ____ ____ ____
9. Portable baskets can be stored and secured   ____ ____ ____
10. Bleachers are at least 10 feet from playing surface   ____ ____ ____
11. Stage area appropriately padded   ____ ____ ____
12. Drinking fountains are recessed   ____ ____ ____
13. Bleachers have side railings, entry aisles with railings   ____ ____ ____
14. Volleyball standards are padded   ____ ____ ____
15. Retractable baskets are regularly inspected and maintained   ____ ____ ____
16. Ceilings at least 20 feet tall   ____ ____ ____
17. Adequate lighting that is protected   ____ ____ ____
18. Seating capacity clearly marked   ____ ____ ____
19. Safety glass in doors leading into area   ____ ____ ____
20. Skylights   ____ ____ ____
21. Adequate secured storage volleyball, badminton)   ____ ____ ____

Comments: _____

_____

D. Aerobic Area
1. Separate classes for different levels   ____ ____ ____
2. Safety or warning signage posted   ____ ____ ____
3. Visible clocks   ____ ____ ____
4. Flooring made of shock-absorbent material   ____ ____ ____
5. Floors clean, free of debris, and undamaged   ____ ____ ____
6. Mirrors secured and unbroken   ____ ____ ____
7. Mats, aerobic steps, and other equipment stored properly   ____ ____ ____
8. Instructor certification(s) and training required   ____ ____ ____
9. Instructor covered by facility insurance   ____ ____ ____
10. Class size enforced, based on space restriction   ____ ____ ____
11. Target heart rate charts posted   ____ ____ ____
12. Area clear of obstructions   ____ ____ ____
13. All obstructions padded   ____ ____ ____
14. Telephone for emergencies purposes available   ____ ____ ____
15. Appropriate climate control and ventilation   ____ ____ ____

Comments: _____

_____

E. Cardiovascular/Circuit Training Area
1. Signage—(warning signs visible and undamaged)   ____ ____ ____
2. Climate controlled   ____ ____ ____
3. Non-slip flooring and drip mats   ____ ____ ____

4. Any restrictions for using area (e.g., age, handicapped)   ___ ___ ___
5. Housekeeping - infection controlled   ___ ___ ___
6. Machine and equipment maintenance exists [Attach reports]   ___ ___ ___
7. Is area supervised?   ___ ___ ___
8. All electrical wiring is concealed   ___ ___ ___
9. All treadmills start at zero MPH and 0% grade   ___ ___ ___
10. Telephone for emergencies available   ___ ___ ___
11. Manufacturer's guidelines followed   ___ ___ ___

F. Strength Training Area
1. Space allocation allows for easy access to equipment ___ ___ ___
2. Signage
   a) Instructional signs visible and undamaged   ___ ___ ___
      (1) Signs emphasizing safety used   ___ ___ ___
      (2) Safety, spotting, warning and acknow-
          ledgement of assumption of risk signs used ___ ___ ___
   b) Entry/exits visible, marked and unobstructed ___ ___ ___
3. Proper environment for weight training
   a) Air exchanges and ventilation adequate   ___ ___ ___
   b) Lights functioning properly   ___ ___ ___
   c) Sufficient ceiling space for overhead lifts   ___ ___ ___
4. Flooring
   a) Non-slip   ___ ___ ___
   b) Shock absorbing   ___ ___ ___
   c) Easily cleaned, repaired, and replaced   ___ ___ ___
   d) Free of debris   ___ ___ ___
5. Wall Covering
   a) Mirror(s)
      (1) Positioned higher than largest weight plates ___ ___ ___
      (2) Secured and unbroken   ___ ___ ___
      (3) Positioned away from activity   ___ ___ ___
      (4) Above and away from dumbbell rack   ___ ___ ___
      (5) Easily cleaned and replaced   ___ ___ ___
      (6) Are cracked or distorted mirrors replaced quickly?   ___ ___ ___
   b) Walls free of protruding objects   ___ ___ ___
6. Strength training equipment maintenance and service
   a) Manufacturer-suggested maintenance program used   ___ ___ ___
   b) Manufacturer's guidelines for repair used   ___ ___ ___
   c) Are service contracts used?   ___ ___ ___
7. Strength training equipment
   a) Weight stacks protected by shields   ___ ___ ___
   b) Collars and clips   ___ ___ ___

         (1) Properly stored   —— —— ——
         (2) In proper working order   —— —— ——
         (3) Corrosion-free   —— —— ——
    c) Do sitting or lying-resistance machines have   —— —— ——
       correct body position illustrations and ins-
       tructions posted on them?   —— —— ——
    d) Weight storage, dumbbell racks, adequately
       positioned, easily accessible   —— —— ——
    e) Benches
         (1) Braced firmly   —— —— ——
         (2) Surfaces cleaned/disinfected regularly —— —— ——
    f) Warning signs visible and undamaged on
       equipment   —— —— ——
    g) Staff in-service training conducted on
       equipment using manufacturer manuals   —— —— ——
    h) Strength machines, weight racks, and anchor
       points securely anchored to wall/floor, where
       required   —— —— ——
    i) Strength machines, squat racks have properly
       functioning safety stops   —— —— ——
    j) Strength machines, weight racks and pulley
       mechanisms   —— —— ——
         (1) Cables not broken or frayed   —— —— ——
         (2) Lubricated   —— —— ——
         (3) No undue metal stress   —— —— ——
         (4) Corrosion free   —— —— ——
         (5) Non-slip material on pedals   —— —— ——
         (6) Non-slip rubber grips on machines —— —— ——
9. Inventory of resistance training machines
    a) Weight stacks   —— —— ——
    b) Hydraulic (e.g., Keiser brand)   —— —— ——
    c) Free weight machines—no chains or cables —— —— ——
    d) Computerized/electronic   —— —— ——
    e) Other: specify: _____   —— —— ——
10. New member orientation given   —— —— ——

Comments: _____

_____

G. Tennis Courts
    1. Playing surfaces free of debris and undamaged —— —— ——
    2. Tennis court nets in good condition   —— —— ——
    3. Wind screens in good condition   —— —— ——
    4. Fences and gates in good condition   —— —— ——
    5. Proper lighting—lights protected   —— —— ——
    6. Warning signs posted   —— —— ——

7. Snow, ice, water removal adequate   ___ ___ ___
8. Equipment securely stored   ___ ___ ___
9. Necessary padding   ___ ___ ___
10. Appropriate distances from endlines to fence   ___ ___ ___
11. Adequate lighting   ___ ___ ___

Comments: _____

_____

H. Playing Fields
   Baseball/Softball
   1. Fields clear of debris   ___ ___ ___
   2. Fences in good condition   ___ ___ ___
   3. Playing surface in good condition   ___ ___ ___
   4. Baseball dugouts in good condition   ___ ___ ___
   5. Backstops in good condition   ___ ___ ___
   6. Storage area free of debris, organized, equipment
      stored, doors locked   ___ ___ ___
   7. Fences taller than six feet   ___ ___ ___
   8. Fences four feet or shorter are covered with a
      protective cover   ___ ___ ___
   9. There is a 10 foot warning track prior to fence   ___ ___ ___
   10. The softball team areas are protected by a fence ___ ___ ___
   11. Easy transition from infield to outfield   ___ ___ ___
   12. Light poles outside of fence   ___ ___ ___
   13. Bleachers have railings and aisles   ___ ___ ___
   14. Bleachers are safe   ___ ___ ___
   15. Adequate lighting   ___ ___ ___
   16. Proper drainage   ___ ___ ___

   Football/Soccer/Field Hockey
   1. Fields have a crown   ___ ___ ___
   2. Goals are padded   ___ ___ ___
   3. Benches are moveable   ___ ___ ___
   4. Scoreboard is located away from field of play   ___ ___ ___
   5. All fences are located at least 20 feet from playing
      field   ___ ___ ___
   6. Bleachers have railings and aisles   ___ ___ ___
   7. Bleachers are safe   ___ ___ ___
   8. Adequate lighting   ___ ___ ___
   9. Proper drainage   ___ ___ ___

Comments: _____

_____

I. Running Track
   1. _____ Indoor   _____Outdoor
   2. Proper signage (directional, safety, other)
   3. Surface inspected regularly
   4. Proper surface   ___ ___ ___
   5. Adequate lighting   ___ ___ ___
   6. Proper drainage, if outside   ___ ___ ___
   7. Proper and adequate storage   ___ ___ ___
   8. Appropriate landing pits   ___ ___ ___
   9. Fences at least 10 feet from the track surface   ___ ___ ___
   10. Appropriate separation of field events   ___ ___ ___
   11. Appropriate runways   ___ ___ ___

Comments: _____
_____

J. Pool
   1. Pool area monitored   ___ ___ ___
   2. Pool area highly visible   ___ ___ ___
   3. Entry/exits visible marked and unobstructed   ___ ___ ___
   4. Adequate number of exits   ___ ___ ___
   5. Walkways undamaged, properly drained, free of
      debris, and standing liquid   ___ ___ ___
   6. Walkways slip-resistant   ___ ___ ___
   7. Emergency telephone or alarm equipped   ___ ___ ___
         a) Emergency phone numbers posted   ___ ___ ___
   8. Ceiling and pool lights covered and functioning   ___ ___ ___
   9. Signs (exit, no smoking, number of users, no diving,
      regulation, and safety rules visible and legible; no
      diving in depth less than feet or less than 25 feet
      of forward clearance)   ___ ___ ___
   10. Pool(s) vacuumed daily or, as needed   ___ ___ ___
   11. Water quality tested and daily pool H_2O analysis log
      posted   ___ ___ ___
   12. Algae growth not visible in pool; water is not dis-
      colored from algae bloom   ___ ___ ___
   13. Water level acceptable   ___ ___ ___
   14. Water depth markings are plainly marked at or
      above the water surface on the vertical wall of the
      pool and on the edge of the deck   ___ ___ ___
   15. Light switches proper and functioning   ___ ___ ___
   16. Adequate ventilation no unpleasant, discernible odors ___ ___ ___
   17. Diving board present   ___ ___ ___
      a) If present, does it have a slip-resistant surface) ___ ___ ___
      b) _____A or _____ B board
   18. Drains maintained and working properly   ___ ___ ___
   19. Ladders secured and undamaged   ___ ___ ___

20. Chemicals:
    a) Stored properly   ___ ___ ___
    b) Labels legible   ___ ___ ___
    c) Labels show appropriate hazard warning   ___ ___ ___
    d) Correctly dispensed into pool   ___ ___ ___
    e) Are employees trained in storage and use of
        hazardous chemicals   ___ ___ ___
21. Storage area free of debris and uncluttered   ___ ___ ___
22. Emergency equipment:
    a) Ring Buoy (one each side)   ___ ___ ___
    b) Extension poles (one each side)   ___ ___ ___
    c) Shepherd's crook   ___ ___ ___
    d) Rescue tube (one each side)   ___ ___ ___
    e) First-aid kit well-stocked and easily accessible   ___ ___ ___
23. Deck and floors leading to pool slip-resistant   ___ ___ ___
24. Decks clean, sanitized twice weekly and algae free   ___ ___ ___
25. Lifeguards
    a) Possess appropriate certification   ___ ___ ___
        What type? _____
    b) Qualified in emergency procedures/rescue   ___ ___ ___
    c) Properly dressed/identifiable   ___ ___ ___
    d) Adequate number and positioning   ___ ___ ___
    e) Given frequent relief breaks and rotated   ___ ___ ___
26. If no lifeguard on duty, is there a surveillance camera
     scanning pool area, proper signage, and rescue
     equipment   ___ ___ ___

Comments: _____

_____

K. Hot Tub
   1. User age restriction   ___ ___ ___
   2. Temperature regulation   ___ ___ ___
   3. Timers functioning   ___ ___ ___
   4. Chemicals used correctly   ___ ___ ___
   5. Warnings list visible and undamaged   ___ ___ ___
   6. Emergency phone   ___ ___ ___
   7. Proper supervision   ___ ___ ___

Comments: _____

_____

L. Sauna
   1. User age restriction   ___ ___ ___
   2. Automatic temperature regulator to shut off heat   ___ ___ ___
      when maximum temperature is reached   ___ ___ ___
   3. Timers functioning   ___ ___ ___

4. Warnings list visible and undamaged   —   —   —

5. Emergency phone/panic button or alarm easily accessible   —   —   —

6. No locking or latching doors   —   —   —

7. Proper supervision   —   —   —

8. Proper maintenance followed   —   —   —

9. Users cannot touch sauna heater   —   —   —

10. Area clean and free of debris   —   —   —

11. Door opens out   —   —   —

12. Window in door   —   —   —

Comments: _____

_____

M. Steam room

1. User age restriction   —   —   —

2. Automatic temperature regulator to shutoff steam when maximum temperature is reached   —   —   —

3. Timers functioning   —   —   —

4. Warnings list visible and undamaged   —   —   —

5. Emergency phone/panic button or alarm easily accessible   —   —   —

6. No locking or latching doors   —   —   —

7. Proper supervision   —   —   —

8. Proper maintenance followed   —   —   —

9. Users can't touch steam head   —   —   —

10. Area clean and free of debris   —   —   —

11. Door opens out   —   —   —

12. Window in door   —   —   —

Comments: _____

_____

N. Therapeutic whirlpool

1. Emergency procedures posted   —   —   —

2. Timers functioning   —   —   —

3. Daily inspection and water testing   —   —   —

4. Proper surface (non-slip)   —   —   —

5. Area free of debris and standing liquid   —   —   —

6. Warning signs posted   —   —   —

7. Inspection log kept   —   —   —

8. Supervised   —   —   —

9. Emergency phone or alarm   —   —   —

Comments: _____

_____

O. Tanning
1. Tanning beds placed in enclosed private area _____ _____ _____
2. Emergency procedures and warning lists visible and undamaged _____ _____ _____
3. Beds disinfected between uses _____ _____ _____
4. Maintenance plan in place (e.g., check bulbs for leakage) _____ _____ _____
5. Strict adherence to manufacturer's suggestions on use of equipment _____ _____ _____
6. Eye protection provided and required _____ _____ _____
7. Waivers signed before use _____ _____ _____
8. Timer coin operated _____ token _____ other _____ _____

Comments: _____
_____

P. Dressing areas, locker/drying/shower rooms
Boys
1. Hallway and locker floors:
   a) Non-skid surfaces _____ _____ _____
   b) Free of debris _____ _____ _____
   c) Proper drainage _____ _____ _____
2. Electrical:
   a) Ground fault interrupters on outlets _____ _____ _____
   b) Emergency power system available _____ _____ _____
3. Lockers
   a) Corrosion-free _____ _____ _____
   b) Free of rough or jagged edges _____ _____ _____
   c) Secured to floor or immovable _____ _____ _____
4. Showers:
   a) Easy temperature control _____ _____ _____
   b) Non-skid floors _____ _____ _____
   c) Signs noting caution _____ _____ _____
5. Locker room maintenance adequate (sinks, floors, mirrors, toilets, urinals sanitized) _____ _____ _____
6. No dripping water/leaks _____ _____ _____
7. Benches, tables, chairs secured _____ _____ _____
8. Adequate size locker rooms _____ _____ _____

Girls
1. Hallway and locker floors:
   a) Non-skid surfaces _____ _____ _____
   b) Free of debris _____ _____ _____
   c) Proper drainage _____ _____ _____

2. Electrical:
    a) Ground fault interrupters on outlets   ——   ——   ——
    b) Emergency power system available   ——   ——   ——
3. Lockers
    a) Corrosion-free   ——   ——   ——
    b) Free of rough or jagged edges   ——   ——   ——
    c) Secured to floor or immovable   ——   ——   ——
4. Showers:
    a) Easy temperature control   ——   ——   ——
    b) Non-skid floors   ——   ——   ——
    c) Signs noting caution   ——   ——   ——
5. Locker room maintenance adequate (sinks, floors, mirrors, toilets, urinals sanitized)   ——   ——   ——
6. No dripping water/leaks   ——   ——   ——
7. Benches, tables, chairs secured   ——   ——   ——
8. Adequate size locker rooms   ——   ——   ——

Comments: _____

_____

Q. Restaurant/bar/lounge/snack bar/concession stand
1. Alcohol served or permitted   ——   ——   ——
    a) If alcohol is served, are state laws adhered to? ___   ——   ——
2. Employees trained in serving alcohol   ——   ——   ——
3. Facility meets health inspection standards and permits kept up-to-date   ——   ——   ——
4. Cooking surfaces and kitchen have automatic fire protection system   ——   ——   ——
5. Area clean, free of debris and grease accumulation ___   ——   ——
6. Proper refrigeration   ——   ——   ——
7. Any glass containers   ——   ——   ——
8. Pest control   ——   ——   ——

Comments: _____

_____

R. Off-premise activities: camps /adventures / excursions/ Special Events
1. Properly supervised
2. Insurance coverage checked in advance and proof furnished by carrier
3. Proper waiver and similar forms signed by participants
    Specify: _____
4. Risks properly explained and acknowledgement of risk forms signed
5. Adequate transportation

6. Transportation insurance obtained   —— —— ——
7. Warning signs properly posted   —— —— ——

Comments: _____

_____

S. Pro shop
  1. Sub-contracted   —— —— ——
  2. Insurance covered
  3. Reputable, insured vendors   —— —— ——
  4. Proper labels and warnings on products   —— —— ——
  5. Proper security   —— —— ——

Comments: _____

_____

T. Beauty salon/masseuse
  1. Sub-contracted   —— —— ——
  2. Insurance covered   —— —— ——
  3. Licensed personnel (if required by state)   —— —— ——
  4. Proper security   —— —— ——

Comments: _____

_____

U. Nutrition Center, Food Supplements, Nutrition Advice
  1. Instructors qualified (i.e., licensed nutritionist on
     staff)   —— —— ——
  2. Any diets recommended?   —— —— ——

Comments: _____

_____

V. Child care center
  1. Give the staff-to-child ratio at this facility   —— —— ——
  2. Special staff requirements for employment   —— —— ——
  3. In-service training offered   —— —— ——
  4. Emergency care training provided to staff (Pediatric
     Medic First Aid—PEDS or Red Cross equivalent cert-
     ification)   —— —— ——
  5. Adequate space allocation   —— —— ——
  6. Signage and rules posted
     a) Language (simple)   —— —— ——
     b) Pictures   —— —— ——
     c) Placed at children's eye level   —— —— ——

7. Flooring
   a) Stain resistant   ___   ___   ___
   b) Non-slip flooring   ___   ___   ___
  Specify type of floor:_____
8. Wall covering
   a) Stain resistant   ___   ___   ___
   b) Washable   ___   ___   ___
9. Communication available to front desk or other
  personnel   ___   ___   ___
  Describe:_____
  _____

10. Security and records
   a) All children clearly visible?   ___   ___   ___
   b) Restricted exit capability (escapable in case
     of fire or emergency)   ___   ___   ___
   c) Child registration (sign-in and sign-out)   ___   ___   ___
   d) Parental release for all children   ___   ___   ___
   e) Continuous supervision   ___   ___   ___
   f) Child's immunization record and medical
     history on file   ___   ___   ___
   g) Accident/incident records maintained   ___   ___   ___
11. Housekeeping
   a) Daily clean-up   ___   ___   ___
   b) Proper sanitation   ___   ___   ___
12. Equipment / activities
   a) Sink and toilet at appropriate heights   ___   ___   ___
   b) Refrigeration   ___   ___   ___
   c) Changing tables   ___   ___   ___
   d) Washable mats   ___   ___   ___
   e) Safe toys and games   ___   ___   ___
   f) Any type of exercise equipment   ___   ___   ___

Comments: _____

W. Martial arts
  1. Is the program for competition training?   ___   ___   ___
  2. Is the program for instructional purposes?   ___   ___   ___
  3. Does your facility host competitions?   ___   ___   ___
  4. Qualified and/or certified instructors
    Specify: _____
  5. Proper acknowledgement of assumption of risk,
    waivers, consent forms executed by students or
    parents   ___   ___   ___
  6. Proper floor covering (e.g., resilient, extra carpet
    padding)   ___   ___   ___

7. Proper signage (contact rules, etc.)   ___ ___ ___
8. Class size enforced   ___ ___ ___
   What is it? _____
9. Any sub-contractors used?   ___ ___ ___
10. Any safety equipment required?   ___ ___ ___
   Specify: _____

   Comments: _____

   _____

X. Sports medicine/training room
  1. Location: _____
  2. Adequate space: _____
  3. Cleanliness: _____
  4. Ice Machine: (# _____)
  5. Telephone: _____
  6. Computer: _____
  7. Refrigerator: (# _____)
  8. Biohazard waste control: _____
  9. Storage
     a. adequate
     b. climate controlled
     c. secured
  10. Adequate HVAC
  11. Team preparation area
     a. tables (#)
     b. Sink
     c. Counter space
  12. Hydrotherapy (Wet) area
     a. Whirlpool (#)
     b. Hot water supply insulated
     c. Electrical supply/GFI/receptacles
     d. Tile floor
     e. Tile walls
     f. Proper drainage
  13. Rehabilitation area
     a. Hydroculator packs
     b. Ultrasound
     c. Electrical stimulation
     d. Free weights
     e. Mechanized weights
     f. Exercise bike(#)
  14. Athletic trainer
     a. On staff
     b. Under contract
     c. Student trainers
       1) Education program (Attach a copy)

15. Health insurance (Limit: _____)

Comments: _____
_____

Y. Transportation
  1. School buses used
  2. School vans used
  3. Personally owned vehicles (POV)
  4. Chartered bus
  5. Drivers
      a. Professionally trained
      b. Coaches
      c. Parents
      d. Students
  6. Transportation policy
  7. Parental release
Z. Other Interscholastic Issues
  1. Interscholastic athletic handbook
  2. Job descriptions
      a. head coach
      b. assistant coach
      c. athletic director
      d. business manager
  3. Athletic training handbook
  4. Strategic plan
  5. Risk management plan
  6. Marketing plan
  7. Financial development plan

VIII. INSPECTOR'S OVERALL RATING AND COMMENTS ABOUT THE FACILITY:

_____
_____
_____
_____

IX. SUGGESTIONS

Minimal changes that you think are necessary and *should* be made for this facility. If possible, please supply photos of each area or situation that you recommend a change to be made.

X. RECOMMENDATIONS

Minimal changes that you think are essential and *must* be made for this facility. If possible, please supply photos of each area or situation that requires a change to be made.

Safety Checklist

The following safety checklist is offered as a shorthand method of assessing a fitness plan and bringing the most critical components into focus (Doughtery, et al., 1993):

1.   Have enough supervisors been provided?
2.   Do all personnel possess the necessary skills?
     certification   % yes ____
     outside training   % yes ____
     in-house training   % yes ____
3.   Have the responsibilities of all supervisory personnel been defined and articulated?
4.   Has the location of personnel been planned to guarantee effective coverage?
5.   Do supervisors have a clear line of sight over their areas of responsibility?
6.   Are there areas that are being under or over supervised?
7.   Is there immediate access to trained first aid personnel?
8.   Are there carefully developed plans for medical emergencies to include telephone access, notifications to be made, etc.?
9.   Are all supervisory personnel familiar with the emergency plans and procedures?
10.   Is there an effective means of communication among supervisory personnel?
11.   Have the participants been made aware, to the maximum reasonable degree, of their responsibilities and obligations?
12.   Have provisions been made to provide follow-up and reminders regarding participant responsibilities and obligations?
13.   Does the supervisor have all necessary medical information on each participant, to include special medical problems, names and telephone numbers of persons to be notified?
14.   Does all fitness activity planning include specific safety considerations?
15.   Has there been careful consideration of the matter of participant readiness such as pre-screening?
16.   Do the participants understand the risks inherent in the activity and the concomitant safety procedures?
17.   Within the reasonable limits of their individual capabilities, do the participants recognize and accept responsibility for their own safety?
18.   Has careful consideration been given to possible activity adaptations to increase safety?
19.   Are there regularly scheduled inspection and maintenance procedures for all equipment and facilities?
20.   Are the results of inspections and completed maintenance procedures recorded and maintained?
21.   Does all equipment meet or exceed appropriate safety standards?

Whom to Contact

For more specific information about ADA requirements affecting public services and public accommodations contact any of the following:

U.S. Department of Justice, Civil Rights Division
Office on the Americans with Disabilities Act
P.O. Box 66118
Washington, D.C. 20035-6118
202/514-0301 (Voice)
202/514-0381 (TDD)

Equal Employment Opportunity Commission
1801 L. Street NW
Washington, D.C. 20507
202/663-4900 (Voice)
800/800-3302 (TDD)

Department of Transportation
400 Seventh Street NW
Washington, D.C. 20590
202/366-9305 (Voice)
202/755-7687 (TDD)

Architectural and Transportation Barriers Compliance Board
1111 18th Street NW Suite 501
Washington, D.C. 20036
800/use-able (Voice)
800/usa-able (TDD)

Federal Communications Commission
1919 M. Street NW
Washington, D.C. 20554
202/632-7620 (Voice)
202/632-6999 (TDD)

Top Twenty Claims Most Common in Lawsuits Against Fitness Instructors, Physical Educators, Personal Trainers, Coaches, Athletic Administrators, Club Owners, Exercise Physiologists

1. Failure to supervise.
2. Failure to use proper learning progressions.
3. Failure to use appropriate equipment.
4. Failure to maintain equipment, and facility.
5. Failure to warn the participant about inherent risks in the use of exercise equipment, or the activity itself.
6. Failure to owe a duty to the plaintiff to keep the premises safe and without hazard.
7. Failure to inspect facility or equipment and conduct reasonable risk management procedures on such.
8. Failure to research equipment purchases for problems or defects in design or appropriateness for activities that are to be conducted in said facility.
9. Failure to take a medical history of participants prior to doing the activity.
10. Failure to require a physical exam before beginning the activity.
11. Failure to instruct users in exercise classes as to how to take their own vital signs.
12. Failure to use proper warm ups.
13. Failure to hire properly credentialed professional staff.
14. Failure to properly evaluate the physical risk factors of the participants to determine the correct level of activity they should be involved with.
15. Failure to advise the participant about exercise and the effects of such on the human body.
16. Failure to provide expert professional instruction advertised or expressly warranted to participants.
17. Failure to provide as expressly warranted, an exercise program best suited for the participants.
18. Failure to require continuing education or other methods for these professionals to update their skills.
19. Failure to properly evaluate the professional staff as to their performance as instructors.
20. Failure to act as a reasonable and prudent professional, meeting the standards of care as promulgated by professional societies, publications or research.

Appendix J

Sample Sponsorship Agreement
Intercollegiate Sponsorship for 2000-2001

◆ ─────────────────────── ◆

University of Hannibal (UH) Enters into this Sponsorship Agreement with Tom Sawyer's Huckleberry Farm, Inc. (TSHF)

TSHF's Objectives for Its UH Sponsorship

There are two major objectives for TSHF in the UH sponsorship agreement:

1. Increase market share and sales volume.
2. Enhance image in travel and entertainment market.

TSHF's Purchase of Sponsorship Rights from the UH

By purchasing sponsorship rights, TSHF was trying to prevent avenues for its competitors—Missouri Huckleberries, Inc., Midwest Huckleberries, Inc., and so on from ambushing its UH sponsorship. For example, if Missouri Huckleberries became sponsor of UH Intercollegiate Athletics, this company could easily fool the public into thinking it was also a UH sponsor.

TSHF's Sponsorship of all UH Teams

TSHF selected sports with high media exposure where it could maximize its UH sponsorship bond and keep out competitors. It sponsored 12 different UH teams.

TSHF's Use of UH Symbols

TSHF has exclusive use of the UH symbols, slogans, and mascot and informed all retailers that this was the preferred logo use. TSHF used the UH logos to create UH-themed packaging, special-edition TSHF decals for merchants, UH pin give-aways, posters, and merchandise premium offers, and to generally enhance the image of TSHF. UH-themed packaging promotions were used to set the UH Huckleberries program apart from competitors.

TSHF's Reason for Using UH Symbols

The UH symbols stand for dedication, quality, and excellence. TSHF hoped that the public image of UH would become associated with the TSHF's product. This could give the TSHF group a competitive advantage in the marketplace.

TSHF's Fund-raising Activities for the UH Teams

Among the TSHF's merchants, fund raising is the one most common promotional activity used. Merchants could use the following fund-raising activities:

- "Pull for the Team" donation-per-transaction program
- Customer-direct donations via UH provided statement inserts
- Donations to UH from annual huckleberry sales
- Per-transaction matching donations
- Fund raising from sales of UH premium merchandise items
- Other client/customer-direct donations

TSHF's Reason for Fund Raising

The company wants to tie in with the national pride and support that midwesterners feel for their UH team and consequently increase sales of products.

TSHF's Rights to the UH football team

One of the specific teams to which TSHF purchased rights was the football team, the most highly nationally televised team in the UH stable. This established a direct association with a highly publicized team, giving TSHF the exposure it wanted on television, magazines, and radio. Everywhere the UH football team competed TSHF was there displaying banners and maximizing its high-profile association with football and UH athletics.

TSHF's Public Awareness Activities

TSHF is prepared to promote public awareness of UH and TSHF in the following ways:

TSHF-arranged ("Win the Mark Twain Bowl") sweepstakes.
Ex-UH athletes used for speeches or demonstrations in employee events, public exhibitions, and advertising.
UH public service announcements to local television stations.
Participation in UH reunions for fund raising.
UH radio contests.
UH promotions at local sport and food retailers.

• Fifty Special UH athletes selected to be TSHF's hosts at the various high profile UH sporting events. News releases were sent to the hometown newspapers of these UH athletes.

TSHF's Sponsorship Guide

TSHF will publish the *TSHF UH Sponsorship Manual*, which was designed to guide TSHF merchants on how to use the UH sponsorship.

TSHF will also support its UH sponsorship with regular bulletins and kits illustrating the TSHF programs and an extensive communications effort.

ABOUT THE AUTHORS

◆ ────────────────────────── ◆

Thomas H. Sawyer, Ed.D.
Professor of Physical Education,
and Recreation and Sport Management
Department of Recreation and Sport Management
Indiana State University
Terre Haute, IN 47809

Dr. Sawyer received his B.S. degree in Health and Physical Education from Springfield College (1968), and a M.P.E. degree (1971) in HPER-A. His doctorate is in Educational Administration from Virginia Polytechnic Institute and State University (1977).

He has worked at Virginia Military Institute (1969-79), University of Bridgeport (1979-81), Montana College of Mineral Science and Technology (1981-84), and Indiana State University (1984-97). He has coached baseball, football, soccer, and track and field. He has officiated high school and college baseball, basketball, football, lacrosse, soccer, softball, track and field, and volleyball. He was an associate athletic director and facility manager. Further, Dr. Sawyer has taught at the collegiate level since 1969.

Dr. Sawyer has been chosen by his peers to receive the following awards: (1) Outstanding YMCA Leader, (2) Outstanding Red Cross Volunteer—CT, MT, IN, (3) Most Valuable High School Football Official in Connecticut 1980, (4) Caleb Mills Distinguished Teaching Award [Indiana State University], (5) Howard Richardson Distinguished Faculty Award [School of HHP, Indiana State University], and (6) Distinguished Faculty Service Award [Indiana State University].

He has written 37 peer-reviewed articles and 70 non-peer reviewed articles; presented 156 presentations at state, district, and national levels. He has also written three chapters in textbooks, and taught four independent study courses. Further, Dr. Sawyer has served as president of the Indiana AHPERD, president of the American Association for Active Lifestyles and Fitness, executive director for the Society for the Study of the Legal Aspects of Sport and Physical Activity, editor of the *Indiana AHPERD Journal and Newsletter*, editor of the *Journal of the Legal Aspects of Sport,* editor of the *JOPERD Law Review*, and Chair of the Indiana State Service Council of the American Red Cross.

Owen R. Smith, Ph.D., CLP

Dr. Smith has been a member of the faculty of Indiana State University since 1982, and chair of the Department of Recreation and Sport Management since 1983. He earned his Ph.D. at the University of Utah in 1974 majoring in Leisure Studies and minoring in Geography with a specialization in resource planning. Dr. Smith also has pursued a career in the reserve military and served as the Morale, Welfare and Recreation Officer for all Marine Corps forces during Operation Desert Storm. Since then he has served as a recreation consultant to the Director, Morale, Welfare, and Recreation Support Activity, Headquarters Marine Corps at Quantico, VA, and to the Commander Marine Corps Forces Atlantic, Camp Lejeune, North Carolina. He has served as a member of the Board of Directors of the Armed Forces Recreation Society, a branch of the National Recreation and Park Association, and was President for 1997. He was recognized as the outstanding alumnus of the Department of Leisure Studies, University of Utah, in 1996.

OTHER TITLES FROM SAGAMORE PUBLISHING

The Wilderness Within: Reflections on Leisure and Life, Second Edition
Daniel L. Dustin

The Wilderness Within is a collection of eighteen essays that explore the meaning of recreation, parks, and leisure in Dustin's own life. Many of the essays are about adventure-based outdoor recreation experiences and are set in the contexts of mountains, forests, deserts, and tundra. More recent essays are based on the realization that much of what makes life interesting flows out of everyday pastimes: visiting with friends, playing games, enjoying good food, listening to music, appreciating the landscape, connecting with family, and self-reflection.

6x9 Softcover • ISBN 1-57167-253-2 • $19.95

Leisure Resources: Its Comprehensive Planning, Second Edition
Daniel D. McLean, Joseph J. Bannon, and Howard R. Gray

Leisure Resources provides detailed information about strategic planning and master planning and about support systems related to these two types of planning. Included in the book as support information is how to create organizational alignment, establishing a program evaluation system, working with surveys, and defining other methods of information gathering. The book is written to be used. It provides examples of strategic plans and master plans. The use of examples and guides allows the reader to develop a comfort level with the processes of planning. This book will find a ready place on any practitioner's reference shelf and be an excellent asset in the park and recreation planning class.

7x10 Hardcover • ISBN 1-57167-025-4 • $44.95

Research Methods in Park, Recreation, and Leisure Services
Ananda Mitra and Sam Lankford

Research Methods in Park, Recreation, and Leisure Services was written to help beginning researchers and practitioners construct research in the pursuit of resolving leisure service problems and issues. This book is a helpful guide in planning and policy studies, market research, and evaluation reports. It also illustrates and illuminates potential contributions of various research methods in the field of leisure services and emphasizes systematic methods for gathering, analyzing, and reporting information.

6x9 Hardcover • ISBN 1-57167-303-0 • $44.95

For more information on these titles call 1-800-327-5557 or visit us at **www.sagamorepub.com**.

INDEX

◆ ──────────── ◆

Product sampling, and corporate sponsor-
    ship, 99
Professional associations, 55. *See also*
    specific organizations
Profitability, 77
Program assessment, 64
Program development, 43, 53–68
    approaches to, 57–60
    components of, 57
    customers' role in, 55
    defined, 53
    factors in, 56
    and program assessment, 64
    and program modification, 65–66
    scheduling in, 60–63
    staff role in, 54–55
    steps in, 57
    for tournaments, 64–65
Program scheduling, 60–63
Program-signal systems, 234
Promotion, 110–115
    campaign for, 112–113
    importance of, 112
    See also Advertising; Personal selling;
        Sales promotion
Pro shops, as source of revenue, 91–92
Protective equipment, purchase requisi-
    tions for, 162
Proximate cause, in negligence cases, 294–
    295
Public Assembly Facilities Planning and
    Management, 278
Public figure, defined, 206
Publicity, 210–212
Public relations, 199–207
    and communications skills, 203–204
    components of program for, 200
    internal vs. external, 202
    legal aspects of, 206–207
    outlets for, 202
    and public service announcements,
        202–203
    and risk management, 334
    selecting agency for, 200
    steps in developing, 200–202, 205
    See also Media relations
Public service announcements (PSAs),
    202–203

Q

Qualified supervisor, defined, 299

R

Rabinoff, M., 312
Racquetball/handball courts
    design considerations for, 247–249
    specifications for, 368
Railey, Jim H., 63, 145, 157, 162, 176, 179,
    184, 188, 203, 273
Ramps, ADA requirements for, 350–352
Reckless misconduct, 292
Recruiting, of customers, 144
Regan, T.H., 103
Rehabilitation Act of 1973, 19, 312
Relative value strategy, 100
Request for Concessionaire Proposal
    (RCP), 89–90
Retirement plans, 21
Revenue bonds, 106
Revenue generation, 87–108
    by child- or adult-care, 94
    by concessions, 88–91, 93–94
    and corporate sponsorship, 95–100
    for facility construction, 103–106
    by hair salons, 92–93
    and licensing, 100–103
    by parking, 94
    by pro shops, 91–92
    by souvenirs and licensed products,
        95
    sources of, 87
Rewards systems, 18
Risk management, 327–341
    benefits of, 329
    and competence of personnel, 335
    components of program for, 328–329
    and contracts, 320
    evaluation of, 335
    and exculpatory agreements, 309
    and identification of risk, 329–330
    and insurance, 335–339
    and risk implementation, 333–334
    and supervision plans, 300
    tools for, 330–333
    treatment of risk in, 330
Roberts, Gary R., 297, 314
Rockne, Knute, 16